After graduating Bachelor of [...]
Babette Smith spent twenty ye[...]
Entertainment industry.

A lifelong interest in history and the discovery that her great grandmother was transported to Australia as a convict, prompted Smith to take up writing full-time. In 1988 *A Cargo of Women: Susannah Watson & the Convicts of the Princess Royal* was published in hardback to critical acclaim. Described as 'A lasting contribution to Australian history' the book was shortlisted for the NSW Literary Awards. Its success encouraged Smith to explore the subject further in popular fiction. In 1991 *A Cargo of Women* the novel took the story to a wider audience. The factual base behind the fiction resulted in one critic hailing it as 'Earthy and honest' and another commenting that 'Its fidelity to history and the convincing picture it gives of the curious sisterhood which bound the women convicts, puts it streets ahead of most...historical fiction today'.

Turning to something completely different Smith is currently writing a non-fiction story of the mother/son relationship twenty-five years after the onset of modern feminism.

For my father, Bruce P. Macfarlan, and
grandmother, Amy Macfarlan...with love

A CARGO OF
WOMEN

SUSANNAH WATSON & THE
CONVICTS OF THE PRINCESS ROYAL

BABETTE SMITH

SUN
AUSTRALIA

First published in 1988 by New South Wales University Press
This edition published 1992 by Pan Macmillan Publishers Australia
a division of Pan Macmillan Australia Pty Limited
63-71 Balfour Street, Chippendale, Sydney

National Library of Australia
cataloguing-in-publication data:

Smith, Babette, 1942-
A cargo of women.

New ed.
Bibliography.
Includes Index.
ISBN 0 7251 0635 2.

1. Watson, Susanah, 1794-1877. 2. Princess Royal (Ship). [3]. Women
convicts – Australia – Biography. I. Title.

994.0088042

Printed in Australia by The Book Printer

CONTENTS

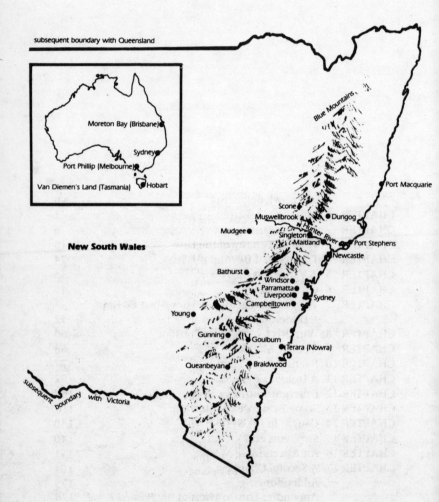

subsequent boundary with Queensland

Moreton Bay (Brisbane)

Sydney

Port Phillip (Melbourne)

Van Diemen's Land (Tasmania)

Hobart

New South Wales

Blue Mountains

Port Macquarie

Scone

Muswellbrook ● Dungog

Mudgee ● Singleton Hunter River

Maitland ● Port Stephens

Newcastle

Bathurst

Windsor

Parramatta

Liverpool

Campbelltown ● Sydney

Young

Gunning ● Goulburn

Terara (Nowra)

Queanbeyan ● Braidwood

subsequent boundary with Victoria

ACKNOWLEDGEMENTS

I owe a great debt to the integrity and initiative of Mr Leslie King and his wife Nancy of Nottinghamshire. Les King not only preserved Susannah Watson's letters, but took the trouble to write to the editor of the *Shoalhaven News* at Nowra, N.S.W. Through the intermediary of the late Mr Crompton Hall of Nowra, a grandson of Charles Watson, I was alerted to this exciting discovery and made contact with the Kings. The news came at a time when my research revealed a giant gap between the end of Susannah's convict days and her, at that time probable, death. Anyone who reads this book will understand the gratitude I feel to Leslie King.

It took me four years to find descendants of John Watson, but when I did they were helpful and enthusiastic, particularly in the fruitless hunt to find an identifiable photograph of Susannah. I am very grateful to Tom and Frances Bourke, Florence and Stan Salkind, Joe Bourke, Ena Notley and her son, Graham. Crompton Hall, the late Jack Moore of Chester Hill, and the late Ella O'Brien of Meadowbank, were all descendants of Charles Watson and all contributed to this book. It is sad they are not here to see the result.

During my research I made contact with Mrs Enid Bohlsen of North-mead and Mr G. Squires of Bowral, who are descendants of Ann Barnett and Catherine Steele respectively. They helped me generously and I am deeply grateful. I will always be interested in the women of the *Princess Royal* and look forward to finding more of their descendants among the readers of this book.

I must express my appreciation to Christine Yeats and the staff of the New South Wales State Archives for their friendly efficiency and helpfulness over several years, and my gratitude to the librarians of the Mitchell and New South Wales State Libraries. Sue Groves of the Nottingham County Record Office and the librarians of the Nottingham Library also gave me invaluable assistance.

It would have been impossible to trace the fate of the women from the *Princess Royal* without the enlightened decision to release the New South Wales Births, Deaths and Marriages pre-1856 registers on microfilm and the pre-1900 Indexes. I am grateful too for the special permission I received from the Registrar and the personal help from Mr Jim Donoghue in my search through the late nineteenth-century records. I must acknowledge also the cooperation of the Department of Health, particularly Dr M. J. Sainsbury who gave me permission to search files under his control.

I owe personal thanks and gratitude to Anthony Rubinstein and Simon and Sally Cowley in London and to Sidney Moore and Dan Margolis in Washington, D.C. In New South Wales the early comments of Doug Howie, Keith Johnson and Malcolm Sainty were very helpful. Bob Cornish caused me to take a second look at some important aspects and Richard Walsh gave me valuable advice.

Although my father began the family research before his death, it was my brother, Robert Macfarlan, who triggered me off when he discovered previously unknown convicts in the family tree. My sister, Rosalinde Kearsley, applied her mind to the logic and the conclusions of the book and gave me encouragement along the way.

Many friends were enthusiastic supporters, including particularly Penny Nelson, Rhonwyn Mooney, Tom Breen, Elizabeth Stephens, Harry Bauer, whose encouragement was critical when my determination faltered, and Prue Lindsay, who armed with camera hotfooted out to the Muringo cemetery near her home at Young, when I finally discovered the location of John Watson's grave.

My husband Graham, my son Joshua, and Wendy Nosworthy, my friend and assistant of many years, bore the heaviest burden of my absorption and earned my grateful thanks for their help. All three of them can regard this book as theirs too.

Babette Smith

CHAPTER 1

INTO THE MAELSTROM

Drunks, whores, pickpockets, burglars, paupers, misfits. Genetic criminals? Moral degenerates? Survivors or victims? The opinion of Australia's women convicts has veered from criminal whore to helpless victim. They have been used to make a case in black and white — Damn the women and uphold the Establishment; Damn the Establishment and uphold the women. They have been vilified, lionised, statisticised and generalised, but no one has yet asked: What were they like as human beings?

Were they strong or weak, helpless or manipulative? Were they proud and scornful or meek and downtrodden? What were their morals — promiscuous or monogamous — and were these by fate or choice? Did they have a sense of family and love their men, their children, their parents? Did they hope for the future, or long for the past? Was transportation for them 'the fatal shore' or a chance for a better life in a new land? Some answers can be found when one group of female prisoners is considered in the detail of its individual lives. As the social stability of the eighteenth century rolled inexorably into the convulsions of the nineteenth, one hundred female children were born at scattered locations across the British Isles. This is the story of those women, whom fate linked by their transportation to New South Wales in 1829. Gathered in from the length and breadth of England, they huddled together for six months on the small tossing ship the *Princess Royal*, to be unloaded and dispersed again across the wide, open spaces of a strange land. Among their number was a dark haired, hazel eyed woman from Nottingham. Her name was Susannah Watson.

It was the twilight of Georgian England. The 'farmer King' George III still reigned over a fundamentally rural country; a country whose workers' lives still centred on the parish of their birthplace, where craft and industry were largely cottage based, and the squalor of London was created by humans rather than machinery.

During the major part of the eighteenth century, most English working men and women had continued to labour at agriculture and the woollen industry as they had done for centuries. Then the development of new agricultural machinery began to replace farm labourers and, allied with new methods of farming, displaced large numbers of people from their rural occupations. As the century drew to a close, many of these went seeking work in the large population centres like London, or settled in the new industrial towns which were developing around the factories and mines, most particularly in the Midlands and the north of England.[1]

New ideas were also taking root. In France, towards the century's end, the people executed their King in the name of 'liberty, equality and fraternity'. While in England, small tradesmen, shopkeepers and mechanics had begun to communicate among themselves and discuss ideas of an equally revolutionary nature. They canvassed the need for Parliamentary reform and the right to vote regardless of property or income. They vowed to spread their views and organise the converted, and placed no qualifications or limitations on membership of their society.[2] They were sowing the seeds by which English working people came to feel an identity of interests between themselves and against their rulers and employers — an idea as revolutionary in paternalistic England as 'liberty, equality and fraternity' was in France.

The women were born at one of those turning points in history. A society, whose shape and texture had remained fundamentally unchanged for hundreds of years, was taking on a new form — a surge forward into a new world. This change was to catch them in the maelstrom and spit them out 12,000 miles away in the lonely bush of a place still called only the colony of New South Wales or, more colloquially, Botany Bay. Their birth gave no indication of the unwitting significance of their lives or the vagaries of fate which would bring them on the *Princess Royal*, bound for Botany Bay.

Susannah Watson's story begins in London. She was born into the noisy, dirty, squalid heart of the eighteenth-century metropolis on 20 October 1794. Her father, 48-year-old William Bidy, had his place in the lower order of society as a maker of blacking for polishing the boots of the upper classes and he and his young wife, Agnes, lived in the district of Westminster.[3] There is no way to be certain whether William Bidy was a craftsman of sufficient standing to keep his family housed, clothed and fed, but the evidence in Susannah's life and character indicates a secure childhood and that her poverty did not really begin until the arrival of her children and marriage.

Most details of Susannah's early life have been buried under the passing of nearly two hundred years. She had one brother, Thomas, thirteen years her junior, and there may have been step brothers and sisters from an earlier marriage of William Bidy's. In a letter written to her daughter in 1875, Susannah refers affectionately to 'your Aunt Mary' but it is not clear whether 'Mary' was a relative of Susannah herself or her husband.[4]

During her childhood, Susannah learnt to read and write and to do both sufficiently well for them to become natural skills rather than something to be laboured over on special occasions. In old age one of her pleasures was to sit in the sun and read, and her writing, which is well formed and firm, enabled her to keep in touch with her children when they were separated by vast distances of bush and ocean. She valued literacy and was concerned her children should share the benefit. In the box containing letters she wrote to her daughters in England, are three small pieces of paper which appear to be exercises in writing which Susannah had set for one of her children. Did her poor daughter cherish these scraps as one of the last tangible links with her mother?

In teaching her children to read and write Susannah may well have continued a family tradition. The opportunities for formal schooling were limited for children of the lower classes, and those schools that did exist concentrated on creating pious and industrious servants. There was minimal attention given to the skills of reading, writing and arithmetic.[5] But William Bidy was literate and could have passed on his knowledge to his daughter. Over 30 years later less than half of Susannah's shipmates on the voyage to New South Wales were literate.[6] Some advantage in her life gave Susannah the chance to acquire skills so many others lacked.

On arrival in New South Wales Susannah described her trade as 'housemaid and needlewoman' and no doubt this was how she earned a living during her young adult years in London. The progress of this career would have been jeopardised when, at the age of 20, she gave birth to her first son. In the written note containing details of the family, which she left with her children in England, she recorded that Samuel Wright Bidy was born in London on 28 October 1814. There is no record of where in London, or who was his father, but with her other illegitimate children Susannah followed the practice of christening them with their father's full name, so it is probable her son's father was called Samuel Wright.

In June 1815 London was briefly the scene of jubilant celebration as the population cheered the victors of Waterloo and the end of the war with France. Some time during these weeks Susannah conceived her second son. He was born on 14 February 1816, and she named him Edward Watson after his father.[7]

Details of Edward Watson, the father, are sketchy. He was nine years older than Susannah, which allows time for him to have been married before, though there is no evidence that he was. He could not read or write and his occupation, when he met Susannah, is unknown.[8] Circumstantial evidence hints that Edward may have been a soldier during the war with France, speculation based mainly on comments of Susannah's in a letter to her daughter. She describes Edward and his brothers as having 'a smell of the gunpowder' but, more to the point, talks knowledgeably about the 'good regiment' her nephew is in and how he should do well as long as he can read and write.[9] Perhaps the reference to the importance of literacy reflects some disadvantage suffered by Edward Watson in the army because he could not read and write.

On 6 February 1817, Susannah married Edward Watson in St Anne's, Soho, where her parents had also married. Built in the seventeenth century, a French-style tower had recently been added to the church, a result perhaps of the number of French immigrants who had settled in the area. Susannah's father was a witness at the wedding, along with James Davies, who was an officer of the parish.[10] In the note Susannah left with her children in 1828 she recorded her marriage took place in 1815. Since only eleven years had elapsed, too short surely to forget, and she recorded the month and day accurately, it seems she was overcome with a desire for respectability and wanted her children to think the marriage predated young Edward's birth which was also noted.

The marriage record reveals that the bride and groom were living by that time in Soho, which was a slum in 1817. The once fashionable district had been deserted by the artistocracy, who moved westwards into the newly developed squares of Mayfair in the early eighteenth century.[11] The nobility were replaced, for a time, by the lesser gentry, but by 1812 the narrow, overcrowded streets and tenements of the area were so despised that the architect, Nash, designed the great curve of Regent Street which divides Mayfair and Soho with the stated aim of providing 'a boundary and complete separation' between the nobility and the poor.[12]

Life for those poor, in London as elsewhere in England, was increasingly hard. The war with France had caused prolonged inflation and high prices for staple commodities such as bread. Wages had risen too, but they didn't keep pace with prices and working families struggled to make ends meet.[13] The end of the war had exacerbated these conditions. The months before and after Susannah and Edward's marriage were a period of extreme economic distress, including enormous unemployment and prices which continued to soar.[14] It was claimed in November 1816 that in the London district of Spitalfields alone, 45,000 people were starving and begging to enter the workhouses.[15] The city was thronged with discharged soldiers and sailors, which added to the unemployment and misery. The overcrowded courts and alleys of the London slums, where the Watsons lived, were a prison of disease and poverty. Crime, drunkenness and prostitution thrived as people struggled to survive or seek oblivion from the appalling condition of their lives.

Within ten months of their marriage Susannah and Edward left London, and by December 1817 they were living in the village of Bulwell outside Nottingham. Young Edward had been weak and ill and on 20 September he died.[16] It could be that his death and Susannah's new pregnancy were the deciding factors in the move.

A circumstantial deduction can be drawn that Edward, senior, was born in Nottinghamshire. If so, the family's move to that county becomes even more understandable. It appeared to offer an opportunity to escape the urban poverty of London, a potentially healthier environment for the family, and the possibility of employment for Edward in what may have been his original trade as a framework knitter. It may also have offered something Edward could not obtain in London — the opportunity for poor relief if they were desperate.

The Poor Laws in 1817 were governed by the Act of Settlement dating back to 1662, when few of the population moved around the country, and provided that poor relief could only be obtained in one parish, usually the place of birth.[17] New arrivals in a parish were supposed to report to the overseer of the parish and the local authorities could reject them and order them to leave, or grant them a settlement certificate. Since poor-relief funds were raised by a poor rate borne by the parish residents, it was in their interests to keep the number of people requiring such relief to a minimum and there were some extreme instances of parish officers forcibly transporting unwelcome settlers many miles away to get rid of them.[18] If the parish of Bulwell in Nottinghamshire was Edward's own, and if he could prove that he was born in the village, either through church records or relatives resident there, then he and his family would have been entitled to settle there and were eligible for assistance if necessary.

So, for whatever reason and possibly a combination of these mentioned, Susannah and Edward left London. Susannah was setting out now on a cycle of events which led with dreadful inevitability to separation from her family and banishment from her country.

In the 23 years since Susannah's birth England had moved down a pathway of change which could not be reversed. The Industrial Revolution had caused the rise of great cities where only towns and villages had existed before. More and more people had flooded into the cities seeking work and aggravating overcrowding and disease. Increased concern for sanitation and drainage and advancements in medical science had not improved the conditions in which the poor lived.[19] The politics of the long war with France, particularly when they coincided with bad harvests, created great economic hardship. Improvements in agricultural production and the development of new manufacturing technologies dislocated or changed forever traditions of labour, crafts and industries, which caused enormous unemployment even as they created new work opportunities.

The material changes led to new ideas and new loyalties. The ties that had bound the small village and town communities for centuries to their local landowners, the attitudes of deference and perceived common interest with the duke or the squire, began to break down. In the big cities, and in the country, members of the working class had begun to feel a common interest with one another and against the rich and powerful.

A whole new way of life was coming into existence and the ordinary people in the first two decades of the nineteenth century reacted in confusion and distress. There were sporadic outbreaks of rioting, destruction and violence and one of the most notorious centres for this kind of demonstration, for opposition to technological change and dislocation to traditional industries, was Nottinghamshire.

PITY OUR DISTRESS

In deciding to move to Nottingham, the Watsons chose a course that was out of the frying pan and into the fire. By 1817, the once pleasant town was as overcrowded and slum-ridden as London. To make matters worse, Edward took up an occupation that was threatened with change on all fronts.

Initially the family settled in Bulwell, a small village on the edge of Sherwood Forest, about four miles north-west of the city. Edward and Susannah's daughter, Hannah, was born there on 22 December 1817, and baptised the next day at the church of St Mary on the hill overlooking the village. It was an unusually quick baptism. Perhaps the baby was ill, or perhaps it was simply that Christmas was only two days away. Edward's occupation is described in the baptismal records as 'framework knitter'.[1]

Framework knitters made stockings. The industry was mainly a domestic one, which had once been respected for its artisan skills and craftsmanship. The knitters operated from their homes or from small workshops attached to the house of a master stockinger or hosier. In the eighteenth century, framework knitting was usually a part-time industry combined with another occupation, such as farming, and another characteristic was a tendency for the knitters to cluster in community groups or small villages.[2] Bulwell was one such village.

A combination of increased demand for silk and cotton stockings rather than wool, cost cutting by the merchant hosiers, and an influx of unskilled labourers seeking work as a result of the agricultural and industrial changes, altered the conditions of the framework knitting industry from a predominantly self-employed, self-respecting, skilled trade, to sweated exploitation by capitalist hosiers and middlemen.[3]

There had been a tradition of protest in the industry for some years as the knitters fought to keep out unskilled labour and methods of work which they believed reduced standards. They had also tried to force the hosiers to pay more for their work. This protest had reached a notorious peak in 1811–12 when the Luddites, a highly organised, almost guerilla group of men, systematically smashed knitting frames in an attempt to force the hosiers to agree to their demands.[4] The violence of the framebreaking had at one time so alarmed the government that 12,000 troops were sent to the Midlands, including Nottinghamshire, to control it.[5] The knitters had also banded together in a sophisticated manner to take their protest to the politicians in London. The villages of Bulwell, and also Arnold where the Watsons subsequently lived, were at the heart of the framework knitting industry and its agitation for improved conditions and the main-tenance of standards.[6]

By 1817 the protest movement on both fronts had passed its peak and the trade had degenerated into sweated labour. However, the tradition of agitation and the desire for economic and political reform lingered on in the area. That very year Bulwell was involved in the abortive political revolt by the villagers of Pentrich across the border in Derbyshire.[7]

Whether Edward Watson was a skilled framework knitter in the old tradition or one of the despised untrained labourers who flocked into the area seeking a means of survival, he and his family undoubtedly suffered from the current state of the industry when they arrived in Bulwell. Framework knitters were working 16 to 18 hours per day and earning only seven shillings a week.[8] The frame had to be rented from the hosier and the knitter was paid for the quantity completed.

The Watsons would have followed the usual practice and worked as one economic unit. It is possible they sometimes rented a second frame for Susannah to operate. She certainly did participate in attempts to earn money and could, in her own words, 'work' lace.[9] This probably meant embroider patterns on it, a common occupation for women and girls in their homes — and notoriously badly paid.[10] As soon as practicable the children would have been employed in helping the production.[11] In 1817 Samuel was only three, but by the time he was six he would have been put to work winding cotton or silk for his parents, and Hannah too would have joined in as soon as she was old enough.

It was a hard and grinding life of poverty, hunger and illness. A contemporary observer claimed you could 'always distinguish a framework knitter because he was so careworn and ill-looking'.[12] Edward was often ill during the next ten years and this was most likely due to the grinding labour of the trade he followed.[13] His periods of illness must have had a devastating effect on the income of the family.

In 1819 there was depression and agitation across the country, and in Nottinghamshire it provoked the stockingers into a remarkable demonstration for a time when trade unions were forbidden. Ex-hausted by the struggle to survive, the knitters tried to organise a general strike. Fourteen thousand of them stopped work and many pulled and dragged their heavy frames and left them on the hosiers' doorsteps. Their action forced over two-thirds of the Nottingham hosiers to sign a statement agreeing to raise the price for stockings, but the workers' funds ran out and they were forced to return to work after nine weeks even though some hosiers had not signed. Within a year the prices were as low as ever.[14]

In 1821 there was another strike and only two dozen pairs of stockings were made for two months in the Midland counties. But this action was no more successful than the demonstration two years earlier. It was a time of enormous distress and in Nottingham 5,000 men paraded daily, led by women carrying banners reading 'Pity Our Distress...We Ask for Bread...Help Our Children'.[15]

It was in these circumstances that Susannah and Edward produced their children and struggled to find a way to feed and clothe them. On 2 May 1820 they had a second son whom they again named Edward. They were then living in Arnold, another framework knitting village near Nottingham.[16] Mary Ann was born on 19 January 1823, at which time the family was living again in Bulwell, and they were still in that village when another son, William, was born on 5 November 1825. By the time their last son, Thomas, was born on 2 January 1828 they had moved into the city of Nottingham.[17] The christian names of both William and Thomas probably reflect Susannah's affection for her father and young brother.

It can be assumed that the family's movement, from village to village and then to the city, was caused by the constant search for work and their poverty, which probably resulted in unpaid rent. The 1820s were marked by particularly harsh winters, which aggravated their circumstances with no heating and insufficient clothes and food.[18] They were fighting a losing battle to survive.

Susannah sought her own remedy and began to steal.

In October 1820, less than six months after the birth of her second son called Edward, she stole a greatcoat belonging to a man named William Lee. The coat was lying in a room in a public house. She took it and pawned it. In court, holding her baby in her arms, she was in floods of tears. Although she pleaded guilty she explained that her husband was ill and she had four small children at Arnold. The tears, which are the only ones she is ever recorded as shedding in court, lend some support to the belief that this was her first offence. Did she cry from a mixture of shock of being caught and remorse at breaking a fundamental code of honesty? There appears to be no record, in either London or Nottingham, of any previous offence and the court believed it was her first offence. So it is possible to conclude that she did not turn to stealing until her family made her vulnerable, by which time she was an adult woman of 25. The court was merciful, according to its lights, and ordered her to be imprisoned in the house of correction for one month's hard labour.[19]

She stole again in January 1821, in the middle of winter, the year men and women paraded in the streets with banners crying their distress. This time the charge was more serious. There were two indictments — for stealing two silver spoons, the property of John Wilcockson; and for stealing a silver can, the property of John Green.

Again, with her child in her arms, she pleaded guilty but her previous conviction at the last quarter sessions told against her. She was given six months for each offence, making a year's hard labour in the Nottingham house of correction.[20]

There is no way of knowing how the Watson family managed while she was in gaol. Years later Susannah referred to the children's 'Aunt Mary' in letters, which lends some support to the idea that Edward had relatives in Nottingham. The twentieth-century notion of the extended family was a reality among the poor, at the time, and it was common for brothers, sisters, their husbands, wives and children to share accommodation, which was often a single room. Perhaps it was the children's aunt who cared for them in their mother's absence. There was certainly some kind of base in Bulwell because the family still lived there years later.

Three years passed, during which time Susannah and Edward's second daughter, Mary Ann, was born. In January 1824 Susannah was in court again. This time her crime had a slightly different nature — she committed it under the alias of Mary Green — and reveals that Susannah was becoming a practised criminal. The evidence claims she stole three and a half yards of cotton lace, the property of Hector Christie, having obtaind it as a piece to work by giving him a false address in Clinton Street, Nottingham, and by stating her husband worked with a Mr Marshall in Coalpit Lane. The lace was obtained from Mr Christie in June 1823, and as the months passed and the completed lace was not returned he started to investigate.

This time, Susannah pleaded not guilty, which is the only occasion she claimed to be innocent. Her defence was that she took the lace to work it, but 'the illness of her husband and the necessities of her family induced her to dispose of it'. Since it is unlikely the evidence that she used an alias and gave the wrong address is totally untrue, it seems Susannah was lying. It appears too that she had planned a cover story to hide the crime. The fact that she pleaded 'not guilty', however, suggests at least a sense of grievance and perhaps victimisation. The court dismissed her defence and found her guilty. She was imprisoned again for 12 months hard labour and ordered to pay a fine of 6*d*.[21]

In April 1824 an Edward Watson, aged 39, stole a one pound note and was gaoled in Nottingham for six months.[22] There is no proof this was Susannah's husband, but the age is right and if it is correct then the family were without both parents for most of 1824.

In November 1825, 12 months after Susannah's release from gaol, William Watson was born, his baptismal records revealing that the family was still living in Bulwell and Edward was still a framework knitter.

For two years, Susannah stayed out of trouble. Then, unexpectedly, a Susannah Watson turns up on trial at the Old Bailey in London. The record reads as follows:

SUSANNAH WATSON was indicted for stealing, on 21st March, 1827, 1 table cloth, value 2*s*., the goods of John Cooke, her master.

SARAH COOKE: I am the wife of John Cooke. We live in Duke Street, St
Giles. The prisoner had some needlework to do for me which she took home
— she used to take her work home in this tablecloth — I missed it and found
it in pawn.

CROSSED EXAMINED BY MR PHILLIPS:

  Q. Did you pay her on Saturday.

  A. No, I was at the theatre and left her money with a woman; but she was
    not paid. I believe she was very poor.

ROBERT MARKS: I live with Mr Jones a pawnbroker of the Tothill Street.
The prisoner pawned this tablecloth with me.

DAVID HENRY: I am an officer and took her in charge; I found the duplicate
on her.

  (Property produced and sworn to)

The prisoner received a good character.

     GUILTY   AGE 29

Strongly recommended to mercy by the Prosecutor and Jury, it being her
first offence.

CONFINE 9 DAYS.[23]

There is no proof this is the same Susannah Watson, but some circumstantial evidence to suggest it may have been. Susannah's father,
William Bidy, died in London on 12 March 1827, at the extraordinarily
old age of 81 years.[24] His death and probable preceding illness provides
a reason for Susannah's sudden presence in the city. St Giles, where
Mrs Cooke lived, is in Soho, and Tothill Street is not far from where
William Bidy was living at the time of his death. The age of the prisoner
is near enough to correct. (Susannah's age on all the documents
concerning her varies within a range of four years, and by 20 years on
her death certificate.) Last, but by no means least, Susannah described
herself several times as a needlewoman and related how she earned
money by needlework. The Susannah Watson who stole from Mrs
Cooke, was a needlewoman.

If this is the same Susannah Watson, then the record sheds light on
her character and circumstance. Mrs Cooke, who probably had no
choice but to prosecute in order to get back her tablecloth, described
Susannah as 'very poor'. And yet Susannah obviously made a sufficient impression to be trusted to take her work home and to cause
both Mrs Cooke and the jury to recommend mercy. There is also the
bald statement that the prisoner 'received a good character', although
it is not revealed from whom.

Susannah returned to Nottingham and to Edward and in January
1828 she gave birth to Thomas Watson and the records reveal that his
father was still a framework knitter and the family lived at Dutch Alley,
in the heart of Nottingham.[25]

The heart of Nottingham by 1828 was diseased and ugly. The city
had been flooded with people from all over the country, who were
looking for work. The population had soared to nearly 50,000 and yet
the town boundaries, encircled by private property rights, had not
expanded. The streets were narrow and twisting and there had been
no control over building or drainage.[26] The cramped back-to-back
houses, so typical of English industrial towns, were uniquely dis-

astrous in Nottingham, due to the local custom of arranging them in narrow courts, closed at both ends and entered by narrow tunnels. There was a common drain down the middle of the court and an inadequate group of privies at one end. The houses consisted of two, or sometimes three rooms, one above the other. Each room was about 11 feet square, with a small storage space under the stairs.[27] By 1828, this was the kind of place Susannah lived in.

In October 1827 the family had been dealt a heavy blow when Edward was caught poaching with four other men. Poaching had always been a source of income and food for the poor and was rife in Nottinghamshire and, indeed, all over England at the time. The penalties were heavy but, with the exception of the landowners, it was not regarded by the people as morally wrong.[28] With the increasing poverty of the working classes during the early decades of the nineteenth century, poaching developed into virtually a class war. There were numerous poaching gangs and they were opposed by the landowners' associations. But the gangs were like a brotherhood, with secret meetings and oaths of loyalty for mutual protection.[29]

Edward's case became a local *cause célèbre* because Sir Robert Clifton's gamekeeper shot and injured one of the poachers and was put on trial for malicious wounding. Feelings ran high in the Nottingham public houses and many people contributed to a collection so the injured poacher could pursue the prosecution. Edward attracted criticism and ill-will when he appeared as a witness for the defence and claimed he thought the keeper was shooting at the dog. He was accused of changing his story and doing a deal for his own benefit. Presumably Susannah, as the wife of someone who betrayed the brotherhood, was also the target for abuse in the months leading to the trial, which did not take place until March 1828.[30]

In the meantime, Edward was sentenced to nine months in the house of correction at Southwell for his part in the poaching gang and Susannah and the children were facing another freezing winter with the loss of their breadwinner.[31] In March 1828 a brief note in the *Nottingham Journal* recorded that Susannah had been caught stealing. She was committed to gaol to wait for her trial at the next quarter sessions.[32]

On 16 April 1828 Susannah faced the court for her day of reckoning. The *Nottingham Journal* reported the details of her case:

THE FOLLOWING PLEADED GUILTY: SUSANNAH WATSON, aged 33, for stealing on the 9th February, two shirts and other things, the property of J. Foster. Another indictment charged her with stealing on the 8th March, a basket and seven brushes, the property of Thos. Hemsley. A third indictment charged her with stealing 2 lb of sugar, 1 lb of mustard and 1½ lb of starch, the property of James Wilcock. It was also charged that she had previously been convicted of felony. She pleaded guilty to the whole. On being called up to receive judgment, the prisoner entreated for mercy, on account of her six children, the youngest of whom was only a few weeks old. When asked about her husband, she shook her head, and declared that her offences arose from her poverty; she could not bear to see her children starving.[33]

The *Mercury* added some further details:

> The prisoner stated that she had six children the eldest 13 years of age and the youngest only 15 weeks old; that she had been reduced to the greatest distress and was driven by necessity to what she had done, though it certainly was no excuse for her. She threw herself on the merciful consideration of the Court. The Recorder in passing sentence, declared that it would be beneficial to her children to have her removed from the country. She had been convicted of felony in two cases; in 1821, and suffered twelve months' imprisonment; she had been again convicted at the Epiphany sessions, 1824, and sentenced to another twelve months' imprisonment; and that between 1821 and 1824 she had been in the House of Correction for three months for obtaining lace under false pretences. The sentence therefore was, that she should be transported for fourteen years.[34]

Did Susannah expect the sentence? She was no fool and must have known the risks she ran. She stole this time on a grand scale, an act of desperation and, perhaps, defiance. The Sessions Crown Minute Book gives a complete list of what she took:

1 Basket	1s.	9 February from John Foster
2 Shirts	6s.	
2 Aprons	2s.	
1 Collar	0s. 6d.	
4 Handkerchiefs	2s.	
1 Pair Stockings	1s.	
3 Shirts	9s	9 February from Thomas Foster
1 Basket	1s. 6d.	8 March from Thomas Hensley
7 Brushes	6s.	
1½ lb Starch	1s. 6d.	8 March from James Wilcox
1lb Mustard	1s. 6d.	
½ lb Blue	2s.	
2 lbs Sugar	1s. 4d.	
½ lb Soap	0s. 3d.	
1 Pint of Peas	0s. 2d.	
½ oz Tobacco	0s. 1d.	
TOTAL	35s. 10d.[35]	

With Thomas in her arms, Susannah was confined to the Nottingham county gaol to come to terms with her fate. She was confronting the greatest emotional agony a mother can face — permanent separation from her children — and made the decision to take Thomas with her.

After the July assizes she was joined by three other women who had been sentenced to transportation. The evidence indicates these three were professional criminals. They were all convicted under the name of Mary Smith, although only the youngest of them was really called

Mary. The other two were Ann or Ellen Burke, their leader, and Ellen Turnbull. None of them was a Nottingham woman. They had arrived by coach from Newark and stolen goods from a shop only yards from where they got out. Ann Burke was so well aware of the criminal law that one of her first actions after being arrested was to arrange for her money in a Hull Bank to be withdrawn for her because, she said, if she was convicted anything in her bank account might be forfeited to the Crown. When all three were sentenced to transportation, young Mary dissolved into floods of tears and pitifully cursed the judge and jury, but Ellen Turnbull reacted angrily. 'What are you crying about, I would not give them that satisfaction,' she snapped at Mary.[36]

The three women made a futile attempt to escape from Nottingham gaol by digging a hole through a wall, but they were caught in the act. They were searched and a letter was discovered which they had written to friends outside:[37]

Dear Friends,

I beg to inform you that our sentence is 7 long years and if we had your relief we could get out of this If you would but come and give assistance at the outside It is the next place fo [from?] the uppanisters [upholsterers?] and the cabinet makers shop under the walk. There is nothing but a thin wall to keep us in and we have it almost ready We only want you to just stall at the outside while we come through Three people will do We are left our own clothes with us and we are the length of a day and nobody comes to us Ellen Burke is got fifty pounds and she wants somebody to came to draw it The one you see Benjamin Cady the better for to come to say that he is Ellen Burke's brother and demand this money and say that he wanted it to support her children You must come to the outside and give 3 knocks at the wall be sure the place you knock at it is the last room under the walk when you come to Clark the cabinet markers... We do not go to bed while 9 o'clock at night and if please God that we are left here the nights will get shorter and there will be no trouble whatever Do not be alarmed at the carrier for his own wife is here and has fourteen years with us

If please god that we are left here a month longer I hope with God's assistance and yours we will I hope be at liberty once more again. We want you to take the last brick out for us that is all

We three women are as comfortable as ever we can wish to be only Mary Smith wants to see Charles the boy Mrs Sticker wants to see her school Mary Collins wants to see that handsome bit a man of hers once more but she hopes that he wont pick that beauty of Birmingham again If it is a thing that we cannot have our liberty it will be for the want of assistance but if we are to go we intend to keep a good case to accommodate you people when you come over So I conclude with our kind love and respects to you all and may God protect you and bring you through life... will ever be the prayers of your sincere friends until death

Mary Smith and Ellen Burk and Mary Collins[38]

Through the spring and summer of 1828 Susannah waited for the order to leave Nottingham. In May she received the sad news that two-year-old William was dead; he was buried at Bulwell on 18 May at the church where he was christened.[39] Perhaps prompted by his death, Susannah was impelled to record the details of her family so they would not be forgotten. A note in her handwriting sets out her birthday, the births and deaths of her children, and her (falsely dated) marriage to Edward. On another piece of paper, a childish hand has copied them carefully and, on the back, the letters of the alphabet. Preserved with these two papers is a third which notes, in Susannah's writing, the death and ages of her parents.[40]

Edward visited her when he was released from Southwell in July.[41] Although years later she referred to 'that cursed poaching that was the cause of my being sent away', she bore him no grudge and described him to her daughter as 'always a kind husband'.[42] Perhaps at this time she tried to make plans for him and the children to follow her to New South Wales, as many wives did their convicted husbands. Susannah believed for the rest of her life that 'it would have been well for him to have followed me',[43] but Edward not only refused to try and follow her, he apparently never communicated with her once she left England. He could not write, but in 1857 he told his daughter Hannah he did not wish to hear from Susannah.[44]

Meanwhile the authorities at the Home Office in London were making arrangements to settle Susannah's fate. The number of female convicts in England awaiting transportation was building up and on the orders of the home secretary, Sir Robert Peel, the ship *Harmony* was chartered in July to take 100 women to Van Diemen's Land, but within a month it became necessary to charter another.[45]

The mayor of Newcastle sent a letter asking when the women in his gaol would be removed and was assured 'it will be soon'.[46] Isabella Errington, Dorothy Huldie and Ann Marshall were unaware their fate was being hurried along.

Some miles north of Nottingham, in York, influential clergymen were being persuaded to intercede for one Ann Simpson, but without success. She would shortly meet Susannah on board the *Princess Royal*.[47]

In the gaol at Guildford, four women had their death sentences commuted to transportation. Jane McPherson, Elizabeth Jones, Catherine Donoghue and Catherine Barrett would also be boarding the *Princess Royal*.[48]

Sir Robert Peel's secretary received a letter from the visiting magistrate at the gaol in Presteigne, a small town on the Welsh/English border. The secretary assured the magistrate that while the law did not authorise females to be sent to the hulks, he would ensure the troublesome dairymaid, Ann Morgan, would be dispatched on the next available transport, which was even then preparing for the voyage.[49]

In late October, the summons finally came. A removal order dated 20 October 1828 authorised the transfer from Nottingham gaol of John Clarke, Matthew Stevenson and William Cocking to the *York* hulk at Portsmouth, and on Wednesday, 29 October, they and the four women convicts were taken away from Nottingham.[50]

In 1876 Susannah reminded her daughter: 'It is 48 years, the day after my birthday, since I saw your face'.[51]

THE FULL PENALTY OF THE LAW

While Susannah and the three Marys waited in Nottingham gaol, fate was curling her tentacles around 96 other women who would share their voyage to New South Wales. Throughout 1828 they were gathered in from all over England. They were convicted in the big cities, including London, Liverpool and Manchester; the large towns such as Bristol, Portsmouth and Newcastle; from the counties of Northumberland in the north to Somerset in the south, to Norfolk in the east and Cornwall in the west. Like Susannah, many of them were born in a different place from the one where they were tried. They came from 50 different birthplaces across England, Ireland and Wales and yet were tried in only 27 centres in England.[1]

The available records of their trials leave a clear impression that, as with Susannah, there was no real miscarriage of justice in the offences for which they were tried. There were no hard-done-by martyrs of political persecution or judicial injustice among them — victims, perhaps, of a grinding circle of poverty and social change, but guilty of theft, false pretences and receiving stolen goods, often in the context of drunkenness and sexual manipulation.

Drink and sex were recurring elements in many of the women's crimes. They were the tools with which the women stole, and on some occasions the weakness through which they were caught. In this they were typical of the lower classes in England. Drinking, for instance, was a way of life. In the eighteenth century the working peoples' addiction to hard liquor had so alarmed the authorities they had passed a Licensing Act in 1751 in an attempt to reduce wholesale drunkenness.[2] But 30 years later anti-Catholic riots in London turned into a massive drunken orgy as the mob broke into a large distillery and ended by drinking raw spirits straight from the gutter.[3] Although the drunken excesses of the previous century had lessened by 1828, the fundamental relationship between the working people, their drinking, and life in the pubs, continued through the industrial changes, war and starvation of the new century.[4] The sale of sex, either professional or casual, was also a way of life for thousands of women. It was often the only 'work' available, their only means to survive, and it was not in itself a crime unless combined with theft.[5] But the increasing self-righteous morality, particularly of the growing middle class, allied quite probably with instinctive male antagonism to being outwitted through sexual vulnerability, meant that crimes involving drink or sex were likely to incur greater wrath from the judiciary.[6]

Margaret Lyons, a 21-year-old Irish girl from Dublin, was charged only with picking pockets but the circumstances told against her. The prosecutor, Thomas Guillam, said he met Margaret and another woman in the street. 'They got hold of my arms and said they wouldn't let go till I gave them a drink.' After visiting a pub, they took him home, robbed him of his money and clothes, including his spectacles, and threw him out the door. But Guillam stayed on the doorstep, shouting, until a watchman came and they forcibly entered the house. Margaret and the other woman were sentenced to transportation for life.[7]

Eighteen-year-old Martha Turner, after drinking in a pub with a sailor, took him back to her rooms and asked him for his money before she went to bed with him. She grabbed the money and ran off. The aggrieved sailor, with the police, tracked her down in a pub the next day and Martha was sentenced to life.[8]

Ann Carrier, Elizabeth Foxall and Mary Harcourt were convicted specifically of stealing from the person (of men) in houses of ill-fame in Birmingham. Both Elizabeth and Mary were given life sentences but Ann was lucky and received only seven years. In the case of Ann Kirby at Bristol, who was sentenced to 14 years, 'the prosecutor got beastly drunk and was then taken by the prisoner to a brothel where he was robbed'.[9]

Catherine Barrett, Mary Hilsley, Mary Palmer and Mary Wootton were all simply convicted of 'stealing from the person', a description which often had a sexual connotation.[10] Susan King, or Forrester, was convicted of stealing a watch from the person. The evidence reveals she met Edward Croft, a labourer, in the street at 3.00 a.m. and went with him for a drink. When trying to persuade him to go home with her, she put her arms round him and, when he refused, ran off with his watch. She was caught in the street and the watch was found in her pocket. Susan claimed Croft was drunk and gave her his watch to pawn, but she was found guilty and sentenced to 14 years transportation.[11]

The details of Hannah Solomons' trial in London, and of Ann Cheeseman and Ann Simpson together at Hull, are indicative of the part sex and drink played and the professional nature of their crimes.

Old Bailey, London. 11 September, 1828.
    HANNAH SOLOMONS and CHARLES BANKS charged with stealing two sovereigns, eight shillings and one sixpence from the person of James Winter.

WINTER: I am a lighterman. I went to a public house and had a beef steak pie, some beer and a gin. I met the prisoner outside. She asked me for gin. I did give her one. I was sober. I went to her lodgings in Bell yard and gave her 3s. 6d. to get some supper. I sat in a chair and went to sleep. I had been up 4 nights and was very tired. I was woken by Banks turning me over. I said: 'You have robbed me.' Banks gave something to Solomons who was sitting up in bed.

Banks and Winter fought and Winter was tossed out the door but he came back with a watchman and found the prisoners in bed together. The room was searched and the money found.

SOLOMONS: He got so drunk he could not stand. He gave me the money for supper. He slept a quarter of an hour while I got supper. He had his things off, got up and put them on and said he was ill-used.

BANKS: I had been to a fair and met Solomons as I returned. She asked me to go home. I did and saw Winter there. I was going to leave. She said: No, don't go away, wake him and he will go.

Someone testified to Banks's good character and, although found guilty, he was only imprisoned for six months. Hannah was sentenced to 14 years transportation.[12]

Quarter Sessions, Hull. July 1828.
ANN CHEESEMAN (20), ANN SIMPSON (16) and SAMUEL RANDALL (22) were charged with stealing £49 from the person of John Smith.

The prosecutor was the master of the trading sloop Nile. On the night in question he fell in with the female prisoners who persuaded him to go to a public house with them where they ordered some liquor. The male prisoner Randall was in the house at the time. Smith and the two females went into a private room where he fell asleep when the prisoners robbed him of the amount mentioned and then ran away. He awoke some time afterwards and found that his property was missing. On the following day through the assistance of a constable he took one of the female prisoners (Simpson) on whom was found part of the property and, by her information, the others were followed to Leeds where they were apprehended. Cheeseman had some of the monies in her possession but none was found on Randall except articles bought for him by Cheeseman. These facts were fully proved in evidence but several parts of the case are unfit to meet the public eye. Two witnesses (Mr Nixon and Mr Jackson, hairdresser, to whom he had served his apprenticeship) gave Randall a good character. The jury acquitted him but found the two females guilty.[13]

The women turned on each other. Ann Simpson betrayed Ann Cheeseman's whereabouts and she, in her defence, claimed Ann Simpson had performed the robbery. The recorder sentenced them to 14 years transportation each and condemned them at length:

Cheeseman had already, at no distant period, been convicted of a similar crime. The whole course of her life had been a continued scene of prostitution and dishonesty. Nothing could be more shameful and disgraceful than her conduct with the prosecutor, even independently of the robbery. Simpson's character was not a whit better. A very short time ago, she had been brought before the Magistrates, and committed to the house of correction for an offence so disgraceful that he [the recorder] was ashamed to mention what it was. She was hardly out of prison before she was engaged in the present crime. He had remarked that her conduct, during the trial, had been distinguished by extreme levity.[14]

Drink was the undoing, or at least the defence, of Ann McGee. She was caught in London taking the clothes off a child and was accused of stealing the frock. She stated: 'I leave myself on the mercy of the Court. I was intoxicated and had the child in the yard not knowing what I was doing.' Margaret Coffin, accused of stealing money from the man she took home with her, said in her defence: 'I wasn't sober. I asked him upstairs and he came.' A journalist who covered Mary Wheat's trial commented after hearing the evidence: 'This woman's life it seems has been a continued scene of dishonesty, induced by an incorrigible propensity to spirituous liquors'. Caroline Thomas was described as 'very drunk' when she was taken in charge by the watchman and it was drink that betrayed Ann Kinsman.[15]

Ann, a 20-year-old dairymaid, accosted a man returning from Blandford Fair in Dorset, diverted him by putting her left hand 'round his person', and used her right to take his money. With the aid of a male accomplice, she got away, but at her trial the following evidence was given:

> Henry Jacob, a constable of Dorchester deposed that in consequence of the prisoners being found in a very drunken state in the streets, he took them into custody and suspecting that some person had been robbed at Blandford fair, wrote to the constable at Blandford, who forwarded his letter to the prosecutor at Shroton; the latter attended at Dorchester and identified the prisoners.

It took several witnesses to prove Ann's guilt and it was only because she and her lover got drunk that she was caught. Her accomplice received two years imprisonment with hard labour, but Ann was sentenced to seven years transportation — whereupon she looked at the prosecutor and said: 'You old rogue, your soul is lost for ever'.[16]

In most cases with a sexual element there is considerable complicity by the male victims or at the very least enormous gullibility, but few of the women defended themselves and the evidence of the victim and a watchman usually decided the sentence. Jane Edwards was one who vigorously argued her case:

> Old Bailey, London.
>   JANE EDWARDS age 25, charged with stealing one handkerchief, value 3s., from the person of James Hodgson.
>   HODGSON: I was in Bath place, New Road, I felt my handkerchief go. I seized the prisoner, she was too strong and pulled it away.
>   PRISONER: I didn't take it from his person. I am an unfortunate girl and was with him half an hour. He told me to feel in his pocket if he had any money. He said 'You hussy, if there was a watchman I would give you in charge'. I have no parents or friends.
>   HODGSON: I wasn't in her company at all, she did drag me across the road and asked me for 2d. I would not give it to her and she took my handkerchief.
>   GUILTY 14 years.[17]

There were many cases of straight-out robbery which involved neither sex nor drink.

Mary Tilley, who was only 17 years old, was convicted of stealing seven yards of ribbon while actually buying two yards of it. Mary Connell, also very young at 19, entered a shop and asked if they had any second-hand shoes. When told 'no' she left, but another customer told the storekeeper she had stolen a pair and she was followed and caught with the boots on her. Margaret Mahoney or Meliar, who was married with three children, was accused of walking out of a shop with two pounds of bacon, but she stated: 'I had the money in my hand. I put the bacon in my basket and he took me directly' (that is, she had not walked out with it). Sarah Quittenton was looking at ribbon in a shop when she was accused of stealing some, but, she claimed, 'I still had a piece in my hand and he [the shopkeeper] knocked it off and said I'd stolen it'. She added, in a pathetic attempt to prove her respectability: 'I rented a house off Mr Hudson eighteen years, but he is dead'. All these women were from London and were sentenced to seven years transportation.[18] Outside London, Elizabeth Stocker, Ann Bowler, Mary Ann Bates and Ann Perks were all found guilty of stealing dress materials, probably in very similar circumstances.[19] Ann Perks stole 90 yards of lace from a box on the counter. She must have expected the death penalty because, when sentenced to life, she said saucily to the judge: 'Thank you my Lord. I want another day to clean myself.'[20] She may have been more thankful than she revealed. Her mother had also been transported.

Nine women robbed houses rather than shops. Mary Wheat was caught in the act:

MARY WHEAT, 33, was indicted for stealing. . . 1 gown, 2 frocks, 2 skirts, 1 flannel petticoat, 2 pairs of stockings and 3 hats the property of John Patterson.

The prosecutor resides in Spinsters Court, Church Lane. At about half past one in the morning a neighbour returning home stumbled over a bundle of things in the passage of her house which adjoins that of the prosecutor. She called up another neighbour and having procured light and having examined the bundle she recognized some of the property as belonging to Mr Patterson. They proceeded to her house and when about to enter the prisoner came out with 3 mens hats belonging to Mr Patterson in her possession. A watchman was called and she was taken into custody. It appears that the door of the house had been left unlocked to enable the son of Mrs Patterson to get in when he came home.

The prisoner on being charged with the robbery and on her defence at her trial, told a long improbable story about meeting a man with the property in his possession who she said brought her to the house. A certificate of a previous conviction for felony at Hull was given in evidence.

Mary was found guilty and sentenced to seven years for this offence.[21]

Mary Haynes, a 26-year-old dressmaker from Bristol, was one of five women convicted of receiving stolen goods. She was originally indicted for stealing with a man named Joseph Monks, but there was apparently insufficient proof of her involvement in the actual robberies.

Although she had no previous convictions, she and Joseph must have been known to the authorities because their room was searched only on suspicion. Items stolen from several houses were discovered and Mary received seven years for one offence, plus seven years for another.[22]

Ann Loydall, aged 34, was convicted of receiving silver tea spoons stolen by her 17-year-old brother, Thomas, for which she got 14 years. Sarah Hazle was also involved in crime through a relative. Her brother-in-law, George Hazle, and two other men stole clothes in Bristol and Sarah was convicted of receiving them. The leader of the men was sentenced to seven years transportation. George Hazle and the third man were sent to prison for 12 months hard labour, while Sarah came off worst of all and was sentenced to 14 years.[23]

The only violent crime was committed by Margaret Hartigan, or Splain, in London. It was reported in the newspapers as far away as Leeds:

CHILD MURDER: On Friday last Margaret Hartigan was put to the bar, charged with the wilful murder of Mary Moore, an illegitimate child of 5 months old, of which Catherine Crawley was the mother. The evidence brought forward proved that on the 20th August last, the prisoner, her brother (8 years old) the mother of the deceased, a Mrs Toomey, and another woman named Anderson, at a house in Crown Court, Whitechapel, were together in an apartment in which three families resided, where also were three of their children. A quarrel arose among them; the prisoner struck Mrs Toomey more than once in the face, and a fight between them was the consequence. The mother of the child attempted to part the combatants when the prisoner struck her — she then took her own child off the bed, leaving the deceased infant with another on it — took up the kettle of boiling water from the hearth and, saying that 'If she could not get her revenge on the woman, she would on the children' — threw the kettle of water against the wall at the head of the bed, which fell on the child. The mother of the deceased snatched it up and dipped it in a tub of cold water: it was carried to the hospital, where it died the next day of the scalding it had received.

Although one of the witnesses claimed Margaret was completely calm about what she'd done, the enormity of it certainly dawned on her in the hours that followed. The watchman who went to arrest her the following morning said she told him 'she had been coming to give herself up. She knew she had done wrong and had been very uneasy all night.' In court, when asked if she wished to speak in her own defence, she replied with a kind of simple dignity: 'I have said all I had to say. I do not wish to say anything now.' She was convicted of manslaughter and sentenced to life.[24]

Georgiana Baxter, a 26-year-old Londoner, was the only prisoner whose background indicates some level of comfort. She lived in an apartment with several rooms, including a drawing room with a piano. Her lover was a member of the 'lesser gentry' with genteel connections and the note he left for a relative, who subsequently prosecuted him, reveals something about Georgiana:

> Honoured Sir, my conscience won't allow me to look my benefactor in the face since I behave so villainous to one who has been like a father. The reason I am absconding, I have stolen a gold watch in the name of Steel and I have had it stolen from me by a woman whom I have loved. Adieu, dear Sir, I remain your unhappy and wretched slave.   Robert Jones.
>   By the time you receive this I shall be numbered with the dead. I have borrowed 2 shillings from the till which my brother will pay for me.

Georgiana was convicted of receiving and sentenced to 14 years.[25]

The reasons for the women's crimes are not often revealed in the reports of their trials.

Sarah Hancock, Dorothy Huldie, Ann Maw, Elizabeth Smith and Margaret Williams were all convicted of pledging or pawning illegally — an offence which is the same as Susannah Watson's crime in London, when she pawned Mrs Cooke's tablecloth which she had used to carry her needlework home. These women had much more in common than the same crime. For one thing, they were older women — four of them aged between 39 and 45 years — which meant they had grown up in the relatively stable period before the worst effects of the war with France and the Industrial Revolution. These four were also among the minority on the *Princess Royal* who could read and write, again, perhaps, reflecting their birthdate when time could be spared for inessentials like education. Only Margaret Williams, aged 30, was comparatively young. An Irishwoman from Londonderry, she was convicted far from home in Liverpool. Three of the five had no previous offences, but Dorothy Huldie and Ann Maw had two each. All of them were married or widowed and all had children. Sarah Hancock claimed she had stolen to pay her rent and the details of Elizabeth Smith's trial in London reveal she was married with three children and was accused of pawning a sheet off her own bed, which was owned by her landlady. Elizabeth pleaded 'distress', a cry that most likely covers a history as tragic in its circumstances as Susannah's.[26]

Mary Mahoney, a young Irish girl, accused her publican employer of deliberately tempting her to steal and the evidence of entrapment creates sympathy for this claim.

Elizabeth Gray, who prosecuted Ann Barnett, revealed they had been in the poor house together. She met Ann crying in the street and Ann asked if she would give her lodging. Ann was convicted of tricking Gray into leaving the house the next morning and stealing clothes while she was out.

Mary Wheat, although described as addicted to drink, begged for mercy because of her children.[27]

Nowhere in the trial records of 31 London women, or in the newspaper descriptions obtained for 34 women in other parts of the country, is there a defence to match Susannah's plea that she could not bear to see her children starving. But Susannah was sufficiently educated to have the power to express herself fluently and vehemently. There must have been others who suffered the same distress in silence. Poverty and overcrowding are revealed throughout the records, but there is also a strong overall impression, not only of people to whom crime was a way of life, but of people who had few personal values. The descriptions of the trials are full of details of trickery, lies, manipulation and disloyalty, as well as drunkenness and prostitution.

In general, Susannah and her shipmates on the *Princess Royal* were a microcosm of all the female convicts transported to New South Wales and Van Diemen's Land. This small sample of 100 women supports, in the main, L. L. Robson's statistical analysis of all the convicts transported.[28] Robson found larceny was the predominant crime, and 86 of the *Princess Royal* convicts were tried for this offence, of which 35 were classified as 'Picking Pockets'. The other offences were receiving stolen goods, pawning or pledging illegally and obtaining goods falsely, for which 11 women were convicted. One woman, Mary Ann Taylor, was sentenced for highway robbery and Margaret Hartigan committed manslaughter.[29] Half the women (51) were sentenced to seven years; 19 for life; 29, including Susannah, for 14 years; and this break-up comes extremely close to Robson's findings.[30]

Robson's statistical analysis led to his conclusion that six out of ten women had former convictions. In this respect, however, the women on the *Princess Royal* differ from the average, for two-thirds of them (68) had none. One-third, including Susannah, had two previous known convictions and Mary Ann Collins from Manchester was the only woman with three former offences.[31] There was considerable inconsistency between their previous record, their crime, and their transportation sentence. Susannah had two former convictions and stole goods worth £1 15s., but nearly all the other women sentenced to 14 years had no previous convictions and their crimes ranged from picking pockets of goods worth three shillings to highway robbery. Most of the women sentenced to life also had no previous convictions and their crimes too ranged widely in value and type.[32] Susannah, it seems, was lucky not to have been sentenced for life.

The punitive attitude of the judges had been reinforced by a recent statute allowing prisoners to be charged with having been previously convicted of felony.[33] The recorder at Hull expressed his determination, where the parties had been previously convicted of felony, to put the full penalty of the law into execution.[34] In Birmingham the judges specifically acted on the principle of transporting for life all prisoners who had been previously convicted.[35] Charlotte Tither had been caught there and her victim knocked down by her male accomplices. In sentencing her to life, the judge said:

> If there was no other reason, the violence that was used to the prosecutor would induce him to remove the prisoner from the desperate connection which she had formed and it was his determination to transport for life everyone where rescue had been made or attempted in the town of Birmingham for really in its present state no one was safe there either in his property or his person.[36]

The chairman of the Somerset sessions reproved

> the too great a readiness on the part of prosecutors, after they had attained the fullest conviction of the delinquent, to appeal most beseechingly to the

Court for an extension of mercy; which, if not attended to, brought down from the public erroneous censure for undue rigour. He hoped such cases only as deserved punishment would be brought before them, when he had no doubt the Court would do its duty.[37]

Duty done, the judges had filled the gaols to overflowing. As the golden English autumn began to turn to winter, the authorities at the Home Office sent out the orders that would make room for more offenders and bring 100 women from around the country to their meeting place on a small ship on the River Thames.

CHAPTER 4

TRANSPORTED BEYOND
THE SEAS

The *Princess Royal* lay at anchor on the Thames at Woolwich in London. She had been built at Yarmouth in 1794, the year of Susannah's birth, and by 1828 was rated only Class E1 by Lloyd's. At 402 tons she compared in size with the twentieth-century commuter ferries which scurry busily across Sydney Harbour. This would be the second voyage to New South Wales for both the ship and her Captain, Henry Sherwood: in 1823 the *Princess Royal* had been chartered to transport 156 male convicts to Sydney.[1]

The women began to embark during the last week of October, and by 25 October Surgeon Superintendent Andrew Douglas Wilson already had four patients in his hospital. He described 42-year-old Sarah Piper from Brighton as 'a helpless object, unfit to take a voyage to New South Wales' and Jane Lyons from Liverpool as 'an unfit object' to be sent to the colony. Both Sarah and Jane, along with Ann Kinsman, were suffering badly from ulcers. But Surgeon Wilson's greatest concern was 50-year-old Mary Pindar, whom he described as 'an old, infirm and helpless woman... fit only for a Hospital or some such asylum'.[2]

By 1828 the ship's surgeon was usually a naval officer who had to ensure the conditions of the vessel's charter by the Navy Board were observed. He was totally responsible for the health and welfare of convicts — a system instituted by the authorities in 1814 as a check on the contractors who owned the ships — and the conditions concerning the convicts were very specific. They included provision for regular cleaning and ventilation of their quarters, the supply of bedding and clothes and the scale of their rations. The amount of time they must be allowed on deck was specified and an area had to be set aside as a hospital.[3] The master of the ship was obliged to comply with the surgeon's decisions concerning the convicts, but he did share one power with the surgeon and that was the right to punish them.[4]

The women prisoners for the *Princess Royal* came on board as they reached London. They were conveyed by coach and in spite of the damp, cold weather, some may have been forced to travel outside with their feet in irons. Certainly many came on board suffering from colds and rheumatism.[5] Susannah and her companions from Nottingham embarked around 31 October/1 November, but whichever way they had travelled, Susannah's iron constitution stood her in good stead and there is no trace of her on the surgeon's sick list at any time during the voyage.

The women were interrogated by Surgeon Wilson on their arrival and then issued with their bedding, cooking and eating utensils, and the regulation clothing. They were, however, allowed to keep their own clothes as well.

The convicts were divided into messes, usually of six people, who would sleep and eat together throughout the voyage. They were allowed to choose their own messmates, but this was influenced by the order in which they arrived on board. Those already there were entered on the muster list and divided into mess groups. From the numbering on the muster list it appears Susannah, naturally enough, messed with the other three women from Nottingham. Probably, 19-year-old Ann Morgan, the Welsh dairymaid, joined the group, and if Surgeon Wilson refused to allow ten-months-old Thomas to count as the sixth, it is likely they also had with them Sarah Bryant, an 18-year-old nurse girl from Somerset.[6]

As the women settled in, the authorities were completing their arrangements for the voyage. Finally, on 7 November, the Home Office advised the commissioners for the navy that the bonds and contracts for transporting 100 females had all been entered into and there was no reason to delay the vessel's departure.[7]

Before they sailed, Surgeon Wilson finally solved the problem of Mary Pindar. He exercised his right to recommend that she was unfit to take the voyage and was given approval to transfer her to the hospital ship at Woolwich. On the afternoon of 9 November she was taken off the *Princess Royal*.[8]

Two days later the *Princess Royal* weighed anchor and moved slowly down the Thames.[9] The hatches were no doubt battened down on the women's quarters, but there were scuttle holes down the side of the ship, which could be opened, and the convicts probably crowded to peer through these for their last sight of London. Susannah's feelings can only be imagined. Had she reached a stage of resignation to her fate which left her unmoved by their departure? Did she feel bitter and glad to see the back of England and its grinding circle of poverty? Or did she ache with desperate worry and longing for Samuel, young Edward, Hannah and Mary Ann?

Agnes Wicks, a nursemaid and sempstress from London, reacted to their departure with hysteria, which landed her in the ship's hospital the following week. Surgeon Wilson concluded her condition was caused by mental suffering and well he might, for Agnes was leaving a young, dependent child behind. Through most of the voyage Agnes was sick with physical symptoms created by her emotional distress and she alternated between long periods of sullen silence and fits of violent sobbing and incoherent muttering about her relatives.[10]

Some women probably viewed their departure with pleasure. The details of the trial of Catherine Turner (alias Dunn) at the Old Bailey indicate she committed her crime on purpose. An Irishwoman from County Kerry, and single, she had two previous convictions and was arrested for stealing 12 pairs of stockings from a shop in High Holborn. John Graham, a linen draper, gave evidence that he followed her down the street and, when he caught her, she told him she had done it on purpose and was glad he had got his property back. A policeman who had been called to the scene confirmed he had heard Catherine say this. She was sentenced to seven years.[11]

Six women had the prospect of joining husbands who had already been transported. Mary Ann Green's husband, Thomas Walton, and Elizabeth Foxall's husband, William Fox, had both sailed for Van Diemen's Land during 1828. Rachael Dagnall's husband Richard and her brother, Jeremiah Andrews, were also both in Van Diemen's Land. Ann Wright's husband, John, had arrived in New South Wales in July 1828, while Ann Shannon's husband, also John, left on the *Mellish* from Falmouth on 2 January 1829, only two days before the *Princess Royal* set sail from the Isle of Wight. Mary Haynes faced a reunion with her husband, James, after nine years; he had been transported by the *Adamant* in 1820, had served his sentence, and was now free.[12]

Later on the day of her departure from Woolwich, the *Princess Royal* was off Purfleet on the Thames. She paused here for two days, possibly to take on a final group of convicts, until she weighed anchor again on 13 November. The next 24 hours were sheer misery for the prisoners as the ship sailed out of the Thames Channel, into the North Sea and round the coast of England to the Downes, off the town of Deal. The weather was damp and foggy and the sea rough, and every woman on the ship was seasick.[13] Susannah and most of the other women had never been to sea before, many would never even have seen the ocean, and they must have wondered how they would bear the voyage ahead. Only Elizabeth Foxall from Liverpool might have felt at home; her records reveal she was born at sea.[14]

The ship remained at anchor for ten days and the women continued to suffer from seasickness and the biting cold. It is likely that the passengers travelling to the colony on the *Princess Royal* embarked at the Downes, as it was common practice for them to delay boarding until the last landfall within reach of London.[15] There were five cabin passengers and at least one steerage. Mr William Baldy and Mr Stephen Owen, both of whom were coming out to New South Wales to work for the government in the Commissariat Department, were accompanied by their wives, and the Owens also brought their maid, Tabitha Buckman. The fifth cabin passenger was Granville W. Chetwynd Stapylton, who was to make his mark as a surveyor in the colony.[16] Within three years of his arrival Stapylton had explored some of the most remote parts of western New South Wales and traced the rivers which form the sources of the Lachlan. He subsequently accompanied the surveyor general, Sir Thomas Mitchell, on his expedition to Australia Felix, but he lost favour with Mitchell, who described him as morose. Stapylton's friend, Robert Russell, described him as being of a good family but of rather dissipated habits, and he records that Stapylton was eventually killed by natives.[17] By contrast with Stapylton, the Owens were very religious and Rebecca Owen's sister was in fact married to the missionary, Rev. Henry Nisbet. The Owens were to live for many years in Parramatta and Sydney, but in 1854 moved to Tasmania where they believed the climate was better for Stephen Owen's ill-health.[18]

To the passengers, the female convicts would have been objects of curiosity and probably contempt. Although the Owens may have attempted a little reformation, it is unlikely that any of them concerned themselves very much with the welfare or feelings of the women prisoners. But, on a ship of that size for so many tedious weeks, both groups observed and gossiped about each other.

There was another addition to the ship's company while they were anchored at the Downes. Early in the morning on 29 November, Susan King (alias Forrester) gave birth to a baby girl whom she called Elizabeth. She never named the child's father, and as the matron of the Female Factory in Parramatta was later to describe her as illegitimate, perhaps Susan, who had been surviving by casual prostitution in London, did not know who he was. Under Surgeon Wilson's care, mother and baby thrived although the surgeon unwittingly encouraged Susan's addiction to drink by allowing her extra rations of wine. When she was discharged from the hospital a fortnight later she persuaded him to continue the extra wine as 'she can't do without it to nourish her'. Later in the voyage, after the additional wine had been discontinued, Susan checked into the hospital complaining she felt so weak she could scarcely suckle her child and the surgeon restored the wine and ordered extra soup for her as well.[19]

On 14 December the ship set sail again, down the English Channel, following the coast of England still. The next day she was running hard past the Isle of Wight and on 16 December anchored at the Mother Bank off the island. There they stayed for over two weeks, probably waiting for the right winds. The passengers no doubt spent the time on the Isle of Wight and celebrated Christmas ashore. Although Surgeon Wilson's hospital records have a curious gap for that period, it is most likely the women remained on board.

On 4 January it was blowing a gale, but it was in the right direction. The ship was sailing again, out of the protected waters of the Solent and through the rough seas of the Needles passage until, on 8 January, she finally turned her back on England and headed into the Atlantic Ocean. She was not to make landfall again for 121 days.[20]

Once at sea, life on board the *Princess Royal* quickly settled into a routine. The women found their sea legs after the initial shock of the English Channel and there was no more seasickness. The cold weather, however, remained a problem and Surgeon Wilson was kept busy with a constant stream of patients suffering particularly from colds and rheumatism. Young Mary Smith from Nottingham, probably vulnerable through distress at her sentence, came down with pneumonia two months after the ship sailed and spent the rest of the voyage in hospital. Susannah and Thomas remained healthy and did not seek the doctor's help for any ailment.[21]

Each day began, usually around sunrise, when the convict cooks went on deck. They were followed a little later by the mess captains who went up to get the rations. It seems reasonable to assume that Susannah, given her age and the status and experience of a married woman and mother, was chosen as captain of her mess. She would have been responsible for obtaining the fair share of rations for her group and doling the food out equally to each of them, as well as ensuring their mess area was tidy and her companions were well behaved.

Food on the *Princess Royal* was probably better and certainly more regularly available than Susannah could have obtained in England. At least for the time being, she did not have to watch Thomas starve. The rations included beef, pork or plum pudding for dinner daily, pea soup several times a week, a pot of gruel each morning with sugar or butter in it, and three-quarters of a pound of biscuit daily in lieu of bread. The women convicts were also issued with tea and sugar and a kettle for each mess. Red wine, and also lime juice mixed with sugar and watter, were issued daily to combat scurvy.

There were chores to be performed each day. The convicts were required to clean their own quarters and the other decks. They did their own washing and ironing and some of them would earn privileges, such as extra food or wine, for helping in the hospital, organising those cleaning the decks, airing and stowing the bedding, etc.[22] On female convict ships the women no doubt were also required to wash and iron for the passengers and crew. Ann Clark, on arrival in Sydney, was assigned as a servant to Mr and Mrs Baldy, which probably indicates she worked for them in some way while they were on board ship.[23]

The female convict ships were also notorious for the relationships which developed between the women prisoners and the crew. In 1829 women convicts no longer travelled on the same ship as male prisoners and this, combined with the rules and regulations imposed by the Navy Board, had reduced the outright prostitution of female prisoners which had occured in earlier years. Neverthelesss, the women were largely at the mercy of the male passengers, officers and crew, even if it was only to exchange sex willingly for extra privileges.

There were strict regulations against fraternisation but, as Peter Cunningham, a pragmatic and sensible surgeon who made six voyages to New South Wales, humorously noted: 'The truly pitiable surgeon who has hitherto endeavoured strictly to enforce the orders...has certainly most justly entitled himself to the full honour of Catholic canonization on his landing'.

Cunningham impartially blamed both the women and the crew for the fraternisation,[24] and it seems that he was right. Unknown, or more accurately unadmitted by Surgeon Wilson, wholesale fraternisation was taking place on the *Princess Royal*. Every member of the 29-man crew was involved with someone and the women responded willingly, although with that imbalance of numbers by no means all of them took part. The indications are that although there was probably considerable promiscuity at the start, the men and women settled into pairs as the voyage progressed.[25] Some of these relationships had long-term results. Harriet Bannister (alias Carrick), a nursemaid from Stafford, formed a relationship with the second mate, John Wright, who stayed in Sydney after the ship arrived and married her seven months later. Mary Williams, a 26-year-old London housemaid, married George Hearn, the ship's carpenter, in Sydney.[26]

Young Mary Harcourt, a housemaid from Warwick, gave Surgeon Wilson a few anxious moments when she collapsed in a state he described as epilepsy. This happened several times and although he suspected she had been drinking, he dismissed it because he thought it impossible for her to obtain any liquor. Someone among the women prisoners betrayed Mary and Surgeon Wilson eventually discovered she had been drinking stolen rum, which had been given to her by some of the sailors. Months later, when writing his report for the Navy Board, he was still so annoyed at being fooled on two or three occasions by 'really alarming' fits, that he described Mary as 'a worthless woman who gave much trouble and withal was most ungrateful'. He extended this complaint to a grumble about female convicts generally: 'They expect as a matter of right to be waited upon as ladies and nursed like children otherwise the Surgeon may anti-cipate being threatened with a complaint against him to...Governor Darling'.[27]

Peter Cunningham describes the generally noisy, quarrelsome, cheeky and insolent behaviour of women convicts. He draws a vivid picture of the way they would flirt with the sailors, use religious tracts which had been distributed to them to paper their curls, and tell outrageous tales or otherwise try to trick any gullible person.[28] There is no reason to believe the women on the *Princess Royal* were any different. The high spirited Catherine Steel and Johanna Brown, who had no qualms about casually bailing up a lady in a London street and snatching her reticule; Susannah Turbitt and Mary Clancey, who deliberately tricked a woman into their room and stole all her clothes while she slept; Margaret Lyons, Mary Ann Smith, Martha Turner and Hannah Solomons, all Londoners and under 21 years, were only a few of those who had used a combination of drink and sex to entice and rob men. Among the older women Sarah Hancock and Ann McGee, in particular, liked their drop of gin and were both drunk when arrested.[29] All of these, and many others, would have provided a volatile and recalcitrant challenge to the men on the ship. But the chief stirrer was Catherine Donoghue, a robust, sandy haired, 18-year-old who described her home as Horsemonger Lane gaol. The extroverted Catherine saw her role to be as noisy and troublesome as possible. If she wasn't bellowing a song at the top of her voice, she was wandering the decks provoking quarrels by her insults and abuse. An exasperated Surgeon Wilson described her as a 'Demon', the greatest blackguard on the ship.[30]

As the voyage continued, the women no doubt fell into groups which reflected common interests or similarities other than the fact they had been sentenced in the same town. Their ages, for instance, ranged from 15 to 48 and age would have been one dividing factor.

Six of the women were under 18. The youngest was Ann Storrett, aged 15, from Northumberland, who was a kitchen girl convicted of robbing an office. With no previous offences, she was sentenced to seven years transportation. A country girl like Ann would have been wide-eyed at the tales of Mary Tilley and Ann Barnett, the two 17-year-olds from London. Also aged 17 was Ann Stokes from Reading, who had been found guilty of housebreaking. None of these three had previous convictions but Mary Fagan, from Liverpool, was being transported for her third offence by the age of 17, and so was Ann Simpson.[31]

There were four women over 40. Isabella Errington, aged 48, travelled down from Northumberland with young Ann Storrett. Isabella, who had no previous offences, had been sentenced to 14 years for receiving stolen goods. Sarah Lovett, aged 43, was convicted in Leicester of stealing a kettle, and Sarah Hancock and Jane Hyde, both aged 45 and both cooks, were country women convicted in London.[32]

There is no evidence who were Susannah's particular friends and only circumstantial conclusions can be drawn. Needlework was one of the constant activities on the ship and there were others on board who, like Susannah, described themselves as needlewomen. There were several of these whose circumstances and background make it possible they were friends. Agnes Wicks, Ann Loydall, Mary Haynes and Georgiana Baxter could all read and write. With the exception of Ann, they were all married or widowed with one child and their ages, ranging from 26 to 36, grouped around Susannah's. They had been convicted for offences ranging from stealing to receiving but, like Susannah, none of their crimes involved drinking or prostitution. Perhaps they sat in a group on the deck, talking while they were mending or making themselves patchwork quilts. Agnes and Georgiana had been convicted in London and could tell Susannah news of life in her home city. Ann and Mary, from Leicester and Bristol respectively, had experienced the effects of industrial and agricultural change on large provincial towns which compared with Nottingham. Mary, whose husband James was already in New South Wales, could give the group details of life in the colony, and perhaps reassure the distressed Agnes, who was reacting so badly to her departure from England. There would have been much debate about their chances for a good future in the colony and, probably, decisions to be made about whether to declare themselves married or single on arrival.[33]

Susannah also had a bond with the other women who had children on the ship. In addition to Susan King and her new baby, there were five besides Susannah with one child on board: Caroline Thomas, Sarah Pitches, Margaret Mahoney, Margaret Hartigan and Margaret Coffin.[34] Why these and no others, it is impossible to establish. The home secretary's correspondence reveals an acceptance by the authorities that women prisoners would be accompanied by children and the *Princess Royal*, like other female prison ships, was chartered by the Navy specifically for 100 women convicts 'and 30 of their children'.[35] There was, however, at least one prohibition concerning children. No female convict was allowed to embark until she had weaned her child 30 days. In some instances this rule caused women to wean their children very early. In 1829 one surgeon complained to Governor Darling of the effects of early weaning, which he blamed for the death of a child who died shortly after her arrival with her mother in New South Wales.[36]

Thomas Watson was ten months old when the ship sailed and probably began to crawl during the voyage, which would have made his mother's life more difficult. Perhaps, however, there were many willing nursemaids. Thirty-one of the women who sailed left approximately 70 children behind and their hearts must have ached at the sight of the seven children travelling with them.[37] Whatever the problems Thomas' presence caused Susannah, he would also have brought her comfort. He was dependent on her, someone else to worry about, someone to cuddle, sing to and laugh with.

James Pitches was Sarah's only child. He was 18 months old and just the right age to be fascinated by a baby, as was Abigail Hartigan, who was aged 14 months. No doubt they helped to entertain Thomas, and each other, during the long weeks.[38]

Caroline Thomas was an Irishwoman, convicted in London of picking pockets. She had been a widow for six years and her only child, Jane, had just turned nine. James Coffin was eight years old and his mother, Margaret, was a country woman from Essex, a 'plain cook' who, like Caroline Thomas, had been convicted in London of picking pockets. Both women appear to have been supporting themselves by prostitution and both were drunk at the time of their offence. Margaret was also a widow, with only one child, so neither woman left immediate family in England.[39] But Margaret Mahoney shared Susannah's unhappiness. She was married with three children, two of whom were left behind with their father, John, in London. Perhaps for support, both emotional and financial, she took her nine-year-old son Richard with her.[40]

From mid-January the weather was warm and, for most of the women, it was pleasant to sit on deck in the sun. But Mary Ann Taylor found the heat oppressive and collapsed after helping to clean the lower deck. Surgeon Wilson found her lying on her berth, red in the face. Two weeks later, she sat too long in the sun on the upper deck and dramatically fainted into a delirious fever.[41]

In March the ship struck choppy seas and their recently acquired 'sea legs' deserted some of the less surefooted women. Sarah Quittenton fell and struck her knee against a bucket. Elizabeth Foxall slipped on the deck and hurt her right side. Agnes Wicks, who was weak anyway from her emotional stress, hurt her spine and Jane Edwards also fell over and 'shook herself very much'.[42]

Towards the end of April, the long voyage began to draw to a close as the *Princess Royal* sailed along the southern coast of Australia. On 6 May it rounded the south-east tip of the continent at Wilson's Promontory and headed northwards. Now they began to see, off the port bow, the long beaches and distant rolling surf of the east coast. They passed the low-lying entrance to Botany Bay with its jagged sandstone cliffs, their tops covered with weatherbeaten, scrubby vegetation. More cliffs, more beaches and, finally, glistening in the bright sunlight, the tall, white tower of a convict architect's lighthouse, standing sentinel at the entrance to Port Jackson. On 9 May 1829 the ship slipped between the dark, rather menacing northern headland and the crashing seas which perpetually eat away at the southern cliffs, into the blue tranquillity of Sydney Harbour.[43]

It was six months since the *Princess Royal* weighed anchor at Woolwich in London. The 35-year-old ship had once again safely completed the long voyage to the other side of the earth. She could deservedly sail proudly up the harbour. Her next voyage, however, was not to end so well. Carrying the first group of assisted, unmarried women migrants to Van Diemen's Land, she ran aground ignominiously on the estuary of the River Derwent at Hobart.[44]

Surgeon Wilson's next voyage also ended in an undignified fashion. Arriving in Sydney in 1832 in the *Asia*, his rheumatism had so incapacitated him that he had to be hoisted out of the ship in a chair.[45] At this moment in 1829, however, he was pleased with himself. He asserted confidently that 'never female convicts landed at Sydney in a more healthy condition' but commented acidly: 'A dose or two of medicine exhibited to a female convict will frequently prevent the necessity of putting her upon the sick list'.[46]

Susannah had avoided a dose of Surgeon Wilson's medicine. She and Thomas had come through safe and well. But they were over 12,000 miles from Nottingham. Susannah's feelings, as she watched the still waters of Sydney Harbour slide past, waiting for the small town to come in sight, must have been a mixture of relief at the prospect of firm ground beneath her feet after the endless tossing of the little ship, and trepidation at what awaited her. But Sydney Harbour, then as now, offers its own tonic. No one can look at it on a sunny, sparkling blue day without experiencing a lift to the spirits, a reaffirmation that it is good to be alive. Why should Susannah have been any exception?

CHAPTER 5

A VERY PLEASANT TOWN

When the *Princess Royal* dropped anchor in Sydney Cove the passengers disembarked immediately. The women prisoners were not so fortunate. Although firm, dry land was invitingly close, they were to spend ten more days on the heaving decks of the ship.[1]

Life was far from dull, however. The arrival of a vessel from home was greeted by swarms of little boats as local residents came out to check for relatives or friends on board. They would circle the ship calling up to the prisoners: 'Anyone from Cornwall?' 'Anyone from Birmingham?' So even someone who only shared a home town was welcomed as a friend and quizzed for news.[2] Two years earlier, if Susannah had read the newspaper in a Nottingham public house, she would have seen a vivid description of the kind of reunion that took place. William Hunt, a Nottingham man who was a private in the Royal Veteran Company, described his arrival in Sydney:

> The first man who spoke to me was a Nottingham man, to ask if we had any from Nottingham belonging to our corps; his heart leapt for joy when I told him I was from Nottingham and while we were talking, John Sinter's son came up, so they helped me with my boxes and luggage...We went to old Jack Slater's the next day, and had a jovial carouse.[3]

The chances are that Susannah met old acquaintances too and felt reassured by something familiar in this strange place. If she was lucky she may have been brought gifts of fresh fruit and vegetables.

The women with husbands already in the colony began their search to find them. John Wright, Ann's husband, was at Campbelltown, too far away to hear of her arrival, but James Haynes was working as a sawyer for William Wells in Sydney and Mary could have sent a message which reached him within hours.[4] John Shannon had arrived three weeks earlier in the *Mellish* and had been assigned to work in Sydney.[5] Although still adjusting to the ways of the colony, perhaps he

too heard that his wife had arrived. Elizabeth Foxall, Mary Ann Green
and Rachael Dagnall enquired in vain. Their husbands were in Van
Diemen's Land and now they discovered just how far away that was
from New South Wales.[6]

After the vast, empty expanse of endless ocean for week after weary
week, the women must have feasted their eyes on the harbour and the
bustling town that was spread across two ridges and down the valley
between. To their left was the castellated tower of Fort Macquarie and,
up the ridge behind it, the imposing buildings of barracks and hospital
with the governor's house, set in spacious gardens, in the foreground.
Crowning the skyline were windmill sails and the spire of St James'
Church. To their right the tip of the land was dominated by a fort called
after Lieutenant Dawes of the First Fleet. Along the top of that ridge
were more windmills, the tower of St Philip's, and some fine houses.
But cascading down the hill was a huddle of small cottages and shacks
in the area known from the earliest days as the Rocks. At the water-
front, money and prestige reasserted itself in the colonnaded mansion
and imposing warehouses of merchant Robert Campbell and the
authority of the three-storeyed commisariat building and the government dockyard and wharf.[7]

The harbour was full of activity. At least a dozen other ships swung
at anchor in the cove — among them the *Vesper*, the *Edward*, the
Reliance, the *Mary* and the *Cumberland*. They were bound for destina-
tions as varied as London, Bombay, Batavia, Calcutta and Raffles Bay.
The *Governor Phillip*, the barque *Alice* and the *Resolution* were preparing
to maintain the links between Sydney, Norfolk Island, Port Phillip and
Hobart.[8] Some were unloading cargo, others taking goods on board.
Boats ferried backwards and forwards between the ships and shore.

Three days after the *Princess Royal* arrived the government officials
and a team of clerks began the long, drawn-out process of mustering
and assigning the women.[9] The muster could go on for several days as
the officials sat asking questions, rows of clerks busily recorded the
women's answers and other clerks who were lining up prisoners
against the tape measure shouted information.[10] Only the year before,
the authorities had tried to relieve the tedium by allowing the band of
the ship *Elizabeth* to play music during the muster,[11] but there was no
similar entertainment on the *Princess Royal*.

The Home Office in England had supplied details of each woman's
trial and sentence, but now the local authorities wanted the kind of
detailed information by which they could be personally identified in
the future. This record, taken on board, formed the basis for the
convict administration. The officials referred back to it constantly
during the following years and usually added notes of further offences
or details of tickets-of-leave and the number of a certificate of
freedom.[12] The convict system, now under the overall direction of the
efficient Governor Darling, had been streamlined since the early
slaphappy days when details provided from England were sparse and
the colony was still so small that it was possible to recognise most of the
prisoners personally.

The colour of the womens' hair, eyes and complexion were recorded, as well as their height. Mary Mahoney's blind right eye, Margaret Lyons' crooked left arm, Ann Maw's hairy mole, Margaret Williams' missing little finger — every small mark and scar was noted down for future reference. Many women had tattoos and these valuable means of identification were carefully described. Ann Barnett had initials and 'I love to the heart' on the lower part of her right arm. Elizabeth Foxall had husband William's name on her left arm. Hannah Solomons was decorated with an anchor, initials and two hearts on one arm, and 'HL I love to the heart' on the other.[13]

Susannah's muster recorded the following details:

NO. 67	Susannah Watson
AGE	34
EDUCATION	Read and Write
RELIGION	Protestant
SINGLE/MARRIED	Married
CHILDREN	5 (one with her)
NATIVE PLACE	London
TRADE	Housemaid & Needlewoman
OFFENCE	Shop Robbery
WHERE TRIED	Nottingham
WHEN	16 April 1828
SENTENCE	14 years
PREVIOUS	
CONVICTIONS	2
HEIGHT	5'1¾"
COMPLEXION	Dark, Ruddy, Pockpitted
HAIR	Dark Brown
EYES	Hazel
	No Marks[14]

All prisoners were required to hand over any money they possessed, which was put in a bank account until they were free. Most of the women had no money but some managed to hide what they had. Ann Burke and Mary Bass handed over £4 each and Georgiana Baxter £2.[15] Both Ann and Georgiana were worldly-wise and gave up only part of what they had. Nearly a year later each was in a position to offer presents to the matron of the Female Factory.[16]

By the following week the authorities had matched up their muster list against applications for assigned servants from private individuals in the colony. The superintendent of convicts had even managed to find a servant — Ann Kirby — for Mrs Windeyer, wife of the chief clerk of police, whose application had arrived after the closing date.[17] Ann was about to become part of a busy household with nine children, but she had gained a place with someone in a position of influence.[18]

On Thursday, 20 May 1829, the master attendant was informed the women would be landed at the dockyard the next day and asked to have boats ready for those who were to travel up river to Parramatta. He was also asked to 'take care that none of the men, or other persons whose presence is not absolutely necessary, are upon the premises'.[19]

Early the following morning Susannah and her shipmates were rowed ashore in small boats and landed at the government wharf on the far right corner of Sydney Cove.

A sense of excitement, mixed with trepidation, must have run high amongst them all as they left the known security of the *Princess Royal*. Some of the women stood quietly, with their belongings ready, watching, keeping their feelings of apprehension, resentment and excitement to themselves. The others, 'the ringleaders' they might have been called by an observer, created noise and confusion. With all the bravado of people trying to establish a sense of importance and simultaneously quell their own fears, they called out to one another, to the sailors, to the onlookers. Lewd and bawdy in language and gestures, disorganised, forgetting things, 'acting up' the difficulty of climbing down a rope or balancing in a dinghy, they performed like actresses on a stage.

As the boats pulled away, those who glanced back for a last look at the old ship could not have foreseen how her name would haunt them to the far corners of the colony. Down the years of their servitude, and in some cases beyond, wherever they went the authorities would identify them by the ship of arrival. They never had a chance to forget her name.[20]

The arrival of a large group of female prisoners was always a matter of interest in the woman-starved colony, even more so because some boatloads in the past had been landed very scantily dressed.[21] In spite of the colonial secretary's orders to keep all unauthorised people away, many of the men employed at the dockyard probably found a vantage point to view the spectacle and assess the 'talent'. In one respect they were disappointed. The women of the *Princess Royal* were so well covered the government decided it was unnecessary to issue them with extra clothing.[22]

On landing at the dockyard the women were mustered again and someone, no doubt, made a pompous and pious speech to them about their behaviour and future prospects. The allocation of assignments then began and the group, which must have achieved some cohesion for all its strange amalgam of characters, now began to split up.

In spite of the authorities' growing conviction that prisoners behaved better if they were assigned to the country areas on arrival, all but 19 of the women from the *Princess Royal* were assigned to employers in Sydney.[23]

Several were assigned to wealthy or influential members of the local society: Ann Dodd to George Sheeker at the prestigious address of Lyons Terrace; Agnes Wicks to William Cox at his mansion near Windsor, 50 miles from Sydney. Sarah Hazel, whose skill was cooking, went to the superintendent of government carpenters and Susannah Turbitt to the surveyor of customs. Elizabeth Smith was assigned to the colonial secretary, Alexander McLeay, and Ann Bowler to Major Thomas Mitchell, the surveyor general. Margaret Bunton went to the attorney, James Norton; Sarah Quittenton and Mary Williams both to another attorney, E. J. Keith. None of these women was likely to have obtained a post in households of this kind in England. On the surface, it would appear they were well positioned for a better future, a chance to use the system to their own advantage. Or were they?[24]

Many women were assigned to small tradesmen and retailers in Sydney. Mary Hart, Catherine Steele and Mary Ann Smith all went to publicans. Ann Wright and Ann Walker both went to Harriet Howell, who ran a laundry business; Caroline Thomas to a ship's chandler; and Ann Simpson to James Robertson, a watchmaker. It appears there was little care taken to match the background of a woman to her employer. Ann Storrett, for instance, who was a dairymaid, was assigned to a Sydney family, so it must be assumed they were all expected to be automatically competent at domestic household chores or child care.[25]

Most of the employers had come free to the colony but some were ex-convicts. Several of these had been in New South Wales nearly 30 years and none of them had been there fewer than ten. Elizabeth Drinkwater, however, who came free herself and was a storekeeper in Parramatta, was married to a man holding a ticket-of-leave.[26] Susan King or Forrester was assigned to her and other women assigned to Parramatta included Sarah Pitches to Andrew Nash, an innkeeper, and Harriet Bannister and Mary Wheat, who both went to James Orr, the clerk of the court at Parramatta.[27]

Mary Haynes and Ann Bullock were both allocated to Andrew Allen, a landholder at Goulburn Plains, and it is likely that Mary's dispatch to what was then one of the furthest corners of the colony was not unconnected with enquiries about her by her husband. It was too early in her sentence for the authorities to agree to assign her to her husband and thus give her what amounted to immediate freedom. Ann Kinsman and Mary Ann Green were the other two assigned far afield, both being allocated to farmers on the Hunter's River north of Sydney.[28]

Sarah Piper and Jane Lyons, Surgeon Wilson's two 'unfit objects', were declared 'not assignable', as was Sarah Clark, who was described as 'sickly and scrofulous'. Sarah Clark, who was only 20, recovered her health and was subsequently assigned to service, but Jane Lyons died in August the following year.[29] Sarah Piper, a cripple who was 40 years old when she arrived, hung on to life for a further 12 years. She was sent to the Convict Invalid Establishment at Port Macquarie in 1838 where she died four years later.[30]

The women assigned outside Sydney were loaded into the master attendant's boat and, escorted at the colonial secretary's insistence by a 'sufficient number of steady constables', were taken up river to the Female Factory at Parramatta for further distribution to their final destinations.[31] The remainder simply walked out of the dockyard with their new master or his agent.

Susannah was assigned to Daniel Egan who was a master builder at the dockyard.[32] He was a young man of 25 and one of the increasing number of native-born Australians.[33]

It was a short walk from the dockyard through the narrow alleys and steep stairs of the crowded Rocks district until, at the top of the hill overlooking Sydney Cove, the streets widened and ran straight and the houses increased in size and comfort. The Egans' residence was in the prestigious gentlemen's section of the Rocks, distinguished by the name of Bunker's Hill. Here Susannah met her new mistress and discovered that Mary Ann Egan, like her husband a native-born Australian, was only 20 years old. Mrs Egan's dismay at seeing Susannah with Thomas in her arms may have been intensified by the age difference or offset by the fact that she badly needed help with her own children, aged two years and 12 months.[34] Perhaps Susannah's personality played a part in convincing her that here was potentially competent help, baby or no, in any event Mary Ann decided not to return her new servant to the government and Susannah settled in and began to discover the nature of her new hometown.

'Fish ho! Fine sand mullet. Snappers all alive. Fat and good oysters ho, all fat, all fat! Fine red apples. Hot rolls, all hot!'

If Susannah and her shipmates closed their eyes and listened to the familiar, raucous Cockney street cries, they would have felt for a moment they were back in England. But only for a moment. When they opened them again, the differences rushed in. Firstly the light, the bright, clear sunlight and the vast, blue sky. Then the space. The whitewashed cottages and two-storey houses spread comfortably along the streets, most with their own gardens full of colourful flowers, fruit and vegetables. And the birds, with bright plumage or queer yellow crests, which hung in cages outside the doors, emitting screeches rather than musical chimes.

The streets were busy, bustling with riders and carriages and the Royal Mail, sounding its horn and clattering importantly off to Parramatta twice a day. But even here was a difference — emblazoned on the Mail's panels was the strange shape of a kangaroo. There were English faces and English voices, but striding amongst them were others — tall, fair, freckled, with broad foreheads, sharp chins and rather flat faces, familiar but strangely different — the native-born, the children of convicts. 'What a powerful effect the climate must have, to change as it does the contour and mould of our children,' said one observer. Did Susannah look at them, so confident in their health and strength, and remember her children, hungry in cold, damp and crowded Nottingham?

Also on the busy streets was a reminder of why Susannah was there — the convict work gangs, the men's irons clanking as they shuffled by in single file, some sullen, some with faces of resigned despair, some surprisingly twinkling. Their grey or yellow jackets, marked with broad arrows and letters PB or CB in black, white and red, singled them out even when they walked through the town alone and unchained.[35]

William Hunt, the Nottingham soldier, thought Sydney was 'a very pleasant town'. He was struck by the abundance of fresh food although he thought it expensive but, he said, 'The working people are paid very well for their labor; tailors, shoemakers, bricklayers and stonemasons can earn from 10s. to 15s. per day'. Like his fellow men and women of the English working classes, William Hunt loved 'a drop of the crea-ture' and regarded it as a major source of pleasure in his life, though he was dismayed that 'women and children [in the army] are allowed no liquor — the worse for me. We draw our liquor every Saturday, which makes a good Saturday night, then goodbye for a week.' He detailed the cost of liquor to his friends: 'Rum is 1s. the half-pint and plenty of good wine at 1s. 3d. per quart; very indifferent ale 9d. per quart . . . public houses are almost as thick together as Nottingham'.[36]

Some of the women of the *Princess Royal* wasted no time in seeking out the liquor and the familiar, convivial atmosphere of the public houses; forgetting, or careless of the fact they were prisoners under sentence and to get drunk, even without stealing anything, would lead to trouble.

Martha Clare was first. The day the women landed she apparently promised her sexual favours for the price of a drink and was caught. She was found guilty of improper conduct and being drunk and sentenced to six months in the third or criminal class of the Female Factory at Parramatta. She thus immediately exchanged the illusion of freedom in a large, open-air gaol for the traditional confines of brick walls and stone cells. She was not alone. In the first three weeks, seven others joined her. Catherine Donoghue, Margaret Hartigan, Martha Gregory, Sarah Lovett, Betty Brian, Ellen Turnbull and Charlotte Smith were all sent to the Female Factory for periods ranging from one month to six weeks for being drunk and, in some cases, with the additional charge of insolence, abusive or disorderly conduct. By Christmas, Mary Palmer, Ann Shannon, Dorothy Huldie, Charlotte Tither and Rachael Dagnall had also been convicted of drunkenness and sent to the Factory, while Ellen Turnbull had been in and out three times for the same offence.[37]

There were women on the *Princess Royal* who were hard drinkers and, in some cases, ended up years later as habitual drunkards. Confined in the enforced discipline of the ship for six long months, it was inevitable some of them would let loose once they landed. They were used to drinking and would not easily show their liquor, so 'drunk' really did mean drunk. Allied with insolence, abuse and dis-orderly conduct, it creates a vivid image of disconnected shouting or singing, foul language, stumbling and weaving as they walked, possibly dancing and suggestively or lewdly throwing their clothes around. Nevertheless, these adjectives were supplied by the disapproving classes who viewed the women without compassion and were pre-disposed anyway to regard them as the refuse of the gutter, with no redeeming characteristics. What to many of the working classes would be called entertainment, would be described by the authorities as disorderly.

One case, involving 15-year-old Ann Storrett from the *Princess Royal*, illustrates very well the difference in point of view. On 20 July 1829 Ann was taken into custody by a constable between 10 and 11 p.m. for being found with another prisoner, Eliza Green, in a disorderly house. The constable gave evidence: 'The house is a disorderly one and a number of people were therein at the time dancing, there was a fiddle playing and the prisoner Stort [*sic*] had a pint of porter before her'.

The picture is one of people harmlessly enjoying themselves, but the police magistrate concurred with the constable's description of a disorderly house. He stated the masters were at fault, not the prisoners, withdrew both women from service and sent them to the first class (non-penitentiary) of the Female Factory for re-assignment. The employers were penalised by being refused any more convict servants and it was April 1832 before William Palmer, Ann's master, was again allowed assigned servants.[38]

Sophia Naylor and Catherine Donoghue were caught for sexual offences. Sophia was charged only ten days after the women landed under the indignantly righteous euphemism of 'highly improper conduct' and again the following year for the same offence. In her case it may have got no further than soliciting. In October 1829, however, Catherine was sentenced to three months in the third class of the Female Factory with the blunt comment: 'Found in carnal connexion'.[39] It was her second offence since she arrived.

The records reveal a rash of early offences committed by the women of the *Princess Royal*. 'Absent without leave' was a favourite charge and one which is, of course, very much open to personal interpretation. A walk to the bottom of the garden to stare down at the harbour at the precise moment her mistress was calling for her services could be regarded as absence without leave. So, more legitimately, could slipping out in the evening to visit a pub or meet a friend. Arguments between mistress and servant over this type of circumstance could result in a charge of insolence, disobedience or neglect of work. In the first six months, Mary Ann Green was charged with being out after hours, Ann Marshall with disobedience, and Caroline Thomas with refusing to work. Louisa Caulfield, Mary Clancey, Mary Hilsley, Rachael Dagnall and Elizabeth Jones were among those who went to the Factory for being absent without leave.[40]

On 19 November Mrs Egan charged Susannah with insolence. She was held in the Sydney gaol for five days and then sent up the Parramatta River to the Factory for six weeks.[41] Insolence is another offence which is open to interpretation, but it is probably no coincidence that Susannah got into trouble at this time. She had formed some kind of sexual relationship with a man called Isaac Moss. It is possible she had slipped out of the house or delayed returning from a message and, in the subsequent argument with her mistress, heated words were exchanged. The nature of the charge, however, indicates Mrs Egan did not know about Susannah's involvement with a man. Although it is not specified in the records, it is probable that Susannah returned to the Egans' service at the end of her sentence.

The more serious charge of absconding from service was brought against Elizabeth Wooller, Margaret Lyons, Maria Allen, Ann Maw, Mary Bates, Ann Dodd and Sarah Hazel.[42] The last two were among those who had been assigned to the upper echelons of colonial society. Sarah fell foul of the superintendent of government carpenters within two months of arrival and Ann Dodd ran away from George Sheeker and his comfortable Lyons Terrace home, as early as 4 August. This was the only offence committed by Maria, Elizabeth, Mary and Ann during the entire period of their sentence, thereby suggesting that the households to which they were initially assigned were unduly harsh or the mistress particularly difficult. All six who absconded received sentences of several months in the Female Factory and were then reassigned. Whoever was her next employer, Ann Dodd conducted herself so well that as early as October 1831 the Sydney bench of magistrates issued her with a ticket-of-leave for 'good conduct in service'.[43] This was a rare accolade which could only have been supplied by her mistress.

It was the little Irish girl, Mary Mahoney, who struck the deepest trouble in the first few months. In September 1829 she was accused of stealing tea, was found guilty and sentenced to one year's transportation to the Moreton Bay penal settlement. One year in a penal settlement rather than the Female Factory was a harsh penalty, but there are no case papers available to shed further light on the details. Held in the Sydney gaol until December, Mary was despatched on the brig *Mary Elizabeth* two days before Christmas, and she served out her time at Moreton Bay until November 1830.[44] She was too early, unfortunately, to benefit from the governor's ruling in 1833 that time spent in the gaol would count as part of a colonial sentence.[45]

Apart from a minor conviction for insolence and neglect of work shortly after she returned from Moreton Bay, Mary committed no further offences in the colony.[46] In April 1839, at the age of 29, she married Richard McGrath, a free immigrant who had arrived the year before. Her application to marry was supported by her employer, Captain Banks, for whom she had worked for two years.[47]

One contributing factor to some of the offences committed by the women soon after arrival was no doubt the presence of the men from the crew of the *Princess Royal*. Those who had formed relationships with women prisoners during the voyage and decided they wanted to stay in the colony worked out a plan to claim the ship was unsafe and force Captain Sherwood to release them from their commitment to sail the ship back to England. In court, they insisted the ship's timbers were rotten. One man claimed he would not trust his old shoes in her outside the heads and another that he was 'not going to sea in a basket'. The captain, however, had arranged for a board of survey to inspect the ship, which declared her seaworthy. With the assistance of the magistrate, who issued dire warnings about the consequences of neglect of duty and the forfeiture of wages, the captain forced the crew to capitulate and return to the ship.[48]

There is no indication how many, or which of the women prisoners were involved in this drama. It was revealed in the Sydney press on 11 June which meant the men, who apparently comprised most of the crew, were at large in the colony during the first three weeks the women were ashore and they must have been, at the very least, a disruptive influence on the women's adjustment to life in Sydney.

Two members of the crew did succeed in staying on. John Wright, the second mate, married Harriet Bannister and George Hearn, a seaman, married Mary Williams later in the year.[49]

ON ASSIGNMENT

The *Sydney Gazette* of 9 January 1830 noted that the female prisoners from the *Lucy Davidson* 'have proved a profitless shipment. Most of the Magdalens were assigned in Sydney and most of those have been returned by their masters as "incorrigibly bad characters"'. Although the newspaper printed no similar condemnation of the women of the *Princess Royal*, a considerable number of them were rejected very quickly by their masters.

In 1829 the community was clamouring for more women to fill the role of servants. To the respectable citizens of the colony, with their large families and multiplicity of household chores, this was the only reason for welcoming another boatload of women prisoners. They put in their applications and quickly snapped up each new arrival, but many of them just as quickly turned the women out again.

In 1830 the colonial secretary reported that almost all the women in gaols were not actual criminals, but prisoners of the Crown returned from private assignment for misconduct. In the 1820s Peter Cunningham had pointed out that many complaints such as insolence, neglect of work, drunkenness, running away, and absence without leave 'were offences which an English bench would not, or perhaps could not take notice of'.[1] But the Master and Servant Act which was passed in New South Wales in 1828 was similar to the one operating in England, providing gaol sentences for offences such as absence without leave and refusal to work. The real difference lay in the colonial employers' contempt for their prisoner servants and, as a result, their interpretation of what constituted these offences. The management committee of the Female Factory confirmed that, still in 1832, in many cases 'persons have been returned for awkwardness or misbehaviour which in free servants would be noticed by a gentle reproof'.[2] In February 1830, beset by the administrative problems and the overloaded gaols this caused, the government resorted to a notice in the *Sydney Gazette*, drawing attention to 'inconvenience caused by the frequent changing of Male and Female servants, particularly the latter'. The notice added there was 'reason to believe they are often returned without any adequate cause' and announced a new measure to reduce the turnover. When returning their servants to government, employers would now have to defray the cost of sending them, in the case of the males to the Sydney police, and for females to the Factory at Parramatta *except* when the magistrates sentenced them for some offence.[3]

This announcement had an obvious consequence. To avoid the expense of their servants' travel, employers of course found reason to charge them with some offence. Not many, however, went as far as one man who returned two women for being pregnant. When it became apparent to the matron of the Female Factory they were not at all pregnant, she swiftly informed the colonial secretary. The police magistrate was called on for details but could only explain that, as the women did not dispute the charge, no depositions had been taken in the case.[4] The suspicion arises that, although being returned to even the second class jeopardised their chances for a ticket-of-leave, the women had agreed to cooperate because their master threatened them with a criminal charge.

When a woman was sent to the Factory for reassignment, or under sentence, the employer usually wasted no time obtaining another servant. In 1831 the colonial secretary attempted to stamp out this practice. He advised Mr Hely, the superintendent of convicts, that employers 'with servants under punishment in the Factory are to receive no others in the interim unless the sentence is of long duration'.[5] Five months later he wrote again to Hely: 'do not submit applications for servants from individuals who continually change the convicts appropriated to them'.[6]

The problem, however, remained unresolved to such an extent that, in May 1832, the managing committee of the Female Factory put its own notice in the government *Gazette*, announcing that all persons receiving female servants were to contract to keep them for one month under penalty of a 40s. fine. At the end of the minimum period, if they wanted to return the women, written notice would be required.[7]

The problems of assignment came down, unsurprisingly, to the fundamentals of human personalities and relationships. Employers who had been convicts themselves could behave one of two ways towards their assigned servants. They could sympathise with someone who was in the same situation as they had been or, filled with a sense of power, they could revenge themselves for their own experience. Those who came free to the colony and regarded themselves as the arbiters of morality and respectability set out to impose their standards on their servants and could display a rigid intolerance in the process.

The character of attorney Edward Keith and his wife, to whom at one time both Sarah Quittenton and Mary Williams were assigned, was revealed by the *Sydney Gazette* in May 1830:

The assigned female servant of Mr Keith was charged by her master with refusing to obey her mistress' orders. The woman would deck herself with lace on Sundays and when desired to remove so many furbelows refused to do so. For this disobedience, she was sentenced to 3 months in the 3rd Class of the Female Factory.[8]

The citizens wanted servants, but their patience was short, their tolerance low, and their standards high. Most significantly, perhaps, assigned servants were virtually a free gift and the employers could afford to be careless of what was so easily obtained and so simply changed. Assignment has often been described as a lottery for the servants. The authorities simply allocated an available woman to an available job. No interview took place. No real attempt was made to match the women's ability or background in the work they were required to do. Consequently assignment was obviously just as much a lottery for the employers and many of them gambled regularly.

The women who provided the raw material for this giant game of chance varied enormously in their potential to satisfy their employers' expectations. A woman straight off a boat from England and suffering the problems of adjustment to a whole new way of life; a woman addicted to drink or beset by personal problems connected with her children, her lover, her husband; or a woman unused to the discipline of regular employment, was unlikely to make a good servant.

Many of the women of the *Princess Royal* changed masters soon after their arrival, some of them several times. Elizabeth Smith, Sarah Quittenton, Ann Simpson, Mary Connell and Margaret Mahoney were all returned to government within the first three weeks. Mr Keith turned Sarah in five days after he received her, but he kept Mary Williams. Alexander McLeay, the colonial secretary, returned Elizabeth Smith, a cook, in six days.[9] In the months that followed, Mary Ann Smith, Hannah Solomons, Susannah Turbitt, Margaret Williams, Elizabeth Foxall, Margaret Coffin, Mary Ann Green and Mary Hart were among those returned to the first class of the Female Factory for reassignment. Mary Ann Charles and Mary Ann Collins were described as 'useless' when they were returned, also to the first class.

Mary Connell, given up on 25 May, was reassigned but given up by her next master on 2 September. Bridget Hainsbury, given up on 13 July, was returned again on 10 September, and Ellen Mears or Myers, turned in first on 26 June, was sent back a second time on 14 December.[10]

In all 25 per cent and possibly more of the women changed masters at least once in the first six months, and this figure does not include those who were charged with an offence and not reclaimed after their punishment expired. Some of these returned to their masters, some did not.

Sometimes a master or mistress displayed an almost perverse persistence in retaining a servant. Ann Walker from the *Princess Royal* was the victim of this attitude. She was assigned on arrival to Harriet Howell, who ran a business as a washerwoman in Lower Castlereagh Street, Sydney.[11] The following list shows what happened to Ann in the years that followed:

1829	May	Assigned to Mrs Howell.
	December	Drunk and disorderly; 6 weeks third class.
1830	May	Drunk and absent; 1 month third class.
	August	Applies to marry; governor refuses because she stated married on arrival. Still assigned to Mrs Howell.
	September	Drunk and absent; 1 month third class.
1831	January	Absent without leave; 1 month third class. Returns to service.
	March	Absent without leave and drunk; 1 month third class. Returns to Mrs Howell.
1832	December	Runaway from Mrs Howell.
1833		No offences recorded but several months spent in the Factory for running away.
1834	February	14 days, third class. Offence not recorded.
	March	28 days, third class. Offence not recorded.
	July	28 days, third class. Offence not recorded.
	October	1 month, third class. Offence not recorded.
1835	September	Ann gets her certificate of freedom.[12]

Whether Mrs Howell actually held on beyond the end of 1832 is unconfirmed. However, the perseverance she showed in the first three years in continually requesting Ann's return demonstrates the power a mistress could exert and the helplessness of the servant. The fact that another *Princess Royal* woman, Mary Ann Charles, also ran away from Mrs Howell the month after she was assigned to her in 1833 lends support to the conclusion that it was Mrs Howell's character which was the determining factor, not her servants'.[13]

The women in assignment were vulnerable to forms of abuse which went beyond an employer's perverse determination to control them. The government's policy was to protect them and this extended, for example, to the regulation that no female prisoner could be assigned to a penal colony unless she volunteered.[14] Instances of abuse of female servants, when discovered, were swiftly dealt with. Magistrates who found a mistress had struck her servant and then charged the girl with insolence cancelled the sentence they had imposed and prohibited the employer from receiving further female servants.[15] A police constable in Goulburn was dismissed for improper and immoral conduct towards a woman assigned in the district, and an employer who refused his servant sufficient food to feed her child also lost the right to have female prisoners assigned to him.[16]

Some unscrupulous employers used their women servants to make extra money. In March 1831, for instance, it was revealed that Timothy Connolly had been exacting 5s. a week each from the two female prisoners assigned to him. How they were earning money was not revealed, but the government put Connolly on the list to receive no more prisoners.[17] Another master and mistress allowed their female servant to go to bed with a man on their premises though it was not stated whether money changed hands.[18] When Mary Collins of the *Princess Royal* was charged with drunkenness and being absent without leave, the examination by the magistrate revealed that the other female servant assigned to her master, Wiliam Saunders, had been cohabiting with a lodger in the house. Both Mary and the other servant were withdrawn and Mr Saunders refused further servants.[19] In each of these cases the main issue is avoided, but there is an implication the women were being used or encouraged to act as prostitutes. The evidence concerning a servant named Mary Ann Waters was much more specific: she went to bed with men at her master and mistress' suggestion to help support their family.[20]

In October 1830 a female prisoner was smart enough to go to the police office before any charge was brought against her. She complained that, after his wife ran away, her master ran a disorderly house. Another woman complained to the bench that her master was taking liberties with her person. Both women were immediately withdrawn from service.[21]

Predictably, Georgiana Baxter from the *Princess Royal* had no hesitation in standing up for her rights. She went to the police on 25 July 1829 to complain about her master, Robert Hardy, who was employed by the Australian Agricultural Company and lived in Kent Street, Sydney. Her main complaint was that she was not being given enough food, but she also revealed that her mistress had 'solicited her to be unchaste' and that she had lent money to both her employers. She was withdrawn for reassignment and the governor decreed Mr Hardy should receive no more female servants.[22]

Insufficient food was also a problem Louisa Caulfield faced in her assignment to Percy Simpson, Esq., a linen and woollen draper of 31 Pitt Street, Sydney. Louisa did nothing about it and the charge was made by a fellow servant, Richard Flanagan, in April 1832, but Louisa supported the complaint and gave evidence that the food they were given was less than the amount specified by government regulations. Louisa and the other servants were withdrawn for reassignment but the government specified there should be no prejudice to their future claims for tickets-of-leave. Mr Simpson was left lamenting in a petition to the governor. He claimed Louisa had lied, as he believed she had done once before when he charged Flanagan with insolence. He also claimed that he had treated Louisa well and she had been with him three years. She had never been sent to the Factory by him, but only through her own misconduct in getting intoxicated and picked up by the constables. He added that all his servants were sorry to leave and told him they hoped he would get them back.[23] Whatever the truth, Simpson did ignore the fact that Louisa had not been with him continuously for three years and had spent possibly as much as six months in the service of Mr R. Walker of Sydney.[24]

The employers, however, did have genuine problems and Mary Palmer from the *Princess Royal* was one who gave her master a fright.

NARROW ESCAPE: On Tuesday night the landlord of the Ship Inn, Essex Lane, observed dense volumes of smoke rolling down from the upper apartments of his house; having made his way, at the risk of suffocation, upstairs, he found it proceeded from the bedroom occupied by his female servant, which he found on entering in flames; the bed clothes and curtains with sundry other articles having ignited, owing to the carelessness of the servant

above mentioned, named Mary Palmer, who had moistened her throat
somewhat two [sic] freely that evening, and having placed the candle too
close to the bed, had laid down, and was shortly wrapped in the arms of
Morpheus; and but for the timely assistance rendered by her master, would
no doubt have shortly become an unwilling 'Suttee'.

Mary was sentenced to three months in the third class of the Factory.[25]

A servant named Ann Walker, who may or may not have been the
Ann Walker of the *Princess Royal*, was charged with dipping her
master's head in a bucket of water and marching off, singing[26]

> If I had a bean for a soldier, who'd go,
> Do you think I'd refuse him, O' no, no, no.

It is noticeable, throughout the records, that many women servants
were not afraid of their employers and would stand up for themselves.
One went to the bench of magistrates and accused her mistress of
mistreating her by throwing a basin of water in her face and striking
her with a poker. She refused to return to her service. The male
magistrate, tentatively adjudicating between two angry women, found
judiciously that although the servant could not prove her case, the
mistress had been at fault somewhat. He sent the servant to the Factory
for reassignment.[27]

Another woman, assigned to a wealthy landowner and his wife,
refused to adopt the meekly submissive attitude of a good servant.
When her mistress asked her to finish the washing by Friday as it was
inconvenient for it to remain unfinished on Saturday, the servant
abused her, stating that she was far superior to her mistress in every
way. She said she always endeavoured to please and was highly
indignant when she was sentenced to 14 days in the cells.[28]

Caroline Thomas from the *Princess Royal* was far from intimidated by
her mistress, Mrs Johnstone of Lockwood Estate at Liverpool. A fellow
servant described the scene in righteous tones:

> Francis Taylor. . . states That on my return with some cattle to the farm after
> sundown yesterday I hear some high sounds took place in the kitchen and I
> saw my mistress and the prisoner *pushing* each other [emphasis added] and I
> don't think she behaved as a servant ought towards a mistress.
>   (Guilty of insubordination. 2 weeks 3rd Class Factory and returned to
> Government.)[29]

This small incident is revealing for the assumptions of equality it
demonstrates between the two women. Although Mrs Johnstone
ultimately resorted to the use of her power over Caroline, before she
remembered her status she and her servant were interacting in a way
unimaginable in England.

The women prisoners came from a society of rigid class structure
and rules of behaviour. Although they were on the bottom of the
hierarchy, barely even part of it, they were not immune to its social
attitudes. Their instinct for recognising class was as keen as that of the
highest aristocrat in England. They knew a real lady from a parvenu.
And all around them in the colony were pretenders to a status which,

the women were aware, they would not achieve at home. In 1833 the *Sydney Gazette* described the case of a servant who was charged with refusing to return to her master's house, and quoted her verbatim:

> It don't signify talking. I can't agree with master and mistress. They won't let me enjoy myself. I always lived with gentlemen and now to descend to a tradesman, horrible, horrible. I won't go back, so let me have my clothes.[30]

The recognition by the women prisoners that in many instances they were working for employers whose background was not substantially different from their own resulted in the creation of the enduring Australian attitude that one person is as good as the next. Historians and others are wrong in emphasising that this national characteristic began only in the male mateship of the bush; it was undoubtedly also established through the domestic battles between mistress and female servant.

Not all relationships between master and mistress and their assigned servants were unsuccessful and some showed considerable resilience. In his diaries, A. B. Spark, a wealthy landowner and magistrate, reveals an acceptance of a long-term relationship which allowed for vagaries in his servants' behaviour and the intrusion of their personal problems. The involvement of his men in a robbery did not end their service in his household.[31] Mary Ann Green from the *Princess Royal* was assigned initially to William Spark of the Hunter River. He gave her back to government but she returned in July 1830 and was still there in November 1831.[32] Louisa Caulfield, as we have seen, returned to Mr Simpson.

Surviving records make it possible to trace almost the entire career of Sarah Lovett as a prisoner. Tall for her times, at 5 feet 5 inches, Sarah's greying brown hair revealed her age of 43 years when she landed. She was a needlewoman by trade, convicted in Leicester of stealing a kettle. In spite of her two previous convictions, she received only a seven-year sentence.[33] The chronology of her assigned service in New South Wales is a good demonstration of the kind of pattern so many others followed and, by implication, reveals something of the behaviour of the women and the attitude of the employers.

1829	May 21	To Charlotte Dick, Pitt Street, Sydney.
	June 1	Drunk; 1 month, third class.
		Assigned to Newcastle.
	September 23	Returned from Newcastle. Neglect of work and insolence; 3 months, second class.
1829/30		Assigned in Sydney.
1830	October 14	Absent without leave; 1 month, third class.
1831	January	Returned to government. To William Smart from gaol on way to first class.
	June 20	Insolent to mistress; 1 month, third class.
1831/32		Assigned Bathurst.
1832	March 19	Bathurst Gaol — returned to government by Mr Sutter: 'No further use for her services'.
	March 20	To Mr McKenzie.
	August 5	Returned to government by Mr McKenzie.

	September 15	Assigned to Mr Town.
	December 4	Returned to government by Mr Town.
	December 10	Sent to first class, Parramatta.
1833	February	Convicted Sydney, unknown offence; 1 month, third class.
	c. August	Assigned to Bathurst.
	November 1	Neglect of duty; 3 days cells Bathurst. Discharged to Mr Strange.
	November 25	Neglect of duty; 6 days cells. Returned to government by Mr Strange. Reassigned to person unknown in Bathurst.
1834	April 18	Charged by Mr Varley with absconding; 14 days cells. Returned to government.[34]

Sarah's career was unspectacular, but typical. No major crimes. No clever manipulation of the system's incentives. Just a continual pattern of petty offences, some of them no doubt generated by the intolerance of her employers. After this extensive evidence of her activities in the colony, Sarah vanished. She never received a ticket-of-leave or a certificate of freedom, which was due the following year, and no one called Sarah Lovett married or died in the subsequent 20 years.

Some women from the *Princess Royal* achieved successful working relationships with their employers. Jane Edwards, assigned to J. P. Lloyd at Liverpool, was still with him more than two years later. Ann Currier, Catherine Barrett and Ann Loydall stayed for nine months with employers, both the Anns until they married and Catherine until she was returned to government without complaint in March 1830.[35]

Agnes Wicks, assigned to William Cox at Richmond in 1829, stayed with him until she received a ticket-of-leave in December 1832. Cox described Agnes as honest, sober and industrious and helped her get permission to marry by promising to keep her and her husband in his employ until they got their tickets.[36]

Jane McPherson was assigned on arrival to Lieutenant McIntosh, an elderly retired officer. After he died she stayed with his widow, who said Jane 'conducted herself with propriety'.[37]

Mary Morris, aged 20, was assigned when she arrived to a young Australian-born mistress, Ann Kennedy, age 25, and her ex-convict husband. They had a two-year-old daughter and Ann worked as a laundress. It must have been a happy household because Mary, who was one of the minority on the *Princess Royal* who had two previous convictions before her transportation, stayed with the Kennedys over two years and committed no offences while she was there.[38]

Ann Bullock, assigned with Mary Haynes to Andrew Allan at Goulburn when she arrived, was still with him in January 1831.[39] The absence of information for six years about Ann Clark may well indicate that she stayed throughout her sentence with Mr and Mrs Baldie, her fellow passengers on the *Princess Royal*. Mary Ann Bates absconded from her first employer, Henry Geesing in July 1829, but she went to work for John and Clara Loveridge about May 1830 and stayed with them nearly two years.[40]

In May 1830 Susannah had been with the Egans one year and the only disturbance in their relationship had been the charge of insolence seven months earlier. But the probable cause of that disturbance had repercussions. Susannah was pregnant by Isaac Moss and the baby was due within weeks. There was only one place to go for female convicts 'lying in', and that was the Female Factory at Parramatta.

THE FEMALE FACTORY — THEY MUST BE KEPT UNDER

Susannah gave birth to a son at the Female Factory on 4 July 1830, and when Rev. Samuel Marsden baptised him he christened him Charles Isaac Watson and defiantly named his father as Isaac Moss.[1] But Susannah's relationship with Isaac Moss is a mystery. It is not even certain which of two men called Isaac Moss was the father of her child. They were father and son and both had been long-time residents in the colony.

Isaac Moss, senior, was transported for receiving stolen goods and arrived in New South Wales by the *Royal Admiral* in 1800.[2] He received a conditional pardon from Governor King within six weeks of arrival, on condition he served in the navy. He spent his time as a seaman on board the HMS *Lady Nelson* and, on her, took part in the first survey of the Hunter River and the annexation of Port Phillip, where he narrowly escaped death from an Aboriginal spear.[3] He subsequently became a self-employed sailmaker and then a publican at the sign of The Cherry Tree in King Street. By 1829 he had become a respectable, but not wealthy, citizen. His wife had died and he was 73 years old.[4]

Isaac, junior, was also a widower and was 34 years old in 1829. He had come free to the colony as a 12-year-old, sailing out on the *Elizabeth* in 1806 under the care of his father's friend Captain Ebor Bunker (of Bunker's Hill).[5] Like many of the colony's youth at that period, young Isaac became a seaman and crewed on local sailing vessels to New South Wales settlements and further afield to New Zealand, Fiji and Tahiti. He was a short, dark haired man with grey eyes and something of a tearaway, unlike his more responsible elder brother, Joseph.[6] In his early twenties young Isaac turned to farming the family land at Salt Pan Creek, a branch of the Cook's River near Liverpool. He got into debt to his father which ended in a dispute in the courts, and under the pressure of the extreme drought conditions of 1826–27 the family sold the land.[7] Isaac returned to the sea and in

1828 was crewing for the shipowner Thomas Street.[8] This circumstance, as well as the age of his father, make it probable that it was Isaac, junior, who was Charles Watson's father. As a seaman, Isaac would have been in and out of the port of Sydney, frequenting the waterside pubs of the Rocks. Most particularly, his brother James and his wife, Isabella, owned The Mermaid public house in Cumberland Street close to the Egans' house.[9] All the circumstances of age, residence and trade, combine to indicate that Isaac would have known and probably been a friend of Daniel Egan.

So, if Susannah first saw Isaac at the Egans' house and subsequently met him again at his brother's pub, what was the nature of the relationship? It could have been a brief sexual connection based on lust or money, or it could have been something emotionally warmer on Susannah's part. It apparently meant little to Isaac. He had no children, but there is no indication he acknowledged Susannah's son or at any time contributed to his support. His view of Susannah would have been governed by her convict status which, as a free man and the son of an ex-convict turned respectable, would have placed her outside his serious consideration. Her marriage anyway created a practical barrier against any future to their relationship because the government would totally forbid their cohabitation.

With two children and no prospects of a permanent relationship with a man, Susannah's future looked bleak. Employers were extremely reluctant to take convict women with one child, and with two her future and theirs were really in jeopardy. For a time she remained in the Female Factory, as was normal for nursing mothers.

The Factory was a solid brick, two-storey structure on the banks of the river at Parramatta. It was surrounded by a 16-foot wall, which was not high enough to prevent escapes and traffic in messages or goods such as rum, tobacco and sugar, which were tossed over the wall to the women from people outside.[10]

The Factory was divided into three classes. The first was for women returned to government without complaint, who were eligible for reassignment. The second was for pregnant or nursing women and for those moved up from the third class for a probationary period. The third class was the criminal division and it was here the women were sent for offences, of all kinds, committed while in assigned service.[11] The Factory operated as a prison, a maternity home, a marriage bureau, an employment exchange and a hostel or refuge for women in transit between jobs. All its inmates, however, were strictly speaking prisoners and the institution was run predominantly as a prison.

Originally built for 300 women, by 1830 it was always overcrowded. It rarely contained fewer than 500 women, plus at least 100 children and sometimes a lot more.[12] Sleeping accommodation was inadequate and there were often fights amongst the women about their bedding. The government laid down specific regulations as to the daily food ration for each woman, but in practice the distribution could be, and was, abused by the Factory authorities and supplies diverted, for instance, to the matron's family.[13]

The Factory, as its name implies, was supposed to occupy the women in productive work, either the services of washing, ironing and mending or the production of wool material and clothes, particularly slop clothing for male convicts. The work of the third class was breaking up stones for building purposes. But the Factory, as a productive unit, was never really successful. The lack of raw materials, delays and disorganisation by the government were recurring problems which affected its production, and the number of inmates often exceeded the work available. Many women escaped work altogether in the Factory due to these reasons or their own 'go slow' attitude which ensured they did little work except personal chores. When Governor Gipps paid an unannounced visit in March 1838 he found the third-class women idle because there were no handles for the hammers to break stones. He added that the women broke the handles as soon as they were supplied.[14]

On a daily basis the matron had the power to punish the women for minor offences, although more serious charges had to be referred to the management committee. Neglect of work, infamous language, abusing an overseer, fighting, breaking a window, trafficking with the workmen, were the kind of transgressions which fell within the matron's authority and were punished by confinement in the cells for periods ranging between 12 and 48 hours. The more serious charge of attempting to escape was referred to the management committee and resulted in a sentence of 14 days to the cells.[15]

There was a rigid degree of personal control over the women's lives, which must have chafed those with an independent spirit. Sleeping during prayers, altering her government cap, or having a pack of cards in her possession, could lead to a woman's confinement.[16]

The resentment of the Factory women against their gaolers sometimes boiled over into a riot. In 1827, for instance, stopping their ration of bread and sugar caused a revolt which resulted in nearly 100 women surging into Parramatta and collecting bread and meat from the residents. Others took off into the bush, pursued by police and soldiers who took several days to round them all up again.[17]

In February 1831, hundreds of women went on the rampage, broke out of the Factory and headed towards Parramatta. The trigger for this riot was apparently a particularly strict overseer. The women seized her and shaved her head, threatening to go to Sydney and shave the head of 'the Governor and his mob' as well. They were stopped by police and hastily summoned soldiers before they reached the township.[18]

In October 1832 the management committee called in the soldiers again to quell the women's 'extremely unruly' behaviour, but a full-scale riot was avoided.[19]

As a method of control the women in the third class were regularly forced to have their hair cut very short. Understandably, this was one of the most hated aspects of confinement in the Factory, going as it does to the very heart of a woman's self-image, and haircutting was the trigger to another major riot in March 1833. The following letter from Rev. Samuel Marsden to the colonial secretary, dated 7 March, described the scene:

> I told you when I was in Sydney on Tuesday that I expected the women in the Factory would excite a riot again. They began Wednesday night to be very troublesome and this morning they struck work — this was also the day for their hair to be cut — they one and all determined not to submit to this operation. No soldiers with their officers were ordered to attend the constables to the Factory. Anderson and I went before, Captain Westmacott gave directions for the soldiers. The women had collected large heaps of stones and as soon as we entered the 3rd Class they threw a shower of stones as fast as they possibly could and at the whole of us. At last they were overcome. Some of them were sent to the gaol and others to the cells and at length their hair was cut. We did not leave the Factory till 4 o'clock. All the three classes were under great excitement.[20]

The haircutting that day was a long and dangerous operation, but the authorities, led by Marsden, were determined not to be beaten. They subsequently recommended one of the inmates for a reduction in her sentence because 'she obliged the Committee at considerable personal risk by cutting the hair of the refractory females yesterday when the paid monitresses refused to do it'.[21] Marsden's personal fury and extremely punitive attitude towards the women was revealed in the comments he added to the colonial secretary:

> It will never do to show them any clemency — they must be kept under — much pains have been taken to bring that Establishment under some proper subordination and a great deal had been done, but all is soon undone and cannot be repaired now without great care. How they will go on tomorrow I cannot say, but they must not do as they please. I have no doubt but all the officers who saw their riotous conduct will be convinced of the necessity of keeping them under the hand of power. We ordered that there should be no wine in the 3rd Class and nothing but bread and water for this day.[22]

Marsden had demonstrated this harsh attitude to the women convicts from his early days in the colony and he influenced, but also reflected, the attitude of the community at large. The Factory inmates were, as Governor Bourke later described them, 'outcast women'.[23]

The women knew and resented their image. During the 1831 riot one of the ringleaders suggested they demolish the press of the *Monitor* newspaper and be revenged on the editor, who 'was always holding them up as the worst and vilest of their sex'. She also revealed her political awareness when she added that Governor Darling would pardon them all for ridding him of his enemy.[24]

But the lives of most of the women convicts were inextricably bound to the Female Factory. The matron, through the management committee, and in later years through the visiting magistrate, could recommend tickets-of-leave and the superintendent of convicts required the Factoy to supply a report on all women prisoners before they were issued with their certificates of freedom. After Samuel Marsden's death, the Factory keeper, Thomas Bell, was for a time required to give his consent to any marriage from the Factory.[25]

Perhaps most significantly, because it was so fundamental, more intangible and there were no real avenues of appeal, by 1830 the matron of the Factory had the power to substantially affect the future of the women in assigned service. It was the matron who drew up the list of women available for assignment, and from mid-1832 she matched up their names to the applications from employers. She could influence the district and type of employment to which a woman was assigned. She submitted her list regularly to the colonial secretary and the superintendent of convicts for approval, so a blatant act of favouritism to a woman with a bad record of colonial offences might be noticed, but the influence and manipulation that could go into the assignment list would be beyond the knowledge of these other authorities.[26] There was, for instance, one case of a woman who managed to serve her entire sentence in the Factory and never go on private assignment. The matron's favouritism then extended to authorising the release of her children from the male orphan school without first obtaining the governor's permission.[27]

A few months before Susannah entered the Factory, some women from the *Princess Royal* had been actively involved in 'buying' the matron's favours. Ellen Turner, assistant matron of the second class, sent the management committee a long list of complaints about the matron, Mrs Anne Gordon, and when Turner was not called to give evidence directly at their enquiry she swore another statement before the superintendent of police at Parramatta and sent it direct to the governor.[28]

Georgiana Baxter and Ann or Ellen Burke were both named among those who gave gifts to the matron. Ann Burke gave her half a yard of muslin and a lace cap, while Georgiana seems to have been rich in useful goods ·for sale or gift, giving Mrs Gordon a piece of sky blue satin, sewing silk and sewing cotton, silk laces, three gauze or silk handkerchiefs and a tablecloth. As well as these outright gifts, Georgiana sold Mrs Gordon, through the intermediary of Ellen Turner, two gown pieces, one of ten yards and the other of nine, some lace, 11 yards of cap ribbon and some bonnet ribbon. Other prisoners, including Ellen Turner herself, gave Mrs Gordon some gold earrings, handkerchiefs, a white gown and material for clothes. Mrs Isabella Kingaby, the matron of the penitentiary division, also received gifts from the prisoners. In the face of these complaints, however, Mrs Gordon prevailed. Even though she admitted to the committee she had taken gifts, they found 'no indication of her giving any preference in her conduct to prisoners'. They insisted that she return the gifts, but recommended, in view of her good record, that no other action be taken against her. The governor expressed his 'extreme disapprobation' but let the committee's decision stand.[29]

Just for a moment the veil lifts and reveals the powerplay and manipulation which took place at the Factory, and was permitted to continue by the authorities' desire for a quiet life. It was an environment where survival of the fittest was paramount. For the timid or undisciplined woman, life could be an endless round of punishment and brutality and ultimately a careless or malicious assignment to private service. Those women who had the personal control to endure the petty restrictions, to bite their tongue and behave respectfully to the matron and overseers, had a chance to manipulate the system to their benefit. But it helped even more if they had money or goods to use as bribes.

Only those women who kept away from the Factory, either by good luck or good management, avoided its tyrannous influence. Yet there is indirect evidence that the women preferred to be there rather than out on assignment and would sometimes commit an offence deliberately to be sent back.[30] It can be claimed, often justifiably, that life in the Factory was the lesser of two evils. The institution did offer protection from the women's great vulnerability, to men particularly, while on assignment. But there were other reasons as well for choosing the Factory. Most importantly, it offered a chance to change assignments if the employer, unlike Mrs Howell with Ann Walker, could be induced to let go. It thus permitted a woman some little control over her life. It was also virtually the only place in the colony where the women could gain the comfort of some kind of group strength and, somewhat variable, solidarity with each other. Finally, it should not be overlooked that the Factory provided an environment redolent of 'home'. In the too spacious colony of New South Wales, it was the nearest thing to the familiar, overcrowded, brawling, raucous atmosphere of an English gaol or even an English slum.

For a brief period of six months Susannah and her two boys were together in the Factory. Then she lost Thomas. At the end of December 1830 he was taken from her and placed in the male orphan school at Liverpool.[31] Whether Susannah agreed with this decision as the only solution open to her is unknown. In any event, she had no choice. All the factors which ruled her servitude were against her keeping him.

The government's rule was that female prisoners' children, who were over the age of three, were to be placed in orphanages with a view to bringing them up as industrious and Christian citizens away from the presumed bad influence of their parents.[32] Thomas was just about to turn three when he left his mother. At this time, in the latter part of 1830 and early 1831, there was also a particularly heavy demand for female servants. The matron of the Factory was constantly requesting the government's permission to move women from the second class into the first for assignment and it was not possible, during that period, to linger as a nursing mother.[33] Employers, however, were loath to take women with children and Susannah still had six-months-old Charles.[34] Early in 1831 she went to work for Thomas Simons, a fisherman in Parramatta. He and his wife, Mary, were both ex-convicts and had two young children, Lucy aged three and Mary Ann who was only 19 months old, so perhaps they were sympathetic to someone with a background similar to their own.[35]

Susannah had been lucky to keep Thomas with her as long as 18 months after she landed in the colony. Within days of setting foot in Sydney, Caroline Thomas, Margaret Coffin and Margaret Mahoney were all separated from the children they brought with them.

Richard Kemp, a ship's chandler in Sydney who was Caroline's employer, wrote to the colonial secretary within two days of her arrival in
his house, asking permission for nine-year-old Jane to enter the female
orphan school. She was admitted five days later and Caroline's distress
at this can be inferred from the fact she was among the earliest of the
Princess Royal women to be sent to the third class of the Factory and was
charged, significantly, with refusing to work and abusing her master.[36]

Margaret Coffin's employer, Prosper de Mestre, also wrote to the
colonial secretary within a week of Margaret and five-year-old James's
arrival and was given permission for James to go to the male orphan
school. James stayed there for six years until he was apprenticed as a
musical instrument maker to Mr Francis Ellard of Hunter Street, Sydney. Margaret's employment with Mr de Mestre lasted six months,
which was relatively long compared to the turnover of some *Princess
Royal* women during that early period. He returned her to government
without complaint at the end of November 1829.[37]

Margaret Mahoney's employer, Rose Casey, who was the wife of
an ex-convict and had two young children herself, simply returned
Margaret to the government for reassignment.[38] It was the Matron of
the Factory, confronted with nine-year-old Richard, who immediately
contacted the colonial secretary requesting Richard's admission to the
male orphan school.[39]

The future for Margaret and Richard was a sad one. Margaret cared
enough for her boy to keep in touch with him and the following year
she got a pass from her master to visit him at the orphanage and set out
to walk from Sydney to Liverpool. On the way she made the great
mistake of stopping at a pub for a drink and fell in with a group of
convict labourers returning in carts to their master's farm beyond
Liverpool. She went with them, apparently in a drunken stupor, past
the turn-off to the orphan school and on to the farm where she was
robbed and raped by three or four men in one of the huts. The
evidence of her degradation as she was dragged by the head from the
hut five hours later, at 2.00 a.m., with her clothes torn to ribbons, is
pitiful.[40]

Margaret faced charges of drunkenness later that year, then she was
assigned to Bathurst at the beginning of 1831. Known in the town as
Peggy Mahoney, the elderly Irish washerwoman appeared regularly
before the bench there for drunkenness, but the magistrates recommended her for a ticket-of-leave, which she received in August 1833
and celebrated by getting drunk again.[41] She obtained her certificate of
freedom when it was due in 1835, but four years later she was
described by the police magistrate in Bathurst as one of the 'bad
females' in his gaol and was sent down to the Factory at Parramatta for
a six-month sentence.[42] Richard stayed at the orphan school until he
was 14 when he was put forward for apprenticeship as a tailor.
Unsurprisingly, his character was described at that time as sullen.[43]

Susannah spent a little over six months in assigned service to the
Simons and then she returned to the Factory. This time she was in the

third class. She had repeated exactly the offence for which she had been transported. On Wednesday, 20 July 1831, she travelled deliberately from Parramatta down to Sydney and went round the town stealing from ten or 12 shops. She was caught on the same day and sentenced to two years in the criminal division of the Factory.[44]

Unless it is assumed that Susannah was simply a kleptomaniac, which the evidence of her life and character as a whole disputes, the only conclusion to be reached is that she wanted to get back to the Factory, and for a long time. Exactly why, can only be guessed at. Were the Simons unkind employers after all? Were they perhaps unable to feed Susannah sufficiently well for her to nourish Charles, whom she would probably still have been breast feeding? Did she, on the other hand, leave Charles at the Factory and see this as a way to get back to him? The records that remain are unclear about the extent to which women prisoners left children under three behind in the Factory when they were assigned, though there is some evidence that they did so on occasions.[45] It is possible this is what she had done and, in collaboration with the matron who was processing women into assignment at a particularly rapid rate, got herself assigned in Parramatta to be within reach of both her children.

There is one other possibility. Thomas was ill and dying at the orphan school. If the Simons gave her a pass, Susannah would have been to visit him. If they refused, she most likely knew anyway from Dr Mathew Anderson, who lived in Parramatta and attended both the Factory and the orphanages. Perhaps she had some mistaken idea that, through the Factory, she could somehow get access to Thomas. If so, it did her no good. Four weeks after she was sentenced, Thomas died. He was buried the next day, 18 August, at St Luke's, Liverpool, and his death certificate grandly and inappropriately described the little boy as 'Scholar of the Institution'.[46]

Susannah must have been devastated. Like many women of her time, she had seen several of her children die, but Thomas was special. He was her only tangible link with her old life and the family in England. He had survived the long voyage with her and been her sole emotional comfort in the trauma of separation and the lonely adjustment to a new life.

It was not until a year later, on 8 August 1832, when half her sentence had expired, that Susannah was ready to try again. She persuaded the matron to let her appear before the management committee to plead for a mitigation of her sentence. The matron supported her by describing her conduct as 'uniformly orderly', so the committee put forward her request to the governor. On 18 August the colonial secretary advised that his excellency had consented and Susannah again went out to try her luck in the colony.[47]

WITH HIS EXCELLENCY'S CONSENT

While Susannah coped with the birth and death of her children and tried again to find a footing for survival in the colony, many of her shipmates were choosing a path which was closed to her. Marriage.

By the end of 1832, when Susannah left the Factory, 40 women from the *Princess Royal* had already married. In the next six years at least another 22 married for the first time in the colony and some had been widowed and married again.[1]

One of the great myths of Botany Bay, which permeated England, concerned marriage. Along with tales of the rags-to-riches rise of ex-convicts went stories of the benefits of being married. Like all good myths, it contained elements of truth in an exaggerated and distorted form. And the time lag for the propagation of the myth meant the reality was already out of date. There were those, in the early days, who were assigned almost immediately on arrival to their free spouse, but by the 1830s the system had hardened, largely in response to these favourable perceptions in England. Just to be a married person carried no benefit at all; it was the availability to marry which mattered. But this misconception continued to lead women prisoners in particular into the error of declaring themselves married on arrival. Friends in England advised them before they left that it was the best thing to do, but it proved their worst mistake.[2]

Marriage was the most important choice open to women prisoners and the women of the *Princess Royal* were not slow to see its advantages. Seventy-two applied to marry while they were still prisoners, some of them applying several times. Ten failed to obtain permission and one, Ann Stokes, did not convert her applications into marriage, although all three were allowed. But 61 women did marry while they were serving their sentences.[3]

Marriage could immediately transform the conditions of the women's servitude through their assignment to their husbands where, although technically still prisoners, they could lead the life of free married women. It could provide protection from harsh or capricious employers and from the vulnerability to sexual abuse in the male-dominated colony. It could lay the foundation for a hopeful future. All around them, the women of the *Princess Royal* had examples of men and women who had been prisoners like themselves but who were now owners of property or businesses, living in houses with space to breathe, eating well, raising children who grew strong and healthy. People from the urban slums, the dispossessed poor from the country-side at home, had a stake in society in a way unimaginable in Britain. And the best chance for the women to share in this unusual bounty was through marriage.

The colonial authorities had their own reasons for promoting the marriage of women prisoners. They were all assumed to be whores and drunkards and it was felt the responsibilities of marriage and family offered the one chance of appealing to their better female instincts and combating their inherent criminal and immoral tendencies. But, beyond their own reformation, they were also seen as having the wider social function of taming the predominantly male society through domesticity. Marriage was seen as a form of social control to consolidate the banished criminals of Britain into a stable and in-dustrious society.[4]

The authorities would go to considerable lengths to facilitate mar-riage. In 1826 Governor Darling had promulgated special regulations to encourage prisoners to marry, promising that married prisoners would be assigned to the same master where possible and that pri-soners who married free persons would be assigned to their spouse.[5] In May 1831 the colonial secretary advised that approval had been given for women from the second class of the Female Factory to marry 'in order to encourage the extension of that rite among them'.[6] In 1832 the Factory committee also publicly expressed its encouragement for the marriage of female prisoners, 'having observed the change which new modes of living and accession of new duties sometimes operate in the character and disposition'.[7] But they were all watchful for signs of bigamy. In 1833, when a man wrote from England enquiring for the whereabouts of his wife, the colonial secretary had it recorded she was married because she had declared 'single' and had tried to marry someone else.[8]

Every marriage application involving a convict had to be approved by the governor and, before going forward to him, it was checked against the records. The men or women who had declared themselves married on arrival came to grief immediately. But there was hypocrisy operating. Many of the male prisoners, particularly in the 1820s before the system tightened, had not declared their marital status. In spite of this, applications were approved so long as the woman had declared herself single. The problem was an insoluble one because the number of the men was so great. The authorities must have been aware that many were committing bigamy, yet they connived at it for their fellow males and took a hard line with the women. The double standard probably began with the muster, where the clerks insisted on a declaration one way or the other from women but often didn't bother at all for the men.[9]

In England, like many of their class, the women's relationships had not always been formalised by marriage. It had not affected their lives there, but they quickly discovered the importance of legal marriage to their future in the colony where, as prisoners, the legalities were essential and the authorities would act swiftly against anyone found simply living with a man. When the Sydney police magistrate discovered one woman had been 'living in a state of fornication for sometime', he sent her to the third class of the Factory for six weeks and recommended her ticket-of-leave should be cancelled.[10] Nineteen-year-old Mary Wotton or Wooten of the *Princess Royal* suffered a similar fate. She was discovered 'living in an improper state with a married man' in May 1831 and was sentenced to six months in the Factory. She and her man had apparently paid Mary's employer to allow them to live together. After her sentence Mary was not allowed to be assigned in Sydney again and was sent to the then country district of Prospect. A year later she applied to marry a self-employed ex-convict shoemaker called Martin Campbell, who was 16 years her senior, but the application was rejected because he had declared himself married on arrival. The authorities did Mary an unwitting service. In 1841 Campbell was convicted of stealing and retransported to a penal settlement for seven years, leaving any dependants he had acquired in the meantime to fend for themselves. Mary got her certificate of freedom at the end of 1835 and six months later married John Brown of Prospect.[11]

The women of the *Princess Royal* who had declared themselves single or widowed were free to choose marriage as their option for the future — and the choice was wide. The imbalance of the sexes in New South Wales had been demonstrated as recently as 1828. In the census that year the colony contained 26,611 males as against 8,987 women.[12] But marriage was as much a gamble as the lottery of assigned service. The right choice of a husband could indeed lead to a secure future, but the wrong choice could result in tragedy and degradation.

Most women met their prospective husbands while on assigned service, though some made marriages from the Factory where men would come in a businesslike fashion to choose a wife. It is hard to establish how many *Princess Royal* women took part in this marriage bureau for strangers. Jane Hyde, who was 50 when she married a much younger man through the Factory, may have done, but the indications are that Elizabeth Stocker and Sarah Bryant, both of whom married from the Factory, were followed there by their prospective husbands.[13]

The businesslike approach of some of the women, and the extent to which their head rather than their heart made the choice of a husband, is demonstrated by those who applied only months apart to marry different men. It is also an indication of the power of choice they had, if they chose to exercise it, among so many available men.

In 1831, dark haired, dark eyed, 22-year-old Maria Allen applied in the same month to marry two different men. One, David Reghan, was 29 and already free, but she finally chose Joseph Woodcock who, although he was an older man at 34 years and still only had a ticket-of-leave, was a sawyer on his own land at Bathurst. Maria had been convicted of housebreaking in Reading, England, and her only offence since arriving had been absconding from her first employer. After her marriage she almost vanishes from the records as a convict. She had no need of a ticket-of-leave and never applied for one. She simply obtained her certificate of freedom three years later. Maria and Joseph settled eventually in Orange, and although they had no surviving children their marriage lasted until his death in 1859.[14]

Charlotte Tither, according to the muster clerk, was a flaxen haired Amazon of 5 feet 11¾ inches. She was another who chose a husband with practical deliberation. In her early twenties like Maria, she had been sentenced to life for picking pockets in Warwick, which was her third offence. With a life sentence ahead of her, marriage must have seemed particularly imperative. She had a chequered career after she arrived in the colony. Charged with drunkenness by Simeon Lord, her first employer, she had replied cheekily that it was because he wouldn't let her go to church. The following year she was sent to the Factory for absconding and ordered to have her head shaved. Her ready tongue got her into trouble again nine months later when she was charged with insubordination, and in October 1831 she was sent down again from Maitland to the Factory for two months. By the time she applied to marry John Meehan, an ex-convict who was a baker in Maitland, the clergyman took the unusual step of describing her character as 'very bad'. The application was rejected because Meehan had stated 'married' so, two months later, Charlotte applied again through a different clergyman in Newcastle. This time her choice was an ex-convict called Thomas McNulty and the application was approved. Charlotte achieved her aim and escaped the system. She appeared no more before the magistrates, obtained a ticket-of-leave in 1843 and, like many prisoners sentenced to life, eventually received a conditional pardon.[15]

Elizabeth Jones, Charlotte Smith and Catherine Barrett were also among those whose lives settled down after marriage. Elizabeth had been sentenced in Guildford, where the judge gave her the maximum sentence of life for picking pockets although it was her first offence. In New South Wales, apart from a charge of absence without leave soon after she arrived, she kept out of trouble until she hit a bad patch, or a bad employer, in 1831. She was sent to the Factory twice that year: in June for drunkenness and abusing her mistress, and in November for an unstated offence. At the end of 1833, after an apparently trouble-free year in assignment, but with two employers, she applied to marry an ex-convict, John Potter. The marriage was stable and they lived in Sydney and produced children at regular intervals. Elizabeth never bothered with a ticket-of-leave or a conditional pardon and was written off the books when she died in 1857.[16]

Charlotte Smith was a widowed laundress from Dublin who had left one child behind in England. She started badly in New South Wales and was charged with drunkenness in June 1829, with being absent without leave in April 1830, and with drunkenness again in August 1830. Early in 1832 she maried Samuel Raynor, a ticket-of-leave holder, and made no further appearances in court. Their marriage lasted until her death 25 years later.[17]

Catherine Barrett's pattern of behaviour was similar to Charlotte's. She was only 20 and single when she arrived and was charged with three offences in the first three years. Then she was assigned to the country and met John Leonard, who worked for the same employer at Lake Bathurst near Goulburn. They were married in 1835 and remained in the rural areas. Twelve years later, when Catherine received her conditional pardon, they were living in Queanbeyan, and by 1854 ex-convict John described himself as a 'settler' at Yass River. Their marriage lasted until Catherine's death in 1880.[18]

Mary Fagan was one of the minority on the *Princess Royal* who had two previous convictions before her transportation. She was only 17 when she was found guilty of stealing hammers at Liverpool and sentenced to seven years transportation. She avoided trouble with the authorities during her first two years in the colony, but was sent to the Factory for three months in June 1831 for 'pilfering and abusing her master'. She subsequently spent 12 months in the Factory after running away from her employer in April 1833, and was sentenced to a further nine months in October 1834 for an unknown offence. After seven years in the colony, she was still only 23 years old when she married James Lockwood, an ex-convict stonemason, in March 1836. Mary never committed another offence, her marriage lasted until James's death in 1860, and seven of her 11 children survived her when she died in 1873.[19]

Most of the colonial husbands of the *Princess Royal* women were convicts or ex-convicts, the great majority being free by the time they were married. Only two women, Mary Ann Taylor and Agnes Wicks, married men still serving their sentence, who did not even hold a ticket-of-leave. In both cases it was the couples' own good records and the support of their employers that gained approval from the government.

Mary Ann Taylor was a dairymaid from Wiltshire and had been assigned straight from the ship in 1829 to Rev. Thomas Reddall at Campbelltown. In the following months she met Joseph Giles, a prisoner for life assigned to the landowner William Howe of Glenee Estate in the same district. They applied to marry as early as October 1829 and both their employers supported them. Rev. Reddall said that Mary Ann 'has conducted herself tolerably well since she has been in my family', while William Howe, supporting Giles, said he 'has been in my employ since his arrival in the Colony and has conducted himself in a proper manner. I consent to his marriage and undertake to receive them both into my service.' Joseph and Mary Ann stayed with him until Joseph obtained a ticket-of-leave at the end of 1834. Mary Ann went with Joseph when he worked as a stockkeeper in the adjoining district of Stonequarry, then they settled in Campbelltown where Joseph became a police constable. They were doing nicely, and had acquired cattle of their own, when Joseph was convicted of stealing a hat in February 1838. He was sentenced to an iron gang for 12 months and lost his ticket-of-leave. The cattle were forfeited to the Crown and were sold. Mary Ann, who fortunately had obtained a ticket-of-leave very early in her sentence, was left to support herself and her young daughter Sarah. Joseph behaved himself so well in the iron gang that the major in charge of the stockade at Campbelltown recommended a remission of his sentence. Still a convict without any privileges, however, he worked as an overseer for one of the street gangs at Liverpool, where he was described as a quiet and laborious man, well spoken of by his superiors. He finally obtained another ticket-of-leave in September 1839 and Mary Ann had hers altered to the Liverpool district so she could join him.[20]

Six women married men who had come free to the colony. Clever Georgiana Baxter was one of them. She married a sailor a few months after she arrived and when he died she already held a ticket-of-leave and survived successfully until she married another free settler in 1836. Harriet Bannister and Mary Williams both married sailors from the *Princess Royal* and the Welsh dairymaid, Ann Morgan, married a soldier who had come to the colony with the Royal Veteran Company.[21] Mary Mahoney, the young Irish girl who was blind in her right eye, had been trapped stealing by her employer in London and was retransported for stealing tea only five months after she arrived in New South Wales, but she married a free immigrant, Richard McGrath, in 1839 and travelled south with him to Port Phillip in 1840. She returned to Sydney in 1845 when she collected her certificate of freedom.[22]

Mary Morris, after a good start in the colony with the Kennedy family in Sydney, married Joseph Spencer, a free immigrant, at the end of 1831. But Joseph died only six months later and Mary, who held a ticket-of-leave, went to live in Bathurst. She had been left pregnant, was obviously struggling to survive, and turned to drink. In August 1834 she was charged with her first offence in the colony, drunkenness and disorderly conduct. She lost her ticket-of-leave as punishment and then the following month her two-year-old son, Joseph, was accidentally drowned at Evans Plains near Bathurst. This progression of tragedies left Mary back where she started, a prisoner without privileges. Her attempt to start afresh had been destroyed through no fault of her own, but her sentence had only a few months to run and in July 1835 she was free. The same month she applied to marry an ex-convict, much older than herself, named William Clarke.[23]

Marriage to a man who had never been a convict proved no real advantage. The personal relationship or circumstances were more important to the women's future. Georgiana and Mary Morris lost their husbands quickly through death, which resulted in destitution for Mary. As we shall see, marriage to men from the crew of the *Princess*

Royal was disastrous for Mary Williams and Harriet Bannister, while Ann Morgan was often in gaol after she was married and even after she was free. Mary Mahoney had overcome her problems before her marriage to Richard McGrath and would have gained permission to go to Port Phillip at his employer's request, even if Richard had been an ex-convict.

Ann Barnett, from the London poorhouse, and Hannah Solomons, a London prostitute, were among those who took the opportunity of a new life as soon as they landed in the colony.

Ann kept out of gaol and the Factory and obtained a ticket-of-leave two years after she arrived. In July 1832 she married Thomas Tollis, who had also struggled to make good. Born in the colony, the eldest son of a soldier in the infamous New South Wales Corps who remained behind in the colony, Thomas and his brothers and sister had all been sent to the orphanages when their parents died. The boys learnt to be shoemakers and this was the trade Thomas followed during his life with Ann. They had 11 children and Ann died in 1885, aged 73 far removed in every sense from her lonely life in London.[24]

Hannah Solomons' life was less straightforward but, given her past, demonstrated that, when a chance for a new direction was available, she took it. Although she was sentenced to 14 years, she obtained an early ticket-of-leave through good behaviour at the end of 1832, and the following year married a self-employed ex-convict named James Box. She was left a widow within three years, but in 1837 married Charles Smith, holding a ticket-of-leave for the rural district of Prospect. The Female Factory report on Hannah, when she received her certificate of freedom in 1842, indicates she had spent a total of two months and 14 days there, but exactly when and why is not revealed. These offences did not apparently occur before her first marriage and may well have been caused by the death of her husband.[25]

Hannah and Ann were not the only women from the *Princess Royal* who took advantage of their situation in a new society. There were others who committed no offences after they arrived and quickly disappeared from the records. Catherine Turner, the Irish woman who said she stole on purpose, found a husband, James Neal, within two years and settled with him in Bathurst.[26] Seventeen-year-old Mary Tilley married an ex-convict policeman, Gregory Howe, and lived in Parramatta raising children until she died, aged 34 in 1847.[27] Bridget Hainsbury married Michael Keefe, from Ireland like herself.[28] Mary Ann Smith from London was given a ticket-of-leave in 1832 for good conduct in service, applied to marry a ticket-of-leave holder the same year, but didn't pursue it. The following year she met and married Robert Mitchell, a free immigrant, when they were both in the service of Alexander Berry on his estate at Shoalhaven, south of Sydney.[29] Mary Harcourt married colonial-born Thomas Wright in 1832 and, except for obtaining a ticket-of-leave in 1838 and a conditional pardon for her life sentence in 1847, had no further dealings with the authorities.[30]

Support from an employer was essential in order to obtain permission to marry. Many masters and mistresses demonstrated goodwill in their supporting letters, even though it often meant they would lose a good servant. The employers of Mary Ann Bates and Mark Brown, her first choice for a husband, did their best for them. John and Clara Loveridge gave their permission because of Mary Ann's good conduct and added: 'She has been here 22 months and has behaved with honesty and sobriety and we are willing to dispense with her services'. Thomas Rayner went even further for Mark Brown: 'He has been in my service for four years and behaved with sobriety and honesty. I feel pleasure to give my consent for he is worthy of it.' Rayner agreed to take Mary into his service as well, but it was to no avail. The governor followed the rules to the letter and refused his consent 'neither prisoner holding any indulgence', that is, a ticket-of-leave. Mary Ann took three years to recover from this setback and it was not until 1835 that she finally married an ex-convict called James Moss.[31]

A powerful and determined employer, however, could override all the rules. Ann Bullock had been assigned from the ship to Andrew Allan, a landholder near Goulburn. There she met James Robinson, a ticket-of-leave holder who was the overseer of another property in the district, and in August 1830 they put in their application to marry. It was rejected because Ann had revealed her marriage when she arrived. Twice more the application went to the governor and each time the Convict Office added the damming notation: 'Female married'. The clergyman, Rev. Thomas Hassall, was being pressured and added on the second application: 'Robinson is in the employ of Captain Rossi who wishes the marriage to take place and states "that the Indent shew the woman to be unmarried"'. Captain Rossi was the superintendent of police in Sydney, but the convict indents were in the hands of the superintendent of convicts who was not prepared to cooperate with his fellow administrator, and 'Female married' was still added to the marriage application. Captain Rossi, however, was a volatile Corsican with true European regard for practicality in marital affairs. He took matters into his own hands and persuaded Rev. Hassall to marry Ann and James. With a small alteration to the surname, there were no repercussions. The Robinsons became Robertson and lived and worked and raised their children undisturbed. But Ann carefully kept away from the authorities and never even applied for her certificate of freedom.[32]

Ann was one of the lucky women of the *Princess Royal*. She and the others, who were able to get themselves married, particularly if it was within the first few years of their arrival in the Colony; who chose their men wisely, either by instinct or good judgment; who kept themselves honest and free of a betraying addiction to drink, found a second chance for their lives. Through the protection and security of marriage, they were able to turn their backs permanently on the convict system, even while they were still technically part of it. Many of their shipmates were still in there, battling for survival.

'FEMALE MARRIED'

'His Excellency does not interfere with the marriage of free persons.'
Thus the colonial secretary relieved the confused mind of one clergyman enquiring on behalf of his flock in 1836.[1]

The clergymen of New South Wales bore a difficult burden, caught
between the precise legalities and procedures of the government, their
personal moral beliefs, and the anxious and persistent importunity of
their congregation. They were on the front line of the marriage battle,
with the unfortunate dilemma of trying to satisfy often irreconcilable
differences. If an application failed, or there was a long delay without
reply, they became objects of suspicion and feared the loss of their
influence among their parishioners. 'When we tell them again and
again that we have not heard from government,' they suspect that 'we
have not written, and because they are poor, we care little for them',
wrote one clergyman.[2] Rev. Samuel Marsden was renowned for his
punitive attitude to the women prisoners, but he was a great believer
in marriage as the path to reformation of the women and he enlisted
the aid of Elizabeth Fry in England in an attempt to have the regulations changed. In 1832 the Quaker reformer replied to him:

> According to Thy wish I have applied to Government respecting the married
> women and it is concluded that the best plan to adopt is not to have any
> account taken of whether the women are married or not, for, as it is only
> their own word that is taken for it, it may as well be taken in New South
> Wales as here, and those who make it clear that they are married certainly
> should be treated as such, but it appears almost impossible certainly to know
> their real condition. Our Under Secretary of State also says that it is a law of
> the country, that any woman who has not heard of her husband for seven
> years may marry again, therefore there is nothing to hinder any under such
> circumstances.[3]

Later in the decade the government adopted the latter reason as
grounds for remarriage, but the change took time and in 1836 it was

still necessary for Rev. Rusden, who dealt with many of the women from the *Princess Royal*, to try and persuade the governor to be more lenient:

> As Maitland is perhaps the very worst place in the Colony for a good looking and unprotected young woman, who is struggling with poverty, treated with unkindness and neglect, and continually exposed to the arts of seduction, I would beg leave...for His Excellency's favourable consideration... for someone who wants to marry.[4]

Rusden's letter encapsulates the main reasons why so many women tried so hard and long to marry in the face of great difficulties and constant rejection. They would go to great lengths to convince the government they were free to marry.

One frequent attempt to provide proof was to swear an affidavit. Rachael Dagnall of the *Princess Royal* tried this. She applied to marry William Compton who was assigned to the brother of Alexander McDougall, her own master. But she had told the clerks on the ship when she arrived that her husband, Richard Dagnall, was in Van Diemen's Land, so she anticipated trouble and went before the Magistrate at Patrick's Plains:

> RACHAEL DAGNALL per Princess Royal being duly sworn deposeth about 10 or 11 years ago my husband was cast for death at Lancaster Castle. I have never heard since what became of him.
>
> Rachael Dagnall, her mark.
>
> Sworn before me at Patrick Plains
> 24 December, 1832. Jas. Glinn, J.P.[5]

The Colonial Secretary replied to the clergyman:

> Rachael Dagnall cannot be allowed to marry William Compton under the affidavit made by her as above as she distinctly stated on her arrival that her husband, John [*sic*] Dagnall, was at Van Diemen's Land.
>
> In some cases His Excellency has allowed credence to affidavits of the above nature where they contain some sufficient proof of the death of the former husband or wife, or where borne by respectable corroborative evidence, but in the present case the variance in Dagnall's statements above pointed out is too palpable to be unobserved.[6]

Rachael was certainly lying in her attempt to marry. Her husband was indeed in Van Diemen's Land and his name was Richard, just as she had told the authorities when she landed. She had also declared on arrival that she could read and write, and perhaps the cross with which she 'signed' the affidavit was the sop to her conscience. For now, she retired defeated, but knowing she had only three more years of her sentence to serve.

Rachael, the only one of that name on the *Princess Royal*, did not have the option of a woman called Hannah Gordon from another ship, who nearly succeeded in a clever impersonation. She applied to marry in the name of Hannah Anderson, a single girl who had sailed out with her from England. Unfortunately for Hannah Gordon, the government's system worked and she was discovered.[7]

But the government system was not infallible. The rigid reliance on the original ships' musters sometimes tripped up the authorities. Mary Williams, who had married and been abandoned by one of the crew of the *Princess Royal*, successfully applied to marry again even though her husband was still alive. The application was approved because the ship's muster revealed she had stated 'single' on arrival and there was no cross check to intervening marriage records.[8] Ann Kirby and Hannah Solomons from the *Princess Royal* both told the truth and described themselves as widows when they applied to marry again. In each case the word 'widow' was conscientiously crossed out and replaced by their original description, 'single'.[9]

Mary Ann Green (or Walton) deliberately tried to muddle the system. When she arrived she had revealed her husband, Thomas Walton, was in Van Diemen's Land. The following year she applied to marry Peter Cheek, and when she was rejected she forwarded a petition which, with very convoluted reasoning, tried to manipulate the government into believing the marriage was a *fait accompli*:

The humble petition of Mary Ann Green most submissively sheweth...

That Petitioner about 9 months ago made application to the Reverend Mr Wilkinson at Newcastle to obtain permission to be united to Peter Cheeck per Hercules...and the Banns of Marriage were accordingly published by that clergyman in the church of Newcastle.

That Petitioner on having applied to be married is informed that some error occurred in the matter at that time and that it will be necessary to renew her application to your Excellency for permission and as your Excellency's petitioner cannot devine the reason for such refusal after considering the clergyman must have obtained your Excellency's leave or he would not have published the Banns, your Excellency's petitioner therefore now most humbly prays your Excellency may be most graciously pleased if any mistake has occurred in the case of the Banns of Marriage having [been] regularly published about 9 months ago, that Your Excellency may be graciously pleased to order the present Clergyman, the Reverend W. Wilton, to unite her to Peter Cheeck...

(sgd) Mary Ann Green

'Not allowed being already married', came the response. Peter Cheek accepted the rejection and he married someone else 18 months later. Mary Ann made no further applications while she was a prisoner.[10]

The attitude of the authorities was not always consistent and the fortune of a marriage application could be affected by a change of governors. Governor Bourke had been in the colony barely a year when Rev. Wilton of Newcastle wrote on behalf of a female prisoner who had stated 'married'. He told the colonial secretary that the woman had a letter from her father, with a Nottingham postmark, informing her that her husband was dead. On the clergyman's representation alone, the governor allowed the marriage.[11] This was an unusual decision. The authorities were increasingly suspicious of letters from home which mentioned dead spouses, and not without reason. Many prisoners, both male and female, went to great lengths to forge such advice. Some wrote to relatives in England, telling them what to say in letters. Others took genuine letters and added, some times in a naively obvious fashion, a sentence informing them their spouse was dead. Occasionally whole letters were forged, but posted in New South Wales which meant the postmark betrayed the deception. Those who could not obtain letters and who did not think their own sworn word would be sufficient, called on their friends in the colony to swear they had known them at home and they were unmarried there. One woman's friend supported her by swearing simply that he had seen her crying in the street when she received a letter telling her of her husband's death.[12]

The sad story of Elizabeth Foxall, from the *Princess Royal*, demonstrates very clearly many aspects of the struggle to marry in the colony.

With striking auburn hair and grey eyes, but rather stout, Elizabeth was only 25 when she arrived in the colony, having been sentenced to life in Birmingham where she and Mary Harcourt were convicted together of stealing money from a man in a house of ill-fame.[13] Her husband, William Foxall, had been sentenced to 14 years a year earlier for stealing a purse, and she told the authorities when she arrived that he had sailed by the ship *William Miles* to Van Diemen's Land.[14] This statement rebounded to haunt the rest of her life.

She was not a healthy woman and spent a large part of the voyage to the colony in the ship's hospital, Surgeon Wilson describing her on the two separate periods she was in the hospital as suffering from 'Contusion'. On one occasion, at least, the bruising was due to a fall in the choppy March seas, but whether drink also played a part is unknown.[15] She had a pattern of ill health in the colony, with several employers returning her 'sick' to government — one of them specified she had a bad leg and was incapable of performing her work.[16] There are, however, indications in the pattern of her employment that she exaggerated illness as a device to change assignments, and in the one instance where it was in her interests to stay with her employer she did so for three years.[17]

Elizabeth had a couple of minor convictions against her — 15 days in the cells for being drunk and absent and six weeks in the Factory for insolence and neglect of work[18] — when, late in 1830 and probably coinciding with the latter offence, she met Richard Barron, a 26-year-old ex-convict. Together they made plans to marry and set up a bakery, but Elizabeth's employers, Mr and Mrs Clayton, refused to give their consent and lose their servant. Eventually, Elizabeth in desperation went before the bench of magistrates who, after hearing the evidence, ordered the Claytons to give their consent within three months or provide a good reason why not. They held out until the last possible moment, but finally supplied the necessary certificate, and in June 1832 Rev. William Cowper of St Philip's, Sydney, sent in the application to marry.[19]

Predictably, it was promptly rejected. Richard immediately responded and wrote a memorial to the governor, attaching an affidavit

from Elizabeth in which she swore she was never married to William
Foxall or anyone else. Richard asked the governor to order an
investigation.[20]

'This matter can be investigated more readily than many of the
kind,' responded the governor when he saw the papers. 'Let enquiry
be made in Van Diemen's Land of Foxall or, if he should be removed,
let enquiry be made as to the fact of his having been a convict there
and whether he reported himself married.[21]

The colonial secretary wrote to his counterpart in Hobart the next
day, 13 July 1832, and when no answer was received by the end of
September he instructed his clerks to send a duplicate, which was
dispatched on 10 October.[22] But the reply was already on its way and
it contained very bad news for Richard and Elizabeth.

William Foxall had done his best for her and a summary of what he
had said was enclosed by the colonial secretary in Hobart.

> Copy: Statement of William Foxall per William Miles, Wire Drawer by trade,
> formerly residing in Floodgate Street, Birmingham. Never was married but
> about three years before he was convicted and up to the period he was
> apprehended he cohabited with a woman called Elizabeth Coates of Stafford
> Street in the above town. This woman he has heard had been transported to
> Sydney since his arrival in Van Diemen's Land, and goes by his name Foxall,
> but he will make affidavit she is not his wife.
>   W. Foxall, his mark
> Before me D. Wentworth,
> 10 August, 1832[23]

The bad news was contained in another enclosure from Josiah Spode,
of the Principal Superintendent's Office (Hobart), dated 25 September
1832:

> In returning the enclosed letter from the Colonial Secretary at Sydney
> respecting Elizabeth Foxall, a convict in N.S.W., I beg leave to enclose a
> statement of her husband (as reported in the...books) by which it will
> appear that although he lived with her they never were married, but it
> becomes my duty to inform you, for the information of His Excellency Major
> General Bourke, that on 3 April last, I wrote, copy enclosed, to the Principal
> Superintendent of Convicts at Sydney, enclosing a letter detained by me
> from Elizabeth Foxall, then residing at Mr Clayton's near the Lumberyard at
> Sydney, being directed to her husband William Foxall, a prisoner in this
> Colony, who arrived in the Wm. Miles, the purport of that letter was to
> deceive the authorities, for I very well recollect that William Foxall was
> therein directed to deny his marriage and that he was to write to the female
> in Sydney and say that they had only lived together in England...
>   P.S. I beg leave to observe that I have delayed this communication until
> now as I expected to have been able to adduce satisfactory proof of the
> marriage, but in which I have not succeeded. J.S.[24]

The moral Mr Spode, conscious of his duty and anxious to
demonstrate that he had indeed sent Elizabeth's intercepted letter to
Sydney in April, enclosed a copy of his letter to Mr Hely, the
superintendent of convicts in New South Wales:

> I beg leave to forward you the enclosed letter from Elizabeth Foxall, a con-

vict now residing as she states at Mr Clayton's near the Lumberyard, and intended for the husband William Foxall, who came to this Colony in the William Miles in 1828. The part I have marked in red ink will fully develop its object and I therefore forward it for your information.[25]

When the colonial secretary in Sydney received all these documents he immediately called for a report from Mr Hely. There was deafening silence for two months, so he wrote again requesting information on 13 December and, yet again, when there was no answer, on 31 December 1832.[26]

Understandably, Richard was getting impatient and on 7 February 1833 he sent another memorial to the governor.

The Petition of Richard Barron sheweth that Your Excellency's petitioner more than 8 months ago prayed through Reverend William Cowper to be permitted to marry Elizabeth Coates alias Foxall and was answered that the marriage could not be allowed, the woman being already married to one William Foxall a prisoner of the Crown at Van Diemen's Land.

Memorialist ventures again to approach Your Excellency and now encloses an affidavit of the said Elizabeth Coates alias Foxall affirming that she was never married to the said William Foxall nor to any other person whatever.

Your Excellency's petitioner further begs to be permitted to produce prisoners, who are now living in the Colony, who will prove the same thing on oath.

Trusting Your Excellency will take the prayer of petitioner into Your Excellency's humane consideration and cause the necessary enquiries to be made, petitioner as in duty bound will ever pray.[27]

'To Mr Hely,' noted the colonial secretary on 14 February, and 'Write again' on 28 February. On 3 April a duplicate of the request for information was sent. 'No answer,' noted the clerk on 30 April. 'Write again,' said the colonial secretary. 'Triplicate-8 May,' responded the clerk. Finally, on 12 May they extracted a reply from the harried superintendent of convicts who carefully ignored the fact the requests had begun in October 1832:[28]

In reply to your letter of 14 February last . . . I have the honour to inform you that I have caused the general letters for 1832 to be referred to, but have been unsuccessful in finding the one named in your letter, nor any replication. I regret consequently that I am unable to furnish any information on the subject.[29]

'I must beg leave,' said the governor when this document and all the others landed on his desk, 'that precis of the case be put into the Report Column as I really recollect nothing whatever about William and Elizabeth Foxall.' The colonial secretary's office constructed a summary and sent it back to him, adding at the bottom: 'For His Excellency's comments on Barron's application which, it is presumed, will be refused'. The governor did what was expected of him and, indeed, what was virtually all he could do given the facts of the case. He refused the application but insisted 'Barron to be informed fully of the grounds of this refusal'. Richard was advised on 5 June and told the details of the decision including the intercepted letter.[30] He accepted the decision and turned his attention elsewhere.

The Claytons had returned Elizabeth to government and she was assigned 200 miles north of Sydney, in Newcastle.[31] There, her distress got her into trouble. Her mistress found she was missing from her room late at night and called a constable. She was found as she left a man's house, 'half dressed' according to the constable who added 'There was no light' as if that settled it. But Elizabeth claimed, significantly, that she went to the house to get a letter written, which was indeed possibly the reason, even if she actually went to pay in kind for a letter previously written. She was sent to the cells for seven days and returned to government.[32]

The truth of the matter cannot be finalised, but the scales tip towards the government's conclusion. Elizabeth and William had every reason to lie, while Mr Spode in Hobart did not, unless his failure to 'adduce proof of the marriage', presumably from William, had made him vindictive. Although the record is difficult to decipher, it appears William did declare himself 'single' on arrival, but this was probably just good tactics. Elizabeth always called herself Foxall or Fox, even in England, never saying 'alias Foxall', which usually reflected a *de facto* relationship. But her written attempt to get William to collude with her rebounded terribly, because this was the same governor who accepted the clergyman's word that a letter was postmarked in Nottingham. The persistence of Elizabeth and Richard and the plethora of sworn statements might just have convinced him to give his permission if it hadn't been for the damning evidence of Mr Spode. The confusion in the Convict Office, which sometimes occurred on other matters, and the long delay it caused, must have aggravated the distress of both parties, and if Elizabeth did lie to Richard and the information of her attempt to deceive everyone about her marriage came as a shock to him, then Elizabeth would have felt the whole misery of his anger, even 200 miles away.

She was returned to government again, sick, at the end of 1833, and sent down from Newcastle to the second class of the Factory, which was probably what she wanted.[33] One can only guess at her attempts to see and talk to Richard, but it was much too late. On 20 December 1833, only a few weeks after Elizabeth returned, Richard married a convict named Sarah McMahon. The witnesses at the wedding were Elizabeth's former shipmate, Sarah Clark, and her husband, Richard Turton, who was a baker like Richard.[34]

Elizabeth soldiered on in a variety of assigned employment until she landed herself in some unknown trouble in June 1835 and was sent to the third class of the Factory for a year.[35] In August 1837 she was assigned to Mr and Mrs John Thurlow in Sydney, and in March the following year she made another assault on the authorities for permission to marry a man named Michael Quindelin.[36] The application was, of course, rejected, so in June she sent a petition to the governor, supported by her present employer and also Mrs Clayton from the past. This time, as well as another sworn affidavit from herself, she had extra ammunition:

> I William Greig maketh oath and sayeth that Elizabeth Fox alias Cootes...
> has been known to me 20 years and upwards. I do certify on her leaving
> England that she was unmarried, I arrived in the Colony in the year 1830.

> Police Office,   William Greig, his
> May, 1838   mark[37]

The governor, by now George Gipps, rejected her for not following
the correct procedure. 'Being transmitted in an irregular manner they
must be returned,' he noted.[38] But Elizabeth didn't give up. She
gathered her forces and sent in the following:

> The humble petition of Elizabeth Coates alias Foxall a prisoner per ship *Princess Royal*, May 1829.
>
> Sheweth that when your petitioner arrived in the Colony she caused, at
> the recommendation of several of her friends, herself to be described in the
> books of the said ship as a married woman in order that she might continue
> to live and be married to one William Foxall, by whom in England she had
> four children and with whom she had resided there 5 years, but who had
> been the year previous to her own conviction, transported as she was
> informed to this Colony.
>
> That your petitioner has since ascertained that the said William Foxall was
> not transported hither but to Van Diemen's Land and that consequently
> great difficulty now arises therefrom in effecting a marriage between your
> Petitioner and one Michael Quindelin of Goulburn Street, Sydney, a stone-
> mason, as it appears by the books that she is married. But as the contrary is
> the fact and as your petitioner and the said Michael Quindelin were truly
> called on the 17th day of March last, your Petitioner therefore humbly
> prays that Your Excellency will be pleased to take her peculiar case into your
> consideration and direct that the marriage be solemnized, or if in any doubt
> should be upon Your Excellency's mind (notwithstanding the affidavit made
> by your Petitioner and sent to Your Excellency on the 12 June last, setting
> out that your Petitioner is not married and which is supported by another
> affidavit which accompanied it) Your Excellency will order enquiry to be
> made and the further affidavit of the said William Foxall acquired in support
> of your Petition's prayer.

> August, 1838   Elizabeth Coates alias
>   Foxall, her mark

Three of her employers came to her support.

> I hereby certify that Elizabeth Coates alias Fox has been known to me during
> the last 7 years and that I have always known her during that time to be
> strictly sober, virtuous, honest and industrious. Whilst assigned to me she
> always behaved to my satisfaction. Assigned to me for 3 years.

> Elizabeth Clayton

> Elizabeth Coates alias Foxall having been assigned to me since August, 1837,
> I consider from what I have observed of her conduct that she is worthy of
> the indulgence she prays for in her petition.

> S. G. Thurlow

I have no reason to believe the above statements to be incorrect, but I have every reason to think that she is a woman worthy of credit.

... Gregory[39]

The colonial secretary's office could not find the affidavits sent in two months earlier because, with terrible irony, they had been filed under 'C' for Coates. In any event the officials reverted to their reliance on the statement made when Elizabeth arrived 'when she had no motive to conceal the truth'.[40] Elizabeth must have reeled from the body blow of the decision as it was finally conveyed to her: 'cannot be granted unless an affidavit from William Foxall can be produced certifying that the applicant was never married to him. The affidavit alluded to in her petition not appearing to have been received.'[41]

She gave up. The hope for a bright future, which had sustained her, withered away. Worn out and worn down, lonely and dispirited, she died at the government hospital, Sydney, less than two years later, at the age of 36.[42]

CHAPTER 10

BEATING THE SYSTEM

Not all the marriage battles with the authorities ended in failure. Mary Palmer triumphed. She had declared herself married when she arrived on the *Princess Royal*, but she did not have a husband in the colony. She also had an advantage Elizabeth Foxall lacked. She had been sentenced to only 14 years, rather than life, and therefore was eventually able to obtain a ticket-of-leave and have some control over her life.[1]

Tall, with brown hair and hazel eyes, Mary was 35 years old and described herself as a 'Plain Cook' when she arrived in the colony.[2] She was obviously a strong-willed woman who spoke her mind and that, particularly when combined with a drink, landed her in the Factory on several occasions. She liked 'a drop of the creature' and nearly burnt down her employer's pub when she was drunk in 1831.[3] A great deal of her assigned service was spent in the country districts south-west of Sydney and it was at Goulburn Plains in 1836 that she caught the eye of William Hickmott, a 40-year-old convict serving a life sentence at Kenmore, the nearby grazing property of the auditor-general, Mr Lithgow. William must have been devoted to Mary because he went to considerable trouble and never faltered in the long battle to marry her.

Mary and William had not one, but two enormous handicaps to overcome. They had both declared themselves married on arrival. In early August 1836 they put in their application through Rev. John Vincent at Sutton Forest.[4] With it went a letter from William's brother in England, which, after reprimanding William for not writing, particularly to his daughter Hannah, went on to say:

> Now William I am now agoing to relate to you very unpleasant news that is concerning the death of your wife after a long and painful illness of 16 weeks. She died on the 4 September, 1833. During her illness she prayed very hard for your welfare and she begged of me to send you word of her death as soon as possible I could for she was very sensible of her death. She was in her sixty five years of age when she died. During her illness her mind

was very much trouble about you as she never heard from you since you left England, which she thought very hard of you, but, thank God, she received a letter from you three weeks before her death which gave her great comfort and she told me she should die happy now...

I have every reason to believe that you will receive this letter for I am going to deliver this letter to a sailor that lodges at my house...and I was saying that I had a brother at New South Wales and there had been three letters sent to you and I could not get any answer from you...He told me if I gave him the letter he would take it to Sydney and put it in the post office there and he would not desert me and you would be sure to have it, for he had taken letters there before and the people that he had taken for had received answers. He goes by the name of Wiliam Cramp here, but sailors have so many names.[5]

Rev. Vincent had sought approval for the marriage from Mr Lithgow and had also taken the precaution of sending him Samuel Hickmott's letter from London. Lithgow responded:

I have no other proof of his being really a widower than the letter which he produced notifying the decease of his wife. It does not bear the English post-mark and, even if it did, this is not positive evidence of the death of his wife, as I understand matters of a similar purport are sometimes sent from the Colony that they may be stamped with the Post Office mark in England with the view to giving an air of credibility to statements which are actually false. I would greatly hope that such a deception is not being attempted in the present case, but it might be desirable to ascertain whether he has any further evidence to adduce.[6]

Vincent noted on the bottom of Lithgow's letter: 'I enquired personally of Hickmott at Goulburn Plains, if he could produce further evidence of the death of his wife. He replied only verbal commiserations, which had been made to him.'[7]

All these documents went, in the first instance, to the superintendent of convict's office for checking against the records. There, someone added:

The accompanying letter, purporting to have been written by Hickmott's brother is of colonial manufacture. One place this states no letter was received from the fellow in the Colony, again it is stated that the dying wife received a letter 3 weeks previous to her death, notwithstanding it goes on to state, that if he could hear from him he would send him a deal of news. How does he come to know his address — if a sailor put the letter in the Sydney Post Office, surely it would bear its mark. The whole is a fabrication.[8]

This hasty and ill-considered comment, in the light of the detailed contents of the letter which explain most of the queries raised, influenced the governor's decision and he noted: 'Not allowed. The letter is a gross fabrication.'[9]

When Mary heard this verdict she went out and got very drunk. But she had worked for the local magistrate, Captain Allman, not long before and he had even informally made enquiries about permission for her to marry. He sympathised with her sad tale and discharged her with a reprimand.[10]

Mary was assigned further north towards Sydney and was working for Mr McAlister at Campbelltown when she received a ticket-of-leave at the end of April 1837.[11] It was valid for the Goulburn district, which would have been at her request, and she returned there to work for the second time at Solomon Moses' pub at Goulburn Plains. Shortly after, she applied to marry again, this time to Lawrence Delaney, a free immigrant who was working for a landholder called Shelley in the Grampian Hills. The application was rejected on the basis of her marriage in England.[12] Mr Delaney's interest withered and died, but William Hickmott came back into the picture.

In November 1838 William and Mary again put in an application to marry, this time through the Presbyterian minister, Rev. William Hamilton, in Goulburn.[13] It was rejected again and they retreated, not to give up but to gather new and irrefutable evidence. William's sister and her husband, Mr J. Byles, who was a solicitor, had recently arrived to settle in Sydney. William requested Mr Byles to obtain proof of the death of Mary's husband.[14]

Eighteen months later, William and Mary made a third application to marry. They enlisted the support of the Church of England clergyman in Goulburn, Rev. William Sowerby, in whom they found a champion who liked and believed them both and was determined not to be beaten. In the following weeks he deluged the government with three separate formal applications. Each time an objection was raised he sent out another with further evidence which refuted it. He fired his opening salvo confidently on 4 June 1840:

> The consent of the Governor is requested to the Publication of Banns between the within named. Mary Palmer is reported married, Certificate enclosed purporting that her husband died in 1827. Wm. Hickmott is reported married, but states to me that Mr Lithgow, to whom he is assigned in company with Mr Atkinson, is in a position to prove the death of his wife by the testament of Mrs Byles of O'Connell Street, Sydney. Contemporary with the reception of this you will receive a communication from Mr Lithgow . . .
>
> PS. Enclosed is a Certificate stating Mr Atkinson's willingness to support the man and his wife if married.[15]

Rev. Sowerby had covered every contingency and among the documents he sent in was the hard evidence many a female prisoner wished for:

> CERTIFICATE OF BURIAL in the Parish of St George the Martyr, Southwark, in the County of Surrey, in the year 1827. No. 2259.
> RICHARD PALMER, St Thomas Hospital, January 5th, 1827, age 52. W.G. Plies, Curate.
> Extracted from the Register 23 September, 1839. sgd. Parish Clerk.[16]

The superintendent of convicts was highly suspicious.

> Mary Palmer ought to be called upon to show how the accompanying printed certificate came into her possession. There is one thing worthy to be remembered, Palmer's supposed husband is stated in it to have been buried 5 January, 1827 and Mary Palmer on arrival in this Colony reported that she was married.

'Write to the Police Magistrate, Goulburn to enquire into the case,' he instructed his clerk.[17]

Mary was called before the magistrate in Goulburn, who reported back that 'she positively affirmed her husband died at St Thomas Hospital and was buried at the time and place noted in the document'. He quizzed her about her inconsistency in stating she was married when she arrived in May 1829, and reported: 'She believes she represented herself as married on arrival, but adds she spoke at random when asked the question by the gentleman'. The Goulburn magistrate also took the initiative of asking his Sydney counterpart to check on Mr Byles. He advised that Mr Byles stated he had obtained the certificate through his agent at Sergeant's Inn, Fleet Street, London. The Sydney magistrate added: 'From the respectability of Mr Byles, I have not the slightest doubt of the truth of his statement'.[18]

Meanwhile, the governor had refused permission for the marriage on the remaining grounds that William was not free. But Rev. Sowerby had written to the auditor-general asking him to testify that William's wife was dead after satisfying himself by speaking to William's sister. Lithgow contacted Mr Byles and received a statement from him that 'the wife of William Hickmott died previous to my leaving England'. Lithgow then complicated the issue by sending this to Sowerby, rather than direct to the colonial secretary as he had been requested to do.[19]

Feeling anxious, William wrote to his employer. His writing was good, but his grammar and spelling rather shaky. The following is a corrected version:

> Sir,   I hope
> you will [be] convinced of my having wife living, as my sister can give you satisfaction that I have not. I have this day made application to the minister for to get married by the consent of Mr C. C. Atkenson [Lithgow's partner]. I hope you will have the goodness to give that satisfaction to Mr Harrington [the colonial secretary] as my sister will give you satisfaction, for I am now the oldest servant you have in Bond. I have been in your service for 8 years and 4 months. I made application for a ticket six months ago, heard no Court [*sic*] it.
> from your most obedient and most humble servant,
> William Hickmott[20]

Rev. Sowerby had forwarded Mr Byles' statement and Mr Lithgow's letter, along with yet another official application, to the superintendent of convicts, but the rejection of his first application crossed his letter. Suspecting something like this might happen, Rev. Sowerby, who had to go away, prepared a third formal application on the prescribed form and left instructions for his assistant to send it off if necessary. It was dispatched but, in the event, proved unnecessary. The police magistrate in Goulburn made his report to the colonial secretary and it was laid on Governor Gipps' desk with the following comment:

> It does not appear from this that Mary Palmer improperly obtained the Certificate of her husband's burial or that the Certificate is a forgery. There is

however still an objection to the marriage...as the man stated on arrival that he was married. 13th [August]
Yes
   G.G. 25th
The enclosed note from Mrs Byles may perhaps be considered sufficient and the marriage allowed. 27th.
   Yes
   G.G. 28th[21]

On 8 September 1840 Rev. Sowerby married Mary Palmer and William Hickmott at St Saviour's Church, Goulburn. No doubt there was a mighty celebration that night at Solomon Moses' pub.[22]

One other woman beat the authorities on the question of marriage. Mary Wheat was lucky because she was dealing with Governor Bourke, whose attitude was more flexible and more trusting. Thirty-two-year-old Mary had truthfully declared herself married on arrival, but on 30 April 1832, soon after Governor Bourke took charge, she sent in the following petition:

> Your Petitioner most humbly presumes to address Your Excellency trusting you will be pleased after the perusal of this her Humble Petition to grant her the favour she now humbly solicits. Your Petitioner begs to state she arrived in this Colony by ship Princess Royal in the year 1829 under sentence of transportation for 7 years, that your Petitioner came under the denomination of a Married Woman but that since your Petitioner arrived in this Colony she has received a letter from her mother in Hull in Yorkshire (which letter she can now produce) stating the loss of her husband (who was a sailor on board the Tolemachns, a private trader which was lost in the Davis Straits.)
>
> That your Petitioner has obtained a Ticket of Leave for her exemplary conduct in her situation with Mrs Blacket of Liverpool to whom she was first assigned and whose signature will accompany this — your Petitoner being now desirous to alter her situation in life, her name with that of John Tiffin a Free Man was published in Liverpool Church but in consequence of your Petitioner arriving as a Married Woman the marriage was not allowed to take place.
>
> Your Petitioner most humbly trusts should Your Excellency be pleased to peruse the Letter as mentioned from Petitioner's mother she feels assured it will prove satisfactory to Your Excellency that your Petitioner is at present a widow and that Your Excellency will be pleased to grant the prayer she humbly requests.[23]

Although the *Princess Royal* muster lists Mary as assigned first to James Orr, the clerk of the court at Parramatta, Mrs Blackett did not dispute that Mary had come to her straight from the boat and she confirmed that Mary had received the letter while in her service and 'I have no reason to doubt as to the correctness of the Decease of her husband'.[24] Strong support was also provided by Rev. John Dunmore Lang. He stated that he had seen the letter and added:

> I believe it to be a genuine document. Were the Petitioner free I should not hesitate on the ground of such a document to solemnize a marriage between her and any unobjectionable person, were there no other reason to stay proceedings and as it is quite impracticable in such cases to procure regular

testimony from church wardens or ministers in the mother country...it appears to me expedient to weigh the evidence actually attained and in such cases as the one in question to permit the party petitioning to marry.[25]

Like Lang, Governor Bourke had no difficulty in leavening morality with expediency. He did not ask to see the letter himself and had no hesitation in granting his approval. Mary and John Tiffin were married ten days later.[26]

The two Marys were the only women from the *Princess Royal* to win this kind of battle. The others who revealed they were married when they arrived and then tried to marry while they were prisoners all failed. Ellen Meares or Meyers tried once and accepted the rejection, as did Elizabeth Smith. Ann Cheeseman, perceiving clearly the freedom marriage could offer, tried three times with three different men over 18 months.[27] Irishwoman Betty Brian tried twice.

Betty was 36 when she was transported for stealing furniture, her third offence, and she left two children behind her in England.[28] She kept out of trouble except for one charge of drunkenness three weeks after she arrived, and in 1831 she had the chance to marry a ticket-of-leave man calleld William Mansfield, who was about her own age and a farmer at Wilberforce. She was in the third class of the Factory when the application went in but she had been returned there, for reasons unknown to the superintendent of convicts, by her master at Windsor, just near Wilberforce.[29] The implication would be that something in her relationship with William got her into trouble with her master. Her application was refused and she was assigned to Sydney where she went through two masters in the following year. In 1836 she was charged with drunkenness again and spent two months in the Factory. In 1838 she obtained a ticket-of-leave and managed to get it valid for Windsor, but she lost it in 1840 when she was sent to the Factory for six months for stealing a child's frock.[30] Back in Windsor again, she applied to marry, this time to Simon Hills who was still a convict and aged 45 like herself. The application was rejected on the basis of Betty's original marriage.[31] She obtained another ticket-of-leave for the Windsor district in 1841, before finally receiving her certificate of freedom in 1844 when she was 49 years old.[32] If she had been allowed to marry the farmer in Wilberforce 13 years earlier she could have avoided the itinerant life of an assigned servant and found consolation for her lost family through a new one in New South Wales.

The inability to marry was a serious blow to all the women, but it was worse for the ones with sentences of 14 years or life. Those who had been sentenced to seven years were in a better position and some most certainly took advantage of it. Rachael Dagnall, rejected when she applied to marry in 1832, turned around as soon as she was free in 1835 and married John McLoughlin under her maiden name of Andrews. Ann Burke was determined to get married and applied three times with three different men in 18 months. She married the third one, an ex-convict named John Jones, immediately she obtained her certificate of freedom. Sarah Pitches never applied while she was a prisoner, but she too married in 1836, the year she became free.[33]

Undoubtedly, others did the same thing.once they were beyond the control of the authorities.

Six women had taken the calculated risk of revealing their husbands were already in the colonies.

Rachael Dagnall, Elizabeth Foxall and Mary Ann Green (or Walton), whose men were transported to Van Diemen's Land, were never reunited with them. In fact it could well have been better tactics on their part to have applied to join their husbands. The government was not unreceptive to applications to reunite married couples, particularly if one of the parties had a ticket-of-leave or was free, and there were instances throughout the 1830s of women prisoners travelling between New South Wales and Van Diemen's Land to join their husbands. But none of the *Princess Royal* women applied to join their men in Van Diemen's Land and nor, apparently, did their husbands seek them out. Richard Dagnall had been transported in 1820, nine years before Rachael arrived, so it is not surprising that no residue of a bond between them remained.[34] But Thomas Walton had been convicted with his wife[35] and William Foxall had left England only months before Elizabeth, so it is more surprising that none of them tried to be reunited. William Foxall had been transported for 14 years and could have obtained a ticket-of-leave around 1836, thus offering Elizabeth an escape from the permanent prison of her life sentence.[36] Mary Ann Walton, however, was free by mid-1835, so probably married someone else. Perhaps the distance between the two colonies was beyond their conception, or they were unaware that any application to be together might succeed. It required the impetus of strong affection to make the attempt.

The three women with husbands in New South Wales had mixed fortunes.

Ann Shannon's husband, John, who was sentenced at the same time she was, dumped her once they were in New South Wales. He had a relatively smooth career as a prisoner and obtained a ticket-of-leave as early as October 1833. Having prudently declared himself single when he arived he was given permission to marry Mary Ann Fitzgerald without any problem the year he got his ticket.[37] Less than two years later he was free, and he quickly established a new life for himself. Poor Ann did not fare so well. She was convicted of drunkenness and insolence only five weeks after she arrived and spent two months in the Factory, but six months after she got out she was sent back again for drunkenness and disorderly conduct. She absconded from one employer in 1833 and had five other offences, with sentences ranging from 14 days to one month in the Factory before she obtained her certificate of freedom when it was due in 1835. But she was in gaol again in Parramatta the following year, sentenced to 14 days hard labour.[38]

A husband and wife who were both prisoners could experience great difficulties in even seeing each other and there is no better illustration than the sad story recounted in the *Sydney Gazette* in 1829. A prisoner named Fletcher was charged with being a runaway and when the magistrate examined him, he found Fletcher had the opportunity of staying in England after he was sentenced, but because his wife had stolen deliberately to follow him and was already on her way to New South Wales he chose to go too. On arrival he was assigned to the country as a shepherd and his wife was assigned in Sydney. The *Gazette* continued:

> The unfortunate couple were alike ignorant of each other's fate for nearly a year after...and when Fletcher did become acquainted with the fact of his wife being here and learnt where she was living, he made frequent and urgent applications to the individual in charge of his master's farm for a pass to go and see her, but without being able to obtain that indulgence...he left his station, saw his wife and was again returning to his duty when he was apprehended...and was sentenced to a road party for absconding. After wearing out a part of his sentence in the gang, he again absconded for the same purpose as before and having once more seen his wife...he came to the Police Office for the purpose of surrendering himself.

There was a happy ending to the Fletchers' story as the magistrates went to some trouble to check the facts and to recommend to the governor that he and his wife be assigned together.[39] John and Ann Shannon could well have been in a similar position, but they were initially both assigned in the Sydney area, so did not have the problems caused by distance.

Ann and John Wright were also both prisoners in the colony. Married, with one child, they had been convicted in Essex, John of stealing money and Ann of stealing fowls. John had arrived in 1828 and by 1829 was assigned to Mr and Mrs Patrick, who kept the busy and successful Marrow Inn at Campbelltown.[40] Ann was assigned, when she arrived, to Mrs Howell's laundry business in Sydney. She had been sent to the Factory in November 1829 for abusing her mistress, but apart from that had an unblemished record when the Patricks applied for her to be assigned to them so she could be reunited with John. The government agreed and Ann went to live with John at the inn in Campbelltown.[41]

Mary Haynes was sent a long way from Sydney when she arrived, but her great advantage was her husband, James, who was already free. Mary had been convicted in Bristol of receiving stolen goods from the man she was living with, Joseph Monks, and sentenced to 14 years. When she arrived in the colony she and Ann Bullock were assigned to the landowner, Andrew Allen, at Goulburn Plains and, like Ann, she committed no offences in the colony.[42] On the evidence of his silent complicity in Ann's illegal marriage, Mr Allen was a reasonable employer who would have agreed to a request for his servant to join her husband. It may have taken Mary some time to contact James, but it can be deduced from circumstantial evidence that in August 1830 she was in Sydney for the first time since she arrived over 12 months before and that this was when she became assigned to him.[43] James had been working as a sawyer for William Wells of Sydney, but he had his own land on a high sandstone ridge overlooking the Hawkesbury Valley at South Colah. They lived there in a small wooden house until James died in June 1862. Mary followed him, dying only six months later at the age of 59.[44] During her sentence she never needed a ticket of leave and never bothered to collect her certificate of freedom.

Not all of the women of the *Princess Royal* who had declared themselves married in England applied to marry someone else in New South Wales while they were still prisoners. Some of them accepted their fate, at least for the time being. Margaret Mahoney, Sarah Lovett, Isabella Errington, Ann Maw, Ann McGee, Martha or Mary Gregory and Sarah Piper were among this group. Noticeably, nearly all of them were older women, thirty-eight years and over. Ann Perks, the youngest at only twenty-seven, was given permission to join her mother in Van Diemen's Land and may have tried to marry there. Ann Bowler and Mary Ann Charles were only thirty-two, but neither applied to marry while they were prisoners and Mary Ann died before her sentence expired.[45]

The 1830s saw the height of the marriage battles between the convicts and the government. The loose arrangements and casual attitudes of the early colonial governments had changed into an efficient administrative system and a determination to bestow morality on the prisoners whether they wanted it or not. But by 1841 even the government was somewhat worn down by the battle and inclined to find a loophole for compromise. In that year the authorities called for advice from the solicitor general in the case of a man who had declared himself married on arrival. The solicitor general reported:

> The Act Geo. IV C31 S22 provides for second marriages after 7 years has elapsed without the parties having intercourse. However, the party marries at his peril and the Governor's sanction will be no protection if it turns out his wife was living and he had reason to believe that.[46]

This nicely removed the onus from the governor and handed it to the convicts, but it was a responsibility and a risk they were happy to accept. In 1835, however, such an attitude was inconceivable to the government and Susannah was one of many for whom the security of marriage was out of reach. She was one of the small group of women who did not apply to marry, but she used her head and found her own solution to the problem.

Some time in the two years after she left the Factory again, at the end of 1832, Susannah met up with John Clarke. They had met before, in circumstances neither would ever forget, both having been moved from Nottingham gaol in the same coach.[47] Like Susannah, he had declared married on arrival, but now this worked for them. They agreed to pretend to be each other's spouse. The fact that they had not made any declaration which indicated otherwise and they were both shown officially as coming from Nottingham, allowed them to carry it off.[48] Susannah began to use the name 'Clarke' and, as John had only a seven-year sentence, she was eventually able to get herself assigned to him as her husband.[49]

It is impossible to pinpoint when their plan to outwit the authorities occurred to them. Exactly what happened to Susannah after the governor commuted her colonial sentence in August 1832 is unknown. She had been described, at that point, as still assigned to the Simons at Parramatta and perhaps they reclaimed her. But 12 months had elapsed. The first boatload of free immigrant women had arrived in New South Wales in 1832 and the intense demand for female prisoners as servants had dried up. She was not assigned, to a new employer anyway, during the remainder of 1832, but in the new year of 1833 she was out of the Factory. Something went wrong for her and on 15 January she was sent to the Factory for three days in the cells for improper conduct. Perhaps this was the reunion with John Clarke.[50]

John Clark was working as a coachman, based in Parramatta. He had arrived on the *Waterloo* in July 1829 and as he had listed his trade as a coachman was assigned to work for the government as a coachman or carter, out of Carters Barracks at the southern end of Sydney town.[51] Early in 1832 he transferred to the private assignment of Mr John Mortimer at Parramatta.[52]

John was seven years older than Susannah, and only two years younger than Edward Watson. At 5 feet 7 inches he was average height for a man of that period, with a ruddy English complexion, light brown hair and hazel eyes. He also had distinctive scars on each eyebrow. Born in Staffordshire, he could read and write and had declared himself married, with two children, when he arrived.[53]

Although supposedly following a trade which had, in theory, not been affected by industrial or technological change in England, John had been pursuing a life of crime, as details of his trial in Nottingham reveal:

> 18 October, 1828. The following pleaded guilty:
>   John Clarke, aged 40, to feloniously stealing, on the 28th September, from the house of Mrs Fellows, on the High-pavement, a coat, the property of the said Mrs Fellows; also a coat, the property of Thomas Arthur; also to a conviction for felony at the Quarter Sessions for this town, on the 15th July, 1824. The Recorder observed, that since this conviction, the prisoner had been in several other jails, and therefore could not expect to remain in the country. Transported for seven years.[54]

John's reputation as a hardened criminal followed him to the *York* hulk in Portsmouth, where the gaoler disregarded his conduct on board and carefully noted against his name: 'Has been in prison 3 times'.[55] John spent four freezing months on board the hulk before sailing for New South Wales in March 1829.[56]

He behaved himself in the colony and, except for one minor offence, stayed out of trouble while he was a prisoner. Susannah's activities, in the meantime, are unknown, but she was certainly involved in a relationship with John by the winter of 1834, when they conceived a child. Susannah returned to the Factory in March 1835, and on the 31st gave birth to a son, she initially christened John Henry Clarke. At the ceremony in May she described herself to Rev. Samuel Marsden as Susannah Clarke and the child's father as John Clarke.[57]

There was one particular repercussion from John's birth. Charles was now a flourishing five-year-old and it could no longer be disguised that he was over the regulation age to go to the orphan school. On 8 June 1835 the matron requested permission from the colonial secretary for 18 children of female prisoners at the Factory to be admitted to the orphan schools, and on the list was Charles Watson, carefully described as three years of age.[58]

Perhaps Susannah favoured the move and had faith that her healthy Australian son would survive the separation better than poor little Thomas. She had been in the colony six years and could now accurately assess her own situation and perceive an opportunity when it was offered. Perhaps she saw the chance to give Charles the benefit of an education, and training for a trade through which he could prosper. But as events would show, she was also aware of the risk of losing her child to the bureaucrats and was determined this would not happen.

Charles went to the orphan school and Susannah left the Factory. Since the demand for female prisoners as servants, particularly those with children, was no greater than it had been two years earlier, it is probable this is the time when she used her supposed marriage to John Clarke and got herself assigned to him. John was entering the final year of his sentence and he was still working for Mr Mortimer at Parramatta. The Clarke 'family' enjoyed 18 months of relative stability, the only hiccup occurring in March 1836 when Mr Mortimer took John before the magistrates and he was sentenced to a flogging of 50 lashes for drunkenness.[59] This incident aside, Susannah was able to enjoy a brief taste of freedom and it is not hard to imagine her energetically setting out at regular intervals to walk the 16 miles to Liverpool to visit Charles.

John's certificate of freedom was officially issued on 30 November 1836 and he and Susannah celebrated in time-honoured style and conceived another child.[60] The celebration was to be short lived, however. John reverted to crime almost immediately, and in April was charged with stealing. He was convicted early in May 1837 and sentenced to two years in an iron gang.[61] Susannah's haven came crashing down.

Although it is impossible to be sure whether Susannah had been working for another employer, or was totally dependent on John, she was now in a very vulnerable position. She had a child aged two and a half to care for, was six months pregnant, and once again she was thrown totally on her own resources for survival. She returned to the Factory some time in the weeks following John's conviction, and on 13 August 1837 gave birth to a daughter. On 17 September she baptised the baby Agnes (after her mother) and recorded she was the daughter of John and Susannah Clarke.[62]

In spite of the competition from free female immigrants Susannah managed to get herself assigned again, or perhaps returned to a previous employer, and by December when the 1837 convict muster was taken, she was working for L. S. Downd in Parramatta. John was also in Parramatta, his sentence in the iron gang commuted, and working for his old employer, Mr Mortimer.[63] There is no trace in the records which reveals how this came about but, although technically free, he was listed in the convict muster as assigned to Mortimer and it may well be that Mortimer had arranged for him to serve out his sentence in his old employment as a coachman.

By May 1838 John was his own master again and had set himself up as an upholsterer in Parramatta.[64] But Susannah was becoming concerned for Charles, who was getting perilously close to the age when the government might apprentice him to a master of its choosing anywhere in the colony. In any event, she took a practical attitude to her children's capacity to earn money from an early age and would have regarded Charles as old enough to contribute to the family's income.[65] No doubt at her urging, John sent in the following petition to the governor:

> The Respectful Memorial of John Clarke, Free, Humbly Sheweth
>   That Memorialist's child Charles Isaac Watson was admitted into the Male Orphan School about 3 years ago and is now of the age of 6 years and 9 months. That Your Excellency's Memorialist is by trade a cabinet maker and upholsterer by whose industry he is able to support his child and bring him up in the paths of Virtue and Religious instruction and by strick attention and persevering attention to be enable to learn him his trade in the same line of business as Memorialist carries on. He therefore most humbly prays that Your Excellency will be graciously pleased to order the said Charles Isaac Watson to be discharged from the school to Memorialist's parental care.
>   May it therefore please Your Excellency to grant this the prayer of your Memorialist and Memorialist as in duty bound will pray.[66]

The memorial, of course, lies on two points. Charles was not John's son, but since the records concerning his dispatch to the orphan school had only named his mother, the truth was sufficiently concealed. Someone had also cleverly remembered that his age on admission to the school had been put back two years and had calculated accordingly so the claim in the memorial was consistent.

The application was supported by Richard Taylor, chaplain of Liverpool, and Thomas Blake, who although only a ticket-of-leave holder, had an excellent reputation in Parramatta and influential contacts through his eight years assigned service to the powerful Macarthur family. The petition was approved without delay and both John and the master of the male orphan school were advised.[67]

But neither Susannah nor John took immediate steps to collect Charles. By September Susannah was back in the Factory. She was not in the criminal division, but the second class, probably because Mr Downd, her previous employer, had returned her and, accompanied by children, she was automatically allocated to the 'mothers' class. This time she couldn't get out again. The Factory was grossly overcrowded and the opportunities of assigned service for women with children had completely dried up.[68] The matron of the Factory took it upon herself to write to the colonial secretary on 11 September 1838

> As the women in the second class are increasing and no appearance of my being able to procure situations for them with their children as formerly had been done, I have the honour to propose for the consideration of His Excellency the Governor, that those who are due for their Tickets of Leave may be granted the indulgence... There are about 30 due for Tickets but having punishments on record against them debars their obtaining them in the regular way[69]

Shortly after, the matron forwarded a list of the women she recommended for tickets-of-leave and Susannah, under the name of Watson, was on it. Her future trembled in the balance. Against the advantage of a ticket-of-leave, the matron was urging that the tickets be issued for country districts, which might well take Susannah far away from John, at Parramatta, and Charles, at Liverpool.[70]

But the matron's direct initiative had avoided the 'proper' channels and the governor referred her recommendations to the visiting magistrate of the Factory, with a request that he investigate. He reported as follows:

> The accompanying letters received from you in my report were sent by the Matron and House Steward without my knowledge and in returning them to you I have thought it right to add another document containing a full and explicit account of the prisoners for whom Tickets of Leave are solicited.
>
> The Matron appeared to treat the question as a mere matter of expediency and, although I am quite ready to admit that these women and their children are very much in the way and that they are a great annoyance within the walls of a prison, I should be failing in my duty were I not to place the case before the Governor in what may appear to me to be its various bearings...
>
> His Excellency will perceive that nine of the ten prisoners recommended have barely completed the period of probation prescribed by law. One of the nine, Sarah Bulpin per Kains, against whom there is no punishment recorded was recommended in the proper course on the 10th May last and I have no doubt she will obtain her Ticket of Leave in a few weeks. She is married and has one child. Susan Watson per Princess Royal is also a married woman and having no punishment beyond 3 days to the cells recorded against her during eight years, I see no objection to her receiving indulgence, but the remaining eight prisoners have been frequently punished, their children are all illegitimate... and I therefore must hesitate before I can in any way be the means of their receiving the same benefits at the same time with those who have behaved well — the commission of the crimes of adultery and fornication having produced the cause from which they now desire equal advantages with well behaved prisoners and greater [than those] who cannot produce an illegitimate infant as a claim for their Ticket of Leave...
>
> I think that arrangements might be made for receiving children into the orphan schools directly they are weaned and the mothers would then become assignable.[71]

The magistrate attached a list, which included these details about Susannah:

Name: Susannah Watson
Ship: Princess Royal

Sentence:	14 years 1829
Married/Single:	Married
No. of children & age:	3 children, one 8 years, one 3½ years & one 13 months.
No. of punishments	1833, Jan. 15, 3 days
	Improper Conduct, Sydney Bench
No. of Places & Names	
Assigned:	John Clarke, husband
District applied for:	Parramatta[72]

The information about Susannah is fascinating, as much for its omissions as for the information it provides. Her two-year colonial sentence, and even her six weeks in the Factory for insolence, have been buried, as has her true record of employment. The Egans, the Simons and any other employers, are completely disregarded. The children's ages are accurate, although no mention is made that Charles was at the orphan school and not crowding the Factory. Most significantly of all, this is the only government document in which Susannah actually claims John Clarke as her husband and the correspondence reveals very tellingly how important the respectable status of a married woman was to a female prisoner. It is hard to believe that Susannah did not have the cooperation of the matron in some of this deceit. Although the internal records of the Factory have not survived into the twentieth century, they were still available at the time. The matron, Mrs Bell, was newly appointed, and in the first flush of enthusiasm was obviously prepared to bend the truth in order to reduce overcrowding. It was to no avail, however. After the visiting magistrate's report, the governor decided not to issue tickets to any of the women and the matter was allowed to drop.[73]

Two months later several children, including John Clarke son of Susan Watson, were recommended for the orphan school which would, the Matron stated, 'cause their mothers to be immediately assigned to private service'.[74] But the request languished, perhaps because the school itself was overcrowded, and the matron put in another list in February 1839, including this time John Watson son of Susan Watson.[75] The governor approved and, on 2 March 1839 John entered the male orphan school.[76]

The decision to identify John as Watson apparently marked Susannah's decision to give up on John Clarke. The week before the matron drew up the new list, John had been caught stealing again. He was charged with robbery and committed for trial at the Parramatta quarter sessions where, in May, he was found guilty and sentenced to three years in an iron gang. Although the sentence was commuted, John vanishes from Susannah's life. There is no indication they cohabited again in any way and even the date of his death is uncertain.[77] Susannah's feelings for him are unrecorded. She had used him with a clear-headed, practical insight, which should have worked to the benefit of them both. But his inability to refrain from crime was the weak link and Susannah decided that, for the time being, she could manage better without the protection of his name.

May 1839 did bring Susannah some good news. She was finally, officially entitled to a ticket-of-leave. Although she wanted it for Parramatta, the government had recently acceded to the wishes of the Parramatta police magistrate that no more tickets-of-leave for women prisoners be granted for that district.[78] So Susannah chose the next best thing and obtained a ticket for the district of Liverpool.[79]

The ticket was actually in her possession by early July and she sprang immediately into action, displaying all the determination and purpose that was characteristic of her. First, she arranged employment for herself with Mrs Emma Blake, the wife of Thomas Blake the baker who supported John's memorial concerning Charles. Next, she persuaded the police magistrate in Liverpool to alter her ticket-of-leave to the district of Parramatta 'so long as she may remain in the employ of Mrs Emma Blake'.[80] Then she got John Clarke to write to the governor again for permission to remove young John from the orphanage, which was granted. Finally, armed with the government's authorisation for the children's release from the school, she went there and collected them.[81]

Mother and sons trudged back along the dusty, tree-lined track to Parramatta and what, they hoped, would be the start of a prosperous and independent future.

A DUBIOUS REFUGE

A woman's relationship with a man could prove a trap rather than offer freedom and some women of the *Princess Royal* found no haven in marriage. They lived in a time when their husbands and society, and they themselves, expected as wives they would be subservient to their husbands. They did not expect the relationship to be equal and accepted as their lot considerable summary control from their husbands and a criterion for behaviour where submissiveness and compliant duty were the ideal. In practice, of course, the realities of human nature often transcended these model roles and a wife could achieve dominance over her husband through force of character, or equality through joint effort in a common enterprise such as a business or a farm. The character of both parties was crucial to achieving a balanced relationship, but if the marriage broke down, the wife was vulnerable because society and the law would be on the husband's side.

Some women of the *Princess Royal* endured considerable violence within their marriages and there were doubtless more cases than came to light in the records. Sadly, wife beating was a common practice, even enshrined in the law which gave to the husband 'by law power and dominion over his wife', including the right to beat her 'but not in a cruel and violent manner'.[1] Its incidence would have been aggravated by the fact that many of the husbands were men of little education, from deprived and brutal backgrounds, whose only real ability to express themselves was physical.

Mary Ann Marshall was an 18-year-old nursemaid from Newcastle-on-Tyne, who had no previous convictions before she was sentenced to 14 years transportation for housebreaking. She could read and write, was not addicted to drink, and committed only one offence while a prisoner, when she was sent to the Factory for disobedience a few months after she arrived.[2] In late 1830 she married a brutally violent man, a 27-year-old ex-convict named Walter Neary.[3] His violence extended beyond his wife and the first time he came to court it was for assaulting his father, Walter Neary, Senior, in July 1833.[4] But six months later Mary Ann was desperate enough to go to the Magistrate herself.

> Mary Ann Neary...I am assigned to my husband, Walter Neary, residing in Pitt Street. The summons was granted me against my husband on Monday last for assaulting me on the Saturday before. Yesterday, whilst I was waiting in the Court for the case to be called he struck me a blow on the mouth with a crutch stick. I went out, when he seized me and dragged me down the street. This day, owing to the crying of my child, I was obliged to leave the Court at the time my complaint was called. I still consider my life to be in danger from the violence of his threats and make this application without malice.[5]

Her father-in-law supported her:

> Walter Neary, Senior...The day before yesterday I saw Mary Ann Neary lying bleeding on the ground in the bakehouse. The defendant, Walter Neary, was standing near her in a great rage and was threatening her. I did not see him strike her, but there was no other person in the bake house.[6]

Her husband was granted bail and less than a month later, on 24 February, Mary Ann was again forced to seek help from the authorities.

> Mary Ann Neary...On Saturday morning [my husband] was drunk and struck me on the head with a piece of iron, which made a deep cut in my head, which bled so profusely that I fainted away from the loss of blood. He has frequently before assaulted me...The assault took place at his father's house...I did not throw any hot water at him, nor did I throw a knife at him.[7]

Walter Neary, senior, supported her again:

> On Saturday morning last the defendant...my son, was drunk and was making use of very disgusting language to his wife. She threw a cup of water over him. He still continued in the same way and she threw a pair of scissors at him. He then struck her on the arm with a pair of pincers and...I saw him strike her with a piece of iron on the head, which cut her head. I did not see her throw a knife at the defendant. It was a piece of wire she struck him with.[8]

Mary Ann dropped both these charges and it is not hard to imagine the pressure brought to bear by her husband. She had three children, so there was little chance of her simply walking out of the marriage, and so long as he was prepared to claim her, as a prisoner assigned to him she could not escape.[9] She applied for a ticket-of-leave at the end of 1835, which was granted although it was early in her sentence,[10] and this gave her the capacity to earn a little money. She continued to live with Walter Neary and in 1838 had another child by him, who only lived a few weeks.[11] The protection her father-in-law could offer came to an end when he was caught robbing a house in June 1838 and was sentenced to 14 years on Norfolk Island.[12] Left defenceless, Mary Ann died in 1841, aged only 29.[13]

Mary Williams (alias Chambers) married Isaac White, an ex-convict who was a brassfounder, only three months after she arrived in New South Wales and spent the next four years constantly running away from him. Only once, in October 1833, was it actually stated that she 'sought protection' from her husband but the obvious implication is he was abusing her continually, although it was not specifically recorded.[14]

In 1831 Margaret Hartigan married an ex-convict, John Smith, who worked for the Australia Company in Newcastle.[15] In October 1835 she went to the Courthouse:

> Margaret Smith... throws herself on the protection of the Police. She complains that her husband is continuously beating her. Yesterday evening he beat me very severely with a thick rope. He has beat me three times within the last month most severely. I am covered with bruises through his ill usage.

John Smith claimed in his defence that his wife was continually getting drunk and the magistrate decided: 'The parties are allowed to take time to see if they can agree better'.[16]

There is some support for John Smith's claim that his wife was always drunk. Only 12 months before a nosy police constable, who lived with his wife in the same house as the Smiths, gave evidence that indicates Margaret was prostituting herself, at least occasionally. The constable charged her with drunkenness and abuse and she was sent to Newcastle Gaol for two months.[17] When she was released she paid the constable and his wife a visit:

> Constable Smith: On Saturday week night last, myself and wife were sitting in our own house when the prisoner was outside. I heard her saying 'Flamming whore, let her go with Buxton again', when my wife heard it. She went out and asked her who she was speaking about. She said: You infernal vagabond, it is you. She said that since that [illegible] she wished me nor my wife or children may never have a days luck as long as we live. She also called me a perjered [sic] Hangman Scoundrel. We live in the same premises, but I do not wish to turn her out. I heard that her husband wishes to buy the premises.

The magistrate obviously had some sympathy for Margaret's resentment and dismissed her with an admonishment.[18]

Ann Simpson and Ann Kinsman were also subject to violence in their marriages. By 1830 they were both assigned to landowners in the Newcastle–Maitland area and both married men who worked for their masters.

Ann Simpson met John Prentice when he was the overseer and she the servant of Mr George Wyndham at Dalwood. John was born in the colony, and had therefore never been a convict, so it appeared Ann was making a good match when she married him.[19] Very young, at only 18, she was literate and had been trained to make gloves. There was someone in England who cared about her and had tried to save her from transportation, but Ann had been leading a criminal life as a prostitute and thief in Hull for some time and had two previous convictions. The judge disapprovingly called attention to her 'levity' during her third and final trial in England.[20] However, she had no offences recorded against her a year after her arrival in New South Wales when she applied to marry John Prentice in June 1830.[21] But only 18 months after the marriage a letter from George Wyndham to the colonial secretary reveals that the relationship had completely broken down:

> I have the honour to inform you that Anne Prentice, formerly assigned to me as Anne Simpson, lately ran from her husband at Maitland to my house; and, arriving in a weakly state, I wrote to him to come and fetch her, but he wrote to me word that he would live with her no more and intended to leave the country. I have thought it my duty to communicate this as the woman may become chargeable to His Majesty's Government. I would indeed be willing to keep her in my service, during her good behaviour (which I cannot answer for) should His Majesty's Government think proper to reassign her to me.[22]

The governor agreed to let Ann stay with Mr Wyndham, but the arrangement didn't last and he returned her, without complaint, three months later.[23] She had a chance for a fresh start in spite of a bad marriage.

Ann Kinsman, a dairymaid born in Cornwall, was assigned straight from the *Princess Royal* to Mr Edward Spark at Dartbrook outside Newcastle.[24] There she met John Hoskins, an ex-convict who worked for her master. In January 1830 they applied to marry and Ann was officially assigned to her husband.[25] This resulted in a confusing and invidious relationship, which was unique to the penal colonies: the nineteenth-century power of a husband over his wife became blurred with the power of a master over his assigned servant.

Many husbands of women who were still convicts assumed they could automatically take their wives before the magistrates even for offences which were personal to their relationship. This occasionally produced humorous results.

> George Hickman sworn: I and my wife went to the Plains [a pub] together and my wife got drunk and would not return with me.
> Prisoner is sorry for it and her husband is willing to make it up. Discharged.[26]

Some magistrates, however, were as confused as the husbands and the government was compelled regularly to write letters to benches all over the country, pointing out the fine distinction which had been ignored by the male assumptions of both prosecuting husband and magistrate.

One husband, for instance, 'returned' his wife for 'general improper conduct' and she was sent to the Female Factory by the Penrith bench in 1832, with the husband agreeing to pay for her maintenance. The colonial secretary, on the governor's behalf, reprimanded the magistrate and pointed out the woman was 'not a regularly assigned servant to her husband as a convict, but married to him for better or worse and he has not the same summary control over her for any offence, not criminal, that a master would have'.[27] But the confusion continued and in 1839 the government resorted to a notice in the newspapers:

> A free husband, who marries a convict, cannot take her before the Bench for an offence, for which convicts alone are punishable and, in relation to the husband, the woman is not a convict, but a wife. In relation to other people, she is still a convict and subject to the usual controls.[28]

John Hoskins also exercised the power of both master and husband. He took Ann before the bench at Maitland in December 1830, eight months after their marriage. She was convicted of 'gross insubordination and assault' and sent down to the third class of the Factory at Parramatta for a one-month sentence.[29] In January 1833 the full disaster of their relationship surfaced again in the court at Maitland:

> John Hoskins charged with aggravated assault.
> Ann Hoskins: I am the defendant's wife. On Christmas last my husband came home with some wine. He gave me some of it to drink. About 2 o'clock, he came home again and beat me in a most unmerciful and cruel manner without any provocation; my body and arms were discoloured from the effects of the beating. I was a little excited with wine at the time.
> William Coleman: I am a surgeon residing at Maitland. About a fortnight ago, I was sent for to examine Mrs Hoskins. I found her head severely cut in several parts, one cut in particular in an angular form. Every part of her body was completely bruised, to such a degree as to render her unable to leave her bed. I would not treat a dumb animal in such a manner.

The magistrate committed John to stand trial at the quarter sessions, but allowed him out on bail. Predicably, one week later Ann agreed to drop the charge.[30] John kept no promises he may have made to her and only weeks later she was sentenced to seven days solitary confinement in Newcastle gaol. He even took his time about reclaiming her and she was not released to his custody until the end of March.[31]

Eight months later Ann ran away from her husband and master and was brought before the bench charged with absconding. She unwittingly brought to a head the confusion among the local magistrates about what to do with convict wives. They sentenced her initially to ten days in the cells at Newcastle gaol, and then to be returned to her husband. But one of them insisted the usual practice was to send a woman to the Factory, with her husband paying for her maintenance, so they changed her sentence and Ann was dispatched to Sydney, with John undertaking to pay £50 for her maintenance.[32]

Governor Bourke was exasperated. The Newcastle and Maitland magistrates had a bad habit of removing 'problem' women from their territory by sending them to the Factory, even though there was a female gaol on the spot in Newcastle. He had previously issued instructions that no woman was to be sent down without his special orders and here was Ann already at Parramatta. He insisted that she must be returned to her husband and his orders obeyed by the magistrates in future.[33]

Six weeks later Ann was parcelled up and sent back to Maitland.[34] On paper the order that she must return to her husband was a tidy solution for the government, but in reality it was a farce. There was no sanctuary in marriage for Ann, nor did her husband want her. Four months later, when she obtained her certificate of freedom, she must have thankfully shed the arbitrary control of husband and government, as she hoped, for ever.[35]

To what extent did these women's characters contribute to the violence and, in some instances, collapse of their marriage? Although the concept of a man using physical violence to his wife is totally repugnant in the twentieth century, it was less so in the nineteenth and, in this context particularly, the potential for violence was probably present among many of the husbands of the women from the *Princess Royal*. It was aggravated by the confusion between the roles of husband and master. We know nothing of the circumstances which prompted Ann Simpson to run away, and although she arrived in 'a weakly state' it may not have been from physical abuse by her husband. Ann's background and subsequent life show little potential for fidelity and loyalty. Six years later John Prentice claimed that after she left he moved to Van Diemen's Land 'in a fit of despair'.[36] Margaret Hartigan's husband claimed she was always getting drunk and we know she was transported for killing a baby in a violent rage. Ann Kinsman admitted she was 'a little excited with wine' when her husband beat her, and even Mary Ann Marshall provocatively threw a cup of water and a pair of scissors at her husband before he hit her. There is no evidence that any of them were totally submissive, innocent victims and with Mary Williams (alias Chambers) there is insufficient evidence to even speculate.

There were other problems, apart from violence, which affected, or were created by the women's marriages.

Jane Edwards had been with her first master at Liverpool for two years when she married at the end of 1831.[37] But in December 1832 she was convicted of drunkenness, and thereafter had several other convictions for the same offence, even losing her ticket-of-leave 'for repeated drunkenness'.[38] As the records of the Liverpool bench for her first three years in the colony have not survived, it is impossible to be certain her convictions for drinking only started in late 1832, but there is other evidence to indicate her drunkenness was caused by distressful circumstances which began at that time. In June her husband, John Smith, was the victim of a brutally harsh decision by the local magistrates, perhaps influenced by the fact the prosecutor was Rev. Robert Cartwright. After church one Sunday evening, two of Rev. Cartwright's servants called in at the Smiths' house and drank themselves insensible. John Smith was convicted of 'harbouring' them, lost his ticket-of-leave and was assigned as a servant over 100 miles away at Bathurst. There was no evidence he had invited them to his house; no indication the evening was more than a sociable get-together. In December, the same month Jane was first convicted of drunkenness, John petitioned the governor, pointing out that he too was employed by Rev. Cartwright and 'could not possibly avoid the occasional mixture of the Reverend gentleman's servants with memorialist's family'. He added that his wife was in service at Liverpool and could not travel to Bathurst. That the sentence was regarded as harsh, even at the time, was evidenced by the unusually large number of local gentlemen who supported the petition and a note from the colonial secretary pointing out that one of them was Cartwright's son-in-law. But the governor viewed it as 'a very serious offence' and stood firm.[39] John remained at Bathurst where he died 18 months later.[40] In this instance the authorities themselves had destroyed one of the marriages they were so keen to promote.

Susan King, on the other hand, was addicted to drink before she was married in 1835, even using her new baby as an excuse to persuade Surgeon Wilson to issue her with extra wine on the *Princess Royal*.[41] Like Jane Edwards, she lost her ticket for getting drunk, and when she died in 1840 the coroner concluded it was from 'disease induced by intemperance'.[42] Martha Clare drank heavily from the moment she landed in May 1829 and continued to do so after she married Thomas Brothers, a labourer holding a ticket-of-leave in Bathurst. Thomas liked 'a drop' too. During their courtship they were before the Bathurst bench together on a charge of drunkenness, but during their married life it was Thomas who frequently turned Martha in to the authorities on a charge of drunkenness or absconding.[43] Martha Turner was only 18 when she arrived in the colony and she married Thomas Buck who, on a ticket-of-leave, earned his living as a brushmaker. She was not convicted for drinking, or any other offence, but the marriage was a failure and in 1838 she lost her ticket-of-leave for 'living in a state of adultery'.[44]

The marriages of two women to members of the *Princess Royal* crew were both disasters, but for different reasons.

John Wright, the second mate, stayed on and married Harriet Bannister in November 1829, but the marriage was not happy.[45] A year later Harriet was found by a constable 'improperly intoxicated with a man in the Domain'.[46] She was assigned to her husband from the beginning, but the relationship had deteriorated so far that he took the precaution of sending her to the first class of the Factory when he crewed on a ship to New Zealand 18 months after they were married. He intended, he said, to reclaim her when he returned, but there is no indication he ever came back.[47] The governor admonished the Sydney bench and told them their action was highly irregular, to which they replied they only wanted 'to preserve the woman from prostitution during the absence of her husband which, from her character, would undoubtedly have been the case'. They created a specific charge of 'illegally at large' and Harriet went to the Factory.[48] She was sent back again for drunkenness later the same year and was assigned from there, early in 1832, to the more rural area of South Creek. But Harriet's life continued to slide. She went through two employers in the first three months of 1832 and eventually managed to get herself reassigned in Sydney. She ran away from a Mrs Wyatt in December 1832 and again in February 1833, then, in July 1833, she died in Sydney, aged 25.[49] Although she had been transported for straightforward shoplifting, with no previous convictions, it is hard not to conclude that the failure of Harriet's marriage was due largely to her pursuit of a life of drink and prostitution.

Mary Williams, a 26-year-old widow with two children left behind in England, married George Hearn from the *Princess Royal*. In October 1829 their chance of happiness was ruined when he was charged — apparently through the malice of his landlord, a publican named Richard Harvey — with stealing a pair of boots. He remained in gaol until his trial in April the following year, when he was found not guilty.[50] Mary, who had been assigned to him, was left to manage as best she could and resorted to prostitution. In March she was 'found in connexion with a soldier' and sent to the Factory for three months. Eighteen months later she was declared 'illegally at large, her husband having left the colony' and was sent to the first class of the Factory.[51] Then her luck changed. In assigned service two months later she met Joseph Irving, and because she had declared single on arrival, they managed to slide past the government watchdogs and get permission to marry.[52] The relationship worked and they were still bigamously happy together six years later.[53]

There were women from the *Princess Royal* who, like Susannah, suffered extreme vicissitudes of fortune through their men's reversion to crime. Three of them had pitifully tragic lives.

Sarah Quittenton was an educated, literate woman. Born in the village of Hampstead outside London, she had been charged (her first offence) with stealing ribbon from a linen draper in the West End, and defended herself by claiming he had knocked it out of her hand and accused her of stealing it. She was a widow, nearing 40 when she landed in the colony, and had left two children behind in England.[54] Assigned on arrival to the pernickety attorney Mr Keith, by 1831 she was working for Mr Lee, a landowner at Bathurst.[55] The only question mark against her record in the colony was a curious incident in February 1830 when she was returned to government after being accused of theft. As the person robbed refused to give evidence against her, the authorities had no choice but to send her to the first class of the Factory. Nevertheless, this would be why she was assigned so many miles away from Sydney. Mr Lee, however, was pleased with her and gave her 'an excellent character'.[56]

In Bathurst Sarah met 45-year-old Daniel Reddiford, transported for seven years in 1819 and long since free. Daniel, a wool sorter and stapler by trade, had prospered since his freedom and had been employed by many prominent landowners. But he was ambitious and by late 1830 decided to set himself up as a manufacturer of cloth.[57] Shortly after, he and Sarah put in an application to marry, which was allowed by the governor. They were married early in 1831 and settled down in a house on Campbell Street, Sydney.[58] The future looked rosy.

Disaster struck four years later. Daniel had overreached himself and, after a struggle to succeed which can only be guessed at, he resorted to theft. On 11 August 1835 a barrow containing 60 pounds of leather was found in a yard in King Street and reported to the police, who took it away. With extraordinarily bad timing, between the departure of the constable with the barrow and his return for further details, Daniel arrived and asked where his barrow had gone. Confronted by the police, he insisted:

> I never had the leather in my possession. I purchased it of a man about 9 or 10 o'clock on the previous night. He borrowed the barrow and told me he had left it at the corner of King and Pitt Streets next morning and had I known it had been stolen, I should never have demanded it.[59]

The owner of the leather swore it was his property, which he had left covered with water the night before, and the barrow was also identified. The case was set down for trial in October and Daniel was released on bail.[60]

But the Reddifords' circumstances must have been desperate. On 18 September Sarah stole a cap from a shop in King Street,[61] and 11 days later Daniel crept through the fence and up to the attic of a neighbour's house, where he stole five sheepskins.[62] This time the evidence was more than circumstantial; he was caught in the act.

> Sarah Wilcox, wife of David Wilcox of George Street states: Last night I heard footsteps coming down from my loft where there is property. I went out and found the prisoner endeavouring to make his way through the fence.

Mrs Wilcox was supported by one of her servants:

> Peter Holmes, Free...states:...I went out and found the prisoner who had put his bundles through the fence. I found five sheepskins removed from the further end of the loft on the landing of the stairs. It was about 5 minutes after I came down myself and I am quite sure the things were removed... Prisoner used to work in the loft. The door was unlocked...Prisoner knew there were skins in the loft. He was employed sorting wool [but] he has nothing to do with skins....[63]

Daniel was now facing two charges at the quarter sessions, but the police decided to concentrate on the more certain conviction for theft of the sheepskins.[64] When the charges were heard the result was devastation for Daniel and Sarah. On 22 October she was found guilty and sentenced to six months in the third class of the Factory;[65] he was tried the following day and sentenced to transportation to a penal colony for seven years.[66]

Life was over for both of them. A year later, on 11 February 1837, Daniel died at Norfolk Island,[67] and in October the following year Sarah's body was found in suspicious circumstances at Campbelltown. The coroner investigated, but found she died of natural causes.[68] He knew nothing about the end of hope and a broken heart.

Sarah Bryant's life in New South Wales was scarcely less tragic, although she was to outlive the worst of her misfortunes.

Born in Bath, the daughter of a musician named Charles Bryant, Sarah trained as a nursemaid but was only 18 years old when she was transported for stealing two gowns, a hat and other clothes. Because she had two previous convictions she was one of those who suffered the heavy penalty of a life sentence.[69] After 15 months in the colony, Sarah had two minor convictions for absence without leave and the timing indicates the second of these — two days and two nights in August 1830 — may well have been caused by an involvement with her future husband.[70] A few weeks later John Foley sought her out at the Factory and they obtained permission to marry, through Rev. Samuel Marsden.[71]

John seemed a good husband. Transported in 1821, he was now 25, had served his sentence and was free. A tailor by trade, which was one of the most sought-after skills in the colony, Marsden described him as 'well recommended as an honest, sober and industrious man'.[72] But John was to prove a mixed blessing for Sarah.

Their life began well. They settled down in Sydney where John was employed by Lewis Cohen of George Street, but this arrangement was disrupted by an argument over a red silk handkerchief which John had given to Sarah. Cohen accused John of stealing it and Sarah sprang to her husband's defence and insisted he had bought it for 5s. Cohen's evidence was nebulous and John was found not guilty.[73] But in the weeks that followed, John appears to have been manoeuvring to avoid financial disaster. In August, Richard Turton, husband of Sarah Clark from the *Princess Royal*, hailed him in the street and as a result of some accusation he made, John called him a liar. Turton swung his fist and gave him a black eye and John called on the police and charged him with assault. It is not hard to imagine the two wives, the bond of their voyage together dissolved by partisan fervour, but as the day of the trial drew near the men had the sense to settle the case before it reached the court.[74]

Some time in 1834 the Foleys moved to Bathurst. By then they had two sons, Charles and John, and their father supported his family.[75] The gentlemen of Bathurst were delighted to have him in the town and commissioned him to make numerous coats and trousers and waistcoats, as well as leaving their old clothes for repair. But John couldn't cope. He began to prevaricate and tell his customers their new clothes weren't ready. Finally, he took advantage of one customer's undertaking to pay John by letting him draw on his father's store. He drew the goods and fled to Sydney.[76] Once there, however, he had nowhere to go, and to his credit did not want to desert his family. So he sat down and wrote a very plausible memorial to the governor:

The Memorial of John Foley, free and Sarah Foley otherwise Bryant, his wife, (a Prisoner of the Crown) sheweth

That your Memorialist John Foley per ship Indoston [*sic*] arrived in the Colony in 1821 and is long since free by servitude — married your Memorialist Sarah on or about the . . . day of September, 1830, who arrived in this Colony in the year 1829 per ship Princess Royal under sentence of Life by whom he has two children now living.

That the mother of your Memorialist Sarah is now residing at Hobart Town Van Diemen's Land and has repeatedly written letters to her said daughter your Memorialist Sarah requesting both your Memorialists to go and reside with her at Hobart Town aforesaid, to which request your Memorialist Sarah cannot comply with, without the permission and sanction of Your Excellency she being yet a prisoner as aforesaid.

May it please Your Excellency to permit your Memorialist Sarah to accompany her husband and her children to Hobart Town for the purpose of residing with her said mother and family.

No. 8 Upper Pitt Street, Sydney
16 September, 1835[77]

He was not lying. Sarah's mother was in Van Diemen's Land, but neither Sarah nor her husband had shown any previous interest in joining her.[78]

The governor approved the application, but the procedure for doing so took time and John was not advised until the second week of November.[79] It was too late. The gentlemen of Bathurst tracked him down and on 24 November he was charged before the bench at Bathurst with 'illegally making away with property entrusted to his care and obtaining property under false pretences'.[80] His case was heard at the quarter sessions in February 1836 and he was convicted and sentenced to five years transportation.[81] John was moved to the *Phoenix* hulk in Sydney Harbour and Sarah and the children remained behind in the female factory at Bathurst.

John then began a series of manoeuvres to avoid being sent to a penal settlement. First, he petitioned the governor with the result that, in October 1836, the colonial secretary asked the sheriff to keep him on the hulk until a decision was made.[82] But the decision was negative and in May 1837, 18 months after he was sentenced, he was dispatched to Moreton Bay.[83] But John had a mind of his own. By November he was back in Sydney to give evidence at a court martial and he took the opportunity to send another petition to the governor.[84] It got lost, and is still lost today, in the bureaucratic confusion caused by the departure of one governor and the arrival of another.[85]

For an unbelievable ten months, John remained in Sydney gaol, unnoticed, until the sheriff asked the colonial secretary what was to be done with him.[86] Aware that time was running out, John gathered all the ammunition he could and on 10 September 1838 sent in yet another petition, this time with the help of Mr Robertson, the colonial surgeon, who knew him at the gaol and also at Moreton Bay.[87]

The Humble Memorial of John Foley per ship Hindostan now confined in the Sydney Gaol humbly sheweth

That he has been in this Gaol in strict confinement since last November having been brought from Moreton Bay to give evidence in a Court Martial then pending, that he had in February, 1836, been tried before the Court of Quarter Sessions. . . and having been found guilty by a jury he was sentenced by His Honour the Chairman to 5 years transportation to a penal settlement and, in pursuance of that sentence, was forwarded to Moreton Bay where he was after a short time employed in the Lumber Yard in making, repairing and altering the clothing of the different prisoners on the settlement, and during the time he was so employed, he conducted himself to the satisfaction of Major Cotton, the then Commandant, as appeared by a testimonial to that effect attached to a memorial of the Petitioner's forwarded to Sir R. Bourke previously to his leaving the Colony and which Petitioner believes was overlooked or mislaid in the hurry consequent on the change then on the eve of taking place in the Government.

That Petitioner had some months ago forwarded a Petition to Your Excellency praying a mitigation of his sentence, to his prosecutor Mr McKenzie at Bathurst, for his signature, but the person to whom Petitioner trusted that memorial never presented it to Mr McKenzie and in consequence this opportunity is the first that Petition has had to address Your Excellency having now for the first time received the recommendation hereto attached from Mr McKenzie.

Your Petitioner therefore most humbly approaches Your Excellency and begs to throw himself and his helpless and unhappy wife and family on your mercy — assuring Your Excellency that, should you be pleased to take his case into your consideration, he will ever feel that gratitude which he knows is due to an act of mercy and Your Excellency may rest assured that he never will be brought before any Bench on any charge of dishonesty.

Petitioner therefore most humbly prays Your Excellency will be pleased to take the circumstances of his case and his long incarceration in this Gaol into your humane consideration and, with your wonted benevolence and bearing in mind the helpless condition of his young and innocent family, that you will be graciously pleased to remit the remainder of his still unexpired sentence and thereby restore him to his family and enable him to protect them from the snares and dangers of the world which on every side beset them and Petitioner will ever in duty bound etc.[88]

The keeper of the gaol, who had also been in charge of the hulk when John was there, certified that his conduct had been 'uniformly good' in both establishments. Even Mr McKenzie, who owned the store at Bathurst from which John stole, added the following certificate:[89]

I beg leave to recommend the prayer of the Petition of John Foley praying a mitigation of sentence to the merciful consideration of His Excellency — the more particularly as I believe his wife and family to be in distressed circumstances.[90]

'What should be done with him, if his colonial sentence be remitted?' asked the governor, Sir George Gipps. After further consideration, he decided: 'Let John Foley, now in Sydney Gaol, be pardoned on condition of serving 12 months with the men of the 2nd Class either at Goat Island or Parramatta. 1st November, 1838'.[91] John had gained a year from his original sentence and, apart from six months at Moreton Bay, had avoided transportation.

Meanwhile, Sarah was in deep trouble. She had remained in the factory at Bathurst and gave birth to a daughter, Margaret, but within months of John's trial she knew she would lose the two boys.[92] The Bathurst magistrate had applied for their admission to the orphan school.[93] After some delay they were finally sent there, arriving on 20 January 1837.[94] Sarah, with the baby, was reassigned to service in Bathurst and there was sufficient local sympathy for her circumstances to cause the bench of magistrates to recommend her for a ticket-of-leave in July that year.[95] But Sarah's world was shattered and her distress was revealed through her behaviour. Over the following months she was repeatedly punished for various offences, and by December, when the ticket arrived in Bathurst, she was in solitary confinement for gross misconduct.[96] The magistrate cancelled her ticket and returned it, unused, to the superintendent of convicts.[97]

Sarah continued in assigned service in Bathurst during 1838 and 1839. She most likely heard from John about the result of his petition and, one way or the other, they would both have learnt of the death of young John at the orphan school in December 1838.[98]

Sarah's behaviour continued to get her into trouble and when she was confined in the Factory in September 1839 the magistrate sought permission for Margaret to be sent to the female orphan school.[99] Sarah's feelings about this are all too easy to imagine. But by the time approval came through, according to the magistrate Sarah's punishment had ended and she and her daughter had left the Factory.[100] It's hard to avoid the conclusion, however, that the magistrate had decided on another solution — either that or Sarah had been returned for another punishment — because only three weeks later he advised she had been sent down to the Factory at Parramatta and described her and several others as 'bad characters'.[101] Among the 17 women who travelled with Sarah were two others from the *Princess Royal*. Margaret Mahoney and Martha Clare (now Brothers) were both free but had been convicted together in Bathurst and were sentenced to the Factory at Parramatta, as a house of correction, for six months.[102] In one fell swoop Bathurst was cleared of its 'troublesome' females.

John and Sarah were reunited in Sydney some time in 1840, and in May that year John collected Charles, now nearly nine years old, from the orphan school.[103] The family, permanently minus one of its members, was together again. But the relationship between the parents had been badly damaged and five years later Sarah ran away from John, who charged her with absconding. She lost the new ticket-of-leave she had obtained in 1843, and was sent to the Factory in April 1846.[104] She was still there the following February when John petitioned for her release, which was approved.[105] The Factory parcelled up her personal belongings: '4 gowns, 2 petticoats, 3 shifts, 1 shawl, 3 handkerchiefs, 1 jacket, 2 aprons, 1 cap, 1 pr. stockings and 1 pr. shoes, 1 bonnett. No jewellery or money.' Sarah made her mark as a receipt, picked up her bundle and rejoined John.[106]

The Foleys moved to Goulburn and Sarah received her third ticket-of-leave for that district in 1849.[107] In 1853 she finally obtained a conditional pardon, the last of the women of the *Princess Royal* to be freed.[108]

Louisa Caulfield's story completes the tragic trilogy of women brought down by their husbands.

The grey in Louisa's dark hair revealed her 43 years when, towards the end of 1833, she married Thomas Hyatt, an ex-convict who was 12 years her junior. They met when Louisa was assigned to Captain Waldron, whose property was only yards from Thomas' farm in the

Illawarra district outside Wollongong, but Louisa was hundreds of miles away in Bathurst when they both put in marriage applications the following year.[109] They settled on the farm, but less than 12 months later Thomas was accused of stealing from a dray which stopped at their house. Louisa, perhaps because she wanted to get out of the marriage, gave evidence which led to him being charged:

Police Office, Wollongong   4 June, 1834
   On 6 May last William Ryan came past with a dray with some of his property on it. Ryan stopped opposite my door and told my husband he had lost a bag of sugar. Ryan told my husband that he should have taken care of it as he promised to do so. Ryan then went home with his goods. Whilst he was gone my husband, Thomas Hyatt, went out and brought in a bag of sugar which was wet. I said, 'Thomas why do you do so'. He made answer and taking up an axe, if I said a word, he would kill me and dig a hole and bury me. I have since hid the axe from that time till yesterday. He then ordered me to give him a knife and he cut open the bag — the outside bag was a common wheat bag with large letters upon it, the letters were black. He then put the bag in the fire and put the logs on it that it might burn and ordered Deponent to the door and watch. Thomas Hyatt then went into the bedroom and emptied the sugar out of the mat bag into a bag of mine, in which bag it is in now. Hyatt then took the sugar out in two different bags, one of the bags he put into the stack and the other in the back, I don't know where. William Ryan again came to my house and said to Hyatt, you must have seen the bag of sugar. Hyatt said you must go and look for it, for I have not been out of the house since. I had some more sugar in the house, that came from Sydney, but the sugar Thomas Hyatt stole from William Ryan was much darker and lumpy — some of it still remains in the house. Hyatt shortly after this went to Sydney. On his return he brought in both bags of sugar. I often told my husband, Thomas Hyatt, that he should not steal from a neighbour and many other dishonest acts he had committed.
(sgd.) Louisa Hiatt[110]

With support from other witnesses, none of whose evidence was as crucial as Louisa's, the case was set for trial at the Campbelltown quarter sessions.[111] There it fell apart and was dismissed as 'not sustainable', probably because Louisa would no longer testify.[112]

The relationship between Louisa and Thomas was in shreds, but she remained officially assigned to him in what must have been the most frightful circumstances. In October 1836 she was brought before the bench at Campbelltown, charged with disorderly conduct, drunkenness and prostitution. The magistrate sentenced her to two months in the third class of the Factory, but had the sense to recommend that she should not be assigned to her husband again.[113] The marriage was over, but Louisa had been broken by it. She died three years later at Parramatta.[114]

Louisa and the two Sarahs would, on a superficial examination of their records, appear to confirm the worst assumptions about the behaviour and character of female convicts. Yet a detailed look at their circumstances reveals that all three were really brought to ruin by their husbands' actions, and the worst of their behaviour can be traced directly back to this. The character of the husbands was fundamental to their lives. Thomas Hyatt was obviously a vicious and brutal man, while Daniel Reddiford's ambition overreached his ability. He was a battler who failed. John Foley was more complicated. Well educated and intelligent, he clearly had a personality which could win people over. But he failed rather than prospered, even though he possessed a trade that was much in demand. Perhaps he was all charm and no substance. When cornered, he displayed a cunning and obsequious ability to survive. The women were victims of personal circumstances of appalling distress, which were aggravated because they were caught in a system which had no room for compassion and too easily passed ill-informed moral judgments. It would be fair to suppose that the governors who were in charge of the colony during the period would most likely have reacted kindly if the full circumstances and motivation had been laid before them. But of course they never were. The very system, not to mention the attitude of the times, prevented such a thing and the women were condemned to struggle in vain and alone.

DIFFERENT JOURNEYS

If some women were fundamentally the victims of other people, there were others from the *Princess Royal* whose own behaviour and character was the major determinant of their fate. It was human nature that created the vagaries in the system, and which made assignment and marriage such a lottery, but the character and attitude of the women themselves was just as important as any external person or authority.

Initially, Ann Wright was positioned to take advantage of the opportunities the system offered for early freedom and a new life, for the lotteries of assignment and marriage had both been drawn in her favour. She arrived in the colony nine months after her husband, John, and after an initial assignment to the Howells laundry business in Sydney she was transferred to her husband's employers, Mr and Mrs John Patrick.[1] John Patrick was an ex-convict who had arrived in New South Wales in 1792, only four years after it was founded. By 1832 he owned the prosperous and busy Marrow Inn at Campbelltown and he and his young native-born Australian wife, Catherine, had four children between the ages of five and 11 years.[2] John Wright was a groom and hardworking by nature, which made him a valuable employee to the Patricks whose attitude and assistance was crucial in arranging for John and Ann to be reunited.[3]

The Wrights were both in their early thirties, country people from Essex — short, sandy haired, with ruddy outdoor complexions. They had both loyally declared themselves married when they landed and they had left a child behind in England. Neither had committed any previous offence before Ann was sentenced to life for stealing fowls and John to seven years for stealing money. By the time they were together again John was within reach of a ticket-of-leave and the chance for a new start for both of them.[4]

Ann was the first to jeopardise their future. She sent the following repentant plea to the governor in an attempt to retrieve the situation:

The humble Petition of Ann Wright a prisoner of the Crown for Life most humbly sheweth—

That His Excellency's Petitioner arrived in the Colony in the year 1828 [*sic*] per ship Princess Royal having been tried and convicted on a charge of Felony and received sentence of transportation for Life.

That on her arrival in the Colony [she] was assigned to Mr Peter Howell of Sydney where she remained until, by her good conduct, she was transferred to the service of Mr Patrick of Airds that she might have the further indulgence of living with her husband who was and now is, assigned servant to Mr Patrick.

That unfortunately on 19 May last, she was induced to indulge in the drinking of ardent [*sic*] spirits and when in a state of intoxication assaulted her mistress and injured her so seriously that she was confined to bed for some time, for which offence Your Excellency's Petitioner was justly sentenced by the Bench of Magistrates to a confinement in the 3rd Class in the Factory for 12 months.

Your Excellency's Petitioner previous to this offence always conducted herself well and should Your Excellency be most graciously pleased to rescind the remainder of the sentence and allow her to join her husband again, she will by strict attention to her conduct endeavour to atone for the past offence. Petitioner is now from her confinement in a very precarious state of health and since her imprisonment up to the present time, required constantly the attendance of the Medical Practitioner of the Factory.

Your Excellency's Petitioner trusts that her prayer will meet with a favourable reception from Your Excellency and that the undermentioned certificate from her mistress whom she injured and also of the Magistrates will induce Your Excellency to comply with her most earnest solicitation of having the remainder of her sentence rescinded for which as in duty bound will ever pray.

29 October, 1832   Ann Wright[5]

Two magistrates supported her petition, as did the local minister Thomas Reddall, and generous support was also provided by her employer:

Campbelltown   20 October, 1832
Should His Excellency the Governor think fit to remit the sentence of Anne Wright, Princess Royal my assigned servant, I should most willingly admit her into my service again, being convinced that her repentance is sincere — the offence of which she was convicted was her only transgression while in my employ and she, up to this time, always conducted herself with propriety.
John Patrick[6]

The governor agreed to remit Ann's sentence and she was returned to the Patricks at Campbelltown, but less than 12 months later her security was put under threat again, this time by John.

20 December, 1833
Petition of John Wright, Prisoner of the Crown.

That Your Excellency's Petitioner arrived in the Colony in October 1828 and was assigned to Mr John Patrick of Campbelltown.

That in the month of August last, your Petitioner was tried before the Worshipful Bench of Magistrates at Campbelltown on a charge of stealing flour the property of his master and sentenced to be worked in irons on the public road for 12 months.

That Your Excellency's Petitioner acknowledges the justice of the sentence passed on him but begs to state at the same time that owing chiefly to the constant...[illegible] and importunities of another individual, who has since been deprived of his Ticket of Leave for misconduct, he was prompted to a commission of the crime for which he is now suffering.

That Your Excellency's Petitioner is married having a wife who is a prisoner of the crown assigned to Mr John Patrick of Campbelltown and Petitioner being consciously aware that his conduct previous to the offence for which he is at present suffering, was honest, trustworthy and exemplary which the subjoined attestations will testify. Petitioner therefore humbly implores the humane consideration of Your Excellency as to his present state of mental anxiety and bodily suffering and grant to him a mitigation of sentence as for which act of clemency Petitioner will ever pray...
John Wright
George's River Iron Gang[7]

Mr Patrick again expressed his willingness to take John back and the local magistrate, William Howe, described Mrs Patrick's 'earnest application' and 'her good character of the man for five years previous to his late conviction'.[8] Thomas Reddall, the minister, expressed his views at length:

From what I have heard of this case I really believe the Petitioner, John Wright, was very artfully led into the offence he was guilty of — I have had general opportunities of observing his industrious habits and I have been informed on creditable authority that he is not addicted to the habit of drunkedness — of the former I can vouch in his favour and, as his master Mr Patrick has, notwithstanding this act of dereliction a very good opinion of the man and is desirous of receiving him again into his employ, I recommend him to the favourable consideration of the Governor.[9]

Within three weeks the governor had agreed to remit John's sentence but, sadly, the papers were then mislaid in the colonial secretary's office. It took a personal enquiry at the office by Mr Patrick, a letter from Rev. Thomas Reddall, another petition from John and further supporting letters from all parties, before the original application and decision was found and put into effect towards the end of March 1834.[10] But the delay had caused great tension between Ann and her employers and on 14 January Mrs Patrick took Ann before the Campbelltown bench for refusing to work. She was sentenced to seven days solitary confinement.[11]

John returned to work at the Patricks, but the damage to the relationship between the Wrights and their employers was severe. John had lost the ticket-of-leave which had been issued but he had never actually received, and he would have discovered this when he returned to Campbelltown.[12] It may well be also that he and Ann blamed the Patricks for the delay in the response to his petition, not believing it was a genuine mistake by the bureaucracy.

At any rate, the situation disintegrated over the next 18 months. Six months after John's sentence was commuted Ann was before the bench again, charged by another servant, William Eggleton, with refusing orders. She was sentenced to one month in the third class of the Factory and returned to government for reassignment.[13] Eggleton was a native-born Australian who had been employed by the Patricks for over six years, but he was a 19-year-old youth, giving orders to a 35-year-old woman, and there may have been mitigating circumstances for Ann.[14] The Patricks intervened again and Ann was returned to them, but the following year Mrs Patrick herself took Ann before the bench with a charge of refusing to work and abusive language. She was sentenced to six weeks in the Factory, but while she was there John's resentment against Mrs Patrick resulted in her taking him too before the bench and charging him with idleness and neglect of work. He was sentenced to one month on the treadmill.[15] The once-positive relationship had become antagonistic and vicious, and the trust and liking on both sides had been destroyed.

No records are available to reveal with certainty how it ended. John Patrick died the following year, in May 1835.[16] When the 1837 convict muster was taken Ann was working for a Mr George Brown in the nearby Illawarra district.[17] John's whereabouts at this time are not recorded. He had been sentenced to only seven years and landed in the colony in 1828, yet he did not receive his certificate of freedom until April 1840 and was still in Campbelltown at the time.[18] The Wollongong bench recommended Ann for a ticket-of-leave in September 1839, and she received it two months before John finally gained his freedom. Thereupon, they vanish from sight, except for one brief moment seven years later when Ann received a pardon in July 1847.[19]

The story of the Wrights and the Patricks demonstrates how human nature, above all else, was the deciding factor in the fate of the prisoners. The government system, combined with a reasonable employer, permitted Ann and John to be reunited and their own good behaviour in the first instance, particularly John's, enabled them to take advantage of the opportunity. Then by their own behaviour they put at risk and, ultimately, damaged what they had achieved. Initially the Patricks displayed kindness, generosity and considerable tolerance towards them, no doubt since John had proved to be a valuable servant, but it is conceivable that John Patrick, as an ex-convict, also had some sympathy for the Wrights' predicament. In January 1834 he demonstrated his concern by calling personally at the colonial secretary's office to enquire about the fate of John's first petition. But by 1834 Mr Patrick was 62 years old and the daily responsibility for running the inn had probably devolved more and more on his much younger wife and the senior servants. Their less experienced management, combined with the Wrights' suspicion and resentment, resulted in a rapid deterioration in the relationship between them all. The long delay before John Wright received his certificate of freedom suggests he was subsequently charged with another serious offence which extended his original sentence.

Within the limits of their status as prisoners in the convict system, the Wrights at one point had everything going for them, but on the evidence of the remaining documents it can only be concluded that they themselves destroyed their advantages.

There were two young women on the *Princess Royal* who began as prisoners on the same basis, but whose very different lives in the colony illustrate vividly the combination of circumstances, including luck and character, which affected the fate of the women prisoners. They were tried together at the Old Bailey in London.

CATHERINE STEEL and JOHANNA BROWN were indicted for stealing, on the 8th August, 1 reticule, value 1s.; 1 scent bottle, value 6d.; 1 thimble, value 6d.; 1 handkerchief, value 1s.; 1 sovereign and 10 shillings, the property of Wright Welby, from the person of Jane his wife.

JANE WELBY:...I had missed my way, and came down Phoenix-street, which comes into George-street, at the top of Holborn — I met the two prisoners and another girl — they each asked me for a penny a piece; I then asked them the way to Tottenham-court-road, and one of them said 'Go and show the lady the way Bet' — Brown went to shew me the way; I said 'Never mind, I can find the way,' but she came up close to me, and snatched my reticule, and said 'That is the way,' and ran off — Steel was close to me at the time, and when I called Stop thief! she struck me; I fell against the wall, and she fell down.

WILLIAM DRAKE. I am a shoemaker. I saw the prosecutrix about eight o'clock, in George-street, St. Giles — she and Brown passed by my door, and when they had gone past four or five yards — Brown stepped up to her, and snatched her reticule from the left arm, and an umbrella from her right — the prosecutrix cried Stop thief! and Steel struck her on the back; I moved from my own door, and asked the prosecutrix if she were frightened; I did not see the property after that, nor see the prisoners taken.

MORRIS NICHOLSON: I took Steel into custody the next day — I told her it was for stealing a reticule the evening before; she said it was Brown, and she got blamed for it; as we were going along, she said if I would go into a house she would tell me where it was planted, and she begged to have half a pint of beer — I said she might have the beer, but she did not tell me where it was.

STEEL's defence: As for Brown, I know nothing of her — I was in liquor, and what I said to the constable I know not.

BROWN's defence: As for Steel, I know nothing of her nor the prosecutrix.[20]

Johanna was only 17 and Catherine — who was approximately 26 — had cleverly put her age back to 19 in the hope that youth would mitigate her sentence.[21] It was to no avail. Both of them were found guilty and although neither had any previous convictions, they were each sentenced to 14 years transportation.[22]

The two women had other things in common. They both described their religion as Catholic and they were both single. Their education was minimal. Johanna in fact said she had none, but Catherine claimed she could read. They were both domestic servants — Johanna a nurse girl and Catherine a kitchenmaid. Neither had been born in London, Catherine coming from Bristol, while Johanna recorded her native place was Portugal and she was, perhaps, the child of an English soldier who fought under Wellington in the Peninsular campaign against Napoleon.[23]

Johanna was the taller of the two — 5 feet 1 inch to Catherine's 4 feet 9½ inches — and she had a ruddy, freckled complexion with brown hair and hazel eyes. Catherine had fair skin, with a large perpendicular scar on her left cheek near her ear, and she too had brown hair and hazel eyes.[24]

When they landed in New South Wales they were both assigned initially in Sydney. Johanna went to Mr T. Durant in Pitt Street and Catherine to a publican, J. Henry, in York Street. From then on, their paths diverged.[25]

Catherine was returned to government by her master within the first six months, but without complaint.[26] She then had the good fortune, which she probably did not appreciate at the time, of being assigned to Thomas Avery in the rural district of Narellan.[27] It was more difficult, more inconvenient, for employers in the country districts to take their sevants before the magistrates for punishment and this made them more tolerant of small failings. There was less temptation for the prisoners to succumb to the convivial atmosphere of a pub and also the police were more intent on catching serious offenders such as bushrangers than bringing in assigned servants for minor infringements or what they judged disorderly conduct.

Soon after she arrived in Narellan, Catherine met Peter Riglin a 36-year-old ex-convict who had established himself as a wheelwright on the Cowpastures Road. They applied to marry in December 1829 and as Catherine was single and had no offences recorded against her their application was approved without hesitation.[28] They married in the new year and Catherine was probably officially assigned to Peter from that time. In the following two years they had two daughters, Caroline and Elizabeth.[29] Then, at the end of December 1833, Peter died.[30]

Catherine wasted no time securing her future. She was assigned to Mr William Wood at Bringelly, where she quickly became involved with a ticket-of-leave holder named John Doran. An Irishman from County Down who had been in the colony since 1821, Doran had spent much of his servitude working at the government establishments of Emu Plains and Wellington Valley, near Bathurst. By the time he met Catherine, he was 37 years old and held a ticket-of-leave for the Penrith district.[31] Only five months after Peter Riglin's death they applied to marry.[32]

On 18 June 1834 Catherine and John were married in the Heber Chapel, Cobbitty, by Rev. Thomas Hassall, who had also married Catherine to Peter.[33] Four months later Catherine gave birth to their daughter, Margaret.[34]

John became a tenant farmer to Charles Badgery at South Creek and Catherine worked as a servant for Captain King at Penrith in the same district.[35] They settled down and Catherine gave birth to several children in the following years. But life was no romantic idyll for any of the women of the *Princess Royal* and Catherine faced the tragedy of most mothers of her day, when two of her children died in 1837 and

1838.[36] In August 1841 her veneer of reformation slipped and she appeared before the Sydney quarter sessions charged with larceny. She was found guilty and sentenced to four months hard labour in gaol, with solitary confinement every four weeks.[37]

Meanwhile, what of Johanna Brown? Theoretically there was no reason why she, too, should not have achieved some kind of freedom, either through marriage or a ticket-of-leave.

She began well and stayed with her first master, Mr Durant, for over two years. When he returned her to government it was because there was 'no future use for her services' and she was sent to the first class of the Factory for reassignment.[38] It was at this point that Johanna's life in the colony went wrong. Perhaps she felt wrenched from the only security she had known since she arrived and couldn't cope with the adjustment to a new household. Either that or her next employer was particularly harsh.

Returned to government on 30 July she was immediately re-assigned, but on 24 August she was before the magistrates charged with being absent without leave and drunk. She was again returned to government and sentenced to one month in the Factory.[39] Assigned again at the end of her sentence, she was returned to government by her next employer on 5 October with the comment that he had 'no further use for her services'.[40] Again she was reassigned, this time to Eliza Edwards who chose her from the gaol where she was waiting to be forwarded to the first class of the Factory.[41] Five days later she was committed by the magistrates to the Factory for a month, but returned to Mrs Edwards when this sentence expired.[42] On 5 December she was sent to the third class of the Factory for another month for 'being picked up in the streets in company with a sailor after hours', and this time Mrs Edwards returned her to government. She had gone through three employers in four months.[43]

The authorities concluded that Johanna would be better in the country and early in 1832 she was assigned to Mr R. Brooks at Denham Court outside Liverpool. She stayed in his service for at least a year and may have seen Catherine during the time, since the Cowpastures Road was not far away.[44] But her service for Mr Brooks came to an end, in circumstances which are unknown, and in 1833 she was assigned again in Sydney. This time her master was a Mr Edward Conneighton. She ran away from him in May 1833, which resulted in another sentence to the Factory.[45]

There is little information about Johanna's life over the next five years and this could well be because she was working peacefully in assigned service and avoiding trouble. She was assigned to Mr Robert Cooper for part of the time and in November 1836, while in his service, was brought before the bench in Sydney and charged with drunkenness. The prosecutor was not Mr Cooper himself. He appears to be a police constable although there is no proof. Johanna was found guilty and sentenced to a month in the third class.[46] When the 1837 convict muster was taken she was working for another master, John Blaxland, in Parramatta.

Towards the end of 1838, Johanna was back in the Factory and on
15 January 1839 the colonial secretary wrote to the police magistrate
at Port Macquarie.

> The Visiting Justice of the Female Factory having recommended 12 priso-
> ners be sent to Port Macquarie for assignment to separate them from the bad
> connections they have formed — they will be forwarded by steamer William
> the Fourth this evening.[47]

Johanna was one of the 12 women on the list and her inclusion is a
significant clue to her character. Allowing for the prejudiced perspective of the authorities who made the judgment, and whose assessment
of 'bad connections' would take no account of loneliness and the need
for friends, it nevertheless indicates that Johanna was a follower rather
than a leader. She was regarded as a woman who could behave well in
conducive circumstances, and her overall record, with its periods of
trouble-free service for the Durants and Mr Brooks, supports this
conclusion. So do the records at the Old Bailey. 'Go and show the lady
the way Bet,' ordered Catherine in the London street, and 'Bet'
obediently responded. Johanna was a girl who apparently needed a
protected environment and someone else to make the decisions for
her. Not very bright. Too eager to please. Easily affected by drink. In
the rough and tough world of the prisoners and ex-prisoners of the
colony she would have been a butt for jokes and an easy target for
tricks and treachery. Alone, she couldn't cope and was lost. And the
more alone and lost she was, the more she drank.

Port Macquarie was no longer a penal settlement when Johanna
went there in 1839. The district had been opened up for settlement
when it was replaced in this role some years previously by Moreton
Bay. It was still used by the government, however, as a place to send
invalid convicts.[48] Crippled Sarah Piper had been there for two years
when Johanna arrived, and was to die there two years later.[49]

Johanna was assigned to Mr Joseph Wilson, and two months later
she put in her first application to marry.[50] Her prospective husband
was 36-year-old Andrew White, an ex-convict working for a Mr Doyle.
Johanna's application was supported by her master who described her
character as good, although he had only a few weeks to form his
opinion. But Andrew White, it transpired, had declared himself
married on arrival, so the application was rejected.[51]

The following year Johanna again applied to marry, and this time
she was successful. In 1840 she married Jonathan Hunt, a convict
holding a ticket-of-leave and working, as she was, for Mr Stacy.[52]

In March 1844 the convict office made out Johanna's certificate of
freedom and sent it off to Port Macquarie.[53] But they needn't have
bothered. No certificate was going to give Johanna freedom. She had
returned to Sydney the previous year and her life was distintegrating
into tragedy.

She had been sent down from Port Macquarie on 26 March 1843
with orders to be imprisoned for one month. This was countermanded
by a police magistrate and she was released the following day.[54] But

she was beyond help. Records from the Sydney gaol over the following years speak for themselves:

1843	April 19	In from Police. Confine 7 days. Out 26 April. Confine free.
	May 5	Confine 1 month.
	September 4	Confine 2 months. Out 4 November, 1843.
	November 11	Confine 3 months. The Police sent her somewhere which is not clear in the records.
	December 15	From [?] Confine 3 months. Out 10 February 1844.
1844	February 12	Confine 1 month. Out 12 March. Confine free.
	March 25	Confine 3 months. Out to General Hospital.
	July 19	Confine 2 months. Out 13 September 1844.
1845	July 25	Confine 1 month. Out 25 August. Confine free.
	September 18	In from Police. Bail discharged at quarter sessions, 29 October 1845.
1846	January 15	Confine 1 month. Out 14 February. Confine free.
	March 21	One calendar month labour. Out same day. Labour free.
	April 22	Confine 2 months. Out 22 June. Confine free.
	July 2	Confine 2 months. Out 3 September. Confine free.
	September 29	Confine 6 weeks. Out 10 November. Confine free.
1847	January 9	Confine 3 months.
	June 26	Could not pay bail of £25. Out 2 August.
	August 13	Confine 6 weeks. Out 24 September.
	September 29	Confine 3 months. Out 15 November.
	November 19	Confine 3 months. Out 19 February, 1848.[55]

The pattern set during these years continued through 1848 and 1849 and in fact for the rest of Johanna's life. But during the 1850s she also began to be admitted regularly into the benevolent asylum for the ill and destitute.[56] As death bore down on her she reverted to the use of her married name, but again and again the old identification recurred — 'per Princess Royal 1829'. Gaol and the asylum were her only home, the police her only family. Recognised by them as one of the regular drunks and paupers of Sydney town, it was the master of the gaol in May 1860 who recommended her admission into the benevolent asylum yet again. She was suffering now from the delirium tremens of alcoholic poisoning.[57]

Two years later, over a hundred miles away, Catherine died at the age of 66. She was in her own home in the village of Pomeroy, outside Goulburn, comforted by husband, children and grandchildren.[58]

Johanna staggered on for another seven years. Two days before Christmas, on 23 December 1869, she was found dead in Darlinghurst gaol. At the inquest the following day the coroner concluded her death was due to 'exhaustion or bronchitis in a constitution broken down by intemperance, exposure and neglect'.[59]

The voyage Johanna and Catherine began together so many years before had resulted in two very different journeys.

CHAPTER 13

SOME EVIDENCE OF AFFECTION

What were the women's feelings towards the people in their lives — their husbands, their lovers, their friends, and their children? What were their hopes and plans? What did they feel about their employers and the magistrates? There is little direct evidence, but a considerable amount can be deduced. Their husbands loom largest, but are also the most difficult to assess.

Susannah took a practical attitude to marriage, as she demonstrated in her arrangement with John Clarke and by her marriages after she was free. More conclusively, looking back over her life years later she said it was the loss of her children, through transportation, she regretted. Her husband Edward was not mentioned in this context.[1]

There is clear evidence that some of Susannah's shipmates chose their husbands with a practical outlook. Marriage, for reasons already outlined, was of vital importance to them. They knew its value and many acted accordingly to ensure they attained this respectable and advantageous status. The unemotional choice of a husband is demonstrated most conclusively by those women, such as Maria Allen and Charlotte Tither, who put in simultaneous or immediately consecutive applications to marry different men. It can also reasonably be concluded that the women who applied to marry virtual strangers within six months of arrival most probably did so for practical reasons. Among these were Georgiana Baxter, who married a sailor in August 1829, and Mary Chambers and Susannah Turbitt, both of whom married in September.[2] None of these women who married so quickly did so through the Female Factory.

The Factory marriage mart is the best known and most infamous evidence that women prisoners married in a businesslike manner, without emotional involvement. Much has been made of the men who went there to choose brides, but the women had the right to refuse and there is no evidence they were coerced to agree. On the contrary, there are descriptions which indicate many participated willingly. One observer assured his reading public that he had been present 'at two or three of these negotiations' and the following was 'a faithful picture' of the women taking part in the Factory marriage agency:

> The girls, all agog for a husband, would show various faces upon the examination [by a prospective husband]. Some, all sheepish smiles and blushes, would look as foolish as all young ladies are supposed to, when a third person happens in upon an interview at which the question has just been popped. Others would avert their faces in a sort of indifference; as, although a refusal is seldom met by an applicant, still these seekers for help-meets are not all of such an appearance as to tempt a woman half way. A third set would most prudishly frown upon the proceeding which pays so little respect to the prescriptive rights of the ladies; while, as if purposely set in contrast to these fastidious ones, others would make attempts, not always successful, or with the best grace, to appear as amiable and pretty as possible, spite of the Parramatta frock and petticoat [Factory uniform], of which they were evidently heartily tired.[3]

Only nine women from the *Princess Royal* were married by Rev. Samuel Marsden, who was the chaplain of the Factory. These included Harriet Bannister, who met her husband on the *Princess Royal*, and Sarah Bryant who the evidence indicates knew John Foley in Sydney. Sarah Hazle was assigned in Parramatta when Marsden married her to a local butcher and there is no indication she was in the Factory when she applied to marry. Elizabeth Stocker's husband had been working as a carrier in Parramatta, where she was assigned, before they married when she was in the Factory; and Betty Brian, who had been assigned in Windsor, applied to marry a farmer from nearby Wilberforce after she had been sent to the Factory. Ann Cheeseman was also assigned in Parramatta when she applied to marry, but since she applied to marry three different men in 18 months it is unlikely she felt much affection for any of them. Hannah Solomons, Ann Kirby and Charlotte Smith were all married by Marsden, but there is insufficient evidence to even speculate on the circumstances. The most likely marriages conducted through the Factory marriage bureau are those of Jane Hyde, aged 50 when Marsden submitted her marriage application to a man aged 36, and Margaret Williams, whose name was submitted by Marsden on a long list of women in the Factory.[4]

As we have seen, the men who married the women from the *Princess Royal* were predominantly ex-convicts. Some such as John Potter, who married Elizabeth Jones, were and remained labourers, farmhands and overseers or servants. Several were employed in the police force, including Gregory Howe, husband of Mary Tilley; James Neale, who married Catherine Turner; and for a while Joseph Giles.[5] A few had a specific trade: Isaac White was a brassfounder; John Foley a tailor; Thomas Tollis a shoemaker; and Peter Riglin, Catherine Steele's first husband, was a wheelwright.[6] Ann Currier married Peter Tyler, a printer who had been at the centre of a major political storm between his employer, E. S. Hall, publisher of the *Sydney Monitor*, and the government.[7] Other husbands were self-employed and probably self-taught in a skill which fulfilled a service for the growing population centres of the colony. James Lake was a butcher, Richard Turton and Walter Neary were bakers, Henry Latham who married Sophia Naylor was a fisherman, and William Mason had a stall in the marketplace. Only Maria Allen's husband, Joseph Woodcock, who was a sawyer, was specifically described as owning his own land when they married.[8]

Some of the women and their men saw each other as a means to a more prosperous future and made plans which were really a joint venture in business. Richard Barron and Elizabeth Foxall were going to establish a bakery. Daniel Reddiford announced his decision to set up as a cloth manufacturer before he applied two months later to marry Sarah Quittenton, but the timing indicates that his relationship with Sarah affected his ambitions and plans. John Hoskins set up as a butcher in Maitland after he married Ann Kinsman, while William Mason changed during his marriage to Jane McPherson from 'having a stall in the marketplace' to being 'a shopkeeper'.[9] Within a month of marrying Mary Bass, Thomas Pearks applied for permission to withdraw the money Mary had brought from England from the savings bank, which may indicate they too had business plans under way.[10]

The evidence of pregnancy as a reason for marriage is inconclusive. The birth records for the period are by no means comprehensive, since many people did not have their children baptised, and the dates may have been distorted by a desire for respectability. Maiden names and aliases are an added complication, as is the possibility that an illegitimate child might bear its father's surname rather than that of the man its mother married. It is likely that some women did marry because they were pregnant, but it is impossible to reach an accurate conclusion, except for Catherine Steele who gave birth four months after she married John Dorman. All that can be said is that no employer or clergyman, in the correspondence which supports the women's applications to marry, gives pregnancy as a moral or practical reason why the marriage should be allowed.

The evidence of affection is equally hard to establish and it is never recorded as a reason to marry. There appears to have been considerable emotional involvement between the crew of the *Princess Royal* and some of the women prisoners. It is implied in the newspaper report of the crew's refusal to leave the colony and Marsden actually comments, on the marriage application of Harriet Bannister and John Wright, that the 'attachment' was formed on the ship.[11]

Another clue to the women convicts' feelings is the evidence they cared about their appearance. The rebellion at the Factory demonstrates their attitude to having their heads shaved, and Peter Cunningham describes the way they would paper their curls with scraps torn from Bibles.[12] (A colonial clergyman who saw this practice in Newcastle gaol was so incensed he insisted that all women prisoners' heads should be shaved to prevent it. The governor, to his credit, responded that he could not punish all for the offence of one.)[13] The women's interest in their appearance implies an emotional interest in the response of the opposite sex, as well as their own self-esteem. Mr

Keith's servant, who insisted on wearing lace on Sunday to the disapprobation of her master and mistress, was dressing as much for a social meeting between the sexes as for herself.[14]

The women had little to hope for and little they could call their own. Their emotions were something personal, something beyond the control of the government, the employers and the clergymen. It would be surprising if they did not give full rein to their feelings when they received some encouragement. For all the women, and particularly the young girls, the attraction of the sexes was one of the few aspects which brought colour and a sense of power and worth into their lives. They had reason to invest emotional energy in their relationships, the more so because they had nothing else. So many charges of absence without leave coincide with an application to marry that a picture forms of hurried meetings and whispered promises in the ineradicable advance and retreat, to advance again, of love and sex. Too many charges of drunkenness and disorderly conduct coincide with the collapse of hope or disappointment in a marriage application, to avoid the conclusion that the women forgot or risked punishment because of emotional involvement with their men. Just one specific proof of this comes to light through the actions of a magistrate who had tried to help.

Margaret Williams from the *Princess Royal* was a slender brunette with grey eyes. She was assigned in Newcastle where she met John Smith, who was still serving his sentence. They applied to marry in December 1830 and were refused because neither 'held any indulgence' — that is, privilege such as a ticket-of-leave.[15] The following month Margaret was picked up by two constables and charged with drunkenness and disorderly conduct. She was convicted and sent, not to the third, but the first class of the Female Factory. The governor could not let this pass and called on the magistrate to explain his sentence.[16] He responded in some detail:

> I have the honour to receive on the 12th your letter of the 1st instant on the subject of the punishment awarded the prisoner described in the margin, who was convicted of Drunkenness and Disorderly conduct on the 18th of last month; and beg to state for the information of His Excellency the Governor, that she was simply returned to the Factory for the following reasons.
>
> She and a Bricklayer here, named Smith, made the usual application to be married about 3 months ago, but did not obtain His Excellency's permission it seems because she and the Bricklayer were both prisoners of the Crown. They therefore enquired whether I would recommend that he should receive a Ticket of Exemption. I expressed myself favourable and, at the time that Williams misconducted herself, I believe they had reason, if not to expect, at least to hope that the indulgence would be obtained and that His Excellency would then permit them to marry.
>
> Being thus led, while their conduct stood well in my estimate, to enquire concerning their plan of life, I learned that he was industrious and had a cottage of his own in the town, that she was a good laundress and that they purposed to keep a shop together, should they be married — under these circumstances I judged that her removal simply, involving as it did the disappointment of her hopes, would be a punishment quite adequate to her offence.

I have to express my regret that I should have caused His Excellency and others this trouble by omitting to send with the warrant of Williams commitment, the explanation of the circumstances of her conviction and punishment.

I have the honour to be, Sir, Your obedient servant.

Geo. Brooks, J.P.[17]

Margaret was returned to assignment in Sydney and 18 months later, aged 33, married George Graburn in what appears to be a Factory marriage. She was one of a list of women in the Factory simultaneously submitted by Rev. Samuel Marsden.[18]

Whatever the basis for their marriage, bonds of loyalty and affection certainly developed and were reciprocated between husband and wife, as the case of Mary Williams and Joseph Irving demonstrated. Mary had 'married' Joseph after the failure of her marriage to the *Princess Royal* sailor George Hearn. Three years after their marriage he made arrangements to bring her two children from England, and in a petition to the governor described Mary not only in the accepted way as 'sober and industrious' but also as 'a good wife'.[19] In 1838 Mary's loyalty and concern for Joseph landed her in the Factory. Her prosecutor, Thomas Clements, described how she went to his shop: 'She abused me and struck me...she struck me repeatedly and called me a Bl...dy witch. I did not call [her] a liar but I did say she never lent me 3 pounds.'[20]

Joseph responded promptly in an attempt to get her back.

The Humble Petition of Joseph Irving of Goulburn Street respectfully sheweth that your Petitioner arrived in this Colony in the year 1827 and, in the year 1832, applied for and obtained the consent of His Excellency the then Governor to intermarry with Mary Williams, Princess Royal 1829 for 14 years, and Petitioner and the said Mary Williams were accordingly married on the 20th day of April in that year.

That in the month of February last (at which time Petitioner was in embarrassed circumstances owing to various losses in his business) a misunderstanding having taken place between your Petitioner and his hired servant Thomas Clements in the course of which in consequence of some irritating observations made by the said Thomas Clements to the Petitioner, Petitioner's wife in a state of great excitement unfortunately and improperly struck the said Thomas Clements, for which offence upon the complaint of the said Thomas Clements, their Worships the Magistrates of the Sydney Bench were pleased on the 10th day of February to adjudge the Petitioner's said wife to six months imprisonment in the Third Class of the Female Factory where she now remains.

That Petitioner and his said wife most deeply lament that she should have so offended, but Petitioner having now released himself from his embarrassments and having the offer of employment wherewith to provide for his said wife and family humbly presumes to hope that Your Excellency will be pleased to restore her to her home and therefore

Most humbly prays that Your Excellency will be pleased to grant your Petitioner's said wife the remission of the remaining part of her sentence. Petitioner assuring Your Excellency that the future exertions and conduct of himself and wife shall be used to endeavour to prove themselves worthy of

the clemency of Your Excellency and as in duty bound Petitioner will ever pray.
Joseph Irving
10 April, 1838[21]

Joseph had taken the trouble to get supporting recommendations from respectable neighbours who knew the couple, and from Thomas Clements who stated he now understood the circumstances which had caused Mary to hit him. The government checked the references, and on receiving confirmation from the matron at the Factory that Mary's conduct there had been 'very exemplary', agreed to her immediate release.[22] Neither she nor Joseph were seen in the courts again.

At a time when her husband Peter Glover had financial difficulties in Bathurst, Elizabeth Stocker got into a fight with another woman and the police charged them both with assault. Elizabeth was sentenced to three days in the cells and Peter was there to collect her when she was released. Elizabeth had no history of drunkenness or disorderly conduct in the colony and it seems possible to deduce that, like Mary Williams, her actions were motivated by loyalty in response to a slur against her husband.[23]

Mary Hilsley's actions indicate deep distress when her husband, John Godfrey, was charged with sheep stealing. She and John had been married over four years and were living in Bathurst when he was committed by the Bathurst bench in June 1834.[24] Mary followed him down to Sydney where he was held in the gaol, but she came to the attention of the police who sent her to the first class of the Factory for assignment. She got herself back to Sydney, but her behaviour around the time John was tried and sentenced to 14 years transportation to Norfolk Island once more attracted the notice of the police who again sent her to the first class of the Factory.[25] Since she was charged with no offence on either occasion, it is possible to conclude it was her distress and attempts to see John which eventually led to the actions of the police.

The most specific evidence of the affection of one of the *Princess Royal* women for her man, is in a note written by Ann Kinsman in gaol.

When the government forcibly returned her to her husband in Maitland Ann may have lived with him for a few months until she became free, but shortly after she found a lover in an ex-convict named Richard Holland. The two of them were implicated with John Boydelle and Robert (Bob) Pete in stealing pigs from John Flemming a tenant farmer of Mr William Sparkes at Maitland.[26] Written on scraps of paper and very much misspelt, the letters between Ann and Richard are so difficult to decipher they cannot be reproduced in their entirety. What can be read reveals a deep affection for one another and a unanimous feeling that they have been persecuted and betrayed, most particularly by the two men charged with them and by someone called Jane, who was probably Ann Simpson, whose real name was Jane Spencer. 'I remain your true [lover] until death' is how Richard closes his letter to Ann. She in turn replies she will be his 'friend until death' and adds 'I hope the time will come when we shall be happy together'.[27] Although the case against Richard was dropped for lack of evidence and Ann was found not guilty, there was no happy ending for them.[28] Richard Holland appears to have died a pauper in 1840, many miles away in Bathurst, while Ann continued to live and work in the Hunter River district.[29]

Ann and Richard's letters reveal they felt surrounded by enemies, including their so-called friends, and no doubt this emotion would have been felt by many of the women from the *Princess Royal*. There are few indications of friendship between them. Ann Perks was the supporting witness for Ann Loydall at her wedding and Margaret Hartigan 'stood up' for Sarah Pitches at hers.[30] The restrictions of assigned service would have made this demonstration of friendship difficult to achieve, but even so, it is surprising how seldom it occurred. Loyalty was not a predominant feature of the women's attitudes to one another. Catherine Steele tried to blame her friend Johanna Brown when they were tried together at the Old Bailey. Ann Cheeseman and Ann Simpson turned on each other at their trial. On board the *Princess Royal* it was another prisoner who betrayed Mary Hart's drinking to Surgeon Wilson.[31] There was little room for trust among the women themselves.

If they felt persecuted at times by their fellow prisoners, they must have felt more so by their employers and the magistrates and clergymen. Yet there are occasional indications of sympathetic relationships between the women and these authorities. The Goulburn magistrate Captain Allman showed his sympathy for Mary Palmer. George Brooks the Newcastle magistrate revealed there had been an ongoing and not unfriendly relationship between himself, Margaret Williams and John Smith, the bricklayer she wanted to marry. Rev. Sowerby demonstrated his support for Mary Palmer and William Hickman, while Rev. Rusden at Maitland, who tried to encourage the governor to allow women to marry because of the many dangers surrounding them, must have revealed something of this sympathetic attitude to Ann Kinsman, Ann Simpson, and Ann Burke, all of whom dealt with him over their marriages. He also helped Sarah Pitches to be reunited with her son James.

The employers were the authorities in closest daily contact with the women and obviously the relationship between both sides cannot be generalised because it varied so greatly according to the personalities concerned. However, it is worth noting that it was to George Wyndham, her former master, that Ann Simpson ran from her husband, and he responded by offering to keep her in his service.[32]

The most direct and unequivocal evidence of the women's feelings is in relation to their children.

Susannah's actions were repeatedly influenced by the needs of her children and her letters in later life reveal her deep and abiding concern and love for them. But there were other women on the *Princess Royal* who also revealed that their children were the source of great love and anguish. In 1833 Mary Smith sent a cry from the heart to the colonial secretary:

Hon. Sir,

I humbly beseech you that you may intercede on my behalf to the Governor of the Colony to obtain a Ticket of Leave for me.

My chief object is in order to support my infant child. In July 1828 I was sentenced to 7 years transportation from Nottingham and arrived in this Colony by the ship Princess Royal in May 1829 and was assigned to Dr Ramsay, was about 11 weeks with him, afterwards was in service of Mr Wentworth and had the misfortune to have a child, a son now two years of age, and the child is now with a nurse and I myself am in the service of Mr Rotten at Maitland.

Although that I did not stay with the first master assigned to, removal was not for any misconduct — by indisposition the first, and Mr Darcy Wentworth having gone to England was the reason of leaving him. I am now addressing a gentleman of the greatest honour and respectability and authority and the parent of children yourself.

May I not solicit you to consider the heart of a mother to my child as his father is not in this colony. I am well able to support him, if once I had a little liberty, having now come to years [i.e., over 21] and advancing in years and having a desire to bring up the child that God was pleased to give me, in the fear of God and a good member of Society, and unwilling that anyone should have anything to do with the bringing up of the child but myself.

My reason of not having formerly applied for the Indulgence through my master, as not long with a master. Through your good disposition recommending my case for compassion to His Excellency the Governor, I rest assured that my case will meet with compassion and Liberty extended to me.

May I entreat your goodness to send me an answer on the subject on receipt.

As aware of your humanity and Christian feelings I am Honored Sir your very humble servant and petitioner

Mary Smith (her mark) 3rd per Princess Royal

P.S. It adds to my uneasiness the child being at Parramatta and myself at Maitland.[33]

Poor little Mary, who calls herself the '3rd'. She was the youngest of the three Mary Smiths convicted in Nottingham, who tearfully cursed the judge when she was sentenced to transportation. It was possibly Mary Smith (alias Ann Burke), the leader of the threesome in Nottingham, who helped Mary write this petition, since she too was working at Walter Rotten's pub in Maitland at the time.[34] They bent the truth a little. She did work for the two masters she mentions, but omits the fact that her assignment to D'Arcy Wentworth was a brief failure. He returned her to the first class with the comment that she was 'useless in service'.[35] Strictly speaking, however, she had no offences against her, but she was assigned the third time well away from Sydney, to Newcastle, where almost immediately she married an ex-convict named John or James Cranfield.[36] John's whereabouts at the time of the petition are a mystery, but he may have been transported to a penal colony. The child too is a mystery, since no such boy was listed as born near the date Mary indicates in the petition.

When he saw her plea, the governor noted that she seemed entitled to a ticket and he told the superintendent of convicts to advise her that she should apply in the regular way.[37] But there is no record she ever obtained one. She received only her certificate of freedom, two years later.[38] Whether she regained possession of her son or not, Mary never did get her life together. As late as January 1844 she was in Newcastle gaol waiting for her trial at the quarter sessions, and again in 1856, over 20 years after she had obtained her certificate of freedom, Mary Cranfield per *Princess Royal* was in Maitland gaol serving a three months sentence.[39]

At this time the government was not unsympathetic to the problems of women separated from their children, and with those under three years of age tried to keep them together; it was later in the decade an official policy existed of taking children away from their prisoner mothers when they reached the age of 12 months. The circumstances which caused Mary to leave her child in Parramatta seem unusual, and would not have been by government order. Indeed, in the early 1830s, even women who had been transported to Moreton Bay were allowed to take their babies with them.[40] The usual fate of a woman with a child was to remain at the Factory, or be returned to it, until she finally found an employer who would accept the child. Although there was an official policy that children over three were better separated from convict parents, this was mitigated by the economic burden of maintaining them and the constant need for places at the schools for really destitute children. As a result, as long as parents could demonstrate they could support their children it was not difficult to obtain their release from the orphan schools. The major problem arose if the child was nearing an age for apprenticeship, by which time an alternative route for its welfare existed which the government was reluctant to abandon.[41]

Susan King's feelings about her daughter Elizabeth, born on the *Princess Royal*, are not on record, but they can be deduced to some extent by her actions. At two crisis points connected with her daughter, Susan applied to marry. When Elizabeth was admitted into the orphan school in May 1832, Susan applied almost simultaneously to be married.[42] Although her application was approved, she did not pursue it and in fact changed assignment, which may have affected her relationship with the man involved.[43] She obtained a ticket-of-leave the following year, but lost it three months later for drunkenness. Then in 1835, only five weeks before Elizabeth died at the orphan school aged six, Susan married George Gilbert. The conjunction of dates indicates Susan struggled, ineffectually and with her efforts jeopardised by drunkenness, to use marriage to help her child. She died only five years later through 'disease induced by intemperance'.[44]

None of the women of the *Princess Royal* who brought children with them forgot those children. All of them tried to keep in touch and some went to considerabe lengths to regain them after the government had separated them.

Margaret Mahoney, as we have seen, intended to visit Richard at the male orphan school and was tragically waylaid.[45] There is no evidence to indicate how much they kept in touch after she was free and he was apprenticed, but a similar case of a mother and her son could well serve to demonstrate the likely fate of Margaret and Richard.

Henry Milhouse, who came to New South Wales with his mother a prisoner, was apprenticed at the age of 11 years to the merchant and magistrate A. B. Spark. In his diaries Spark reveals considerable pride and some self-satisfaction in the growth of the undernourished boy whom he carefully measured and weighed each year and whose training and progress in his household he watched closely. Henry's mother, who was ill and desperately poor, kept in touch with Mr Spark and he with her. He visited her when she was 'in very indigent circumstances', and when she died he arranged her burial. Henry saw his mother occasionally and was very distressed at her death. He said about her: 'She would have taken the bread from her own mouth to have given it to me', a description which might well have applied to the mothers of the *Princess Royal*.[46]

Caroline Thomas and her nine-year-old daughter Jane had been separated only days after they arrived in the *Princess Royal*. Caroline's career as an assigned servant was interspersed by at least five sentences to the Factory, usually for drunkenness and some times for insolence or abuse.[47] She never obtained a ticket-of-leave, but shortly before she became free in 1836 she married Jacob Myers, a convict still serving his sentence. Caroline was 39 and Jacob 14 years younger.[48] It is very likely they did a deal of some kind — Jacob, who was serving a life sentence, to gain the benefit of Caroline's freedom; and Caroline to recover Jane. The Myers remained in the Liverpool district, but 18 months later, in July 1837, Caroline died.[49] That mother and daughter had been reunited in some fashion was proved when Jane married, also at Liverpool, in 1839. One of the witnesses was her dead mother's husband.[50]

Margaret Hartigan had managed to keep her daughter Abigail with her until February 1831, when she was three and a half years old and the Matron of the Factory arranged for her to go to the orphan school.[51] Later that same year Margaret was married in Newcastle to John Smith, an ex-convict, but as the Newcastle bench books reveal Margaret had a difficult marriage and she did not apply for Abigail until she was granted a ticket-of-leave eight years later.[52] In March 1839, when she finally sent a petition to the governor, she was told Abigail had been apprenticed the previous September.[53] Abigail had in fact been sent to work as nurse and housemaid for Thomas Buxton, a Newcastle shopkeeper, and as Margaret's ticket-of-leave was for nearby Maitland it is likely they were ultimately reunited.[54]

By the 1830s the government's system for reuniting ex-prisoners with their families in England was well established and many men, particularly, applied to bring their families out. There was no official barrier to women making the same application and when Sarah Hazel married in February 1832 she wasted no time in sending a petition direct to the governor.[55]

Your memorialist Sarah Hazell per ship Princess Royal most respectfully solicit, as she is now married to Mr James Lake Butcher of Parramatta as per certificate annexed from the Reverend Mr Forrest and having a young Son in England that require the attention and advice of a parent being left quite friendless depending upon for support from an Institution at Bristol

Your memorialist trusts from her good conduct since her arrival in this Colony and being in circumstances able to support her Offspring at the request of your memorialist Husband

Your memorialist humbly beg that her memorial will be laid before His Excellency the Governor trusting that His Excellency will condescend to order a Certificate from the Colonial Secretary's Office to accompany her Petition to the Home Secretary to restore the youth to his Parent a Mother

Your memorialist humbly pray — from her servitude as a nurse at the orphan school, which her good conduct can be testified by the Archdeacon, and the ability of her Husband being in circumstances able to support her Son, that Your Excellency will be pleased in sanctioning her son being restored to an afflicted Mother to relieve a distressed Parents mind, wishing to save her Son from a Bad end — for the want of early tuition in being brought up in the fear of the Lord

which your memorialist will ever feel in duty bound to pray...
Sarah Lake[56]

The governor stuck rigidly to the rules and insisted that she should apply through the proper channels on the proper printed form.[57] Whether Sarah's son ever arrived is unknown. She stated on arrival in 1829 that she had left three children behind in England,[58] and it is possible she was attempting to bring all of them to New South Wales but trying for a free passage for one of them. What is certain is that, once safely married herself, her thoughts turned immediately to the family she left behind.

Ann Bowler's thoughts were also with her family in England. She was married and left six children behind when she was transported for shoplifting in Birmingham. Although she had two previous convictions, she escaped a life sentence and received 14 years.[59] Her record in New South Wales was impeccable throughout her servitude, although she was constitutionally sickly and unfit for hard work. By the end of 1831 she was caring for the children of her employer, who had died while Ann was in her service, and one of her referees for a ticket-of-leave described her as 'a mother in every sense to the family'.[60]

Ann received her ticket-of-leave in mid 1833 and had held it without interruption when in December 1836 she sent the following petition to the Governor:[61]

The respectful memorial of Anne Bowler most humbly sheweth that she arrived in this distant colony under sentence of transportation for the term of 14 years per ship Princess Royal, Sherwood Master, in the year 1829

That she now begs leave most humbly to approach Your Excellency with the most unbounded respect in succinctly laying the following ardent desire of Your Excellency's memorialist before you, reposing a hope that Your Excellency will view her case as one deserving the boon she so imploringly solicits

That as above stated Your Excellency's memorialist arrived in the year 1829 and was in May of the same year assigned to the Surveyor General of the Colony Major T.L. Mitchell

That your Memorialist by living an honest, sober and industrious life with steadiness of conduct and correctness of deportment received a Ticket of Leave on the 20 August 1833, the benefits of which she has since increasingly continued to enjoy

That from sentence of her transportation (14 years) Memorialist has (under expiation) served so much as 9 years in July next, which leaves little more than 4 years to entitle her to a Certificate of Freedom and having continued (as will appear from the appended papers) to conduct herself with uniform propriety and decorum your Memorialist humbly trusts that from the foregoing reasons Your Excellency's Memorialist hopes she is worthy the clemency and humane consideration of Your Excellency .

That she is now becoming in years and when torn from home with all its endearments left with husband and 6 children, 3 of whom are girls and 3 boys, the younger being 9 years, who she is very eager to rejoin for their protection and support having heard that their Father has lately died, and the family left altogether unprovided for — and to enable her to proceed thither for such parental purpose your Memorialist most humbly and dutifully prays that Your Excellency will be graciously pleased to extend to Memorialist the indulgence of an Absolute Pardon for which act of Your Excellency your memorialist will as in gratitude and duty bound ever pray No. 13 opposite Mr. Hynd's, Sussex Street
30 December, 1836[62]

Ann was rejected on the grounds that she had not been in the colony for long enough to justify 'such an indulgence', but she persevered and in January 1840 she received her absolute pardon, which entitled her to return to England.[63]

Sarah Pitches had a very chequered career in the colony before she was able to regain her son James. And when she did, it was just in time. He had reached the age for apprenticeship.

A short, skinny, dark haired Irishwoman, with a ruddy, freckled complexion and hazel eyes,[64] Sarah's face was marked with scars on either side of her forehead and a large one across her left cheek. She had been born in Londonderry and was 29 years old when she was convicted of housebreaking in Cambridge, England. As she had no previous convictions she was sentenced to seven years.[65] When the *Princess Royal* docked she was assigned to Andrew Nash, a well known innkeeper at Parramatta, and she managed to keep her son with her for their first year in the colony.[66] But in mid-1830 Sarah was in the Factory and the matron put forward James's name as a child old enough to be admitted to the orphan school.[67] He was, in fact, barely three.

Sarah spent the next two and a half years working in Sydney for various employers. In August 1831 she was sent to the third class of the Factory for one month for being drunk, and in November 1832 she ran away from her then mistress, Mary Elliott of York Street, Sydney, for an unknown reason.[68] She was finally discovered, four days later, hiding in an oven in the military barracks.[69] After this she was assigned to Newcastle, and in January 1835 her master took her to court and charged her with insolence.

The Reverend Mr Threlkeld being duly sworn says: The prisoner has been a very good servant for sometime. I had occasion to reprove her for improper connection which I conceived was going on between her and a married man. Her mistress sent for me to see the shameful state she had done her washing repeatedly. I stopped her tobacco in consequence and she sent repeated insolent messages by the children to her mistress. I was in my study the day before yesterday and heard her say to her mistress, she would not do any more of the bloody work for any of the bloody... something which I could not hear. I went to her, when she told me she would go to work when I gave her the tobacco.

In reply to a question by the prisoner: I saw the clothes several times include to [two? of] my own shirts.

The prisoner had no more questions to ask. 14 days cells, to be returned to master.[70]

Sarah was going through a very bad patch. A few months later, however, she was free and could do as she wished,[71] but on 8 October she was in court again, charged with drunkenness.

Constable Rouse states: Between 9 and 10 o'clock last night I found the prisoner drunk on Mr Reid's premises in company with 6 or 7 of Mr Reid's assigned servants. They were sober. No person complained of her except Langham, who complained that her language near his door was disgusting — he had thrown water on her to drive her away. She is a habitual drunkard.

Samuel Langham...states: Last night between 8 and 9 o'clock, the prisoner was near my door. She was drunk and used abominable language in the hearing of my family, her expressions were obscene. She called Mr Reid's Baker a Bloody Bugger.[72]

Sarah made no defence and was found guilty. She was given the option by the magistrate, George Brooks, of entering a surety to be of good behaviour for six months or to be committed to gaol for one month. Without any money, she had no choice but gaol.[73]

In 1836 it appeared Sarah's luck had turned. William Turvey, a widower, asked her to marry him. William may well have been the married man of whom Rev. Threlkeld so disapproved and it could have been an emotional involvement with him that was the cause of Sarah's behaviour during 1835. His wife Harriet died of heavy drinking in December 1834, and on 10 October 1836 he and Sarah were married in Newcastle with Margaret Hartigan, now Smith, as Sarah's witness.[74] The governor, it may be remembered, did not interfere in the marriage of free persons, so Sarah's bigamy passed unnoticed.

Sarah went with William to live in Maitland and her thoughts turned to James who was now over ten years old. She persuaded William to send in the following petition to the governor on 5 June 1839:

The Memorial of William Turvey, Free of Maitland, humbly sheweth that he was married by Reverend Wilton to Sarah Pitchers, Widow, whose son is now in the Orphan Asylum at Liverpool

That Memorialist has a very good lucrative trade and more work than he can do, that he has bound himself to support her son upon transfer from the Asylum, to teach him his trade and to bring him up to man's estate soberly,

virtuously and in the fear of God and the laws
  The Memorialist begs to refer Your Excellency to the subjoined Certificate
and as in duty bound will ever pray[75]

William then swore the following statement to verify his good intentions:

> I William Turvey, Free of Maitland, the present husband of Sarah Pitchers,
> Widow, do hereby bind myself to support her child, James Pitchers, by her
> former marriage, upon his transfer from the Orphan Ayslum at Liverpool, in
> an honest, creditable and comfortable manner, to teach him my trade of a
> whip thong maker and that he may be enabled to get his own livelihood and
> to see that he be virtuously brought up to attend divine service and to be
> taught his duty to God and Man.[76]

The application was supported by the local magistrate and by Rev.
Rusden, who certified he had enquired into William's ability to support James and recommended His Excellency grant the petition.[77]

  The master of the male orphan school was asked his opinion and he
reported that James was now 12 years of age and had been in the
school for nine years; his character was good and he was fit for an
apprenticeship. On this basis the governor allowed James to be apprenticed to William, and he left the school in July 1839 for a reunion
with his mother.[78]

  But fate had far from finished with Sarah. She had only four years
of contentment before she was dealt a double tragedy. In May 1844
William died, aged 66, and his loss was compounded terribly when
only six months later James died at the age of 18. The boy and his stepfather were buried by Rev. Rusden.[79]

  Sarah lived on in Maitland and eight years later Rev. Rusden married Sarah Turvey, widow, to William Price.[80] The tough little Irishwoman had somehow survived the ups and downs life threw at her
and she died peacefully, with her husband beside her, many years later
in 1868. In her death she deserted the Rev. Rusden's church and
returned to the faith of her native land. She was buried by a priest in
the Roman Catholic cemetery at Maitland — a long, long way from
Londonderry.[81]

CHAPTER 14

CAUGHT IN THE SYSTEM

Once free, the women could take steps to redress the worst tragedies of their lives. They could marry and perhaps find happiness and security, or they could try and regain their children. But a number of the *Princess Royal* women, including Susannah, extended their original sentence by committing further offences in the colony. None equalled Dorothy, the wife of Thomas Huldie, alias Ann the wife of Thomas White. Sentenced originally to seven years transportation, she served over 11 years.

Dorothy, or Ann as she called herself, was 39 when she landed in New South Wales. A literate woman of some education, she was married and left three children behind in England. She had been convicted in Newcastle of unlawfully pledging, which was her third offence, but she was sentenced to only seven years.[1]

Drink was Ann's main undoing. Convicted of drunkenness in September 1829, she was charged again with repeated drunkenness a year later and sentenced to the Factory for one month.[2] But her master wrote the following letter to the colonial secretary, dated 13 November 1830:

> I have the honour to solicit your favour in allowing my female servant Ann Huldin (Princess Royal), who was yesterday sentenced by the Magistrates to a months confinement in the Female Factory, to return to her duty, she being now sensible of her error and has promised to conduct herself better in the future.
> I have the honour to be, Sir, your obedient sevant,
> Benjamin Lloyd
> Lieutenant 39th Regiment

Ann's sentence was remitted and she was returned to Lieutenant Lloyd.[3] But she didn't keep her promise. Only a week later she was again convicted of drunkenness, and this time her employer returned her to government.[4]

In the new year she was assigned to Wiliam Cox at Richmond, but within a few months was in serious trouble. In August 1831, as she waited in gaol, she wrote a petition to the governor.

The humble petition of Ann Huldie per ship Princess Royal, now confined in H.M. Gaol, Sydney, most respectfully sheweth

That your Petitioner arrived in the Colony in the year 1828, under sentence of 7 years transportation and was an assigned servant to William Cox Snr., Esq. JP, of Clarendon for the last five months. That, about 2 months since, your Petitioner was tried before the Worshipful Bench of Magistrates at Windsor and sentenced to 3 years to a penal settlement for some articles of wearing apparel the property of Mr Cox and begs to state that it was the first and only crime imputed to her since she has been in the Colony and that she acknowledges the justice of her trial, but solemnly declares herself innocent of the charge alleged to her

Your Petitioner begs further leave to state that her fellow servant, a woman named Nanny (free), was the person who committed the offence for which I am charged with, she was intrusted with the keys of the press where the articles were taken from and they were never intrusted to me nor were they ever in my possession. That on the date the said Nanny had taken the articles from the press, she was intoxicated in liquor and concealed the articles in my bed in the nursery, where her bed also was and likewise another female servant's bed, but your Petitioner's bed was closest to the Press — and it fully appears that the said Nanny only concealed the articles in Petitioner's bed but meet [*sic*] her any opportunity of removing them after, but being too drunk had forgotten where she put them.

Your Petitioner begs further leave to state that if she had taken these articles (which was impossible as she never had the keys) and would conceal them in her own bed, she would not request Mary Gough, a free and confidential servant of the family of Mr Cox, to lay down on Petitioner's bed, when she would be aware that if she had anything concealed therein, the said Mary Gough would immediately communicate it to Mr or Mrs Cox — and the latter had candidly expressed in the kitchen that she was fully sensible of your Petitioner's innocence — and the said Nanny, which had taken those articles, had been subsequently committed and tried (but acquitted) at the late Quarter Sessions held at Windsor, charged with two carpenter's rules and two silk handkerchiefs found under her bed, but in consequence of others having access to the same apartment she was acquitted.

Your Petitioner therefore humbly hopes Your Excellency will be graciously pleased to take her case into your humane consideration and that you will be pleased to mitigate her sentence to any less period that may be to Your Excellency's judgment best meet and Your Petitioner as duty bound will ever pray

(sgd.) Ann Huldie[5]

The possibility that Ann was the victim of injustice is negated by her known addiction to drink and the number of her subsequent offences for larceny. The governor did not call for the case papers to check all the details she mentioned, but he sought the views of William Cox, who responded:

I do not think that Nanny committed the theft, but that it was done by Petitioner, who has given way to drinking to [*sic*] much to be intrusted when spirits is to be had. She was convicted on the clearest evidence and the other woman was acquitted.

Mr Cox, senior, was one of the most respected and influential residents of the colony and in the world of gentlemen his word was sufficient. 'No answer' (to the petition), noted the governor.[6]

Ann was on her way to Moreton Bay before this decision was reached, and she remained there for the full three years of her sentence, returning to Sydney on 15 August 1834.[7] Under different circumstances she should have been eligible for a ticket-of-leave by that date and looking forward to the final year of her servitude. But the colonial sentence was additional, and in the years that followed she committed other offences which extended her term. It was December 1840 before she finally obtained her certificate of freedom.[8] The next month she was in gaol again for stealing. Tried at the quarter sessions, she was found guilty and sentenced to six months hard labour in the Factory.[9]

In the following years Ann spent more time in gaol than out of it. In September 1843 she was sentenced to a year for larceny, of which the governor remitted the final five months.[10] But this merciful action did not help her. In circumstances no doubt of destitution and poverty, she continued to steal. In 1846, after yet another sentence to the Factory, she married an elderly man named Richard Challenor but he only survived three years. Ann remained single until she died in 1859.[11]

Catherine Donoghue — Surgeon Wilson's 'Demon...the greatest blackguard in the ship' — was another who compounded her problems. She was in trouble from the beginning. Barely five feet tall, with a ruddy, freckled complexion, sandy hair and blue eyes, she was an 18-year-old single girl from Guildford. She had been caught with three other women, stealing a hat and jacket 'from the person', and although the *Princess Royal* muster does not list any previous offences for her, she received a life sentence which would imply she had been caught before. Surgeon Wilson conveyed a vivid picture of the way she would stride around the deck of the *Princess Royal*, provoking quarrels or singing at the top of her voice.[12] In New South Wales she continued to go her own way. Less than three weeks after she arrived she was sent to the Factory for being drunk and disorderly. Four months after that she was 'found in carnal connexion' and back in the Factory for three months. In May 1830 she served another sentence for disobedience and was then assigned 200 miles north to Port Stephens.[13] Most probably she decided herself she wanted to get back to Sydney and, through her behaviour, compelled her master to return her. By November she was on her way to the first class of the Factory. However, she got drunk on the trip from the gaol in Sydney to Parramatta, a not uncommon occurrence for women prisoners, and when she arrived at the Factory she was sentenced to a month in the third class.[14] In 1831 she is absent from the available records, but 1832 reveals a pattern to her assignment, which cannot realistically be blamed on five different employers:

January—March	House servant to Michael McCormick, Castlereagh Street, Sydney.
April	Housemaid to Major Poole, 39th Regiment, Parramatta.
June	House servant to T. Moore, Wilberforce.
July	Laundress to Patrick Fennell, Campbelltown. Returned for absence during the night without leave. Third class, one month
October	Laundress to Daniel O'Brien, Pitt Street, Sydney.[15]

In 1833 the Government sent her to Port Macquarie, even further away from Sydney, but by October she was in trouble there too. Her background in England and her experiences in the colony had obviously made her bitter and angry and she and another woman, Ann Cahill, per *Palambam*, let loose that anger on the authorities in Port Macquarie. They were part of a group who had been brought before the court there for insulting the colonial surgeon 'in the execution of his duty attending the corporal punishment of two male prisoners who had been sentenced to receive 50 lashes each'. As the surgeon was giving evidence describing the abuse which had rained down on his head during the flogging, Catherine and Ann physically launched themselves at him and the presiding magistrate, shouting that they wished they could 'find a knife to whip into the B......'. Another magistrate was immediately called in to try the case and he, deciding that the bench had not the power to pass 'a sufficiently severe sentence', sent the two women to Sydney for trial before the quarter sessions.[16] The government sent them right back again, with a letter censuring the magistrate for such a sentence.[17] Less than ten days later they sailed yet again for Sydney, now under sentence of 12 months hard labour in the third class of the Factory,[18] and the governor, who had expected them to remain in the local female factory at Port Macquarie, gave up and let them proceed to Parramatta, although he instructed the colonial secretary to advise the authorities in Port Macquarie not to send women under punishment to Sydney in future.[19]

Circumstantial evidence indicates that Catherine and Ann had some provocation in Port Macquarie. The relationship between prisoners and gaolers there was volatile at the time and beyond the ability of the local authorities to remedy or control. There was some aspect of the flogging they were watching which was either particularly harsh or unjust and which caused them and six other prisoners to abuse the surgeon. The week after the women attacked the surgeon and magistrate in court, two male prisoners on trial for larceny were charged with throwing bricks at the magistrate.[20]

Catherine served her 12 months sentence during 1834, but there was no future for her at the end of it. She died of an undisclosed cause in the Factory hospital in June 1835.[21] There is no indication that she was severely victimised by the convict system. She was among the minority on the *Princess Royal* who were literate, and by character she was neither timid nor downtrodden. But she found nothing in New

South Wales to change her anger and resentment into a positive determination to play the authorities at their own game and come out ahead.

Ann Stokes, at 17, was even younger than Catherine when she was transported. She had been convicted of housebreaking at Reading, and with no previous convictions she had been sentenced to seven years. But she served ten.[22] She too had a disastrous career in the colony, but overall, her record indicates a simple inability to cope with her life and a recurring tendency to petty theft, which continually led to her punishment. The chronology of her servitude is a gruelling circle of assignment and punishment:

1829	May	Assigned to Ann Harley, Windmill Street, Sydney.
1830	July	Theft; third class, one month.
1831	April	Third class, 3 months.
	October	Absconded from service, third class 6 weeks.
1832	April	Runaway from escort to Parramatta.
	June	Assigned Redmond Connor, Camden.
	September	Runaway from Redmond Connor.
	October	To Newcastle for service.
	November	Assigned to W. M. Townshend, Wollombi. Applied to marry Peter Dalton. Allowed. Did not proceed.
1833	January	Sent to Sydney to give evidence and returned Newcastle.
	February	Before Newcastle Bench for slander. Prosecutor Mrs Hostun. Case dismissed.
	February	Charged with theft by employer, Mr Kemp; 7 days cells.
	March	Assigned to Mr McDougal, Patricks Plains. Charged by overseer with leaving the house without leave. Acquitted but returned to government.
	April	Sentenced to 9 months in Newcastle gaol.
1834	January	Assigned to Mr Francis Beattie Newcastle.
	March	Absent during the night; 21 days cells, Newcastle gaol, and returned to government.
1835	February	With Mr Beattie (still/again?) applied to marry Patrick Reddy. Allowed. Did not proceed.
	March	Returned to government.
	March	Assigned Mr Muckleton, Newcastle. Returned. Assigned Surveyor Ogilvie, Maitland.
	July	In Newcastle gaol. Return to Mr. Ogilvie.
	August	In Newcastle gaol — sentence 2 years hard labour. Sent to Factory at Parramatta.
1836–37		Factory, Parramatta.
1837	May	To Newcastle for service.
	September	In assignment to Major Crummer, 14 days cells, Newcastle gaol for disorderly conduct (see below).
1838	December	In Newcastle gaol. Certificate of freedom.

| 1839 | July | Although free, sent in application to marry Charles Pain, also free. Did not proceed.[23] |

There was something about Ann that provoked trouble. Not a rebellious, high temper; or proud insolence; nor an addiction to drink. It would appear to be more a naive stupidity, which made her personally undisciplined and caused her to do or take what she wanted, without really understanding the consequences. It also made her an easy victim for spite or officiousness. The following extract from the Newcastle Bench Book, 3 September 1837, gives some illustration of her character:

> Eliza Blunt, assigned to Major Crummer, sworn says: The second day I was in Major Crummer's house, I saw a pair of stockings on the prisoner's legs marked KC. She told me Mrs Crummer had given her two pairs. Mrs Crummer missed two pairs last Sunday week and I told her the prisoner had them. The prisoner took out the name from the stockings. She also had a cap and 3 towels of the Misses Peters. She told me the Misses Peters had given them to her. The prisoner took the things. They were offered to Mrs Crummer, but she would not take them back. I saw the prisoner wearing the things.[24]

By implication, neither Mrs Crummer nor the Misses Peters wanted to pursue the prosecution and Eliza Blunt had obviously kept quiet until put in a situation where she might have been charged with theft herself. The problem for the magistrate was the nature of the charge, since Ann had not run off with her mistress's property and was still living in the house. She was initially described as 'improperly making use of Mrs Crummer's property', but this was altered to 'disorderly conduct' and she was sentenced to 14 days solitary in the cells of Newcastle gaol.[25]

Ann's applications to marry while she was a prisoner were supported by her employer each time, but sadly she had always moved on to another assignment before the approval came through. There is no escaping the conclusion that for Ann, more than most, marriage might have been the real solution. Serving three years more than her original sentence, she was still only 27 years old when she received her certificate of freedom.[26] There is no certainty about what became of her after she ceased to be a prisoner, but it is likely she was the Ann Stokes who married John Hunt in 1842 at Muswellbrook.[27] She appeared no more in the records of local gaols, nor is there any immediate record of her death, so perhaps she found, at last, a peaceful and happy life.

The tragedy of Catherine Donoghue and Ann Stokes, two young girls with their very different personalities, demonstrates how the assignment system could grind the prisoners down relentlessly if their characters prevented them from coming to grips with it.

The stories of Ann Cheeseman (alias Ann Bates) and Ann Simpson, two very tough characters, show how the women themselves could manipulate the system endlessly, but in the end they too were ground down and beaten. They had been convicted together in Hull in circumstances, and with established backgrounds, which revealed crime and prostitution was a way of life, possibly a chosen path. But if there was friendship between them, it did not survive their trial when they betrayed each other. In New South Wales assignment took them in different directions.[28]

Ann Cheeseman made it clear from the beginning that she was not going to accept her servitude or cooperate with the authorities. She may have been involved with one of the crew from the *Princess Royal*, because on 11 June, the day they all appeared in court, she was charged with absconding or being absent from service and was sent to the Factory for three months.[29] From then on barely a year passed without Ann facing some charge. In 1830 she was charged with drunkenness in February and insubordination in September, both offences resulting in a month in the Factory.[30] In the middle of 1831 she was sent to Newcastle and assigned to surveyor Ogilvie where she remained for a year and a half with only one offence, resulting in ten days solitary confinement in Newcastle gaol.[31] But by the end of that year she was back in the Factory, and in 1833 went through at least two employers in Parramatta.[32] She spent most of 1834 in the Factory, having been sentenced in January to 28 days, in May to 52 days, and in August to two months.[33] May 1835 brought another sentence of two months and the following year, in October 1836, she absconded from an employer and was sentenced to another two months.[34]

Seeing the route to freedom through marriage, Ann Cheeseman put in three applications. The first was to an ex-convict who had settled at Maitland and her request was supported by her then employer, Ogilvie, who described her conduct as very good.[35] She was rejected because she had declared herself married on arrival. She tried again the following year over a six-month period for two different men. The first was an elderly resident of Parramatta who had arrived as a convict in the *Hillsborough* in 1799, and the second was a 19-year-old boy who had come free to the colony. Both applications were rejected.[36]

By 1839 she was again assigned in the Newcastle district, and the chronology of the following two years shows how far her life had disintegrated. She was also by now either ill or using illness to manipulate her employers.

1839	October 31	Medical aid in Newcastle gaol.
	November 20	Seven days cells, Newcastle gaol and returned (by employer).
	December 10	Assigned Major Crummer.
	December 15	Gaol hospital.
1840	January 5	To Major Crummer.
	February 16	Gaol hospital.
	March 1	Assigned Mr White.
	October 18	Returned to government, first class.
	October 25	To Mr McDougall
	October 31	To Mr Boyce, Lake Macquarie.
1841	January 17	Returned to government.
	January 22	To R. Macdonald, Maitland.

February 2	Cells, Newcastle gaol. Possibly returned to government.
May 16	To Mr Dalglish
June 1	Fourteen days cells.
June 14	From cells to first class for assignment.
August 10	To Police Office.
August 14	Forwarded to Hyde Park Barracks, Sydney 'to be identified'.[37]

There are gaps in Ann's records and at times uncertainty about the precise accuracy of the gaol clerks' records. There is also very little detail of the reasons she was so constantly in trouble and there must have been occasions when her employers were to blame. But the overall pattern is undeniable and puts the responsibility back in Ann's court.

She could, if she wished, conform to the behaviour of a good assigned servant, as is indicated by her 18 month stay with Mr Ogilvie in 1831–32, and the relatively peaceful period from mid-1835 to late 1836. Her applications to marry and her choice of husbands are proof of her attempts to use the system in that respect, while the fact that she did not pursue marriage once three refusals over 18 months proved it was fruitless shows she was not foolish.

By 1839 Ann Cheeseman was either in the grip of an illness, possibly caused by excessive drinking, or she was furiously displaying her contempt for the system and everyone who represented it, and this culminated in a performance in 1841 which so confused the authorities they sent her to Sydney for identification.[38] There is one tentative clue to the way she could behave, which confirms the conclusion of contempt for the system. On 2 June 1831 an employer in Sydney returned a Mary Ann Bates, per *Princess Royal* from Yorkshire, to government with the comment she was 'useless in service being insane'.[39] Neither of the Mary Bates listed on the *Princess Royal* muster had any connection with Yorkshire, but Ann Cheeseman alias Ann Bates was convicted there and she was being turned in from assignment at that time. Three weeks later Ann Cheeseman passed through the Sydney gaol again on her way from Parramatta to service in Newcastle.[40]

The descriptions of her trial in England make it clear Ann Cheeseman was not insane, as do many of her actions in New South Wales. But she may well have used insane behaviour to confuse and manipulate the system in the colony. At no time did she commit an offence which risked substantially extending her sentence, and once back in Sydney she begins to fade from the records. Within a year of her return from Newcastle she applied for a ticket-of-leave, which was granted for the Windsor district in December 1842. In February 1844 her official certificate of freedom was issued and she disappeared into the melee of the rapidly growing colony.[41]

Ann Simpson, meanwhile, had been following a not dissimilar course. She had been offered a helping hand by her former employer, George Wyndham, who obtained permission for her to stay in his service when she ran away from her husband, John Prentice. When that arrangement failed and Ann returned to government for assignment some months later in March 1835, she was on a path which led only downhill.[42] An extract from the Newcastle Bench Book in July 1838, illustrates the kind of conflict she experienced with her employers.

> Ann Simpson alias Prentice, alias Levingston per Princess Royal...
>
> Jonathan Warner, Esq. sworn deposeth: On the morning of the 27th July, [sic] soon after daylight, the prisoner left my service without leave and I have not seen her since, till now.
>
> Sworn this 2nd day of July [sic] 1838.
>
> The prisoner states in her defence that she was unwell and not able to do her work and Mr Warner refused to send any person with her to Newcastle.
>
> Mr Warner further states on his former oath that the prisoner was not unwell on the previous day to her absconding and on the previous Saturday, she left the house and was brought back by Constable Moses Carole under the effects of liquor from which she was obliged to keep her bed next morning and most part of the day.
>
> Guilty. Sentenced to undergo Solitary Confinement in the cells at Newcastle for 14 days and to forfeit to the Benevolent Asylum the 4 shillings taken from her person.[43]

Ann had been with Mr Warner for over six months and this was the second occasion he had taken her before the Bench.[44] He returned her to government, and after she served her 14 days she was re-assigned to another employer in Maitland.[45] In October she was in gaol again and, two months after that, yet again.[46] In January 1839 she was returned to government.[47] Some time during 1839 she served a sentence in Newcastle gaol and at the end of it managed to convince the authorities that she was waiting for her husband to collect her. Finally, in September 1839 the Newcastle police magistrate wrote to the colonial secretary asking what he should do with Ann and Susan Whitely (or Farrell), whose husbands had not applied for their release.[48]

The magistrate's question brought to a head one of the perennial problems experienced by the government. The authorities encouraged marriage as a means of reforming women prisoners, but also with the intention of removing the economic burden of their support from its own funds. Husbands were supposed to withdraw their wives promptly after a sentence in gaol or pay their maintenance, but both requirements were often ignored. The governor, Sir George Gipps, decided to enforce the law, and since the relevant Act of Council was uncertain about the Newcastle gaol/factory but precise about the government's power in relation to the Parramatta Factory, he ordered the women down to Parramatta. The colonial secretary asked the magistrate to find the husbands and extract payment for the time their wives had been in gaol since the expiration of their sentences.[49]

The magistrate at Maitland found both Timothy Farrell and John Prentice.[50] Timothy Farrell told the magistrate that his wife had been away from home at least a week, had been found drunk in East Maitland and sent by the bench to gaol. She 'has served me this trick four times before', he said, but he agreed to take her back.[51] John Prentice, however, was adamant he would not have Ann back and the magistrate reported:

> I have ascertained that his wife absconded from him six years ago and, in a fit of despair, he left the colony and resided in Van Diemen's Land from whence he has lately returned. His wife, in the interim, has been repeatedly assigned to private service. He seems resolved not to live with her again and, as he has no property, it would be impossible to recover any penalty that might be imposed.[52]

The governor accepted the inevitable and 'from the misconduct of Ann Simpson' as reported by the magistrate he ordered that she should be detained in the Factory at Parramatta without indulgence of any sort.[53] If Ann, knowing John Prentice had returned to the neighbourhood, had tried to use him, it rebounded on her viciously. She remained in the Factory, but the overcrowding there became critical following the end of transportation and of assigned service. In July 1841 she was issued with a ticket-of-leave for Goulburn and by December 1844, when she received her certificate of freedom, she had worked her way even further afield to Queanbeyan.[54]

Both Ann Cheeseman and Ann Simpson used the system in a way that expressed their resentment of their servitude and their contempt for the authority of magistrates and employers. Ann Cheeseman's career, particularly, demonstrates the kind of perverse control a prisoner could achieve within assigned service. They were strong-willed women who would not be controlled and, as such, deserve sympathy for the conflict this created with a society where subservience, or at least its pretence, was the way to freedom. Their tragedy was their very success was so short-term and so self-defeating. Caught in a spiralling daily battle, they failed to take stock of the future and plan an escape route for their own benefit. As a result they served out every single year of their sentence, where a different behaviour pattern could have resulted in a high level of freedom, even while they were still prisoners.

CHAPTER 15

SURVIVORS AND VICTIMS

Catherine Donoghue and the four Anns — Huldie, Stokes, Cheeseman and Simpson — were among the few women who failed to use the system to their benefit. As early as the end of 1833, 41 of them had taken advantage of the system by marriage or tickets-of-leave and were effectively free. All but a few of these had no further contact with the authorities except on personal matters concerning children and marriage, or obtaining their certificate of freedom.

Marriage of course was open to all single women, regardless of sentence, but early in 1829 Governor Darling established a scale for tickets-of-leave, which brought them too within the reach of all the women and offered a chance for relative freedom to those who could not marry. Female prisoners with sentences of seven years, 14 years and life, were eligible for the tickets at the end of two, three and four years respectively and the key to obtaining them was good behaviour.[1] Eight women from the *Princess Royal* who were on 14 year sentences had tickets-of-leave by 1833, thus reducing their servitude enormously. Among them was Georgiana Baxter, who received hers 'for good conduct in the married state'. Her quick marriage to a free sailor had paid off for her. Along with Mary Ann Taylor, Hannah Solomons and Jane Edwards, who were married and also got tickets, she officially achieved a double freedom. But Ann Bowler and Isabella Errington, who were also on 14 year sentences, could not marry, so their tickets gave them freedom when the alternative path was closed.[2]

Isabella Errington is one of the mysteries of the *Princess Royal*. Forty-eight years old with striking auburn hair and a freckled face, she had been convicted in Newcastle-on-Tyne of receiving stolen goods.[3] She was assigned on arrival to William Hodges, an ex-convict publican in Sydney, and the reason for her ticket in 1832 was specifically described as 'good conduct in service', so she was probably still with him.[4] Thereafter she disappears from the record, never featuring on any other assignment list, never passing through the gaols, never collecting her certificate of freedom. She was not a young woman when she landed in the colony, but there is no record of her death in the subsequent 40 years. When she arrived she declared herself 'the wife of William Errington' but she did not say he was in New South Wales or Van Diemen's Land.[5] Perhaps he was and she went to live with him after she obtained her ticket, or perhaps 'Errington' was an alias and she lived and died under another name. There is one other possibility, but no confirming proof. English records reveal an Isabella Gibson married William Errington in Northumberland in 1807. In New South Wales in 1836 an Isabella Gibson married Henry Bath at the Scots Church, Sydney, and ten years later Isabella Bath died.[6] If this is the same Isabella, she beat the system resoundingly, successfully passing herself off as free when she was not and marrying without the governor's permission and despite her declaration when she landed.

There is no specific explanation as to why only these eight women took advantage of the opportunity to lighten their 14 year sentences through tickets-of-leave. In the first instance they had to apply and it was no doubt a combination of the women's ability to perceive the main chance, and the suggestion of others such as magistrates, husbands, employers or friends, that made them send in their applications. Some women like Susannah knew it was hopeless, because they had colonial convictions of a more serious nature, or a continual pattern of petty misbehaviour.

In the light of the relative freedom which was within her reach, Susannah's shoplifting in Sydney is inexplicable unless it was connected with one of her children. She was not an undisciplined woman, nor was she addicted to drink. Her career as a prisoner could have been vastly different if she had not been burdened by children. Her decision to bring Thomas to New South Wales, understandable as it was, proved to be an error and her easy fertility was a further handicap. But it is unlikely she would have assessed her situation in this way. The wellspring of her adult life was caring for her children and, if she did perceive the disadvantage they were to her, she would have dismissed it from serious consideration. It is difficult to establish how many other women from the *Princess Royal* were similarly burdened with illegitimate children after they arrived in the colony. The casual attitude to baptism that was prevalent, and the different names under which some were christened, make it impossible to prove without the assistance of their descendants. However, the general comments of contemporary observers, the records of large numbers of children who were always in the Factory, and the constant pressure for places in the orphanages, indicate many women prisoners did become pregnant and among them, no doubt, were some from the *Princess Royal*.[7]

By 1839, when Susannah finally got a ticket-of-leave, over a third of her shipmates had officially obtained their certificates of freedom. With one exception, they had all been sentenced to seven years and most had committed no offence which extended their servitude. The exception was Georgiana Baxter, who in 1839 obtained a conditional pardon from her 14 year sentence, which gave her all the rights of a free person so long as she remained in New South Wales.[8] When the women's time expired they simply applied for, and received, the precious document. A few, however, were very casual and applied months or even years later, while others through death, distance, or simply because it no longer mattered to them, never bothered at all to get a formal certificate.

A high percentage of the women from the *Princess Royal* found a new life very quickly after they arrived in the colony. Eighty-one of the 100 were assigned in Sydney when they landed, and as even those returned without complaint went through the gaol on their way to the Factory for reassignment, the Sydney gaol entrance books are a reliable indicator, by omission as much as for those women who do pass through, of their success or failure to settle in the colony. Combined with the somewhat sporadic records of other gaols and benches, with marriage applications and details of tickets-of-leave and certificates of freedom, it is possible to say that 27 per cent of the women found transportation to New South Wales a sufficiently positive experience to immediately change their way of life for the better. They can be traced by marriage, ticket-of-leave and certificate of freedom applications, but they found an incentive to stay out of trouble. The records of another 30 per cent have some kind of charge against them — ranging from a number of minor offences, such as absence without leave, to one major crime such as theft. The evidence indicates their offences were isolated and after marriage (e.g., Charlotte Tither), or when the particular problem vanished (e.g., Hannah Solomons between marriages), they led lives of sufficiently good behaviour, and presumably therefore positive experience, to keep them out of contact with the authorities.[9] On these women's record, if their lives fell to pieces they would have come to the attention of the officials again.

Death removed approximately 15 per cent during the first decade after their arrival. Jane Lyons, Surgeon Wilson's 'unfit object', died the year after she arrived.[10] Mary Bishop, who did not appear on the surgeon's hospital list at all during the voyage, died at the Female Factory hospital in April 1830, aged 41.[11] She had been convicted in Portsmouth of stealing a bed from a house, had two previous offences, but was only sentenced to seven years, which hints at a story of great distress for the elderly widow with six children.[12] The Factory sold her clothes after she died and their description conveys a vivid picture of Mrs Bishop with her hazel eyes and sandy, greying hair:[13]

    One gown
    One petticoat
    One shift
    One shawl
    One pr. stockings
    One pr. shoes
    One handkerchief (old)
    Black Willow Bonnett

By her lights she was well dressed, and her clothes fetched the third highest amount on the list at 15s. 6d.[14]

Susannah Turbitt and Mary Hart, both of whom had married, died in 1832 and 1833 respectively. Jane Bailey, still single, also died in 1833. Mary Hilsley, left destitute and distraught after the transportation of her husband John Godfrey in 1834, returned to Bathurst on a ticket-of-leave, but died in the female factory there in 1837.[15] Harriet Bannister, who lived hard on drink and sex, died in 1833, and Caroline Thomas and Susan King, both heavy drinkers, died in 1837 and 1840 respectively.[16] The tragic quartet of Sarah Quittenton, Louisa Caulfield, Catherine Donoghoe and Elizabeth Foxall, were all dead by 1840.[17]

By 1840 there was only a small core of about 11 women from the *Princess Royal* whose lives were still governed by the convict system. Jane Edwards had lost the ticket-of-leave she received in 1833 through repeated drunkenness. She did not try to marry again after she lost her husband and continued to work as an assigned servant in the Liverpool district. She finally received a second ticket in 1842 and her freedom in 1843. Betty Brian, who lost her 1838 ticket for stealing a child's frock, remained in assigned service until she was granted a second ticket at the end of 1842. Ann Kirby had a blameless early record in the colony and married Thomas Linwood in 1831. After her husband died she tried to marry a man who had a wife in England, and this relationship brought her before the attention of the authorities again. She lost the ticket-of-leave she had received only three months earlier, because of 'highly immoral conduct', and was sent to the Factory.[18] The three women were all free by the beginning of 1844, although Ann Kirby never collected a certificate.[19]

There were only two women with life sentences still actively in the system by 1840. Sarah Bryant had lived through the worst of her troubles in Bathurst, and that year she rejoined her husband John Foley in Sydney. But she was to lose her second ticket-of-leave in 1846 when she absconded from him, and did not receive her pardon until 1853.[20] Martha Turner's marriage to Thomas Buck, which occurred as early as March 1830 and had effectively kept her out of assigned service, had failed by 1837. The following year she lost her ticket for living in a state of adultery. When it was finally restored three years later, she made an attempt to rid herself of the chafing restrictions of her life sentence.[21]

The humble Petition of Martha Turner now Bucks most respectfully sheweth

That your Excellency's Petitioner was tried at the Sessions of Old Bailey in 1828 and having been convicted of House Robbery was sentenced to be transported for Life.

That pursuant to sentence Petitioner arrived in this Colony on the ship Princess Royal in the year 1828 [*sic*]

That very shortly after Petitoner's arrival in this Colony she with the consent of H. M. Government entered into the Holy estate of Matrimony with Thomas Buck, who is still living although Petitioner is in the assigned service of Mrs White of George Street, Sydney

That Petitioner having now been 12 years in the Colony and having endeavoured by good conduct to make some reparation to Society for her
previous offence humbly prays that Your Excellency will be pleased to take
those considerations complete with the accompanying certificate and
recommendations into your humane consideration and mercifully recommend her to Her Majesty for a Conditional Pardon.

Martha Turner now Bucks
Sydney, March 10, 1840[22]

Martha had collected supporting references from two Sydney
merchants William Carter and Alexander Young, from her employer,
from the superintendent of police, and from the Presbyterian minister
Rev. McGarvie. The police magistrate Charles Windeyer certified she
had no record of any conviction in the colony. But the superintendent
of convicts turned up the cancellation of her previous ticket-of-leave
and sent a note to the governor that her request was 'not recommended in consequence of having lived in a state of adultery and the
restoration of her ticket having been so recent. (April 1840).' 'Refused'
the governor noted obediently and Martha was condemned to another
six years servitude as the best years of her life passed her by.[23] In
January 1847, when she was 36 years old, she was finally granted a
conditional pardon.[24]

In 1840 Ann Huldie ended the 11 years she served for her seven year
sentence, but as a free person immediately returned to gaol for larceny.
Johanna Brown married at Port Macquarie in 1840. Ann Cheeseman
was at the height of her manipulation of assignment in the Newcastle
district, and Ann Simpson was in the third class of the Factory. In June
1840, Susannah joined her there.

A brief announcement in the official *Gazette* and a note scrawled on
her ticket-of-leave revealed that Susannah had been sentenced to the
Factory for six months for 'obtaining bread under false pretences'. Her
hard-won ticket was also cancelled.[25] The high hopes she held when
she returned to Parramatta with the children had come crashing down.
There are no details at all to shed light on this offence, the reason for it,
or the circumstances in which it occurred. It can only be speculation
that either the relationship with Mrs Blake, who ran the bakery, failed,
or Susannah simply could not earn enough to support herself and the
children. Increased immigration, and an economy that would turn into
a full-scale depression two years later, had made it more difficult than
ever for female ticket-of-leave holders to find work and Susannah was
not alone in her failure to support her children. Three months later a
magistrate tried to help a woman in a similar situation, although she
had only one child. But the government took a hard line and refused to
admit her child into the orphanage. The woman lost her ticket-of-
leave and both she and her child were returned to the Factory for
assignment.[26] Charles was now ten and it would be in character for
Susannah to have found a job for him when they settled in the town.
Neither he nor John reappear in the orphan school records so presumably they stayed in Parramatta when she returned to the Factory.
Agnes, who was not quite three, went with Susannah and the danger

of losing her to the orphanage then arose.

While Susannah was in the Factory, the transportation of convicts to New South Wales officially ended, and in November 1840, the last ship unloaded its cargo of male prisoners at Sydney.[27] The colony had received 80,440 prisoners, of whom only 12,460 were women.[28] Transportation to Van Diemen's Land did not end for another 12 years and it was 1867 before the last convict ship sailed for Western Australia, closing a chapter in the country's history.[29] In total 163,021 prisoners were sent to Australia, including 24,960 women.[30]

What happened to Susannah at this point, is very uncertain. The assignment of prisoners took some time to fade out and the Female Factory was more overcrowded than it had ever been. Her sentence expired at the end of 1840, but it is unknown whether, encumbered by Agnes and possibly John, she managed to get herself a place again before the assignment of women prisoners to Sydney ceased four months later in April 1841, and to other parts of the colony, including Parramatta, in December.[31] One result of the end of assignment was that employers and their female servants became much more careful to preserve their working relationship, because now, if a woman was sent to the Factory, she did not return to her master and in fact could not get out of the institution.[32] The Factory overcrowding continued to increase and in July 1842 reached a peak of 1,203 inmates in a building originally designed to house 300.[33] Governor Gipps began to authorise more and more tickets-of-leave, but finding the women who received them could not survive economically and were constantly returning to the Factory, he then introduced a form of modified assignment, whereby women were placed in service, but for wages.[34] This paid assignment came into effect in February 1843.[35] Susannah never received a second ticket-of-leave and there is evidence she was out of the Factory before paid assignment was introduced, so, on balance, it appears she left the Factory at the beginning of 1841 after her sentence ended.

What difficulties she endured during the following year can only be imagined. But it culminated in tragedy when, on 4 January 1842, four-year-old Agnes died at the Parramatta hospital.[36] Poor Susannah had to cope with the loss of the little girl who had provided some consolation for her lost daughters in England. Twelve months later she took steps to ensure greater security for herself and the boys.

On 21 January 1843 Susannah married a 46-year-old ex-convict named William Woollard. They were married in the Presbyterian Church at Parramatta in the presence of their employers, Miss Ann Blair and Mr Ewebank Lough.[37]

Susannah was still a prisoner and it would have been necessary for her to obtain the governor's permission. As the application has not survived, there is no direct evidence of the grounds she used. However, there are two possibilities. Two years earlier the solicitor general had stated the government's position in a case of a man who had declared 'married' on arrival. He referred to Act Geo. IV, C31 s22, which 'provides for second marriages after 7 years have elapsed without the parties having intercourse'. But he added 'the party marries at his peril and the Governor's sanction is no protection for the man, if it turns out his first wife is living and he had any reason to believe that'.[38] Susannah's application to marry may well have been approved on these grounds. The second and more likely possibility is simply that, her reputation as John Clarke's wife being sufficiently well known to the residents of Parramatta, she could establish she was a 'widow' when he died.[39]

The protection of a man again transformed Susannah's situation, as it had done for so many others. William was a short man, with greying hair and a dark complexion, who had been in the colony for over 20 years. Born in Essex, he was tried there in 1820 and was sentenced to transportation for life.[40] Working as a gardener and labourer in the rural districts of the colony for most of his sentence, he received a conditional pardon in 1842.[41] He settled in Pennant Hills, in the Parish of Marsfield outside Parramatta and continued to earn his living as a gardener.

In July 1844 Susannah obtained her certificate of freedom,[42] sixteen years after the day, in April 1828, when she had stood in the court at Nottingham and told the judge she could not bear to see her children starving. She had survived all her setbacks and had indeed come out ahead. The children, who proved such a burden, now consisted of two strongly growing sons, who provided her with an Australian family.

The family lived in Pennant Hills throughout the 1840s, during which time Charles was apprenticed and learned the trade of a printer.[43] In July 1849 William died, but his death could no longer place the family in jeopardy.[44] Charles was nearly 20 and employed as a printer and journalist. John was 14 and capable of earning a living. With Susannah's own energy and needlework skills, they could at last take care of themselves.

Some of Susannah's shipmates were not so fortunate. Unlike Susannah, freedom did not mean the end of their troubles.

The Welsh dairymaid, Ann Morgan, who had married Private Patrick McMahon in 1830, ended her seven year sentence in May 1835. Over the following six years she was regularly in Sydney gaol until she could raise the bail to get out again. There are no details of her crimes, but the records indicate her husband was still alive.[45] Martha Clare, who had married Thomas Brothers at Bathurst in 1830, was sent down to the Factory at Parramatta with Margaret Mahoney after they were both free, described as 'bad characters'. Martha was sentenced to six months in 1839 for escaping from the factory in Bathurst and 'for being a rogue and a vagabond'.[46] Her problem was drink. She had been convicted many times in the town and was obviously motivated by a sense of resentment towards one of her targets, as the following case from February 1836 demonstrates:[47]

Mr William Boyler being duly sworn states: I am residing on Bathurst Plains. On Friday last, the prisoner came to my dwelling house in a state of intoxication and commenced a volley of abuse towards me in a most . . . [il-

legible] manner, which has been repeatedly the case.
    28 days cells on bread and water.[48]

At the end of her 1839 sentence Martha returned to live with her husband at Kelso near Bathurst. He died in 1842, but she lived on in the town until her death in 1851.[49]

In 1841 Catherine Steele suddenly regressed and was sent to the Factory for four months for larceny. Sarah Clark, who had a steady marriage to baker Richard Turton and a virtually trouble-free servitude, received a conditional pardon in 1840 but was charged with perjury by the supreme court in July 1842. The result is not clear, but she was apparently released on a bond to be of good behaviour.[50] Margaret Coffin was in trouble in 1842 as well, but it no longer mattered to her. In September the government cancelled the ticket-of-leave it had just dispatched for her to the bench at Hunter River. The reason was her absence from the district. Unknown to the authorities Margaret had slipped down to Liverpool the previous year. It is probably no coincidence that this was the location of the orphan school, and perhaps she went to try and find out what had happened to James, who had in fact been apprenticed in Sydney some years earlier. While in Liverpool she fell ill, and on 1 October 1841 she died there. She was still a prisoner and the clergyman carefully noted she came 'per ship Princess Royal'.[51] But nobody made the connection when she failed to collect her ticket-of-leave and it is possible James never knew what happened to his mother.

Mary Wheat, who successfully persuaded Governor Bourke to let her marry John Tiffin, had received her certificate of freedom in 1835. But her husband died in 1838 and Mary's life again became a struggle to survive. She was in gaol at the end of 1840, she was sent to the Factory for an unknown offence, in late 1846 and in March 1847 she was in gaol again, and while there was accused of stealing from another prisoner. At her conviction in England Mary was described as having 'an incorrigible propensity to spirituous liquors', but there is insufficient evidence to establish whether drink was her undoing in New South Wales.[52] What is certain is that freedom in a new land had brought little change to her life and circumstances. Transportation had produced nothing but the devastating wrench of separation from her two young children in England.

Little Mary Smith, 'the 3rd', who travelled from Nottingham with Susannah, was one of the saddest figures in the long years of her 'freedom'. Like Johanna Brown she was one of life's victims, was pulverised by the system and by society in general and was never able to get on top of her circumstances. As late as 1856 she was in gaol for three months in Newcastle.[53]

Ann Kinsman, by contrast, began life as a strong character betrayed by drink. Her marriage in New South Wales and the beatings she received from her husband, damaged her physically and no doubt mentally as well. The psychological persecution continued when she and her lover were tried before the Maitland quarter sessions for stealing pigs, although on this occasion she was found not guilty. Her husband John Hoskins died in 1838 at Maitland and her lover Richard Holland apparently in 1840 at Bathurst, but whether this latter relationship had survived and Ann was with him is unknown. In May 1846 she married a man named Phillip Field at Clarence Town, northeast of Maitland.[54] Seven years later they were living in nearby Dungog and on 22 March 1853 Ann was brought before the Bench there:

> Ann Field, alias Hoskins, Freed.
> Charged by Constable Conway with wandering about without having any visible means of support, contrary to the Act of 13 Vic. No. 46 s.3 Convicted on the 2nd section, 15 Vic. No. 4 and sentenced to be sent to Maitland Gaol as a place of safety and correction for 40 days and her husband meanwhile to pay the expence of conveying her to gaol, to which he consents.[55]

The tragedy behind this cold and formal summary is devastating. The once proud Cornish farmgirl, who told her prosecutor in Dorset his soul was lost forever, had been ground right down. Although still described as strongly built, her ruddy, freckled complexion had turned sallow, her brown hair was mixed with grey and she had acquired a distinctive scar across the bridge of her nose. She was sent to Maitland gaol, where the 40 days 'in a place of safety and correction' somehow transformed into '40 days hard labour'.[56]

At the end of her 40 days, they sent her down to Sydney to the Tarban Creek lunatic asylum, where she was admitted as a pauper suffering from mania with delusions.[57] She lingered on, and when Tarban Creek closed she was transferred with other patients to the Female Factory. The once infamous building had now become an asylum for the destitute paupers who had long ago outraged society by their bawdy, recalcitrant behaviour. In 1861 Ann finally died a lonely death in the old building which had once been the heartbeat of the female convicts' ordeal.[58]

As Ann moved towards her end, other women were coming in from the far corners of the colony. Some of them were surprising survivors. Mary or Martha Gregory, 'the wife of John Gregory' as she stated on arrival, showed up at the Benevolent Asylum in 1854. She had been among the older women on the *Princess Royal*, aged 38 when she was transported. Her life as a prisoner had been unspectacular, but interspersed with regular offences for drunkenness, and when she entered the protection of the Benevolent Asylum she was infirm and destitute.[59] She was joined there only two months later by one of her original shipmates, Ann Maw, who was aged 40 when they sailed. Both were married in England and left children behind and there are no identifiable records which indicate either remarried in New South Wales.[60] Perhaps age had given these two some resilience or endurance which helped them to cope with life as prisoners, though an uncharitable observer would probably describe them as 'two old boilers'. Ann died in the asylum in 1858 and Mary, who had left but returned again, followed two years later in 1861.[61]

In January 1860 Rev. Sowerby performed one last service for Mary

Palmer, when he recommended her admission into the Benevolent Asylum. Mary and William Hickmott had spent some of their last years together in the goldfields town of Bells Creek, not far from Braidwood. William died there in March 1853 and by 1860 Mary, who was 67, was blind and destitute and could no longer cope alone. She turned to her old mentor and he responded as he had done for her so positively before. Mary died at the Hyde Park Asylum in October 1863.[62]

Nine months after Mary entered the asylum she was joined by Ann Simpson, who was suffering badly from dysentery. Ann was by now 51 years of age and a far cry from the 17-year-old who connived with Ann Cheeseman to seduce and rob a man in Hull. There is an indication that she married again in Goulburn after she obtained her ticket-of-leave for that district in 1841, although her husband John Prentice was still alive in Maitland. Perhaps the clerks checked the records and found she had declared 'single' on arrival. In any event, the governor gave his consent to the marriage of an Ann Simpson to John Stone in 1842 and the ceremony was performed by the Goulburn clergyman Rev. Sowerby.[63] But 18 years later Ann had not changed. In the space of two years in Sydney, she used three different clergymen to gain admission to the benevolent asylum four times. As death approached she began to use her real name, Jane Spencer, for the first time since she arrived in the colony, but she was still tellingly identified by 'ship Princess Royal'.[64] She finally died in the asylum in 1867 and the authorities compromised and registered her death as Jane Simpson.[65]

Those women from the *Princess Royal* who died a sad and lonely death in an institution, still linked to their convict days by their ship of arrival, were far outnumbered by those who died among their families, in most cases with no indication of the reason for their presence in the colony. A few can be traced.

In 1860, seven years after she received her conditional pardon, Sarah Bryant was finally free in every sense of the word. In July her husband John Foley died at their home at Diamond Swamp, Binda, near Goulburn.[66] Barely a year later, Sarah married a settler named Francis Tunnicliff and her daughter, Margaret, now married herself, was a witness at the wedding.[67] Sarah had nearly 20 years of a new life before she died, amongst her family, in 1879.[68]

Mary Ann Taylor remarried after Joseph Giles died in 1847 at Denham Court near Liverpool.[69] Sarah Hazel and her husband, the butcher James Lake, moved from Parramatta and had been living in the country town of Scone for over ten years when Sarah died there in 1853.[70] Ann Clark never put a foot wrong from the day she landed and was assigned to her fellow passengers Mr and Mrs Baldie. She had declared herself single to the muster clerks, but her husband George Phillips recorded on her death certificate that her parents' name was Birchell. He had been 'married' 22 years to Ann when she died in 1856.[71] Elizabeth Jones outlived her husband John Potter, and it was their 24-year-old son who recorded her death aged 46 in November 1857.[72] Mary Fagan's husband, James Lockwood, died in 1860 and some time in the subsequent 13 years Mary succumbed to melancholia. Her children arranged for her to enter the Gladesville mental hospital and she died there aged 61 in 1873.[73] The turbulent teenage years of the girl who left Liverpool aged only 17 must have seemed very remote after more than 40 years in New South Wales. Mary Tilley, the wife of policeman Gregory Howe, died in Parramatta in 1847, and although she was free the clergyman noted she had come to the colony by the *Princess Royal*. Jane Isabella Mason, née McPherson, can be positively identified by her christian names. She died in 1856, proudly described as 'the wife of a shopkeeper'.[74] The young thief from Surrey had found herself a stake in the community of New South Wales. Ann Bowler, armed with her absolute pardon, may have returned to England. There is no evidence to prove it, but there is no record of her death or remarriage in New South Wales for the subsequent 40 years. The end of the story for many who turned their transportation into success is lost in uncertainty. Only their descendants can positively reveal how their lives ended, can prove the connection between a great-grandmother and a young convict who arrived on the *Princess Royal*. Susannah's story, however, can be followed to her final destiny.

As many of her shipmates neared their end, Susannah was about to begin a new life. Shortly after William Woollard's death in July 1849, she married again. On 26 March 1851 Susannah Woollard, widow of the Field of Mars, married John Jones, widower of Castle Hill, at St Andrew's Church, Parramatta.[75] Her timing was coincidentally superb. Two months later the colony was galvanised by the discovery of gold and Susannah's marriage left both her sons free to join the rush to the goldfields. By the time she was widowed again, five years later, they were established in the Braidwood district, 150 miles inland. Concerned for Susannah's safety alone in Parramatta, they insisted she should join them.[76] So at the age of 62, she set out on a new journey.

AN AFFECTIONATE
MOTHER

On 28 June 1857 Susannah Watson wrote from Braidwood to her daughter, Hannah, in England:

My dear daughter,

You will be Surprised at not hearing from [me] Before this but I did not Receive your Letter till the 4th of this Month though it was Lying in Sydney post Office since January Last   the reason I have Left Sydney and Gone Two Hundred Miles Further up the Country to a place called Braidwood your Brothers did not Like me being their by myself and sent for me up Last August to be with them as they have a Little property their   Dear Hannah I am sorry to hear that you have been so ill and so bad off I gave your Letter to your Brothers and they Both Desired me to tell you to answer has [as] quick as possible the Mails are a very short Time Coming Now and let me know Wether you would Like to Come out with your Children to be with me and if you do they will pay the Deposit money for your passage   you must send the age of your children   I have been to the Court House about it   Dear Hannah I should have sent you some Money but we Cannot send lefs than Five pounds and that we Must get a Check from one of the Banks in Sydney as our Notes wont pafs in England   But send as soon has you Can and I will get one up and send in my Next Letter if God spares me — I am pretty well in Health Thank God for [it] and very Comfortable.   I live in one of Charles Cottages with a fine peice of Land to it and Nothing to do but mind my poultry and...their things...   I want for Nothing that they can get for me only very Lonely as i am mostly by myself as they work some miles from me   they are builders   but sometimes i dont see them but once a Fortnight   thiere Obliged to Come then to their Lodge as they Both Belong to the Grand United Order of Odd Fellows and Friendly Brothers   Dear Hannah you Must Make your Mind up at Once and Let me know   I should wish very Much for you to Come   we see some accounts how bad of [off] they are in England   we take the papers twice a week   this is a most plentifull I may say since its been Made Free a Extravagant Country   things are plentifull   plenty of work but short of people to do it   Wages is very high   a Labouring Man wont star [start] less than 10s a day your Brothers

Gives 10s a day to their Man or 1.10 a week and find them Board and
Lodging a woman to wash Gets 5 shillings a dozen and Needlework is very
high   i Earns a Good deal myself a Making Sun Bonnets your brothers dont
want me to do it but it amuses me and keeps me in pocket Money the
Reason work is so high in this part — its the Market Town for the Southern
Diggins   the Araluen diggins is only 14 miles from me the Majors Creek 12
and the Little River diggins 7 miles, where your Brothers are Building   Dear
Hannah I am very sorry that there should be any uneasyness between your
Father and Sister and am also sorry that they did not wish to hear From
me   your Father always was a kind husband to me the only fault I [had?] to
Find was Following that Cursed poaching which was the Cause of my being
sent away but only for. . . [you?] Children it was the Best thing Befell me   it
would [have] been well for him to have followed me.
S. Watson

Direct for me to care of Charles Isaac Watson, Braidwood, New South
Wales[1]

Susannah was nearly 63 when she wrote this letter, active, independent, taking a lively interest in the world around her, and keeping
track of conditions in England. No earlier correspondence has survived,
but how many letters she must have written in the nearly 30 years
which had passed since she left England. Letters asking about the
welfare of the children. Letters trying to persuade Edward to come to
New South Wales and bring the children to the greater opportunities
she saw there. She had obviously written before to tell the family
about their Australian brothers, but there is no real indication whether
she ever got an answer. Did she get news of the family from their Aunt
Mary, or did she just stop writing into a vacuum. Hannah was 10 when
Susannah left England. She was old enough to remember and old
enough to have learnt from her mother how to read and write, unlike
Mary Ann, who was only six years old in 1828. Perhaps Hannah did
reply to an earlier letter, even though her father disapproved, but there
is something about the details of Susannah's answer in 1857, particularly towards the end, which indicate this was the first letter she
had received from her family. In despair, Hannah turned to her mother
for comfort across thousands of miles and Susannah responded with
loving generosity.

As the months passed Susannah must have waited with anxious
excitement, making plans for her daughter, checking at the post office
to see if a letter had arrived. But it never came. And it was ten years
before Susannah learned that Hannah was dead.

The family were all still living in Bulwell. Hannah was at Joiners Hill
in the village when she died on 25 August 1860.[2] She would have
received Susannah's letter, but it was too late for her to take the
opportunity it offered. Her exact circumstances are unknown, but it
appears she had formed a long-term *de facto* relationship when she was
15 with Emmanuel Birkin, by whom she had six or seven children.[3]
She was ill and in a desperate situation when she wrote to Susannah so
it is likely Emmanuel had died. Her address indicates she may have
been living with his relatives.[4]

Mary Ann was 35 in 1857. When she was 22 she had married Reuben Povey, a framework knitter of Radford.[5] They had a son, Edwin, before Reuben died of typhus less than four years after their marriage.[6] Mary Ann returned to Bulwell and a year later married another framework knitter, William Kirk.[7] When Susannah wrote in 1857 they were living in Main Street, Bulwell, with young Edwin Povey now ten years old and their daughter, Sarah, aged nearly three. Living with them was Edward Watson.[8]

There is an indication, but no proof, that Edward may have 'remarried' in 1838.[9] He didn't have to petition or argue with His Excellency the governor for permission to commit bigamy, but by 1857 he was 'widowed' again. He was 73 years old and cantankerous, which may have led to Hannah's description of the 'uneasyness' between her father and sister. In later life Edward had earned his living as a cotton glove maker and this was his given occupation when he died, aged 75, on 26 November 1859.[10]

His real widow was still flourishing across the ocean in Braidwood. The Australian family was doing well. But Charles and John had not struck great quantities of gold. As thousands flocked to the goldfields and the elusive nuggets became harder and harder to find, Charles had the sense to change course. One observer commented:

> There was no newspaper printed in Braidwood and there was a digger in Araluen by the name of Charley Watson, who was a tinsmith by trade, and who also had a knowledge of printing. As Watson was not very successful on the diggins, he made up his mind that he would go to Braidwood and start business as a newspaper proprietor. So he accordingly had a printing plant sent up from Sydney and started a paper, which I think he called the *Braidwood Observer*. Thus Charles Isaac Watson was always ever after styled father of the Press in Braidwood.[11]

The newspaper Charles founded about 1854 was not the 'Observer' but the *Braidwood Dispatch*. A natural entrepreneur, he kept it for only two years, then sold it and turned to building houses in partnership with John.[12] When the population growth slowed and the town began to consolidate, he turned again, and in 1859 began his second newspaper, the *Braidwood Daily News*.[13]

Susannah meanwhile, had settled in. When Charles set up the *News* he was permanently close at hand, and as he was still a bachelor she kept house for him. John, however, was moving on. Over the next ten years he covered hundreds of miles as he followed the lure of gold across New South Wales.

Susannah became a member of the Anglican parish of St Andrew's and met an old acquaintance from Parramatta, Rev. James Allen, who became the rector of Braidwood in 1845 after he left the Presbyterian Church and converted to the Church of England.[14] Rev. Allen must have had all the fervour of a convert and there was no one more receptive to his ministrations than the ex-prisoners with their colourful and disreputable pasts. Under his influence, and no doubt with the increasing confrontation of old age, Susannah's faith in God became a major tenet of her life. She had never been God-less. With an eighteenth-century working-class acceptance of *de facto* relationships and illegitimate children, she had nevertheless married in the church when possible. And unlike many of her generation, she had also taken care that each of her children was baptised.

Through the church, and also through the Grand United Order of Oddfellows, Susannah and Charles became friendly with the parish clerk, John Boden Yeates, and his family. Like Susannah, John Yeates was an ex-convict. He had been caught pickpocketing in Fleet Street and was sentenced to seven years transportation in 1837.[15] Only 25 years old and single, he had been assigned straight off the ship to the Braidwood district where he worked for a ship's surgeon turned landholder, Dr Robert Huntley, at his property Farringdon.[16] John's life as a prisoner had none of the fierce struggles to survive that Susannah experienced. A year after his arrival he married Mary Driscoll, an Irish immigrant servant of the Huntleys, and they settled down to raise a large family.[17] A shoemaker by trade, he had his own business in Braidwood when Susannah and Charles met him and the influence of his wife Mary and Rev. James Allen had combined to turn the carefree London thief into a pillar of moral rectitude and religious faith.[18]

Life in Braidwood for Susannah was comfortable, lively and enjoyable. Thousands of people were still coming into or passing through the district. The town was growing and its activities were increasing. Charles was an active and vocal member of the community, involved in balls and race meetings, serving on the hospital committee, attending his Lodge meetings.[19] Through his many activities, Susannah acquired a little status, which at times was probably an uncomfortable glory. Charles fought vehemently against any injustice, particularly to the working man, and in the process made a number of enemies.[20] She no doubt lived quietly in the background and confined herself to church activities and the companionship of the friends she had made. In 1861 Charles married John Yeates' eldest daughter, Eliza, and Susannah soon had two Australian grandchildren, young Charles and Walter, to bring a new interest into her life.[21]

In 1867, out of the blue, came another letter from England. This time it was written by Mary Ann — or rather written for her, since she had never learned to write. Susannah responded promptly, but now she too needed someone else to do the actual writing for her.

Dear Daughter,
I received your most welcome letter, and should have answered it much sooner if [it] had not been for the inclemency of the weather, it being winter time with us here in Australia, and all mail communication between Braidwood and Sydney being stopped. The former place you must remember is distant from Sydney 200 miles.

You cannot imagine how happy I was to receive a letter from you, dear daughter, not having heard from you [*sic*] for ten years. My son Charles, who has been proprietor of a newspaper in Braidwood for about nine years, where he has, I am sorry to say, met with great loss, he has removed from

Braidwood to a place called Shoalhaven, which is 90 miles from Braidwood, and the same distance nearer to Sydney. I am still living in Braidwood having been prevented from joining Charles at Shoalhaven owing to the great prevalence of floods, of which there has been a great many this winter. To give you an idea of what an Australian flood is, I may tell you that whole towns have been under water and that a boat could be rowed for 20 miles across the bush. I hope with God's permission soon to be able to join him. Both your brothers are married and have two children each. I wish you would let me know if grandfather [your father?] Edward Watson is living, or if dead when he died; have you heard from your brother Samuel, whether he is dead or alive. I also wish you would tell me whether you have heard of Aunt Mary and how she is getting on. I send you a photograph of myself. Perhaps you will be able to recognise your poor old mother, who is now in her seventy-third year. I enjoy very fair health, thank God, but my eyesight is not very good. I hope you are all quite well. When you write again dear daughter, you must let me know how all my old friends are (if there are any alive).

I must now conclude, dear daughter, I hope, with the blessing of God, to be able to write you a longer letter next time (if you answer this). Give my love to your husband, and children, and accept my most sincere love and blessing dear daughter. God bless you all.

I am, dear daughter, Your affectionate Mother...Susannah Watson[22]

Mary Ann's letters have not survived, so it is impossible to know what prompted her to write so unexpectedly. It may have been simply that, having reached the age of 44, she had matured sufficiently to forgive her mother's 'desertion'. In the ten years which elapsed since her mother heard news from Hannah, Mary Ann had experienced her own share of tragedy. Following the loss of her father and sister, her second husband had died, leaving her pregnant with his son.[23] But she was remarried, almost immediately, to yet another framework knitter, a 54-year-old widower named Abraham Birks.[24] Abraham lived at Joiners Hill, Bulwell, and may well have been a relative of Emmanuel Birkin, Hannah's 'husband'. Mary Ann's letter arrived in Braidwood just in time to reach Susannah before she moved.

What caused Charles's 'great loss' is unknown, but he was often sued for libel by upright members of the community who felt insulted through the columns of his newspaper and perhaps one of them obtained a heavy verdict. However, his wife Eliza always maintained to her family that they moved because bushrangers made the Braidwood district too dangerous.[25] Charles kept the *Braidwood News* and founded another paper, the *Shoalhaven News*, based at the township of Terara beside the banks of the Shoalhaven River on the New South Wales south coast.[26] Susannah joined the family there towards the end of 1867. On 29 December 1868 she wrote again to Mary Ann:

My dear and affectionate daughter.

I received your ever welcome and affectionate letter and indeed I cannot tell you how glad I was to hear from one of my dear children so many thousands of miles away from me. Dear daughter, you cannot tell what happiness it gave me to receive your dear likeness. To think that I should live to gaze on that dear face again, although so altered since I parted from you all.

Although I am now turned 74 years of age, it is the wonder of every person how active I am. I have not enjoyed very good health of late owing to my knee cap being split and at the change of weather I cannot bear to stand on it the pain is so great, but God is good to all who put their trust in him.

The person you speak of, Charles Berkin, did not come to Sydney. He went to Van Demons [sic] land, that is a week's sail from Sydney. Some time after his wife came, expecting to meet him in Sydney with her son. She then applied to a Mrs Hanell, late of Bulwell, whose husband had some influence with the Government, through him ascertained he was in Hobartown, and working with a shoemaker, and by the very excellent character he bore, the Government intended to send his wife and child by the first vessel to him. But while she was waiting in Sydney for a vessel, she took sick and died, but Mrs Hanell fitted the boy out and put him under the charge of the Captain, and sent him to his father, and that is the last I have heard as I have not seen Mrs Hanell for many years.

Dear daughter, your husband's father and mother I know well, although he must have been quite a boy when I left, and thank God you are so happy. Your brother John I have not seen for nearly 4 years. He is married and got three children, but I have not seen one of them, he being so many hundreds of miles away. Your brother Charles lives close to me and has got three children, the first and only one of my grandchildren I have seen. He pays my rent and helps me all he can. I have no more to say this time. Hoping you will be spared to receive this letter. Remember me to William and Charlotte Berkin, hoping they are well. Give my kind love to your husband and kiss all my dear grandchildren for me, and accept the same from your widowed mother.

S. Watson

Write as soon as you can, as I don't expect God will spare me much longer and address the same as before.

Mary Ann answered this warm letter almost immediately, but this time it was Susannah who delayed replying. She was suffering from the injury to her kneecap, which caused her great pain and increasingly incapacitated her. The accident had happened in Braidwood in June 1867 when Susannah had fallen into a posthole. The knee was shattered but, characteristically, she made light of it and ignored the advice of friends that she should go to a doctor in Sydney.[27] During her first year at Terara, she spent three months confined to a sofa. The enforced idleness irked her, but she tried to make the best of it, writing:

> I have felt it very wearisome, lying here so long after having been used to such an active life, but the winter has been very mild and the weather is delightful at present with rather an early spring, which makes matters more cheerful.[28]

But the weather was the nemesis of the residents of Terara and nine months later it wreaked havoc on the small township. The settlers of the Shoalhaven plains were still discovering the boundaries nature set for them, floods being a recurring danger. But the rain of April 1870 produced the greatest flood of all and the damage to Terara was devastating.[29] An observer, possibly Charles, reported:

The spot where once stood the post office, the telegraph office, the steam company's store and wharf, where all was life, business and activity, is now one vast and vacant blank, and forms part of the Shoalhaven River. The streets are turned into innumerable gullies, sand banks and creeks, fences are washed away, and the formation of the town completely destroyed.[30]

Susannah and the family escaped with their lives, but their home and business were ruined and many treasured personal possessions were washed away. Eliza Watson managed to save the photographs of her dead parents, and Susannah salvaged her precious certificate of freedom, although it was tattered and stained by muddy water.[31] In the months that followed, more heavy rain and floods compounded their problems. Charles, the eternal optimist, made plans to rebuild, but he was struggling financially and burdened by a growing young family. Susannah was now increasingly an invalid and they decided she should live with John, who was a widower with two young children. He moved from Bathurst to Queanbeyan, and once Susannah had settled into her new life with him she wrote to Mary Ann.

My dear daughter,
   I have been looking for a letter from you for a long time and should be so glad to hear from you once more before I die, which I think will not be long . . . for I must tell you that I have been quite an invalid for two years and unable to put my foot to the ground and now I feel that it is going into my body. The Lord only knows how long I have to remain in this state of suffering, but it cannot be very long, so do my dear child write to me as soon as you get this, perhaps I may get it.
   We had a great deal of rain and heavy floods all last winter before I left Terrara and nineteen houses were washed away. Your brother Charles lost a great deal and was left very poor. John came over to Queanbeyan and I followed him with my bad knee five hundred miles by land and water, but it was too much for me at my great age. I had the bronchitis afterwards, which brought me very near death's door, but God in his mercy spared my life. We have a nice little cottage close to the town and John gets about as much work as he can do. I have his two little motherless children, Henry aged seven and Alice five years. Charles wife has four children living but has lost some. I should be so glad if you would send me Sarah's likeness. I should like to see it so much and John would like to have it. I have not heard of James Elliot as Launceston is nearly a week's sail from Sydney and we are living over two hundred miles from Sydney. Be sure and write to me as soon as you get this and believe me
   Your ever affectionate mother,
   Susannah Watson[32]

Strangely, Susannah doesn't mention that John had remarried only a few weeks before.[33] Perhaps she succumbed to the very human urge to make herself sound needed and important. On the evidence of later letters, she and John's new wife, who was also named Susannah, co-existed peaceably enough in what was probably a very small house. She dictated the letter, so the other possibility is that the date is wrong or a sentence missed out.

John was working as a baker, a trade he had followed earlier when he was living in Wellington near Bathurst. But he was a jack of all

trades and turned his hand to many different ways of earning a living
as opportunity offered or circumstances demanded.[34] They lived
contentedly in Queanbeyan for the next four years and Susannah
continued her correspondence with Mary Ann.

In February 1872 she was delighted to receive a letter and a
photograph from her English grand-daughter, Sarah. She responded,
signing herself 'your affectionate "Grannie"', and sent a letter at the
same time to Mary Ann.

> My dear,
>   Many thanks for your joint letter, which I received some time ago. I was
> indeed glad to hear from you, but I should have liked to have had better
> news of you. I was truly sorry that you had been ill so long and sincerely
> trust by this time you have quite recovered your health, which is the
> greatest of all blessings.
>   I am still alive you will find, but a great sufferer still with my leg and I fear
> without any relief until God pleases to remove me to himself, which I pray
> may be soon. It is a dreadful thing to feel so helpless and a burden to
> everybody, but it is my lot and I must try to bear it patiently for Jesus sake,
> who has borne so much for me. My little grandchildren are a great comfort
> to me and I have many reasons to be thankful. God grant I may be so. The
> children say they hope to see you and all their relations some day and they
> send their love to 'Auntie'. I hope you will get the Carte de Visite safely and
> trusting this will find you all well and with love from all relations here to all
> at Home, I remain my dear Mary Anne,
>   Your loving mother... Watson
>   We are all well here and hope you are all the same. Write as soon as you
> receive this and let me know you have received this — God bless you.[35]

She kept remembering things she wanted to say and before this letter
was posted she put in another note asking what had become of
Hannah's children 'as it is a very long time since I have heard anything
of them'.[36] On 7 November she wrote again:

> My dear daughter,
>   Your very welcome letter of May 28th came safely. I am glad indeed to
> know of your welfare. I am sorry you have been ill, but hope you are better
> now.
>   I could not get Charles's likeness to send you this time as there is no artist
> where he lives, but I have sent you one of his houses. He is sitting down
> reading the proof sheet of his paper (called the 'Shoalhaven News'). The
> apprentice stands behind him holding the roller. Little Charley, with white
> trowsers, stands in front. The woman in the doorway is your brother's wife's
> sister and her husband standing by the porch. They were well the last I
> heard. I shall be glad to have Edward's likeness. I hope Sarah is still doing
> well. You must give her my best love and hope she will write to me. But my
> dear daughter, you must never expect to see me again in this world. I am
> quite a cripple now and much too old to think of crossing the water again.
> My sight too is failing very much, so that I cannot see to write but have to
> get a young lady who comes to see me to do it. I have just completed my
> seventy eighth (78) year. How good has God been to me all my life long.
> Though he sends trouble and affliction, he cheers us with the light of his
> presence and give us a hope of heaven through the merits of our precious
> Redeemer. God in mercy grant that you and me, with those we love, may

know what it is to have our sins forgiven, to love the Saviour who died to save us, that when we have done with the toil and trouble of this life we may enter in by the gate into the heavenly city.

If you want to know your age, your birthday was in January 19th, 1822.

We have had rather a severe winter this year, but the weather is lovely now and a prospect of an abundant harvest in our part. There is great excitement with the gold, zinc and copper mines. Some are making money at them, but many are not. Johnny gets a fair share of work, but so often suffers from lumbago. I hope you will write soon and let me know how you are all getting on. Johnny sends his love and accept much from,

Your affectionate mother,
Susannah Watson

Old age was creeping up, but Susannah's reflections were philosophic rather than painful. The confused forgetfulness of old age, however, resulted in Mary Ann being given a birth date which was a year out. It is also difficult to know whether the reference to 'Edward's likeness' should have been Mary Ann's son Edwin, or is in fact Susannah's own son Edward, whose fate is never mentioned. But Susannah, the great survivor, was not done yet, and the letters continued with increasing frequency. In the new year of 1873 Mary Ann wrote to tell her that her son, Samuel Wright Bidy, was in Australia. Susannah responded:

I have heard nothing whatever of your brother, Samul. Altho' we may both be in Australia, we may be as far [apart], as if in different countries from the wide extent of the territory. I am glad to hear such a good account of all your family — tell them something about their Grandmother and don't let them forget her: for she preserves a lively remembrance of all who were dear to her at Home. John is most industrious and is now clearing his way and getting on pretty well, but he has to work very hard as the children are rather small to earn much yet and his wife is only now recovering from a severe attack of rheumatism, which confined her for several months. Our good pastor never forgets me and sends his Buggie [sic] to bring me to Church on Sacrament Sunday, whenever I am able to attend. We have lately had an assistant Minister ordained for Queanbeyan, a Mr Evans from Oxford College, where he graduated. In this far away humble little spot, it is a great thing to have two clergymen as in so many places they are without the blessing of even one and a lady friend of mine, who has lately returned from Queensland, and was situated on a fine station, where they were 180 miles away from a church, a clergyman, or a doctor. She went up to be with her only daughter in her first confinement and had to do everything herself, there was only one white resident on the station and she just did the washing. All however went prosperously and by the good hand from God upon them, she brought them all back with as fine a little grandson as could be seen...my leg...is very bad again...but in other respects my bodily health is wonderfully good and I am able to sit in the sun and read and sew. This country affords splendid fuel, as much wood as we want, for the trouble of bringing it in. What a mercy this would be at home. I have heard that coal is 40 to 50 shillings per tunn.

I shall always be very glad to hear from you and trust that our Heavenly Father will preserve us all to meet in His Kingdom of Glory when time and trouble are no more. With kind love to your husband and children, I remain your affectionate mother...S. Watson[37]

There is a slightly more formal tone in this letter, perhaps influenced by whoever was writing it for Susannah. It could even have been the 'good pastor' who sent his buggy to take her to church. But for her age it is remarkable for the breadth of its contents and the activities and interests it reflects. In April 1874 she wrote again.

My dear daughter,
   I have received your last kind letter of December 4, with the enclosed photograph, which I like very much. I have shown it to several who say it is just the stamp of a nice little English maiden, soft and gentle in appearance and in this way unlike the young people of this Colony, whose general character is self-sufficient independence, carelessness of rebuke and want of respect to those whose age and position demand reticence and submission.
   I am sorry to hear of your accident, but hope by this time you are quite recovered. My bodily health I am thankful to say is wonderfully good, when we consider that if spared till next October, I shall be 80 years of age. I have been trying Holloways ointment with my leg and am happy to say with considerable success. They greatly relieved the pain and is causing it to heal and look so much better in so much that I am beginning to have some faint hopes of getting about a little once more. I should be so thankful to be able to walk to church. It would make me feel comparatively young again. I am happy to say my daughter in law is very much better than she was. Her rheumatic attacks are not frequent, nor by any means severe, so with care I trust she may be preserved from any return of her former illness — she is looking particularly clear and well. John is always busy. He has now his own cart and horses and is employed as a carrier. I shall hope to get Edwin's photographs next time and should be very glad if you could let me know whether your father, Edward, left either wife or family and, if so, what has become of them. A respectable middleaged man named Percival has come amongst us here, to get employment and support. He comes from the neighbourhood of Nottingham. Do you know anything about a person of this name? He speaks of returning to England, if so you will try to see him and he will give you an account of me. My spirits are...fairly good and I am able to read my Bible daily, and other books when the print is large. I cannot expect to be very much longer in this changeful world, but my hope for Eternity rests on the finished work of my God Redeemer, whose servant and follower I desire to be. Give my love to all the young people and please tell me when you write, something about your sister's children. John and his wife unite in kind wishes for you all and, believe me, my dear Mary Anne, Your very affectionate Mother...S. Watson[38]

The burden and restrictions of old age crept into this letter, aggravated perhaps by a clash with the younger generation just before she began to dictate it. But as always, Susannah found escape through reading and comfort in her increasing religious faith. Late in 1874 John moved the family to Gundaroo, at the time mooted to be the next stop on the extension of the railway from Goulburn, and Susannah wrote to Mary Ann in the new year:

My dear daughter,
   I duly received your very welcome letter about a month ago — and was glad to learn from it that you and yours are all well. I am glad to say that I am very well for my age, thank God. I am now old and cannot expect to live long, so that I quite agree with you that we are never likely to meet one

another again in this world. However, let us try to make the best use of the time granted to us in preparing for a better and happier world, where there will be no more parting, 'where the aged cease from troubling and the weary are at rest.'

I am glad to say I live with John and, as far as he can supply my wants, he lets me want for nothing. You will see by this we are not living in the same place as when I last wrote to you. We are now living at Gundaroo, about 25 miles distant from where we were living when I last wrote you. Last month John bought ½ an acre of land in the town and has erected a temporary house on it and that is where we are now living. He is employed at present getting material for building a new Court House and, as soon as he has completed this he intends to get material for to build a good substantial house on his own ground. I have not heard from Charles for a long time. I intend to send him a letter in a few days, to see how he is getting on, and how he has not written to me for so long a time. I am sorry you do not write me oftener. You must know that a letter from you always gives me great pleasure and, instead of getting one only every 2 or 3 years, I would like to hear from you every 2 or 3 months, if it were possible... You say Sarah is 21. Well that is a nice youthful age. I have seen many ups and downs since I was that age, but while I get my few wants supplied that is all I now care for and I hope that God will still provide for me as he has done in the past... Wishing that God may bless and prosper you and yours while you are in this world and at last that we may all meet in that Happy Land far, far away, is the earnest prayer of your affectionate mother... Mrs Watson[39]

John never did build the substantial house, but moved on again to a place called Boulder Hill, six miles from Gunning. He wrote to Mary Ann and assured her that 'it has been much better for Mother than the last place I was at. We have a very nice Minister, who is very attentive to Mother and she is among my wife's friends.' They were living near young Susannah's brother-in-law, Mr Bean, who owned the prosperous Frankfield Inn on the Great South Road from Sydney to Melbourne.[40] According to Susannah John was 'the Inspector of the Roads', but he was also farming and looking forward to a good harvest from his two acres of wheat.[41] With her usual alert interest in what was happening around her, Susannah told Mary Ann:

There is a railway near to our place. It will soon be completed to Gunning, that is the nearest township. The engine passes by every day with ballast and sleepers for the railway and the train is expected to be running by here in a month or two.[42]

Susannah's sight was growing very dim and she had also become slightly deaf, but there was nothing wrong with her mental faculties.[43] Six months later she wrote again, commenting on the news Mary Ann had sent of an ill relative and the lack of word from Samuel, and responding to conditions in England:

I am sorry to hear of work being so dull and provisions so dear. We think it hard some times and things aren't half so dear. My dear daughter, I have not forgotten my home for I am often with you.... Dear Mary Ann, your brother Charles had something of the same complaint as Harriet with tape worms and the Doctors gave him up and I cured him myself.[44]

She enclosed a separate piece of paper with the recipe for her home
medicine: 'As much gun powder as will cover sixpence. Mixt with
brown sugar to a treecal. Give her this much every 2 nights for 3
nights.'[45] Whether Mary Ann used the recipe or not, her relative
Harriet lingered on, a perpetual invalid for another five years.
Susannah's mind remained lively, and across the thousands of miles
of ocean she humorously teased her grand-daughter Sarah in a letter
to Mary Ann:

> My dear daughter,
> I received your kind and welcome letter and was happy to hear from you.
> Hoping this will find you all in good health as this leaves us all in good
> health, except myself. I still remain about the same. My leg is very painful at
> times. I should have written before this, but we have removed into Gunning
> as your brother, John, is working for the Railway Line. It is more pleasant
> where we are living now, for we can see the train pass the house 3 or 4 times
> a day. The English Mail comes from Melbourne by rail, a distance of 600
> miles overland. I am glad Harriet is much better and I hope she will soon be
> strong again. I am sorry Edwin and his wife could not agree. But it seems
> that he has a smell of the gun powder as well as your father and uncles. If he
> can read and write he is all right, for it is a good regiment he is in. I should
> like to know what family Edwin's wife belongs to. Give my kind love to Sarah
> and tell her I hope she has made a better match than what Edwin did — if
> not, I expect she will enlist for a sailor and then she can come and see me.
> This letter leaves Sydney by this mail on Friday the 20th, on my birthday. I
> am 82 years old. It is 48 years, the day after my birthday, since I saw your
> face, which I hope I will see in heaven. Albert and Henry and Alice send
> their love to you so I conclude with our kind blessing to you all. Your brother
> John and his wife sends their kind love to you. So no more at present, from
> your affectionate mother,
>   Susannah Watson
>   Don't forget Thomas' likeness.[46]

On 7 March 1877 Susannah wrote her last letter to Mary Ann:

> My dear daughter,
> I received your kind and welcome letter on Sunday 4th and was happy to
> hear from you all, hoping this will find you and all your family in good
> health, as this leaves us all at present, thank God for it. I am sorry to hear
> that Harriette is no better, but I hope she will be better by the time you get
> this. I am very glad to hear that Sarah has got a good husband. I should like
> to see you myself, but it is impossible to think of it as I am too old, but I hope
> and trust that we will meet in that Bright Land, where there will be no more
> hurting. My health is about the same as when I wrote last. My leg is worse
> and my eyes is failing me very much.
> I am very proud of the card you sent. There is a great difference between
> December in this country and England. While you have the frost and snow,
> we have it scorching hot that we can only keep a bit of meat. My dear, I am
> sorry that we forgot to say something about your husband. I should have
> liked for him to have been near to us on Sunday last, as the water is very
> scarce at present. I must inform you that your brother John's wife has got an
> increase in the family. They have got a fine son and he was christened on
> Sunday last. His name is George Edward. He was born on 30th January. If
> Abraham had been here to fetch some water, it would have saved us the

trouble of taking the child to the Church to be christianed. My dear daughter, don't think I forget you. My thoughts is on you night and morning. I should like to know if Hannah's children are living anywhere near you and I hope you are friendly with them.

Your brother John and his wife and family send their kind love to you all. I have given the card to Henry James and I will be so glad to get William's likeness. So I must conclude with all our best wishes and love.

I remain your affectionate mother,
Susannah Watson

And remain an affectionate mother she did. Until the very end of her life the love for her children, which had burdened but sustained her, remained the pivot of her existence. Her care for their welfare was her main concern.

But the end of her long life had arrived. In the following months she deteriorated rapidly, and by July was completely helpless and in great pain. In late October, near her birthday, she slipped into a coma for a few days. Then her strong lifeforce exerted itself and she rallied briefly. Born in the careless mortality of the eighteenth-century Georgian age, by the time of her death she was a true nineteenth-century Victorian and her deathbed was worthy of Charles Dickens. The night before she died she asked John to read to her from the Bible: 1 Corinthians 15, 'The last enemy that shall be destroyed is death'; and John 13, 'The servant is not greater than the Lord; neither he that is sent greater than he that sent him. . . A new commandment I give unto you, That ye love one another.' Then she sang the hymn 'Here we suffer grief and pain'. The next morning, 28 October 1877, 'with kind friends standing by her bed', she sang part of 'Rock of Ages cleft for me, Let me hide myself in thee' and, shortly after, she died.[47]

That same evening, her friend Mr Saxby sat down and wrote to Mary Ann.[48]

A SECOND CHANCE

How is Susannah to be judged? Was she simply a criminal who repented? Was she a victim of social change who, tossed by fate, found a capacity to endure? Or did she contribute to the vicissitudes of her life, but in the end surmount them?

On the evidence, she was a strong-minded and intelligent woman, who was active in every sense of the word. Physically energetic, she worked hard without resentment, and even when her sons offered her the chance to be idle she didn't take it, preferring to be productively occupied. Mentally active, she would take steps to find a solution to the problems of her life when passivity might have been much safer. Faced with a dying child, she could not sit by and succumb to grief, but found relief in action, whatever the risk.

It is possible to trace the hardening of her attitude from one of frightened shock at her first transgression, to cool calculation and very deliberate action in the face of desperation and a growing sense of injustice. She was too intelligent, and her comprehension of the world around her too good, not to understand the inequalities in society, the gap between 'the haves and have nots', and she obviously came to feel that in desperate circumstances there was justification for stealing. Apart from the first time she stole a coat, hers were never snatch-and-grab crimes, but rational acts performed with clarity of purpose. She displayed an increasing determination to survive, even if it meant theft, lying to the authorities, and manipulation of people in positions of influence. She was not a prostitute, but she had no qualms about swapping sex for security, which were the terms of her arrangement with John Clarke and which resulted in her marriages to William Woollard and John Jones. Like many of her shipmates, sex was her only currency.

The force of her personality undoubtedly affected the course of her life. In the first instance it led her to steal with deliberation, but in other ways it worked for her. In Nottingham, with her two previous convictions, she could easily have received a life sentence: the new Act really called for it and judges in many other trials were governed by this. It can only have been the force of Susannah's personality and the eloquence of her plea for mercy which decided the judge to give her 14 years instead. It was personality that kept her employed at the Egans when other employers returned their servants with children. It was personality which influenced the management of the Female Factory — her personal plea before the committee for mitigation of her sentence; her success in keeping Charles out of the orphanage until he was five; her inclusion in the abortive 1838 attempt to obtain a ticket-of-leave. Once she had adjusted to life in Sydney and come to understand the local society, she displayed an ability to use her persuasive powers to work the system.

Circumstances, combined with facets of her character, made Susannah a very independent, very strong woman. By the time she was transported she was angry. Angry with Edward, who let her down by his poaching, and angry with a society where her children were forced to starve. Perhaps this anger, which propelled her into criminal action again, also sustained her in the emotional wrench of separation from home and family. But when the *Princess Royal* dropped anchor in Sydney the immediate anger behind her actions in Nottingham would have long since dissipated, and in those early months in the colony she must have faced moments of great loneliness and anguish. It is a measure of her personal strength that she never sought oblivion through drink. None of the men in her life ever truly provided her with an emotional refuge, and she learned to depend only on herself, but she found the strength to endure through the dependence of others — her children — on her.

It is her children, who provide some of the clearest evidence of Susannah's character. Their characters bear testimony to hers. From her they learnt the loyalty of family and were conscious of an obligation for her care of them which each, in turn, repaid in her old age. 'Zeal in a good cause is commendable' was one of the homillies she had used to teach her children to write, and presumably she chose it because it meant something to her.[1]

Throughout his life, her son Charles exemplified this maxim. He fought the good fight with a zeal which, after his death, resulted in the iconoclastic magazine, the *Bulletin*, gleefully describing him as 'top scorer in the matter of libel actions'.[2] He had absorbed his mother's perceptions of the plight of the working classes and acted according to her principles, which became his own. He was also an idealist and he founded the *Shoalhaven News* with the stated aim of a wider good which revealed not only his and his mother's love of reading, but also indicated what Susannah might have believed had her life been different. Charles' motto was from Shakespeare's *Henry VIII*: 'Be just and fear not. Let all the ends thou Aim'st at be thy Country's, thy God's and Truth's.'[3] Unlike his mother, Charles had the privilege of living by principles rather than threadbare survival. He died young, at

55, as a result of an impulsive act of gallantry which was totally in character.[4]

John was a battler, a practical man, although he followed his dreams for ten years around the goldfields of New South Wales. His essential simple decency shines through in the letters he wrote to his English sister after their mother's death and he displayed all his mother's energy in a flexible ability to survive and in his constant care for his family. He also inherited her longevity. Born in the Female Factory at the height of the convict system, he lived through the death of Queen Victoria and Australian Federation, through World War I and the coming of the aeroplane and the motor car, to die aged 88 in 1923.[5] He continued to correspond with his sister in England until Mary Ann, who survived the early privations of her life, died aged 70 in 1893.[6] Her descendants met some of their Australian relatives in Nottingham during World War I.[7]

In old age, as Susannah began to look at her life from a moral perspective rather than simply one of survival, she revealed some repentance for the sins which, in a Christian sense, she had committed. But she was by no means overwhelmed with guilt. She found the courage to face death through the comfort of belief in the afterlife, but she did not condemn herself for past transgressions. Nor was she bitter. On the contrary, she revealed a philosophic acceptance of 'the many ups and downs since I was that age' — that is, 21 — and concluded that she had 'many reasons to be thankful'. It says as much for her character as for the new country where she ended her life, that she regarded transportation as a positive rather than a negative experience.

If this was Susannah's character, about which there is so much detailed evidence, what of her shipmates? Were they drunks, whores, thieves, misfits, outcasts? Genetic criminals? Moral degenerates? Are these the terms which should describe Australia's female convicts? Were they survivors or victims? Was transportation for them a positive or a negative experience? There are few black-and-white answers, because these were human beings.

Yes, they were all thieves. They were not victims of injustice. They stole. And their offences cannot be dismissed in relation to the item stolen, or its contemporary value: a handkerchief worth a shilling was a valuable item in the early nineteenth century. The seriousness of their crime, however, cannot be assessed against their sentence. The English penal code was still harsh in 1828, although it had been considerably reformed since Australia was colonised 40 years earlier when more crimes carried the death penalty. But transportation was the next after death. It was a brutal punishment and, even given the then value of what they stole, it was out of proportion to the crime, most particularly in the case of the women of the *Princess Royal*, so many of whom had no previous conviction.

For nearly all of the women, crime and criminal attitudes were, or had become, a way of life. They used lies and tricks and manipulation and drink and sex to steal. And then sometimes used them again to try and escape the consequences. Survival was what counted and the indulgence of morality, at the expense of survival, was out of the question. With their background and low level of education, it is unlikely that many of them perceived their actions as 'wrong'. They just got caught by someone with the power to punish them. But some among them comprehended their situation more fully and resented it. Like Susannah, they understood the gap between the haves and have nots, the powerful and the powerless: 'Don't give them the satisfaction,' snapped Ellen Turnbull to a tearful Mary Smith. Others expressed their anger through cheek: 'Thank you my Lord,' said Ann Perks, 'I want another day to clean myself'.

To the question — were they drunks and whores? — the answer must be a resounding yes, many of them were. But not all. Of the total 100 women of the *Princess Royal*, there is evidence or a strong indication that approximately 24 of them were whores to some extent either in England or in New South Wales. Eight of them were specifically revealed at their trials to be living as professional prostitutes. At least another 11 to 16 were selling themselves, it appears, on a more casual basis...to steal. And specific details have not been obtained for every woman. In New South Wales available records indicate three cases of prostitution and one of soliciting, although the evidence is circumstantial. The most specific relates to Harriet Bannister, Margaret Williams (soliciting), Louisa Caulfield and Mary Williams or Hearn, with considerable implication that Margaret Hartigan, Ann Simpson and several others sold themselves on occasion. But as historian Henry Mayhew found through his extensive investigations among the London underworld, 'to be unchaste among the lower classes is not always a subject of reproach'.[8] There is little doubt that most of the women from the *Princess Royal* accepted that sex was their most valuable, if not their only currency, and used it accordingly and without qualms. It could be exchanged for lifelong security, for escape from penal servitude, as payment for a letter written, or for a few drinks and some fun. Sex was their only real source of power and manipulation, even though it lay paradoxically at the heart of their greatest vulnerability. Sometimes they must have had feelings of personal distaste or revulsion, but life in the overcrowded, starving slums of England would not have developed in them a sense of inviolate personal privacy, and nor were they restricted by the Christian concept of personal morality that had begun to be propagated so vigorously by the upper and middle classes but which had not yet fully permeated the working classes. 'Prostitute' was a description too easily applied to the women by the upper social strata, for whom prostitution really meant all female sexual activity outside marriage. Mayhew described the lower-class attitude when he commented: 'many of them draw a distinction between those who live by promiscuous intercourse and those who confine themselves to one man', and he also found plenty of evidence that actual prostitution was regarded by its practitioners simply as one form of work. As one woman told him, 'she did not on the whole dislike her way of living: she didn't think about the sin of it; a poor girl must live'.[9]

As to their being drunkards, the evidence is more extensive and more specific. There is hard evidence of one or more convictions for drunkenness for 32 of the women and, given the gaps in the surviving records and the practice in many instances of recording the sentence but not the offence, this is almost certainly only the tip of the iceberg. But the women and the men convicts who came to New South Wales brought with them from England a tradition of hard drinking as an escape and a recreation and the tradition took root and flourished from the beginning of the colony. The role of drink was vividly described by a woman in the London slums who said : 'When I am sad I drink. . . I am very often sad, although I appear to be what you call reckless. . . there's nothing like gin to deaden the feelings'.[10] On the confined stage of the small community of New South Wales the relaxation their drinking created for the women prisoners collided spectacularly with the increasingly vigorous middle-class concept of female modesty in behaviour, language and attitudes.[11] But the classification of the women convicts as whores and drunkards was not just a pre-emptive moral judgment; it was most definitely based on fact. Unfortunately, this widespread judgment condemned them all without exception.

So if thieves, whores and drunkards is a generally accurate description, are there mitigating circumstances? The answer here must also be a resounding yes. Conditions for the working class in England were appalling. English society was experiencing a major transformation into an industrial nation and the impact of the changes was aggravated by the economic effects of the war with France and, during the 1820s, particularly harsh winters. The majority of the women of the *Princess Royal* were under 30 years of age and they had been born right in the middle of this turmoil. Most of them would never have experienced any social or family stability. Ann Barnett and Jane Edwards, for instance, were totally alone in a brutal, insecure world, and those who did have relatives were still forced to live in grossly overcrowded, disease-ridden, lodgings. Economic circumstances resulted in a population that was constantly on the move, so there was little stability even in geographic location. Concepts of personal and financial security, of building and creating a future, were beyond their reach. They had to live from day to day, concerned only with a roof over their heads and something to eat. It was survival at its most primitive, so it is not surprising they used sex to earn money and drink to dull their senses. And the opportunity to break out of this vicious cycle of poverty and deprivation was non-existent, particularly for people whose intelligence and education was circumscribed by their background, while the traditional class structure of English society reinforced passivity, acceptance and hopelessness.

There is some evidence of personal tragedies which may have forced certain of the women into a life of crime. Mary Palmer's husband, as she proved so conclusively, had died only the year before she was convicted, which was her first offence. William Foxall and John Wright had been transported the year before their wives. Was it this which forced Elizabeth into prostitution and Ann to steal fowls? Elizabeth

Smith, a 40-year-old widow with three children, was convicted of illegally pawning a sheet. She pleaded 'distress' as the reason for her crime. Some of the young girls probably knew no other way of life and it was almost a game they played. Others, befuddled by drink, stole almost unwittingly. But if all the women could be investigated in the same depth as Susannah, how many of their stories would reveal a similarly tragic combination of circumstances leading them to crime? In England, without a doubt, the women of the *Princess Royal* were victims of forces beyond their control.

But what about New South Wales? Were they victims there? They certainly arrived under the handicap of their background, and the negative assumptions about all women prisoners which were held by colonial society.

They found a government system which operated, in general, with a high degree of efficiency, and was designed to regulate their employment, their behaviour, their morals and, through marriage, their future. The first shock for the women was the degree of regulation they faced in what at first must have appeared relative freedom for them. They discovered to their cost they must not only work where they were told and commit no crimes as they were understood in England, but one of their major recreations, drink, and their sex lives, were subject to punishment. Coming to grips with the local rules for their behaviour was the first major adjustment they faced, which some never made and others took years to understand. Those who achieved it quickly fared best.

They were all at the mercy of their employers, many of whom were capricious with expectations which took no account of their servants' background and with a too easy, too ready power to punish. This, at least, was a syndrome the women understood. The shopkeepers of England were just as quick to turn to the police as those in the colony. The Masters and Servants Act, passed in New South Wales in 1828, was similar to the one in England for free servants. It provided gaol sentences for offences such as absence and refusal to work and was the basis for the employers' expectations of their assigned servants. The difference lay mainly in the general attitude to the prisoner servants who, one woman said, were 'treated like dogs and worked like horses . . . seldom spoken to without an oath or "as devils" more than human beings'.[12] However, for every bad master there was a good one, and there are many instances of masters behaving fairly or even kindly towards women prisoners. Assignment was one of the two major areas where luck affected the fate of the women of the *Princess Royal*.

The women were not entirely helpless, however. They had some ability to seek redress and control their lives. One way, which many obviously used, was to get themselves sent back to the Factory by committing one or more offences until the employer gave up. Another way was to complain to the magistrates. This required courage and confidence and easy access to the court. Assignment to a country property made it virtually impossible, but in Sydney a considerable number of women complained to the bench about their employers and

were successful in obtaining reassignment. Apart from specific matters
like rations, one of the women's best weapons was to turn the
authorities' morality back on them as a news item from 1829 indicates:

> On Tuesday last a female prisoner went to the Police Office and requested
> that she be returned to Government. In her complaint she stated that she
> was assigned to the mistress of a notorious brothel on the Rocks, that her
> fellow servant, also a prisoner, was kept for the same disgraceful purposes
> and the same was expected of her and thinking such a house not a fit place
> for a modest woman, she resolved to apply to His Worship. (She was sent to
> the 1st Class of the Factory for reassignment.)[13]

On the evidence of the available records, and within the perspective
of their times, most magistrates tried to be fair to the women. George
Brooks' attempt to help Margaret Williams in Newcastle, Mr Allman's
attitude to Mary Palmer when she got drunk, the Sydney magistrates
who withdrew Georgiana Baxter and Louisa Caulfield for insufficient
rations and who blamed Mr Palmer for Ann Storrett's presence in a
'disorderly' house, are just some of the examples which applied to
women from the *Princess Royal*. If anything, the female prisoners'
greatest threat came from over zealous, usually ex-convict police
constables who picked them up on the street and charged them with
absence, drunkenness or sexual misconduct. But the women were
often their own worst enemies and many were, in fact, guilty of all
these offences.

If assignment was a lottery, the key to using it, surviving it or
becoming a victim of it, lay much in the character of the women
themselves. It was this that sorted out the survivors from the victims,
and here the fate of the women of the *Princess Royal* diverged sharply.

There were some women who could not or would not refrain from
stealing, and who extended their troubles by committing another theft
in New South Wales. There were others who were hot tempered and
fought back when it would have been more prudent to remain meek.
Many took the very human risk of slipping out to meet friends, lovers
or husbands. But those with a propensity to drunkenness were always the most vulnerable. They ran foul of their employers, were targets
for the police, prey to sexual assault and, in the case of Margaret
Mahoney, to rape. It was drunkenness that lost Susan King and Jane
Edwards their chance of escaping the assignment system through a
ticket-of-leave. Disintegration was cumulative and in several instances
continued well beyond the end of the convicts' original sentence.

The cliché 'You can't buck the system' was never more true than
when it applied to the convict system in New South Wales, which was
tailor-made to degrade women who were weak and simple minded, or
strong and rebellious. Catherine Donoghue and Johanna Brown, who
represented these extremes, were both destroyed by the system. But
Catherine turned her back on the cooperation or even marriage which
might have benefited her, and Johanna was one of life's victims, who
was unlikely to have survived any better in England. Ann Kinsman
was destroyed by her life in New South Wales, but although the

convict system was a contributing factor, it was by no means the sole reason.

But for those who were not addicted to drink and had some self-control over their actions and their tongues — for those motivated to succeed, transportation could turn into freedom quite quickly. Some of them, such as Georgiana Baxter and Ann Bowler, manipulated their sentence with considerable skill. They used the opportunities the system offered — obtained tickets-of-leave and conditional pardons, influenced their assignment by good behaviour or manipulation, and those who could escaped into marriage.

Marriage was the second great lottery in the women's lives in the colony. Their declaration of an availability to marry was the first throw of the dice, their choice of husband the second, their own character the third. There is no doubt that some of the women became victims of the system through their inability to marry, while others escaped it almost entirely by marriage. But there were some who, within marriage, fell victim to brutal men or to their husbands' regression to crime. In some cases the women's own behaviour, their addiction to drink, their casual immorality, exacerbated their troubles. The loss of a husband through death or retransportation could leave a woman as destitute and vulnerable as those in the worst of assigned service. Like assignment, marriage had its pros and cons, but on balance it provided the women with a viable escape from penal servitude.

There is no simple answer to the question of whether the women of the *Princess Royal* were victims of the convict system. On the evidence available, it appears that although some were, most were not. Because they were prisoners the master–servant relationship was worse than in England, if the women had a job there, which most did not. But they were not completely without redress. In addition, the incentives in the system such as tickets-of-leave, along with the option of marriage, offered opportunities for an early escape which many took. The inability to marry could be a tragedy, which was caused by the system, but most overcame this when they were free. Those who came to grief were not simply victims of the system, and a crucial ingredient in their fate was their own character.

Were the women moral degenerates and genetic criminals? The descriptions of female convicts which have come down through the years are virtually unanimous in their picture of degraded, dissolute, worthless people. And although many people believed life in New South Wales provided the opportunity for reform, the theory that 'the criminal classes' were a race apart, irreclaimable and perhaps even genetically determined, was highly regarded and much discussed during the nineteenth century.[14] A belief in their inherent worthlessness offered contemporaries one explanation for the women convicts' behaviour. But one of the women's few defences against their life as victims of society in general, and authoritative males in particular, was defiantly raucous, bawdy, cheeky, generally recalcitrant behaviour. They had to pretend not to care. They even had to convince themselves they didn't care, in order to survive their lives. Nobody ever considered that it might be an act, and such a good one it even fooled the actresses themselves.The idol of women as 'God's police' was held up before them and, since they could not possibly live up to it, their defence was to refuse to pay it homage and to shock the idol's worshippers by their behaviour. But they did care. They cared how they looked. They cared about their wholesale reputation as 'outcasts'. They cared about their children. And although many married with a practical attitude, most undoubtedly did care about their men. The proof that they cared, that their crimes and their morals were fundamentally the result of their circumstances, can be found in the lives of so many of the women who, given the opportunity of a traditionally moral and upright life, the chance of a future, took it and vanished permanently from the criminal records.

Finally, was transportation a negative or a positive experience in the women's lives? The fates of Mary Smith "the 3rd" and Mary Wheat demonstrate there were certainly some for whom the enforced voyage across the world produced no improvement in their circumstances. But it is not only the fate of the women which provides an answer to this question. Elizabeth Foxall's tragedy, for instance, was not transportation — she was working as a prostitute in a Birmingham brothel when she was convicted — but that she recognised a second chance in New South Wales and was prevented from taking it. Ann Simpson had apparently sought her life of theft and degradation in Hull before she was transported. In the colony she continued a course she set at home. The women who suffered a tragic fate in New South Wales were not, in the main, the victims of transportation *per se* but of their own characters and background, of their husbands, and of a middle-class morality which was increasingly affecting attitudes to the working classes both in England and New South Wales. The great trauma of transportation was the separation from loved ones, most particularly dependent children, and the agony this caused cannot be underestimated. But by 1829, enough information had reach England in the years since Australia was founded for the voyage itself to an unknown land to be less daunting than it once was. Although Surgeon Peter Cunningham might confess that New South Wales was the only place he was ashamed to admit having visited,[15] there were also positive expectations about the colony, among the English working class at least.

Through the layers of official records which remain about the people of New South Wales in the 1830s, the researcher catches a glimpse of real life. An impression builds of a gigantic reunion unofficially taking place, as parents and children, brothers and sisters, husbands and wives, uncles, aunts, cousins and friends catch up with one another and, in the main, successfully re-establish their lives and relationships. The government, which could on occasions be so unrelentingly harsh, could also be a sucker for the moral plea, the repentant sinner, the distraught female, the responsible family man. The word passed round among the tough, street-wise inhabitants of the colony that the authorities could be outwitted or manipulated to a person's benefit —

and they passed down to their descendants a tradition of kudos in outsmarting the government. Those still prisoners knew how to move around when they wanted to, how to change employers. They turn up in districts where they are not supposed to be. They are listed as ticket-of-leave holders or free when they are not. Inexplicable marriages occur. Aliases come and go with a frequency that successfully blurs the trail and confuses the movement of a single individual through the system. Some people never die — at least so far as the register is concerned. Beyond official policy and official records the prisoners made lives for themselves in spite of the system. In there with the best of them, working the system, were Susannah Watson and many other women of the *Princess Royal*.

Australia offered the women from England a chance they could never obtain at home. At its most fundamental, it offered a better climate, more easily obtainable food, and simply more living space. In spite of increasing immigration, their employment prospects and remuneration were better than they could have obtained in England. Labour was scarce and wages high by comparison with home. But Australia offered more. It offered the opportunity to move up, to become part of society economically and socially, rather than the disregarded fringe. It is unlikely that any of the women from the *Princess Royal* ever rose to riches and status — although some were well positioned when the gold rush began. In the main, no doubt, they remained comparatively poor and lived out their lives in small urban houses or slab huts in the country, scratching for a living. But there was space around them, fresh air to breath, and their children grew strong and healthy and ran free. They spawned a generation who were generally poorly educated and uncultured, but healthy, competent and confident, with increasing pride in themselves, in their strange brown land, and with belief in their future. In Australia the child of Ann Barnett, a girl from the London workhouse, could become the archdeacon of the diocese of Maitland.[16]

The specific feelings of the women from the *Princess Royal* about their transportation are not on record, with one exception. But their actions and the eagerness with which they married, and the speed with which many of them moved out of the convict system, indicate they agreed with the views of some male convicts which are on record:

> This is a very fine country, not a finer in the world and a very wholesome climate.
>
> You may very clearly see what an opportunity there is for well conducted persons.
>
> This is the best country under the sun. I am very thankful to my prosecutors for sending me here to the land of liberty and freedom.[17]

These men, all writing in the 1830s, echoed the feelings of a female convict who as early as 1806 told the daughter she left behind in England: 'This my dear is the most healthful country in all the Globe...do not lose a moment's time when you receive this but use all your interest and endeavours to come to the Garden of the world.'[18]

What the women from the *Princess Royal* thought, and what Australia offered their descendants in the longer term, is probably no better demonstrated than through Susannah's story. The final irony of her life occurred 82 years after her death. In 1959, wearing the curled wig and red robes with which Susannah herself would have been all too familiar, her great-grandson was sworn in as a judge of the Supreme Court of New South Wales.[19] His career on the bench included periods in the Criminal Court when, with the full weight of the crown and the law of England on his side, he meted out punishment to murderers and thieves alike. His great-grandmother had indeed won through to the other side. Her faith in 'this plentifull country' had been triumphantly vindicated. In 1857 Susannah delivered her verdict and she can, with justification, speak for her fellow travellers. In spite of the anguish of separation and the misfortunes she suffered in New South Wales, transportation, she said, 'was the best thing befell me'.[20]

On the evidence of Susannah Watson and her shipmates from the *Princess Royal*, transportation, for most of the convicts, was not the fatal shore at all, but a second chance.

ADDENDUM

As I had hoped, the publication of *A Cargo of Women* put me in touch with more descendants of women from the *Princess Royal*.

Despite a difficult, sometimes violent marriage, Mary Ann Marshall and Walter Neary left numerous descendants whose respectability and status increased with each generation. Their son, Walter, settled at Wattle Flat near Bathurst and was already a well-known carrier of goods between Sydney and country districts when the discovery of gold at the Turon fields offered him new opportunities which he was not slow to take up. Mary Ann's grandson, Henry H Neary, fought with the 2nd Light Horse Regiment in Egypt in 1915. A well-educated cultured man, Henry Neary published a book of reminiscences and poetry in 1940 called *Ghosts of the Goldfields*. His grandchildren reprinted the book in his memory in 1983.

Ann Storrett, the youngest girl on the ship, has many descendants from her marriage to ex-convict James Jaye. A tinsmith and blacksmith, her husband became a prosperous citizen of Bathurst. The premises of Jaye & Jordan and, later, Jaye & Freeman, feature in a number of nineteenth century photographs of the town. In a fascinating letter to his son, James Jaye detailed his wife's family background as well as his own because, he said, 'in a young country like this a man who bears a family ought, I think, to let them know something of their origin to enable them to recognise a friend and detect an imposter...' There was no mention of convicts anywhere in the letter. According to Jaye, Ann's father was a sergeant in the Scotch Grays, and was so disconsolate when his regiment left for Waterloo without him, that he committed suicide. Ann's mother then married a man who was a tin and slate worker. Jaye's letter also dropped a hint which led to my discovery that Ann's brother Peter was transported to New South Wales in 1836. Aged 21, his trade was described as tin plate worker, a strong indication that a family reunion, if not family co-operation, occurred between brother

Peter and husband James, which may well have been the foundation of a successful business.

Her daughter's married name of Skelly was the clue that made descendants of Sarah Bryant think she might belong to them. Together, we were able to link up the information to prove she did, but the puzzle of her mother's presence in Tasmania has not yet been solved.

Ann Bullock's descendants provided details of her theft of two half sovereigns and some silver coins from the person of William Green in Derby, a crime containing the common elements of much drink and gullibility on the part of the victim. James Robinson or Robertson, later to be Ann's husband, was sentenced to death for stealing a horse in London. In New South Wales, he remained involved with horses as an overseer on properties in Goulburn, Yass, Burrowa and Young, but he was working at his original English occupation as a gardener when he died in 1864 aged 76 at a property called Carumbi near Young. Ann was not mentioned on James' death certificate and her descendants are still searching for details of her death.

Mary Harcourt, wife of Thomas Wright, the son of a convict who arrived on the Second Fleet, died at their property Phoenix Park at Morpeth, New South Wales in 1880 aged 76. Husband, Thomas had predeceased her in 1861. Descendants informed me that Mary suffered all her life from the epileptic fits which so puzzled Surgeon Wilson during the voyage of the *Princess Royal*. Members of the family still own Phoenix Park.

The end of the story for Margaret Hartigan and her daughter Abigail was revealed by her descendants' research. My conclusion that they had been reunited despite the many years of enforced separation by the authorities was proved correct. Abigail took her stepfather's name and he was a witness at her marriage as Abigail Hartigan Smith to ex-convict Edward Brummell in 1849. Abigail died aged only 48 in 1876 survived by five children. Her mother Margaret, and husband John Smith had died some years earlier after producing approximately ten children of their own, seven of whom survived. John, who had worked as a fisherman and a timbercutter over the years, was described as a labourer when he died in 1861 aged 74. Margaret, transported for manslaughter, described as a tailoress on her convict indent, was registered as a storekeeper of Watt Street, Newcastle, when she died in 1869 aged 61 years.

Descendants were not the only sources of extra information about the women of the *Princess Royal*. In Professor Alan Atkinson's fine book, *Camden*, which was published in 1988, I discovered Georgiana Baxter, now Mrs John Lefevre, behaving in a characteristically forthright fashion. The local Bench Book records her quarrel with the butcher in the town's main street and, on another occasion, her accusations that her manservant had stolen a silk handkerchief which she gave him to pay for her bottle of rum. Georgiana had chosen well in her second colonial husband. Although bankrupted in the recession of the early 1840s, John Lefevre subsequently acquired power and status in Camden under the patronage of the powerful Macarthur family. As a master carpenter, he carried out all the joinery work for the town's church, post office and hotel in the 1840s and he both designed and constructed the roof of St John's church which still stands today.

A fellow researcher, Ralph Hawkins, contributed a fascinating detail to the story of James and Mary Haynes. He rang me to say their grave was in the Uniting Church, Cherrybrook in north-west Sydney and recited the inscription which stands over Mary: 'With patience to the last she did submit, And murmured not at what the Lord thought fit'.

Some mysteries remain. Catherine Turner alias Dunn has so far successfully thwarted all attempts by her descendants to discover her last resting place. She did indeed marry James Neal/Neil as detailed in *A Cargo of Women* and they produced a number of children to whom the line can be traced, but Catherine herself vanished after the marriage of her daughter Ann in 1847. She witnessed that wedding under the name of Catherine Dunn, so we suspect a name change has confused her trail at least temporarily.

The mysterious Isabella Errington remains a source of great interest to me. On obtaining more details of her English crime, I discovered she was well known in Newcastle-on-Tyne under the name of Bella Beamson. This information sent me hurrying to the births, deaths and marriages index once more, but no Bella Beamson is recorded in the register. My original conclusion still stands.

My tentative conclusion about the death of John Clarke has been disproved by Mrs Marilyn Maddocks who was good enough to let me know that the John Clarke 'accidentally shot' at Newcastle, was in fact a relative of hers who was visiting the colony. The fate of Susannah's 'pretend husband' remains to be tracked down.

Susannah Watson's existence is indisputable, but her birthplace is so far undiscovered and the grave in the Church of England cemetery at Gunning, New South Wales was apparently unmarked. However, I was fortunate in discovering the house where she died. Positioned near the new railway, it was originally built in 1876 as an hotel for John Watson's brother-in-law, Joe Bean. The building subsequently became a guest house and has gone down in local history books as 'The Old Boarding House'. It still stands, althought enlarged, at No 1 Warataw Street, Gunning, and is now a private residence.

This edition of *A Cargo of Women* will take the story to a wider audience. My file stays open on the women of the *Princess Royal* and I would welcome contact from anyone with further information about them.

Babette Smith
P.O. Box 161
Neutral Bay NSW 2089

APPENDIX

THE CONVICTS OF
THE PRINCESS ROYAL

The following summary biographies are drawn from all the sources listed in the bibliography, but the first paragraph of '1829' information is almost entirely from the Princess Royal Muster with occasional interpolations from other sources. The Muster, for instance, contained no information at all about the seven children on board except for noting their existence, so their names, ages, etc. come from elsewhere as documented in the chapter footnotes. Once or twice, usually concerning the fate of a woman or her issue, I have included information which is not academically proven but hoping it will help descendants.

One cautionary note for amateur historians. The chronological flow of each woman's life is by no means complete. The biographies need to be read thoughtfully and the gaps in time noted to avoid making wrong assumptions. It also needs to be remembered that gaps of information can represent not only a woman's behaviour or location in the colony, but the survival or loss of particular records.

Abbreviations used in the Appendix are as follows:
R&W, Read and write; R, Read; TL, Ticket-of-leave; 3cl, third class; FF, Female Factory; CF, came free; BC, born in the colony; FS, free by servitude; VDL, Van Diemen's Land; Prot., Protestant; Cath., Catholic.

MARIA ALLEN
1829: 20 Single Prot. *Educ* R&W *Native* Reading *Trade* All work *Trial* Reading 20 July 1828 *Offence* House breaking *Sentence* 7 years No previous convictions *Heights* 4'11½" Ruddy pockpitted complexion Dark brown hair Dark brown eyes

1829 May		To D. Howard, Sydney
	Aug	Absconded from Howard Sentence 4 mo.3cl FF
		Assigned Henry Donahy
	28 Oct	[*sic*] Transferred from Donahy to David Dyer
1830		To Archibald Campbell, Bathurst
1831 Jan		Applied to marry (a) Joseph Woodcock (b) David Reghan
	Mar	Married Woodcock, FS, sawyer

1835 Sep   Certificate of freedom
1859 Jan   Joseph Woodcock died Orange, N.S.W. Wife Maria still living Her real maiden name 'James'

JANE BAILEY

1829: 27 Single Prot. *Educ* R, *Native* Liverpool *Trade* All work *Trial* Liverpool 27 July 1828 *Offence* Receiving *Sentence* 7 years No previous convictions *Height* 5'¾" Ruddy complexion Brown hair Dark brown eyes Small scar right corner of mouth one left cheek and raised mole on left jaw
1829 May   To William Hutchinson, George St, Sydney
1831 Sep   TL, Sydney
1833 Mar   Died Sydney hospital

HARRIET BANNISTER alias CARRICK

1829: 26 or 22 Single Prot. *Educ* R&W *Native* Wolverhampton *Trade* Nurse girl *Trial* Stafford 16 July 1828 *Offence* Shoplifting *Sentence* 7 years No previous convictions *Height* 4'10½" Ruddy freckled complexion Light brown hair Dark brown eyes Small scars on right forehead and right cheek
1829 May   To James Orr, Parramatta
      Nov   Married John Wright, 2nd mate, *Princess Royal*
1830 Nov   6 weeks 3cl FF — improperly intoxicated with a man
1831 Jun   Illegally at large, husband at sea See Chapter 11 for details
      Nov   2mo. 3cl FF — offence unknown
1832 Feb   To Charles Marsden, South Creek
      Mar   To Mrs Barnes, Parramatta
      Dec   Runaway from Mrs Wyatt, Sydney
1833 Mar   1mo. 3cl FF
      Jul   Died Sydney

ANN BARNETT

1829: 17 Single Prot. *Educ* R *Native* London *Trade* Nurse girl *Trial* London 26 October 1828 *Offence* Stealing bonnets *Sentence* 7 years No previous convictions *Height* 4'11" Ruddy fair and pockpitted complexion Light brown hair Hazel eyes 'I love to the heart' on lower right arm
1829 May   To Joshua Holt, Sydney
1831 Nov   TL, Sydney
?   To Wolfe & Co, O'Connell St, Sydney
1832 Aug   Married Thomas Tollis, BC, shoemaker
1836 Apr   Certificate of freedom
1880   Thomas Tollis died.
Ann Tollis age 73, died 16 August 1885 at Gerrard Street, Alexandria, Sydney
Issue: 2 daughters, 7 sons, including Archdeacon Walter Tollis of Maitland

CATHERINE BARRETT

1829: 20 Single Prot. *Educ* R *Native* London *Trade* All work *Trial* Guildford 1 August 1828 *Offence* Picking pockets No previous convictions *Height* 5'1½" Ruddy complexion Brown hair Blue eyes Scar on forehead and two small ones right side of nose
1829 May   To Thomas Meehan, Liverpool
1830 Apr   Still with above Applied to marry Thomas Smith Allowed but marriage did not occur
1830 Oct   6 weeks 3cl FF and returned to government — absconding
?   To David Allen
1831 Mar   6 weeks 3cl FF and returned to government — absent without leave and drunk

1832 Apr   To Rev. G. Erskine, Sydney
1833 Feb   2mo. 3cl FF — offence unknown
?   To William Sherwin, Lake Bathurst, Argyle,
1835 Oct   Still with above Married John Leonard, TL, overseer Mr Sherwin
1847 Jun   Conditional pardon
1880 Aug   Died Yass, N.S.W.
            Issue 4 sons including James, Patrick and Thomas

MARY BASS

1829: 24 Single Prot. *Educ* R *Native* Essex *Trade* Nurse girl *Trial* Essex 21 July
1828 *Offence* Shop robbery *Sentence* 7 years No previous convictions *Height* 5'
Ruddy complexion Brown hair Brown eyes Raised mole on upper nose
1829 May   To Thomas Cooper, Point Piper
1829 Nov   To Frances Brown, Pitt St
1830 Mar   Married Thomas Pearkes/Parkers, TL
1835 Jun   2mo.3cl FF cause unknown
1838 Jun   Certificate of freedom

MARY BATES

1829: 19/20 Single Prot. *Educ* None *Native* Stafford *Trade* Shoebinder *Trial*
Warwick 15 Oct/Jul 1828 *Offence* Stealing silk *Sentence* 7 years 2 previous
convictions *Height* 4'10½" Ruddy freckled complexion Brown hair Light
hazel eyes Small scar over right eye Tattoo 'BF' on upper right arm
1829 May   To Henry Geesing, Pitt St, Sydney
     Jul   Absconded from above
1830 May   To John Loveridge, Sydney
1832 Apr   Still with above Applied to marry Mark Brown, Bond. Refused
1834 Feb   TL, Liverpool
1835 Feb   Married James Moss, FS
1836   Note on TL butt indicates ticket torn up, 'Bates free' No certificate
            of freedom was issued

MARY BATES

1829: 39/40 Married 2 children Prot. *Educ* R *Native* Shropshire *Trade* All work
Trial Warwick 14 October 1828 *Offence* House robbery *Sentence* 7 years 2
previous convictions *Height* 4'9½" Ruddy freckled complexion Red hair Hazel
eyes
1829 May   Lieutenant Scarman, Sydney

1832 Jan—   To Catherine Ryan, Sydney
     Jly   No TL or certificate of freedom

GEORGIANA BAXTER

1829: 26 Widow 1 child Prot. *Educ* R&W *Native* London *Trade* Needlewoman
and nurse *Trial* London 26 September 1828 *Offence* Receiving (lover's ring)
Sentence 14 years Previous convictions illegible *Height* 5'0½" Ruddy complexion Brown hair Brown eyes Mole and horizontal scar on left cheek
1829 May   Robert Harvey, Sydney
     Aug   Withdrawn on own complaint Reassigned to H. Thomas, Sydney
     Aug   Married William Taylor, CF per *Mary*, seaman
1832 Jul   TL, Sydney
1836 Oct   Married John Lefevre, CF per *Lady Rowena*
1837   Muster — unlisted under any name
1839 Oct   Conditional pardon
1842 Sep   Certificate of freedom

1879 May   Death of husband John, a carpenter
    Nov   Died Camden, N.S.W.

MARY BISHOP
1829: 40 Widow 6 Children Prot. *Educ* R *Native* Hampshire *Trade* All work *Trial* Portsmouth 11 July 1828 *Offence* House robbery (stealing bed) *Sentence* 7 years 2 previous convictions *Height* 5'1¾" Ruddy freckled complexion Sandy grey hair Hazel eyes 2 moles right cheek, scar on right hand and little finger
1829 May   To Isabella Ryan, Sydney
    Dec   2mo, 3cl FF drunkenness & neglect of work
1830 Apr   Died in FF, Parramatta

ANN BOWLER
1829: 32 Married 6 children Prot. *Educ* R *Native* Birmingham *Trade* Housemaid *Trial* Warwick 15 July 1828 *Offence* Shoplifting *Sentence* 14 years 2 previous convictions *Height* 5'0½" Pale freckled complexion Brown hair Grey eyes
1829 May   To Major Mitchell, Sydney
    Aug   To Henry Thorn, Sydney
1830 Oct   To Hannah Fowler, Sydney
1831 Nov   To Mr Hyndes, Sydney
1833 Aug   TL, Sydney
1837   Muster — TL, Sydney
1840 Jan   Absolute pardon

BETTY BRIAN (BRYAN, O'BRIEN)
1829: 34 Married 2 children Cath. *Educ* R *Native* Kildare *Trade* All work *Trial* Lancaster 21 July 1828 *Offence* Stealing furniture *Sentence* 14 years 2 previous convictions *Height* 5'1¼" Ruddy freckled complexion Brown hair Hazel eyes Scar left eyebrow, chin and small one left arm
1829 May   Eliza Crampton, George St, Sydney
    Jun   6 weeks 3cl FF drunkenness
    ?   To W. Fitz, Windsor
1831 May   From above to 3cl FF, cause unknown
    Jul   Applied to marry W. Mansfield, Parramatta, TL
1832 Jan   To J. McLoughlin, Sydney
    Jul   To W. Lackay, Parramatta
    ?   To Mrs Austin, Sydney
1836 Dec   2mo. 3cl FF drunkenness
1838 Nov   TL, Windsor
1840 Apr   TL cancelled — stole child's frock 6mo. 3cl FF
    Dec   Applied marry S. Hills, B, Windsor — refused
1842 Dec   TL, Windsor.
1844 Feb   Certificate of freedom. Still at Windsor

JULIA BRIAN
1829: 36 Married 3 children Cath. *Educ* R&W *Native* Cork *Trade* Plain cook and all work *Trial* London 17 September 1828 *Offence* Stealing clothes *Sentence* 7 years No previous convictions *Height* 4'11" Ruddy freckled complexion Dark brown hair Light hazel eyes Small raised mole under left eye
1829 May   To Mr Manning, Sydney
1831 Aug   TL, Sydney.
1835 Sept Certificate of freedom

JOHANNA BROWN
1829: 18 Single Cath. *Educ* None *Native* Portugal *Trade* Nurse girl *Trial* London 11 September 1828 *Offence* Stealing reticule *Sentence* 14 years No previous

convictions *Height* 5'11" Ruddy freckled complexion Brown hair Hazel eyes
Scar over right eye and on right arm
See Chapter 12 for further details

SARAH BRYANT

1829: 18 Single Prot. *Educ* R&W *Native* Bath *Trade* Nurse girl *Trial* Somerset 18
July 1828 *Offence* Stealing clothes *Sentence* Life 2 previous convictions *Height*
5'0½" Ruddy slightly pockpitted complexion Brown hair Brown eyes Scar on
left thumb

1829 May	J. Edwards, Sydney
Nov	Given up by Master
1830 Jan	1mo. 3cl FF — absent without leave
Mar	Transferred from Mr A. Block to Mr James Mordane
Aug	6mo. (or weeks) 3cl FF — absent without leave
Nov	Married John Foley
1853 Dec	Conditional Pardon
1860 Jul	Husband died 1861 Remarried Francis Tunnicliffe
1879 Feb	Died Binda, Goulburn Issue: 1 son (Charles), 1 daughter (Margaret m. Skelly)

See Chapters 11 and 15 for details

ANNE BULLOCK

1829: 23 Married No children Prot. *Educ* R *Native* Litchfield *Trade* Dairymaid
and all work *Trial* Derby 21 August 1828 *Offence* Picking pockets *Sentence* 14
years No previous convictions *Height* 5'1" Ruddy freckled complexion Dark
brown hair Dark brown eyes Scar over right eye

1829 May	To Andrew Allan, Argyle
1830 Jul	Applied marry James Robinson, TL. Refused
1831 Jan	Still with Andrew Allan
Jun	Marries Robertson [sic]
1837	With husband working for James Chisholm, Goulburn

Known issue: 2 daughters (Elizabeth and Caroline) 1 son (James)

MARGARET BUNTON

1829: 19 Single Prot. *Educ* R *Native* Norfolk *Trade* Housemaid and nurse *Trial*
Norfolk 25 April 1828 *Offence* Picking pockets *Sentence* 7 years 2 previous convictions *Height* 5'3" Ruddy fair freckled complexion Light brown hair Hazel
eyes Tattoo on upper right arm

1829 May	To James Norton, Sydney
1829 Oct	3mo. 3cl for escaping from FF
1830 Oct	To Benjamin Singleton, Williams River
1830 Nov	Married William Cooper, FS, Maitland
1841 Oct	Certificate of freedom, Queanbeyan
1844–45	Probable convictions for drunkenness in Queanbeyan

LOUISA CAULFIELD

1829: 40 Widow No children Prot. *Educ* R&W *Native* Kent *Trade* Cook *Trial*
London 18 June 1828 *Offence* Stealing watch from person *Sentence* 14 years
Previous convictions? *Height* 5'4¾" Dark ruddy pockpitted complexion Black
to grey hair Dark hazel eyes Small dark mole on tip of nose

1829 May	To Percy Simpson, 31 Pitt St, Sydney
1830 Jul	1mo. 3cl FF — absent without leave
1831 Feb	1mo. 3cl FF — absent. Returned to government by Mr Walker
Apr	6 weeks 3cl FF
Oct	1mo. 3cl FF — Absent/drunk

Dec	2mo. 3cl FF — offence unknown
1832 May	Withdrawn from P. Simpson — insufficient rations
June	Assigned to Captain Waldron, 39th Regiment
	Absconded from Captain Waldron
1833 Aug	Still with Captain Waldron
Sep	Married Thomas Hyatt, FS, Farmer, Wollongong
1834 Jun	Gave evidence against husband for theft
1836 Oct	2mo. 3cl FF — disorderly conduct, drunkenness and prostitution
	Not to be assigned to husband again
1839 Oct	Died Parramatta Hospital

MARY ANN CHARLES

1829: 32 Married One child Prot. *Educ* R&W *Native* Falmouth *Trade* All work *Trial* Surrey Boro. 1 September 1828 *Offence* Picking pockets *Sentence* Life No previous convictions *Height* 5'5" Dark ruddy complexion Dark brown hair Hazel eyes Two small scars over right eye

1829 May	To Major D'Arcy, Sydney
Aug	Returned to government — useless in service
1832 Oct	To Mary Weller, Sydney
1833 Apr	Runaway from Mrs Howell, Sydney
May	2mo. 3cl FF — absconding
Sep	1mo. 3cl FF — offence unknown
1834 Oct	4mo. 3cl FF — offence unknown
1840 Jan	Died in the Parramatta hospital

ANN CHEESEMAN alias BATES

1829: 20 Married No children Prot. *Educ* R *Native* Manchester *Trade* Nursemaid *Trial* York 16 July 1828 with Ann Simpson *Offence* Picking pockets *Sentence* 14 years 2 previous convictions *Height* 5' Ruddy freckled pockpitted Dark brown hair Hazel eyes Scar on nose and lower lip

1829 May	To Mr McLoughlin, York St, Sydney
1829 Jun	3mo. 3cl FF — absconding from above
1830 Feb	1mo. 3cl FF — drunk
1830 Sep	1mo. 3cl FF — insubordinate/neglecting work
1831 Aug	To Surveyor Ogilvie, Maitland
1832 Jan	Still with above Applied to marry W. Harris, FS Refused because she was married on arrival
Jun	10 days solitary confinement Newcastle gaol
1833 Mar	With Mary Paterson, Parramatta Applied to marry John Webb, FS Refused
Jul	With Mrs Porter, Parramatta Applied to marry Charles Jones, CF Refused
1834 Jan	28 days 3cl FF
May	52 days 3cl FF
Aug	2mo. 3cl FF — charged by Sydney police
1835 May	2mo. 3cl FF from Sydney police
Nov	2mo. 3cl FF — absconding
1837	Muster — with A. L. Kentish, Sydney
1838–41	See Chapter 14 for details
1842 Dec	TL, Windsor
1844 Feb	Certificate of freedom prepared but not immediately received by Ann
Apr	At Windsor — applied marry William Dunkley, TL Refused because she declared married on arrival
1850 Apr	Probable marriage to William Malpass

MARY (ANN) CLANCEY
1829: 21 Single Cath. *Educ* R&W *Native* London *Trade* Nurse girl *Trial* London
26 October 1828 *Offence* Picking pockets *Sentence* 7 years No previous
convictions *Height* 4'9" Ruddy complexion Brown hair Light brown eyes 'WC'
on upper right arm

1829 May	To W. Hayward, Castlereagh St, Sydney
Aug	1mo. 3cl FF — absent without leave
1830 Jan	To Newcastle for assignment
Apr	Returned 2cl FF — pregnant
Aug	Returned from service — not wanted
1831 May	To John Rossi, Liverpool
Jul	1mo. 2cl FF — intoxication and insolence
Dec	Returned to government from assignment
1832	To J. Redmond, Sydney
Apr	Runaway from J. Redmond
Oct	To J. Brackenreg, Sydney
1833 Feb	6 weeks 3cl FF — insolence
Jun	2mo. 3cl FF — offence unknown
Sep	6 weeks 3cl FF — offence unknown
1835 Dec	Certificate of freedom

MARTHA CLARE
1829: 36 Widow One child Prot. *Educ* R&W *Native* Essex *Trade* All work and
needlewoman *Trial* London 12 September 1828 *Offence* Private stealing *Sentence*
7 years No previous convictions *Height* 5' Dark ruddy complexion Dark brown
hair Dark brown eyes Small scar in centre of forehead

1829 May	To Cornelius Prout, Sydney
May	6mo. 3cl FF — drunk, improper conduct
Aug	To Mr Cobb, Newcastle
Nov	1mo. 3cl FF — committed Patersons Plains, insolent and insubor-dinate
1831 Jan	To Robert Jones, Tailor, Sydney
Mar	1mo. 3cl FF — drunk and disorderly
May	1mo. 3cl FF — drunk and disorderly
	Returned to government by Mr Jones
1831	Assigned to William Boyler, Bathurst
Sep	48 hours cells — drunkenness
Dec	6 days cells — absconding
1832 Mar	Still with William Boyler Married Thomas Brothers, TL, at Bathurst
1833 Aug–Feb 1836:	12 convictions at Bathurst, mainly for drunkenness
1838 Oct	6mo. 3cl FF for escaping from Bathurst factory and for being 'a rogue and a vagabond'
1839 Aug	6mo. 3cl FF at Parramatta — offence unknown
1842 Sep	Thomas Brothers died at Kelso, Bathurst.

Martha Brothers died Bathurst hospital, 12 February 1851, buried Kelso

ANN CLARK
1829: 26 Single Prot. *Educ* R *Native* Bath *Trade* All work *Trial* London 5
September 1828 *Offence* Shoplifting *Sentence* 7 years No previous convictions
Height 5'1" Ruddy complexion Brown hair Hazel eyes Scar inside right arm
over joint

| 1829 May | To William Baldie (passenger *Princess Royal*) |
| 1831 Nov | TL, Sydney |

1835 Jan   Married George Phillips, TL
    Dec   Certificate of freedom
Ann Phillips died 7 August 1856 at 636 Parramatta St, Sydney Husband George Phillips, a dealer Maiden name Birchell [*sic*]

SARAH CLARK
1829: 20 Single Prot. *Educ* R&W *Native* Stroudwater Gloucestershire *Trade* Spinner All work *Trial* Somerset assizes Wells 13 August 1828 *Offence* Picking pockets *Sentence* 14 years 2 previous convictions *Height* 5'5½" Pale pockpitted complexion Brown hair Grey eyes
1829 May   Not assignable — sickly and scrofulous
    ?   Assigned in Sydney
1830 Jan   Returned to government 1st class
    May   With John Morgan, Sydney Applied to marry Francis Keefe, FS Allowed
    Sep   Married Richard Turton, FS, Baker, Sydney.
1836 Jun   TL, Sydney
1840 Feb   Conditional pardon
1842 Jul   Charged with perjury Supreme Court
    Aug   Certificate of freedom. Living with Mr Sutherland

MARGARET COFFIN
1829: 31 Widow 1 child with her (James aged 5½ years) Prot. *Educ* R&W *Native* Essex *Trade* Plain cook *Trial* London 10 September 1828 *Offence* Picking pockets *Sentence* 14 years *Height* 5'3" Ruddy freckled complexion Brown hair Brown eyes
1829 May   To Prosper de Mestre, George St, Sydney
    Jun   James to Orphan School
    Nov   Returned to 1st class, FF
1830 Jun   Returned to 1st class, FF. Assigned to Mr Hutchinson
1831 Dec   1mo. 3cl FF — offence unknown
1832 Jan   To Mrs Mitchell, Sydney
    Mar   To W. Bruce, Sydney
1835 Dec   James apprenticed as music instrument maker to Francis Ellard, Hunter St, Sydney
1841 Oct   Margaret died at Liverpool
1842 Mar   Ticket of Leave for Hunter area cancelled for absence from district

MARY ANN COLLINS
1829 28 Single Cath. *Educ* None *Native* Manchester *Trade* All work *Trial* Manchester 21 July 1828 *Offence* Picking pockets *Sentence* 14 years 3 previous convictions *Height* 4'9" Ruddy complexion Brown hair Hazel eyes Scar left eyebrow blue mark on nose, left cheek and left...mole on left cheek
1829 May   To Michael Farrell, Sydney
    Aug   Returned to 1st class — useless in service
    ?   To Mrs Ward
1830 Jan   To William Saunders
    Oct   6 weeks 3cl FF — drunk but employer (Saunders) also punished
1831 ?   To George Smith
    Jun   To W. Hayward
    Jul   1mo. 3cl FF — absent and drunk
    Sep   1mo. 3cl FF — insolent
1832 Jan   To Dennis Hasset, George St, Sydney
    May   To Sergeant R. Martin, 17th Regiment, Sydney
1833 Jan   6mo. 3cl FF — charged by Sydney police, offence unknown

?	To Mr John Cooper, Sydney
Oct	10 days 3cl FF — insolent
1834 Mar	30 days 3cl FF — charged by Sydney police, offence unknown
Jul	35 days 3cl FF — offence unknown
	No TL obtained
	No recorded marriage application
1845	Free by Factory Report (No certificate of freedom issued)

MARY CONNELL

1829: 19 Single Cath. *Educ* R *Native* Cork *Trade* Straw bonnet maker *Trial* London 17 September 1828 *Offence* Shop lifting *Sentence* 7 years No previous convictions *Height* 5'3" Ruddy pockpitted and freckled complexion Brown hair Hazel eyes Small scar over left eye ES on left arm Scar on back of hand

1829 May	To James Rooke, George St
May	Returned to government 1st cl FF
Sep	Returned to government 1st cl FF
1830 ?	In Newcastle area
Apr	Travels to Sydney at request FF committee
1831 Nov	To D. Ryan, Sydney
1832 Jun	To John Cobb, Hunter's River
1833 Jun	Sent from Merton down to FF Parramatta
1835 Sep	Certificate of freedom

ANN CURRIER (CARRIER)

1829: 19 Single Prot. *Educ* R&W *Native* Wolverhampton *Trade* Housemaid and nurse *Trial* Warwick 9 August 1828 *Offence* Picking pockets *Sentence* 7 years No previous convictions *Height* 4'9" Ruddy fair complexion Flaxen hair Hazel eyes Small scar on forehead between eyes

1829 May	To Sarah Wyie(?), Sydney
1830 Jan	Transferred from S. Wyer [*sic*] to M. Smith
Sep	To Captain H. Steel, Sydney
1831 Jun	Still with above. Applied marry John Ward, BC Marriage did not proceed
1832 Mar	TL, Sydney
1833 Apr	Married Peter Tyler, TL, printer
	No certificate of freedom obtained
	Peter Tyler died 6 July 1842

RACHAEL DAGNALL

1829: 24 Prot. Married No children (Husband Richard Dagnall and brother Jeremiah Andrews in V.D.L.) *Educ* R&W *Native* Chester *Trade* All work *Trial* Liverpool 5 May 1828 *Offence* Picking pockets *Sentence* 7 years 2 previous convictions *Height* 4'10¼" Ruddy freckled complexion Brown hair Hazel eyes Scar over right eye Mole on left cheek 'FAWA JA' on left arm 'JSRD' on upper part plus other marks

1829 May	To Elizabeth Board, Sydney
Jun	6 weeks 3cl FF — absent without leave
Aug	3mo. 3cl FF — drunk and insolent
1830 Sep	1mo. 3cl FF — absent without leave
1831 Feb	1mo. 2cl FF and returned to government — absent from service
1832 Dec	With A. McDougall, Maitland Applied to marry William Compton, Bond Refused
1835 May	Certificate of freedom, Mudgee
Sep	Rachael Andrews married John McLouglin at Maitland

ANN DODD
1829: 22 Single One child Prot. *Educ* None *Native* Chester *Trade* Kitchenmaid
Trial Chester 14 April 1828 *Offence* Housebreaking *Sentence* 7 years No previous
convictions *Height* 5'2¾" Ruddy pockpitted complexion Brown hair Brown
eyes Dark mole on each cheek and on left side of chin

1829 May	To George Sheeker, Lyons Terrace, Sydney
Aug	Absconded from above
1832 Mar	TL for good conduct in service
1835 Apr	Certificate of freedom
Nov	Married John Hutchinson, BC

CATHERINE DONOGHUE
1829: 18 Single Cath. *Educ* R&W *Native* London *Trade* Housemaid *Trial*
Guildford 31 July 1828 *Offence* Picking pockets *Sentence* Life No previous
convictions *Height* 4'11¾" Ruddy freckled complexion Sandy hair Blue eyes
Horizontal scar over left eye Dark mole on right cheek

1829 May	To Mary Johnstone, Sydney
Jun	6 weeks 2cl FF — drunk and disorderly
Oct	3mo. 3cl FF — found in carnal connexion
1830 May	1mo. 3cl FF — disobedience
May	Assigned to Port Stephens
Nov	Returned from Port Stephens — service not required
Nov	1mo. 3cl FF — drunk
Dec	To J. B. Harwood
1832 Jan	To Michael McCormick, Castlereagh St, Sydney
Apr	To Major Poole, 39th Regiment, Parramatta
Jun	To T. Moore, Wilberforce
Jul	To Patrick Fennell, Campbelltown
Sep	1mo. 3cl FF — sentenced at Campbelltown
Oct	To D. O'Brien, Sydney
1833 Feb	To Port Macquarie
Oct	12mo 3cl hard labour FF — assaulting the magistrate
1835 Jun	Died at FF hospital, Parramatta

JANE EDWARDS
1829: 27 Single Prot. *Educ* R. *Native* London *Trade* All work *Trial* London 11/26
September 1828 *Offence* Picking pockets *Sentence* 14 years No previous convictions *Height* 5' Ruddy fair and pockpitted complexion Brown hair Blue eyes

1829 May	To J. P. Lloyd, Liverpool
1831 Aug	Still with above Married John Smith, TL
1832 Jun	Husband assigned Bathurst and ticket cancelled
?	Jane assigned to Mrs Page, Liverpool
1832 Dec	1mo. 3cl FF — drunk
1833 Jul	TL, Liverpool
1834 Jul	Husband dies at Bathurst
Dec	TL cancelled for repeated drunkenness
?	Assigned to Mr Scurr, Campbelltown
1835 Oct	1mo. 3cl FF — offence unknown
1836 Dec	14 days solitary at Campbelltown
1837	Muster — employer Thomas Reddall, Campbelltown Jane described as TL
1842	2nd TL, Liverpool district
1843 Sep	Certificate of freedom, Liverpool

ISABELLA ERRINGTON the wife of William Errington
1829: 48 Married Prot. *Educ* R *Native* Northumberland *Trade* All work *Trial* Newcastle 3 August 1828 *Offence* Receiving *Sentence* 14 years No previous convictions *Height* 5'0½" Ruddy freckled complexion Auburn hair Hazel eyes Cannot pronounce the letter 'R'
1829 May   To William Hodges, Sydney
1832 Jul   TL for good conduct in service
1836   Possible marriage to C. H. W. Bath, Sydney, and daughter, Eliza, born 1837

MARY FAGAN
1829: 17 Single Cath. *Educ* None *Native* Liverpool *Trade* All work *Trial* Liverpool 27 July 1828 *Offence* Stealing hammers *Sentence* 7 years 2 previous convictions *Height* 4'10½" Ruddy freckled complexion Brown hair Dark grey eyes
1829 May   To Mary Box, Sydney
1831 Jun   3mo. 3cl FF — pilfering/absent
1832   Ann Reynolds
1832 Mar   To David Smith, Sydney
1832 Apr   12mo. 3cl FF — runaway
1833   Runaway from T. Callanan, Sydney
1834 Oct   9mo. 3cl FF
1836 Feb   At Mrs Bayley, Sydney
1836 Mar   Married James Lockwood, 26, FS
1837   Assigned husband
            No TL or certificate of freedom obtained
James Lockwood died 15 November 1860 at Shadforth Street, Paddington, Sydney Mary Lockwood died 22 March 1873, Gladesville hospital Issue: 7 children.

ELIZABETH FOXALL
1829: 25 Prot. Married (Husband William Fox to V.D.L. per William Miles) *Educ* R *Native place* At sea *Trade* Housemaid *Trial* Warwick 12 August 1828 *Offence* Picking pockets (in a house of ill-fame) *Sentence* Life No previous convictions *Height* 4'10" Ruddy complexion Brown hair Dark hazel eyes 'WILLIAM FOXALL' on upper left arm Letters on upper part of right Scar over left eye
1829 May   To Sarah Wapples, Pitt St, Sydney
     Dec   Returned to government 1cl FF, sick
1830 Jan   To Mr Downes
     Feb   To Mr Faulkland
     Jul   15 days cells — drunk and absenting
     Nov   6 weeks 3cl FF — insolent and neglecting work
     ?   To Elizabeth Clayton
1832 Jul   Still with above Applied to marry R. Barron Refused — See Chapter 9 for details.
1840 Feb   Died at the government hospital, Sydney

MARY ANN GREEN or WALTON
1829: 24 Married One child Prot. (Husband Thomas Walton to V.D.L. per Georgiana) *Educ* R *Native* Cheshire *Trade* All work *Trial* Chester 14 April 1828 *Offence* House breaking *Sentence* 7 years No previous convictions *Height* 4'9½" Ruddy complexion Brown hair Hazel eyes Raised mole under left corner of nose
1829 May   To William Spark, Sydney
     Jul   3mo. 3cl FF — out after hours

Oct	Returned to government 1st class FF
?	To S. Cooley
1830 Jan	To James Wells, Sydney
Mar	To William Summerfield
Jul	With William Spark again at Hunter River
	Applied to marry Refused because declared married
1831 Aug	Still with William Spark Again applied to marry Refused permission
1832 Mar	Ticket of Leave, Newcastle
1835 Jun	Certificate of Freedom. Probably settled Melbourne

MARTHA GREGORY the wife of John Gregory

1829: 38 Married 8 children Cath. *Educ* None *Native* Cambridge (but born Queens Co Ireland) *Trial* Essex 14 October 1828 *Offence* Stealing shoes *Sentence* 7 years 2 previous convictions *Height* 4'11" Ruddy freckled complexion Brown hair Hazel eyes Small scar left side of nose

1829 May	To Vabian Solomon, George St, Sydney
Jun	1mo. 3cl FF — offence unknown
Sep	1mo. 3cl FF — drunk and absent
Oct	Returned by master to 1st class FF
1830 Jan	Returned by master to 1st class FF
Mar	3mo. 3cl FF — drunk
Oct	1mo. 3cl FF — drunk and absent
1831 Mar	With Mr Shairp, North Shore — 1mo. 3cl FF — drunk
Oct	1mo. 3cl FF — drunk and absent
1832 Sep	To Edward Hunt, Sydney
1833 Mar	1mo. 3cl FF — offence unknown
Dec	28 days 3cl FF — offence unknown
1834 Jun	2mo. 3cl FF — offence unknown
Oct	10 days cells Parramatta gaol
1835 Mar	1mo. 3cl FF — offence unknown
1837 Mar	Certificate of freedom.
1861 Jan	Died at benevolent asylum

BRIDGET HAINSBURY

1829: 25 Single Cath. *Educ* None *Native* Connaught Ireland *Trade* Kitchenmaid *Trial* Stafford 19 July 1828 *Offence* Stealing bottles *Sentence* 7 years No previous convictions *Height* 5'2" Ruddy freckled complexion Sandy hair Grey eyes Small scar on left eyelid

1829 May	To Alexander Thompson, King St, Sydney
Jul	Returned to government 1st Class FF
Sep	Returned to government 1st Class FF
1830 Nov	With Thomas Deane, Kent St, Sydney
	Married Michael Keefe, FS Wollongong Probable issue includes: Ellen, Mary
	Probably settled Wollongong
1837 Jun	Certificate of freedom collected Sydney

SARAH HANCOCK

1829: 45 Widow 1 child Prot. *Educ* R&W *Native* Exeter *Trade* Cook *Trial* London 19 September 1828 *Offence* Unlawfully pledging *Sentence* 7 years No previous convictions *Height* 5'3" Ruddy freckled complexion Grey hair Hazel eyes

1829 May	To Mary Wyatt, King St, Sydney
1833 Aug	TL, Parramatta
1839 Apr	Possibly employed as infirmary nurse at female orphan school

1840 Jun   Sydney gaol 6 weeks (13th)
           From gaol to hospital (18th). Returns to gaol (29th)

MARY HARCOURT
1829: 20 Single Prot. *Educ* R *Native* Birmingham *Trade* Housemaid *Trial*
Warwick 9 August 1828 *Offence* Picking pockets (in house of ill-fame with
Elizabeth Foxall) *Sentence* Life No previous convictions *Height* 5' Ruddy
complexion Brown hair Dark hazel eyes 'ZY' heart darts and 'MH' on right arm
'WH' on left
1829 May   To John Reddall, Molles Plains
     Nov   Applied to marry William Platt, FS Allowed
           Did not proceed — Platt transported Moreton Bay
1831 ?   To Rev. Meares, Pitt Town
1832 Jan   Married Thomas Wright, BC. Settled Morpeth, NSW
1847 Dec   Conditional pardon

MARY HART
1829: 38 Single Prot. *Educ* R *Native* Londonderry *Trade* All work *Trial* Liverpool
27 July 1828 *Offence* Picking pockets *Sentence* 7 years No previous convictions
Height 5'2" Ruddy freckled complexion Brown hair Blue eyes Large scar under
left eye and on nose and perpendicular one upper lip
1829 May   To James Byrne, Gloucester St, Sydney
     Jul   Returned to government
1830 Feb   Returned to government
     Oct   With Mr Moses, Innkeeper, Penrith Married Jacob Winter, FS, at
           Castlereagh
1833 May   Died Bathurst

MARGARET HARTIGAN or SPLAIN
1829: 21 Single 1 child with her (Abigail 14 months — father William Splain in
London) Cath. *Educ* R *Native* London *Trade* Tailoress *Trial* London 11
September 1828 *Offence* Manslaughter *Sentence* Life No previous convictions
Height 5'0½" Ruddy pockpitted complexion Brown hair Blue eyes Large burnt
scar inside right arm
1829 May   To Lydia Walker, Castlereagh St, Sydney
     Jun   6 weeks 2cl FF — drunk and disorderly
1831 Feb   With Mr Pawsey, Newcastle — charged with absence without
           leave. Admonished.
           Daughter, Abigail, in Parramatta, admitted to female orphan
           school
     Nov   Still with Mr Pawsey — married John Smith, FS
1834 ?   2mo. Newcastle gaol — drunk and abusive
1835 Jan   Charged with abusive language, Newcastle. Admonished
     Oct   Sought protection from husband's brutality
1837 Nov   Charged with stealing — dismissed
1839 Feb   TL, Newcastle Altered for Maitland. Applied for Abigail from
           orphanage, but Abigail apprenticed (1838) to Mr Buxton, New-
           castle
1847 Apr   Conditional Pardon

MARY HAYNES
1829: 26 Prot. Married 1 child (Husband James per Adamant 1820 to N.S.W
Now free) *Educ* R&W *Native* Bristol *Trade* Dressmaker *Trial* Bristol 14 October
1828 *Offence* Receiving *Sentence* 14 years No previous convictions *Height* 4'10½"
Ruddy freckled complexion Dark brown hair Dark blue eyes Scar right side

upper lip and over left eye Scar corner right eyebrow and small one right cheek
1829 May   To Andrew Allan, Esq., Argyle
1841   Census — James Haynes, Parish of South Coolah, (*sic*) Parramatta
              district
1846 Jan   Certificate of freedom
1862 Jun   James Haynes died at South Colah
    Nov   Mary Haynes died at Sydney (Maiden name Mary Robberts)
              Surviving issue: 1 daughter

SARAH HAZLE

1829: 40 Widow 3 children Prot. *Educ* R *Native* Hertford *Trade* Plain cook *Trial* Bristol 14 July 1828 *Offence* Pledging *Sentence* 14 years No previous convictions *Height* 5′1″ Ruddy complexion Dark brown to grey hair Light hazel eyes Scar over outer corner of left eye
1829 May   To William Bradridge, Sydney
    Jul   6mo. 3cl FF — absconded from above
1831 May   1mo. cells on bread and water — stealing
1832 Feb   With Mr Ellis Married James Lake, FS, Parramatta.
1837   Muster — in government employ, Bathurst
1843 Jul   Certificate of freedom, Scone
Sarah Lake died 4 July 1853 at Scone Wife of James Lake
James Lake, butcher, died at Scone 7 February 1860

MARY HILSLEY

1829: 21 single Prot. *Educ* R&W *Native* London *Trade* All work *Trial* Surrey Boro. 4 September 1828 *Offence* Picking pockets *Sentence* 14 years No previous convictions *Height* 4′8″ Ruddy complexion Dark brown hair Dark hazel eyes Scar over left eye and corner of right 'GEORGE COLLABY' heart and dart on upper right arm 'PJ/MPJI' heart and darts on left arm
1829 May   To Daniel Whitehead, Pitt St, Sydney
    Aug   1mo. 3cl FF — absent without leave
    Sep   Returned to government 1st Class FF
1830 Jan   With Captain Steele, Bathurst Married John Godfrey, FS, carrier
1834 Jun   John charged with sheep stealing. To Sydney
    Aug   Mary to 1st Class FF per Sydney police
    Sep   John transported Norfolk Island
    Dec   Mary to 1st Class FF per Sydney police
1835   In Sydney
1836 Mar   TL for Bathurst
    Sep   Applied to marry John Primmir, FS
            refused — man married
1837 Mar   Died at the Bathurst factory

DOROTHY the wife of THOMAS HULDLE (HULDIE/HULDIN) alias ANN the wife of THOMAS WHITE

1829: 39 Married 3 children Prot. *Educ* R&W *Native* Northshiels *Trade* Nurse *Trial* Newcastle 16 October 1828 *Offence* Unlawfully pledging *Sentence* 7 years 2 previous convictions *Height* 4′11″ Dark ruddy complexion Brown hair Hazel eyes Nose inclined to left
1829 May   To Mary Weedon, 15 Harrington Street, Sydney
    Sep   1mo. 3cl FF — drunk and insolent
1830 Nov   With Lieutenant Lloyd, Sydney
            1mo. 3cl FF — repeated drunkenness — remitted
    Nov   1mo. 3cl FF — drunk and absent
1831 Jul   With William Cox, Windsor — 3 years transportation to Moreton

	Bay — theft
1834 Aug	Returned from Moreton Bay Assigned to J. Weston
Oct	From Hospital to 1st Class FF
Nov	From Police to 1st Class FF
Dec	From Sydney Police 1mo. 3cl FF
1836 Jun	With William Lawton, Parramatta — disorderly conduct 2mo. 3cl FF. 1837 Muster with C. Windeyer, Sydney
1840 Dec	Certificate of freedom
1841 Jan	Tried quarter sessions, Sydney, for larceny Guilty 6mo. hard labour, FF
1842 Jan	Tried quarter sessions, Parramatta, for larceny Not guilty Discharged
1843 Sep	12mo. 3cl FF — larceny Remitted after 10 mo.
1846 May	From Sydney police/trial — FF — offence unknown
July	Married Richard Challenor, Sydney
1849	Husband died
1859	Ann died, Sydney

JANE HYDE

1829: 45 Single Prot. *Educ* R&W *Native* Cobham *Trade* Plain cook and all work *Trial* London 19 September 1828 *Offence* Stealing plates *Sentence* 7 years 2 previous convictions *Height* 5'1¼" Dark ruddy complexion Dark brown to grey hair Dark brown eyes

1829 May	To Charles Driver, Castlereagh St, Sydney
1830 Feb	To James Underfield, Ashfield Park
1831 Jan	10 days cells at FF — absent without leave and drunk
1835 Mar	Applied from FF to marry James Taylor, FS
	No certificate of freedom issued

ELIZABETH JONES

1829: 18 Single Prot. *Educ* R&W *Native* London *Trade* Housemaid *Trial* Guildford 31 July 1828 *Offence* Picking pockets *Sentence* Life No previous convictions *Height* 5' Ruddy freckled pockpitted complexion Black or dark brown hair Dark brown eyes

1829 May	To R. Harvey, 25 Pitt St, Sydney
Sep	1mo. 3cl FF — absent without leave
Oct	Returned to government 1st Class FF
1830 Jul	Returned to government 1st Class FF then assigned to John Dibbs, Sydney
1831 Jun	3cl FF (length of time unknown) — drunk and abusive to mistress
Nov	1mo. 3cl FF — offence unknown
1832 Jan	To Maria Dowling, Woolloomooloo
Oct	To Daniel O'Brien, Pitt St, Sydney
1833 Dec	Applied to marry John Potter, FS
1834 Mar	Married Potter — brickmaker
	No TL No certificate of freedom
1857 Nov	Died at Sussex Street, Sydney
	Issue included son John, daughter Jane

SUSAN KING or FORRESTER

1829: 29 Single 1 child (Elizabeth born on ship) Prot. *Educ* R&W *Native* Maidstone *Trade* All work *Trial* London 18 June 1828 *Offence* Stealing watch from the person *Sentence* 14 years No previous convictions *Height* 5'1¼" Ruddy fair complexion Light brown hair Hazel eyes Scar over left eye and one under corner of right

1829 May   To Elizabeth Drinkwater, Parramatta
1830 Aug   1mo. 2cl FF — drunk and abusive
1832 Jan   To S. Simpson, Castlereagh Street, Sydney
    Apr   Elizabeth to female orphan school
    May   Applied to marry Edward Sinnott, CF, discharged soldier Allowed but did not proceed
    May   To George Pearce, Upper Pitt St, Sydney
    Jul   To W. H. Petit, Bathurst St, Sydney
1833 Aug   TL, Sydney
    Oct   2mo. 3cl FF — drunkenness and insolence
           Ticket cancelled
1835 Feb   With Ann Goodwin, Sydney
    Mar   Married George Gilbert, FS, carter
    May   Elizabeth died Orphan School, aged 6
1840 Sep   Susan died Sydney

ANN KINSMAN (sometimes KINGSMILL)

1829: 20 Single Prot. *Educ* R *Native* Cornwall *Trade* Farm servant and dairymaid *Trial* Dorset 14 July 1828 *Offence* Picking pockets *Sentence* 7 years No previous convictions *Height* 5'0½" Ruddy freckled complexion Brown hair Brown eyes Flat nose Scar left cheek and eye Raised mark right arm Scar right forefinger
1829 May   To Edward Spark, Dart Brook (Hunter River)
1830 Feb   Still with above Married John Hoskins, FS See Chapters 11 and 15 for further details
1835   Richard Holland, lover, Maitland
1846   Married Phillip Field, Clarencetown
1861 May   Died at Parramatta lunatic asylum
           Possible issue, son Henry Kingsmill (1831)

ANN KIRBY (real name probably KIRLEY or KILEY or REILLY)

1829: 20 Single Cath. *Educ* None *Native* Waterford Co. *Trade* Housemaid *Trial* Bristol 14 July 1828 *Offence* Robbing person *Sentence* 14 years No previous convictions *Height* 5'4" Ruddy freckled complexion Light brown hair Hazel eyes
1829 May   To Mrs Windeyer, Castlereagh St, Sydney
1830 Feb   1mo. 3cl FF — absent without leave
    Sep   1mo. 3cl FF — improper conduct. Return to government
1831 Jun   Married Thomas Leonard/Linwood, FS
1837   Muster as 'Ann Reilley' at George Howell's Richmond
1839 Apr   TL Windsor. Cancelled in May for 'highly immoral conduct'
    July – Second TL Windsor. Applied marry Patrick Day FS.
           Refused – 'man married'
1841 Dec   Ticket cancelled for absence from muster

SARAH LOVETT

1829: 43 Married Prot. *Educ* R *Native* Leicester *Trade* Needlewoman *Trial* Leicester 18 July 1828 *Offence* Stealing kettle 2 previous convictions *Height* 5'5" Ruddy freckled and pockpitted complexion Dark brown to grey hair Brown eyes
1829 May   To Charlotte Dick, Pitt St, Sydney
See Chapter 6 for details

ANN LOYDALL

1829: 36 Single Prot. *Educ* R&W *Native* Leicestershire *Trade* Sempstress and nurse *Trial* Leicester 22 March 1827 *Offence* Housebreaking *Sentence* 14 years

No previous convictions *Height* 4'8" Ruddy fair complexion Light brown hair Light hazel eyes Brown mark on left eye Scar left temple Scar inside right arm Raised mole right upper lip Scar in right eyebow

1829 May	To William Davis, Kent St, Sydney
1830 Apr	Still with above Married James Winter, FS, police constable, householder in Kent Street
1841 Apr	Certificate of freedom, Sydney

JANE LYON
1829: 39 Single Prot. *Educ* R&W *Native* Liverpool *Trade* Buttermaker *Trial* Liverpool 27 July 1828 *Offence* Stealing blankets *Sentence* 7 years 2 previous convictions *Height* 5'1" Ruddy freckled pockpitted complexion Brown hair Hazel eyes Large raised mole over right eye Large brown mark on each cheek

1829 May	Not assignable Scrofulous and lame,
1830 Aug	In assigned service to Mr Ralph
	Died at Sydney hospital

MARGARET LYONS
1829: 21 Single Cath. *Educ* R *Native* Dublin *Trade* Nurse and housemaid *Trial* Middlesex quarter sessions 23 October 1828 *Offence* Picking pockets *Sentence* Life No previous convictions *Height* 4'11½" Ruddy freckled and pockpitted complexion Dark brown hair Hazel eyes Left arm crooked broken Scar corner of right eye

1829 May	To Thomas Wood, George St, Sydney
Jun	3mo. 3cl FF — absconding
1832 Jan	To Mary Raine, Parramatta
1834 Sep	14 days 3cl FF — offence unknown
1835 Jun	2mo. 3cl FF — offence unknown
1836 Jun	From Liverpool to Sydney for trial
Aug	To FF — details unknown
1840 Dec	With Henry Shadforth, Esq., Mulgoa
	Married John Jackson, CP
1849 Jan	Conditional pardon

ANN the wife of John McGHEE (or McKAY) alias ANN BROWN
1829: 39 Married 2 children Prot. *Educ* R&W *Native* Dublin *Trade* Laundress *Trial* London 11 September 1827 *Offence* Stealing child's frock *Sentence* Life No previous convictions *Height* 5'1" Ruddy freckled complexion Light brown to grey hair Hazel eyes

1829 May	To Elizabeth Raine, O'Connell St, Sydney
1830 Oct	Drunk and absent Cells 10 days on bread and water and return to her service
1831 May	1mo. 3cl FF — offence unknown
1838	TL, Parramatta
1850	Ticket cancelled for absence from district, but reissued, absence being explained

JANE McPHERSON
1829: 20 Single Prot. *Educ* R&W *Native* London *Trade* Needlewoman *Trial* Surrey boro. 31 July 1828 *Offence* Picking pockets *Sentence* Life No previous convictions *Height* 4'9" Ruddy freckled complexion Light brown hair Light hazel eyes 'ETHOMAS Edward Thomas' on left arm Small scars centre forehead left side nose and corner left eye

| 1829 May | To Lieut. McIntosh, Cumberland, Sydney |
| 1830 Apr | 15 days 3cl FF — absent without leave |

1831 Jan   Still with Mrs McIntosh
      Feb   Married William Mason, FS, dealer
1837   Not listed convict muster
1844 Dec   TL, Sydney
1851 Aug   Conditional pardon
1856 Apr   Died at Sussex Street, Sydney

MARGARET MAHONEY or MELIAR (MEELEY/MEALEY)
1829: 40 Married to John Mahoney 3 children, son Richard age 9 with her on
Princess Royal Prot. *Native* Sligo or Dublin *Trade* Washerwoman *Trial* London
11 September 1827 *Offence* Stealing bacon *Sentence* 7 years 2 previous convictions *Height* 5' Dark freckled pockpitted complexion Brown hair Blue eyes
Scars left eyebrow under left eye over right eye on nose
1829 May   To Rose Casey, 9 Hunter St, Sydney
      May   27th: returned to FF. Richard sent to male orphan school —
               admitted under name Meeley
    ?   Margaret assigned to Mr Phillips, Sydney
1830 Jul   Drunk and raped at Bringelly (see Chapter 7)
      Sep   Drunk and absent without leave — 10 days cells
      Nov   1mo. 3cl FF — drunkenness
1831 Mar   With Thomas Everden, Bathurst — drunk Admonished
      Nov   Still with Everden Drunk and abuse Fined 5s.
1832 Sep   With Mr Piper Drunk — 2 days cells
1833 Aug   10th: drunk — 3 days cells
               20th: TL, Bathurst
               20th: drunk — 3 days cells
1835 Nov   Certificate of freedom.
               Richard apprenticed to James Bibb, blacksmith
1839 Aug   Margaret convicted of drunkenness at Bathurst — 6mo. 3cl FF at
               Parramatta

MARY MAHONEY
1829: 19 Single Cath. *Educ* R *Native* Cork *Trade* All work *Trial* London 18
September 1828 *Offence* Robbing employer *Sentence* 14 years No previous
convictions *Height* 5'1½" Ruddy freckled pockpitted complexion Brown hair
Hazel eyes Mole between eyes Blind of right eye
1829 May   To Elizabeth Clayton, George St, Sydney
      Sep   Stole tea — retransported Moreton Bay 12mo.
1830 Nov   Returned to Sydney Assigned to Joseph Moore
      Dec   2mo. 3cl and returned to government — insolence/neglect of duty
1837   Assigned Capt. G. Banks, Cumberland St, Sydney
1839 Mar   Still with above
      Apr   TL, Sydney
               Married Richard McGrath, CF, 1838 per Magistrate
1840 Jan   Ticket altered to Port Phillip
1843 Nov   Certificate of freedom issued Collected in Sydney 1 October 1845

ANN MARSHALL
1829: 18 Single Prot. *Educ* R&W *Native* Newcastle *Trade* Nursemaid *Trial*
Newcastle 3 August 1828 *Offence* Housebreaking *Sentence* 14 years No previous
convictions *Height* 5'2¾" Ruddy freckled complexion Brown hair Light hazel
eyes
1829 May   To James Warman, Sydney
      Sep   1mo. 3cl FF — disobedience
    ?   To Hannibal Macarthur, Esq., Parramatta

1830 ?	To Mrs McGilveroy of Sydney
Nov	Married Walter Neary, per *Asia*, FS, Baker
1834 Jan	Assaulted by husband (see Chapter 11)
1835 Nov	TL, Sydney
1841	Died Sydney Known issue: 2

ANN the wife of William MAW alias ANN GILMORE
1829: 40 Married 2 children Prot. *Educ* R&W *Native* Dorsetshire *Trade* All work
Trial Southampton quarter sessions Portsmouth 17 October 1828 *Offence*
Unlawfully pledging *Sentence* 7 years 2 previous convictions *Height* 5'3½" Dark
freckled complexion Sandy to grey hair Hazel eyes Hairy mole left side upper
lip Horizontal scar on left cheek

1829 May	To Henry Donohoe, Pitt St, Sydney
Aug	Runaway from David Dyer
Nov	1mo. 3cl FF — drunk and absenting
1830 Apr	1mo. 3cl FF — drunkenness
?	To James Whittaker
1831 Mar	3mo. 3cl FF — absent without leave and highly improper conduct
	Returned to government by Whittaker
1835 Dec	Certificate of freedom

ELLEN MEARS or MAVORS/MEYERS/MEARY/MORRIS/MURRAY
1829: 26 Married Prot. *Educ* R&W *Native* Chelsea *Trade* Nurse girl *Trial* Surrey 2
January 1828 *Offence* Stealing watch *Sentence* Life No previous convictions
Height 5' Pale freckled complexion Brown hair Green to dark hazel eyes Two
raised moles left cheek and small scar underneath

1829 May	To Jane Blofield, Upper Pitt St, Sydney
Jun	Returned to government 1st class FF
Dec	Returned to government 1st class FF
	Possibly assigned to Hannah Wheeler
1834 Mar	With Mrs Tyne at Castlereagh Applied marry George Palmer, TL
	Governor refused permission
1837	Convict muster — with Richard Hibble, Penrith

Other possible surnames — Grant, Gleeson See male orphan school — Robert
Gleeson alias Myers

ANN MORGAN
1829: 19 Single Prot. *Educ* R&W *Native* Radnorshire *Trade* Dairymaid *Trial*
Radnor 18 April 1828 *Offence* Stealing watch *Sentence* 7 years 2 previous convictions *Height* 4'11½" Ruddy freckled complexion Brown hair Grey eyes Scar on
left elbow Small scar over right eye...

1829 May	To Abraham Kern, cabinetmaker
1830 Mar	To Lieut. William Ball, Royal Veterans, Windsor
Aug	Married Private Patrick McMahon, CF per *Orpheus*
1832 Jun	Husband purchased land Lot 10 Mount Tomah
1834 Oct	3mo. 3cl FF — offence unknown
Nov	TL, Sydney
1835 May	Certificate of freedom
Dec	Bail from Sydney gaol
1836 Sep	Trial Discharged on own recognizance
1839 Aug	Bail from Sydney gaol
1841 Oct	Bail from Sydney gaol
1852	Probable death Sydney age 42

MARY MORRIS
1829: 20 Single Cath. *Educ* R *Native* Liverpool *Trade* All work *Trial* Manchester
21 July 1828 *Offence* Robbing master *Sentence* 7 years 2 previous convictions
Height 5'1½" Ruddy freckled pockpitted complexion Brown hair Light hazel
eyes Dark mark inside left arm joint Scar inside top left hand

1829 May	To Ann Kennedy, Goulburn St, Sydney
1831 Jun	TL, Sydney.
Aug	Still with Kennedys Married Joseph Spencer, CF per *Ceylon*, Clerk
1832 Apr	Husband died at Newcastle
1834 Aug	Working for G. Bush, Esq., Bathurst Charged with drunkenness — admonished and ticket cancelled
Nov	6 days cells — charged by matron of Bathurst factory with disorderly conduct
1835 Jan	2-year-old son, Joseph, accidentally drowned
Feb	Working at Bathurst factory Absent without leave — admonished
Mar	Drunk and disorderly — fined 5s. Reassigned to government service, Wellington Valley.
Jul	13th: applied to marry William Clark, FS. Allowed but did not proceed
	26th: Certificate of freedom.
1842 Oct	At Bathurst applied to marry William Cloft or Clough, TL. Refused until she proved her widowhood Did not proceed
1844 Mar	Married John Holmes, TL, at Bathurst

SOPHIA NAYLOR or HUNTER
1829: 20 Single Prot. *Educ* R *Native* Newcastle-on-Tyne Northumberland *Trade*
Housemaid nurse and all work *Trial* Northumberland 3 March 1828 *Offence*
Picking pockets *Sentence* 7 years 2 previous convictions *Height* 4'5¼" Ruddy
freckled complexion Brown hair Blue eyes Nose short and a little cocked By
1835 lost all front upper teeth

1829 May	To C. Nott, Sydney
May	31st: 6wk.3cl FF — highly improper conduct
1831 Jan	2mo. 3cl FF and returned to government — absconding and taking a pair of boots
Oct	With William and Ann Wells, Sydney Applied to marry Henry Latham, FS, fisherman Did not proceed
Oct	1mo. 3cl FF — offence unknown
1832 Apr	Runaway or absent without leave from Mrs Wells
Jul	Assigned to J. D. Nicholls, Pitt St, Sydney
Dec	Reapplied to marry Henry Latham Application also lodged Newcastle
1833 Jan	Married Henry Latham
1835 May	Certificate of freedom

MARY PALMER
1829: 35 Married (Husband Richard died London 1827) 1 child Prot. *Educ*
None *Native* Plymouth *Trade* Plain cook all work *Trial* Surrey boro. 1
September 1828 *Offence* Picking pockets *Sentence* 14 years No previous
convictions *Height* 5'6" Ruddy complexion Brown hair Hazel eyes

1829 May	To James Brackenreg, Sydney
Jul	3mo. 3cl FF — drunkenness and abuse
1830 Jan	Transferred from Brackenreg to Thomas Day
Apr	1mo. 3cl FF — abusing mistress Returned to Day
1831 Feb	1mo. 3cl FF — insolent to her master
	Returned to government by Thomas Day

Jul	3mo. 3cl FF — drunk and insolent — set fire to master's pub
1832 Jan	To Thomas Icely, Bungarabee
1833 Mar	3 days cells, Parramatta gaol — offence unknown
1835 Jan	Stealing — confined in Goulburn
1836 May	To Captain Allman, magistrate, Goulburn
Aug	With Solomon Moses, publican, Goulburn
	Drunk — reprimanded
1837 May	With J. McAlister, Campbelltown
	24 hours solitary — absent without leave. TL issued for Goulburn
1838 Sep	With Solomon Moses, Goulburn
1840	Married William Hickmott (See Chapter 10)
1863 Oct	Died Hyde Park benevolent asylum.

ANN PERKS (PARKS)
1829: 27 Married 1 Child Prot. *Educ* R *Native* Stafford *Trade* All work *Trial* Warwick 9 August 1828 *Offence* Shoplifting (stealing silk) *Sentence* Life 2 Previous convictions *Height* 4'11½" Ruddy fair complexion Light brown hair Grey eyes Scar at corner right eye Large inoculation scar on left arm

1829 May	To Thomas Howell, York St, Sydney
1831 Apr	2mo. 3cl FF — offence unknown
Jul	With M. A. Johnson in Sydney
Aug	13th To V.D.L. per Snapper with Governor's permission to join mother Phelis Herring

SARAH alias CHARLOTTE PIPER
1829: 40 Married No children Prot. *Educ* None *Native* Brighton *Trade* Unserviceable *Trial* Lewes 4 September 1828 *Offence* Stealing coats *Sentence* Life 2 previous convictions *Height* 4'10½" Ruddy freckled complexion Brown hair bald (*sic*) Light hazel eyes

1829 May	Not assignable — cripple
1837	Convict muster — with Jeremiah Walters
1840	TL, Port Macquarie
1842 Apr	Died at Port Macquarie

SARAH the wife of James PITCHES (PETCHES)
1829: 29 Married (Husband James) 1 child James age 18 months on Princess Royal Cath. *Educ* None *Native* Londonderry *Trade* Barmaid *Trial* Cambridge 14 July 1828 *Offence* House breaking *Sentence* 7 years No previous convictions *Height* 4'9½" Ruddy freckled complexion Dark brown hair Hazel eyes Scar on each side forehead Large scar across left cheek

1829 May	To Andrew Nash, Innkeeper, Parramatta
1830 Jun	James to male orphan school
Sep	1mo. 3cl FF — improper conduct
1831 Aug	1mo. 3cl FF — drunk
1832 Jun	To Mrs Mary Elliot, York St, Sydney
Nov	Runaway from Mrs Elliot
1834 ?	To Rev. Threlkeld, Newcastle
1835 Jan	14 days cells — insolence Returned to master
Jul	Technically free
Oct	1mo. Newcastle gaol
1836 Oct	Married William Turvey, Newcastle

See Chapter 13 for further details

SARAH QUITTENTON (QUIDENTON/WHITTINGTON)
1829: 39 Widow 2 children Cath. *Educ* R&W *Native* Hampstead *Trade* All work

Trial London 19 September 1828 *Offence* Stealing ribbon *Sentence* 7 years No previous convictions *Height* 5'3½" Ruddy pockpitted complexion Brown hair Brown eyes Small scar near centre of forehead

1829 May	To E. J. Keith, Attorney, Pitt St, Sydney
May	26th: returned to government — 1st Class FF
1830 Feb	Suspected of theft Returned to government
?	To William Lee, Bathurst
1831 Feb	Married Daniel Reddiford (see Chapter 11)
1838 Oct	Died at Campbelltown

ANN the wife of John SHANNON
1829: 30 Married (Husband in N.S.W. per Mellish) 1 Child Cath. *Educ* None *Native* Down Patrick *Trade* Housemaid *Trial* Liverpool 27 July 1828 *Offence* Picking pockets *Sentence* 7 years No previous convictions *Height* 4'10½" Ruddy freckled pockpitted complexion Brown hair Light hazel eyes Nose broken and scar underneath left side

1829 May	To John Morris, Market St, Sydney
Jul	2mo. 3cl FF — drunkenness and insolence
1830 Feb	1mo. 3cl FF — drunk and disorderly
1832 Jan	To J. Walsh, Sydney
1833 Apr	To R. Connor, Wilberforce
Apr	Runaway from above
Oct	14 days 3cl FF — offence unknown
1834 Sep	28 days 3cl FF — offence unknown
Nov	1mo. 3cl FF — offence unknown
1835 Aug	1mo. 3cl FF — offence unknown
Nov	Certificate of freedom.
1836 Feb	14 days hard labour Parramatta — offence unknown

See Chapter 10 for further details

ANN SIMPSON
1829: 17 Single Prot. *Educ* R&W *Native* York *Trade* Gloveress *Trial* Hull 16 July 1828 *Offence* Picking pockets *Sentence* 14 years 2 previous convictions *Height* 5'2" Ruddy freckled complexion Hazel eyes

1829 May	To James Robertson, Sydney
Jun	Returned to government — 1st Class FF
?	To George Wyndham, Esq., Maitland
1830 Jun	Still with above Married John Prentice, BC, overseer to George Wyndham

See Chapters 11, 14 and 15

CHARLOTTE SMITH
1829: 29 Widow 1 child Cath. *Educ* R&W *Native* Dublin *Trade* Laundress *Trial* Lewis 4 September 1828 *Offence* Shoplifting *Sentence* 14 years No previous convictions *Height* 5'2½" Ruddy freckled complexion Brown hair Blue eyes

1829 May	To Joseph Thompson, 31 Princes St, Sydney
Jun	6wk 3cl FF — drunkenness
1830 Apr	6wk 3cl FF and returned to government — absent without leave
Aug	3mo 3cl FF — drunk and absent
1832 Mar	Married Samuel Raynor, TL for Mulgoa
1837	Convict muster — working for George Cox, Bathurst
1839	Samuel and Charlotte still with George Cox
	Samuel received Conditional Pardon
1857 Oct	Died Broomby, Mudgee (see Chapter 8)

ELIZABETH SMITH

1829: 40 Married 3 children Prot. *Educ* R&W *Native* Exeter *Trade* Cook *Trial* London 19 September 1828 *Offence* Pledging illegally (a sheet off the bed at her lodgings) *Sentence* 7 years No previous convictions *Height* 5'4½" Ruddy complexion Dark brown to grey hair Hazel eyes Raised moles on each cheek and right and left corners of nose

1829 May	To Alexander McLeay, Esq., Colonial Secretary, Macquarie St, Sydney
28 May	Returned to government — 1st Class FF
Dec	With Andrew Gardiner, Bathurst Applied to marry John Barber, FS, bullock driver Application rejected
1832 Dec	With William Crockett, Campbelltown 1mo.3cl FF — charged with absconding by Crockett
1840 Jan	Certificate of freedom

MARY SMITH alias TURBULT (sometimes ANN or ELLEN TURNBULL)

1829: 28 Married 2 children Prot. *Educ* R *Native* Manchester *Trade* All work and needle *Trial* Nottingham 16 July 1828 *Offence* Shoplifting *Sentence* 7 years No previous convictions *Height* 5'2¾" Ruddy freckled complexion Brown hair Hazel eyes

1829 May	To Samuel Bate, 46 Pitt St, Sydney
Jun	1mo. 3cl FF — drunk and disorderly
Jul	6wk. 3cl FF — drunkenness
Sep	To Mr Mossman Applied to marry William Littlewood, TL — refused
1830 Feb	6wk. 3cl FF — drunkenness
Jul	2mo. 3cl FF — absent without leave
1831 Mar	Illegally at large in Sydney Sent to Magistrates, Parramatta, to be dealt with
1835 Sep	Certificate of freedom

MARY SMITH (the 3rd)

1829: 20 Single Prot. *Educ* R&W *Native* Manchester *Trade* Nursegirl *Trial* Nottingham 16 July 1828 *Offence* Shoplifting *Sentence* 7 years No previous convictions *Height* 4'10" Ruddy freckled complexion Brown hair Dark brown eyes Dark raised mole over right eye and another right side of chin

1829 May	Dr David Ramsay, Dobroyd, Petersham
Jul	Returned to government 1st Class FF To Mr Wentworth
Sep	Returned to government 1st Class FF — useless in service To Mrs Fennell, Newcastle
Dec	Married at Corinda to James or John Cranfield, FS, employed at St Helier
1830 Dec	Birth of daughter Ellen Cranfield at St Helier, Maitland
1833 Mar	With Walter Rotton, publican, Maitland
1835 Sep	Certificate of freedom
1842 Jun	Tried Maitland quarter sessions for receiving stolen goods Not guilty
1844 Jan	In Newcastle gaol for trial at quarter sessions
1856 Jul	3mo. in Newcastle gaol — offence unknown

MARY ANN SMITH

1829: 21 Single Cath. *Educ* None *Native* London *Trade* Housemaid *Trial* London 1/7 June 1828 *Offence* Picking pockets *Sentence* 14 years No previous convictions *Height* 5'2" Ruddy pockpitted complexion Brown hair Hazel eyes Raised swelling over left eye

1829 May To Catherine Clarkson, 7 Hunter St, Sydney
     Jun   Returned to government — 1st Class FF
1832 Jul   TL Sydney for good conduct in service Applied to marry Charles Hancock, TL. Marriage allowed but did not proceed
1833 Jan   Ticket altered to Airds district
     Aug   Ticket altered to Shoalhaven district — Employed by Alexander Berry
     Oct   Married Robert Mitchell, CF, employed by Mr Berry

MARY ANN SMITH alias AMY (or ANN or ELLEN) BURKE

1829: 32 Married 3 Children Prot. *Educ* R *Native* Dublin *Trade* Laundress *Trial* Nottingham 16 July 1828 *Offence* Shoplifting *Sentence* 7 years 2 previous convictions *Height* 4'9½" Ruddy freckled pockpitted complexion Dark brown hair Hazel eyes Nose inclined to right Scar of cut over left eye
1829 May To Stephen McDonald, 24 Princes St, Sydney
1832 Jan   To H. Howell, Sydney
     Aug   To R. Lethbridge, Maitland
1833 Sep   With Walter Rotton, publican, Maitland
           Applied to marry Samuel Davis, TL — refused
1834 Mar   In Newcastle gaol — applied to marry William Clarke, BC — refused permission
     Sep   With J. B. Squires, Maitland Applied to marry John Jones, TL, employed by A. McLeod — refused
1835 Feb   Still with Mr Squires Reapplied to marry Jones
     May   Married John Jones
           Certificate of freedom due 1835 but never issued

HANNAH (sometimes ANNA) SOLOMONS

1829: 20 Single Prot. *Educ* R&W *Native* London *Trade* All work *Trial* London *Offence* Picking pockets *Sentence* 14 years No previous convictions *Height* 5'1½" Florid freckled complexion Red hair Hazel eyes 'BMGSHC' 2 hearts anchor and 'BS' on upper left arm 'HL love to the heart' on upper right JS and 5 dots between left thumb and forefinger
1829 May To John Tolkard, 26 Kent St, Sydney
     Aug   Returned to government — 1st Class FF
1832 Dec   TL, Windsor
1833 Sep   Married James Box, FS
  ?   Husband died
1837   Convict muster — TL, Parramatta
     Oct   Married Charles Smith, TL, servant, Prospect
1842   FF report of Dec 1842 says total of 2mo. and 14 days against Hannah's name Date and offences are not stated
1843 May Certificate of freedom

CATHERINE STEEL

1829: 26 Single Cath. *Educ* R *Native* Bristol *Trade* Kitchenmaid *Trial* London 26 September 1828 *Offence* Stealing reticule *Sentence* 14 years No previous convictions *Height* 4'9½" Fair complexion Brown hair Hazel eyes Nose inclined to right Large perpendicular scar on left cheek near ear
1829 May To J. Henry, 1 York St, Sydney
     Jun   Returned to government — 1st Class FF
     Dec   With Thomas Avery, Narellan
1830 Jan   Married Peter Riglin, FS, wheelwright
1833 Dec   Husband died Assigned to William Wood, Bringelly
1834 Jun   Married John Dorman, FS

1837   Convict muster — working for Capt. King, Penrith
1841 Aug   4mo. hard labour, Sydney gaol — larceny
1862 Jun   Died Goulburn
See Chapter 12 for more details
Maiden or English married name possibly Stevens or Connor

ELIZABETH STOCKER
1829: 18 Single Prot. *Educ* R&W *Native* Bristol *Trade* Nurse girl *Trial* Bristol 14 July 1828 *Offence* Stealing cotton *Sentence* 7 years 2 previous convictions *Height* 4'8" Ruddy slightly pockpitted complexion Brown hair Blue eyes 'WA' heart 'ESHP' on left arm 'CI' on right upper arm Ring and spots on fingers Dark mole right side of cheek
1829 May   To Rev. Thomas Reddall, Campbelltown
1831 May   Returned to government — 1st class FF
1832 Feb   Assigned to James Fellows, Parramatta but in FF for unknown
              reason
     Mar   Married Peter Glover, FS
1833 Nov   3 days cells Bathurst — assault
1834 May   Husband a debtor, Bathurst gaol
1836 Jun   Certificate of freedom

ANN STOKES
1829: 17 Single Prot. *Educ* R *Native* Reading *Trade* All work *Trial* Reading 25 July 1828 *Offence* Housebreaking *Sentence* 7 years No previous convictions *Height* 5'0½" Ruddy fair complexion Brown hair Dark brown eyes Small scar on right upper lip
See Chapter 14 for details

ANN STORRETT (STORT/STODHART)
1829: 15 Single Prot. *Educ* R *Native* Lecas *Trade* Kitchen girl *Trial* Northumberland assizes 3 March 1828 *Offence* Robbing office *Sentence* 7 years No previous convictions *Height* 4'11" Fair freckled complexion Light brown hair Blue eyes Scar at top of nose and two small ones over right eye
1829 May   To William Palmer, Sydney
     Jul   Found in a disorderly house Withdrawn for reassignment —
              master punished
1831 Jan   To Mr Pelcher, solicitor, Maitland
     ?   At Dalwood, Hunter River
     Mar   4 days solitary and returned to government
     Apr   To Mr Dixon, Newcastle
     Dec   3mo. 3cl FF — offence unknown
1832 Mar   To Mary Bell, York St, Sydney
     Sep   To Edward Hunt, Sydney
1833 Jan   6 weeks 3cl FF offence unknown
     May   With W. Byrne, Campbelltown. 1mo. 3cl FF and returned to
              government — refusal of orders
1834 Sep   With Mr Kennerly, Campbelltown 7 days cells for refusing orders
     Oct   Still with above. 2mo. 3cl FF and returned government —
              refusing orders and insolence
1835 Dec   Certificate of freedom.
1836   Runaway from unknown employer, Bathurst
1837 Apr   At Bathurst married James Jaye, TL, who was employed by J. W.
              Richards
1863 Dec   Found dead at Bathurst due to 'exposure to cold while labouring
              under great mental and bodily weakness'

MARY ANN TAYLOR
1829: 21 Single Prot. *Educ* R *Native* Wiltshire *Trade* Dairymaid *Trial* Berkshire Assizes Reading 14 July 1828 *Offence* Highway robbery *Sentence* 14 years No previous convictions *Height* 5'4" Ruddy freckled pockpitted complexion Brown hair Hazel eyes

1829 May	To Rev. Thomas Reddall, Campbelltown
Dec	Married Joseph Giles, bond, assigned to William Howe Transferred to Mr Howe also
1843 May	Certificate of freedom
1848 May	Married William Banford after death of Giles

See Chapter 8 for details. Known issue: Harriet Giles (1841)

CAROLINE THOMAS
1829: 34 Widow (Husband Thomas died 1823) 1 child with her Jane age 9 Prot. *Educ* R&W *Native* Dublin *Trade* Cook and all work *Trial* London 23 October 1828 *Offence* Picking pockets *Sentence* 7 years No previous convictions *Height* 5'1" Ruddy freckled complexion Dark brown hair Hazel eyes 2 scars right wrist Small scar under left lower lip

1829 May	To Richard Kemp, George St
28 May	Jane admitted to orphan school.
Jul	3mo. 3cl FF — refusing to work and abuse
1831 Feb	1mo. 3cl FF — drunkenness
Aug	1mo. 2cl FF and returned to government
Dec	2mo. 3cl — offence unknown
1832 Jan	To R. C. Lethbridge, Parramatta
Jun	To John Palmer, snr, Parramatta
1833 Jan	with Mr Johnstone of Lockwood, Liverpool
	2wk. 3cl FF and returned to government — insubordinate (pushing mistress)
1835 Jan	Married Jacob Myers, bond, Liverpool
1836 Aug	Certificate of freedom
1837 Jul	Died at Liverpool
1839 Oct	Daughter Jane married John Kent, Liverpool

MARY TILLEY
1829: 17 Single Prot. *Educ* R&W *Native* London *Trade* All work *Trial* London 17 September 1828 *Offence* Shop Robbery *Sentence* 7 years No previous convictions *Height* 4'11" Ruddy pockpitted complexion Brown hair Dark hazel eyes Scar over right eye

1829 May	To Sarah Ward, 47 Pitt St
1830 Feb	Returned to government — 1st Class FF
	Transferred to John Guider or Garvee
Apr	Married Gregory Howe (Hough), FS, Sydney police
1831	Husband served in police on Norfolk Island
	Mary accompanied him and son William born there
1835 Sep	Certificate of freedom
1837 Jan	Husband rejoined police force at Parramatta
1847 Jan	Died in childbirth at Parramatta

CHARLOTTE TITHER (TETHERS/TEDDER/THEODORE/FETHERS/FISHER)
1829: 21 Single Prot. *Educ* R *Native* Wolverhampton *Trade* Housemaid *Trial* Warwick assizes Birmingham 9 August 1828 *Offence* Picking pockets *Sentence* Life 2 previous convictions *Height* 5'11¾" Ruddy fair complexion Flaxen hair Hazel eyes 'DTHAT' left arm 'MLPIGT Love' heart and 'JH' upper right arm

1829 May	To Simeon Lord, Sydney

1829 Aug   2mo. 3cl FF — drunk and insolence
1830 May   3mo. 3cl FF and head shaven — absconding
1831 Feb   To service of John Palmer, Maitland
    Mar   3mo. 3cl FF and returned to government — disobedience and
           gross insubordination
    Jul   To Mr Dangar, Port Stephens
    Oct   To Parramatta — 2mo. 3cl FF — offence unknown
1832 Jan   Richard Williams, Sydney
    Mar   James White, Ravensworth near Maitland
    Jun   Applied to marry John Meehan, FS, Maitland — character stated
           as 'very bad' — disallowed
    Aug   With George Wyndham, Maitland
    Sep   Married Thomas McNulty (McMantly), FS
1843 Sep   Ticket of Leave, Maitland
1847 Apr   Conditional Pardon

SUSANNAH TURBITT
1829: 20 Single Prot. *Educ* R&W *Native* London *Trade* All work *Trial* London 26
October 1828 with Mary Clancey *Offence* Picking pockets *Sentence* 7 years No
previous convictions *Height* 4'10" Dark ruddy complexion Dark brown hair
Dark brown eyes Scar on nose and left arm Dark mole right forehead, raised
mole right rear nose
1829 May   To James Raymond, Sydney
    Aug   Transferred to James Byrne
    Sep   Married Daniel Bullock, FS, sawyer
1832 Jan   Died Sydney

CATHERINE TURNER alias DUNN
1829: 28/34 Single Cath. *Educ* R&W *Native* County Kerry *Trade* Laundress
Trial London 26 October 1828 *Offence* Shoplifting (possibly on purpose)
Sentence 7 years 2 previous convictions *Height* 5'1¾" Dark ruddy complexion
Light brown hair Hazel eyes
1829 May   To R. H. Rafsey, George St, Sydney
1831 Nov   TL Windsor Altered to Bathurst February 1832
1832 Mar   Married James Neaill (Neale/Nail) FS, Bathurst
1833 Feb   Daughter Anne born Charlotte Vale, Bathurst
1834 Oct   Husband joined Bathurst police.
1835 Mar   Daughter Catherine born Bathurst Plains
    Nov   Certificate of freedom

MARTHA TURNER
1829: 18 Single Prot. *Educ* None *Native* London *Trade* All work *Trial* London 18
September 1828 *Offence* Picking pockets *Sentence* Life No previous convictions
Height 4'9½" Ruddy fair freckled complexion Fair hair Dark hazel eyes 'MF'
and 'W' upper right arm 'HWDWW' upper left
1829 May   Assignment illegible
    Nov   With John Collins, Sydney Applied to marry John Clayton —
           allowed but did not proceed
1830 Mar   With Mrs Glenn, Sydney Married Thomas Buck, TL, brushmaker,
           of Kissing Point
1837   Convict muster — with husband at Parramatta
    Dec   TL for Sydney district
1838 Oct   Ticket cancelled for living in adultery
1840 Mar   With Mrs White, George St, Sydney

	Apr	2nd TL, Sydney
1847	Jan	Conditional pardon
	Jun	Possible marriage to Charles Brodie in Melbourne

ANN WALKER

1829: 30 Married Prot. *Educ* R, *Native* London *Trade* All work *Trial* London 19 September 1828 *Offence* Street robbery *Sentence* 7 years No previous convictions *Height* 5′ Dark ruddy freckled complexion Dark brown to black hair Brown eyes Hairy mole left corner mouth Speck on left eye

1829 May   To Harriet Howell, Lower Castlereagh St, Sydney

See Chapter 6 for further details

SUSANNAH WATSON

1829: 34 Married 5 children (1 with her — Thomas Watson age 18 months) Prot. *Educ* R&W *Native* London *Trade* Housemaid and needlewoman *Trial* Nottingham 16 April 1828 *Offence* Shop robbery *Sentence* 14 years 2 previous convictions *Height* 5′1¾′′′ Dark ruddy pockpitted complexion Dark brown hair Hazel eyes

1829	May	To Daniel Eagan, Bunkers Hill, Sydney
	Nov	6wk 3cl FF — insolence
1830	Jun	2cl FF — for lying in. Charles Watson born
	Dec	Thomas to orphan school
1831	Jan	Assigned to Mr Simons, Parramatta
	Jul	2 years 3cl FF — shoplifting in Sydney
	Aug	Thomas died at orphan school
1832	Aug	Shoplifting sentence remitted
1833	Jan	3 days cells, FF — by Sydney bench, improper conduct
1835	Mar	John Henry Clarke Watson born
1837		Convict muster — with L. S. Downds, Parramatta
	Sep	Agnes Ellen Watson born
1838	Sep	Failed to obtain TL
1839	Jul	TL, Liverpool — altered to Parramatta
1840	Jun	6mo. 3cl FF — obtaining bread under false pretences
1842	Jan	Agnes died Probable death of John Clarke
1843	Jan	Married William Woollard
1844	Jul	Certificate of freedom
1851	Mar	Married John Jones
1856	Aug	Moved to live in Braidwood
1867–		Lived Shoalhaven
1870		
1877	Oct	Died Gunning, N.S.W.

MARY WHEAT (sometimes WEEKS)

1829: 32 Married (husband a sailor drowned on ship Tolemachns in Davis Straits) 3 children Prot *Educ* R *Native* Hull *Trade* All work *Trial* Hull 16 July 1828 *Offence* Picking pockets (stealing from a dwelling house per English newspapers the *Hull Packet* and the *Hull Advertiser*) *Sentence* 7 years 2 previous convictions *Height* 4′9′′ Ruddy pockpitted complexion Dark brown hair Brown eyes

1829	May	To James Orr, Parramatta
1829	?	With Mrs Charlotte Blackett, Liverpool
1831	Nov	TL, Liverpool district
1832	Jun	Married John Tiffin, FS
1835	Oct	Certificate of freedom
1838	Apr	Death of husband

1840 Nov	2mo. Sydney gaol — offence unknown
1846 Aug	Through Sydney gaol for trial — to FF Offence unknown
1847 Mar	In Parramatta gaol — offence unknown Tried for stealing a shawl from another prisoner

AGNES WICKS
1829: 28 Widow 1 child Prot. *Educ* R&W *Native* London *Trade* Nursemaid and sempstress *Trial* London 16 September 1828 *Offence* Obtaining goods falsely *Sentence* 7 years No previous convictions *Height* 4'11" Ruddy complexion Dark brown hair Hazel eyes

1829 May	To William and Elizabeth Cox, Richmond
1831 Jun	Married Samuel Leicester, bond, cabinetmaker, also assigned to William Cox
1832 Dec	TL, Windsor
1835 Nov	Certificate of freedom

MARGARET WILLIAMS
1829: 30 Widow 1 child Cath. *Educ* R, *Native* Londonderry *Trade* Nurse *Trial* Liverpool 27 July 1828 *Offence* Pawning illegally *Sentence* 7 years No previous convictions *Height* 5'0½" Ruddy freckled pockpitted complexion Brown hair Grey eyes No little finger on the left hand

1829 May	To Jane Lyons, George St, Sydney
Jul	Returned to government — 1st Class FF
Oct	1mo. 2cl FF — drunkenness
1830 Feb	To Rev. Wilkinson, Newcastle
1831 Jan	Still with above Forbidden to marry John Smith, bond, because neither had TL
Feb	Drunk — to 1st (*sic*) class FF
Feb	Assigned to F. Durand, Sydney
May	To B. Levy, Sydney
Oct	To J. Foley, Sydney
1832 Jan	To Mary Dell, Sydney
May	To Mary Barley, Parramatta
Sep	Married George Graburn from FF
1833 Sep	2mo. 3cl FF — improper conduct (soliciting)
Dec	1mo. 3cl FF — offence unknown
1835 Aug	Certificate of freedom
1839 Jan	To Sydney from Liverpool for trial at Supreme Court

MARY WILLIAMS
1829: 26 Widow 2 children Prot. *Educ* R. *Native* London *Trade* Housemaid and needlewoman *Trial* London 23 October 1828 *Offence* Picking pockets *Sentence* 14 years No previous convictions *Height* 4'7½" Ruddy freckled complexion Brown hair Hazel eyes Raised mole on left cheek

1829 May	To Edward J. Keith, Sydney
Sep	Still with above — married George Hearne, CF cabinetmaker and crewmember of the *Princess Royal*
Oct	Husband in Sydney gaol charged with theft
1830 Mar	3mo. 3cl FF — found in connexion with a soldier.
Apr	Husband tried and found not guilty
1831 Oct	Illegally at large her husband having left the colony — sent to 1st Class FF
Nov	To Mr Joseph Foley, Sydney
	1mo. 2cl FF — offence unknown
Dec	Still with Mr Foley Applied to marry Joseph Irving, FS

1832 Apr   Married Irving
1835 Nov   Living Sydney — applied for assistance in bringing children to N.S.W.
1838 Feb   6mo. 3cl FF — assault
            Remitted April on husband's petition
1847 May   Certificate of freedom

MARY WILLIAMS alias CHAMBERS
1829: 24 Single Prot. *Educ* R *Native* Birmingham *Trade* Glasspolisher *Trial* Stafford 16 July 1828 *Offence* Shoplifting *Sentence* 7 years No previous convictions *Height* 5'0½" Ruddy freckled complexion Light brown hair Hazel eyes Scar under chin
1829 May   To Joseph Bigg, Phillip St, Sydney
      Aug   Still with above. Married Isaac White, FS
1830 Feb   2mo. 3CL FF — absent without leave
      Oct   1mo. 3cl FF — absenting from husband
1832 Jan   3mo. 3cl FF — offence unknown
  Jan–Mar   To Robert Foster
      Nov   Runaway from husband
      Dec   Runaway from husband
1833 Jan   6mo. 3cl FF
      Jun   1mo. 3cl FF
      Sep   Sought protection from husband — discharged
      Dec   1mo. 3cl FF
1836 Apr   Death of husband, Isaac White, brassfounder of Kent St, Sydney
1837 Aug   Possible death of Mary
            Certificate of freedom due 1835/36 — never issued

ELIZABETH WOOLLER
1829: 30 Single Prot. *Educ* R&W *Native* London *Trade* Housemaid *Trial* London 23 October 1827 *Offence* Picking pockets *Sentence* Life No previous convictions *Height* 5'1¼" Ruddy freckled and pockpitted complexion Brown hair Hazel eyes Scar over left eye
1829 May   To William Clark, O'Connell St, Sydney
      Jun   3mo. 3cl FF — absconding
1830 Mar   Returned to 1st class — ill and unfit for service
      Apr   To Rev. Threlkeld, Newcastle
      Jun   Returned 1st class — unfit To FF hospital
      Aug   Returned by master
       ?   To Mr Cooper, Sutton Forest
1831 Jan   Still with above Married Mathew Flynn, FS

MARY WOTTON (sometimes WATSON or WOLTON)
1829: 19 Single Prot. *Educ* None *Native* Birmingham *Trade* Barmaid *Trial* Warwick Quarter Sessions 14 July 1828 *Offence* Picking pockets *Sentence* 7 years No previous convictions *Height* 4'11" Ruddy complexion Light brown hair Hazel eyes 'ACE' upper left arm 'JLE' on lower Small scar over left eye
1829 May   To John Flood
183?   To James Byrne, Sydney
1831 Apr   6mo. 3cl FF — living in improper state with a married man and with master's connivance
            Not allowed to be assigned again in Sydney
1831 ?   To George Stephens
1832 Jan   To M. A. Kenyon, Prospect
      May   To Edward Lakeman, Parramatta

1833 Jan   Still with above Applied to marry Martin Campbell, FS Refused —
            man married
1834 Sep   14 days cells — absconding
1835 Dec   Certificate of freedom
1836 May   Probable marriage to John Brown, FS, of Prospect

ANN WRIGHT
1829: 30 Married (Husband John Wright to N.S.W. per Marquis of Hastings
1828) Prot. *Educ* R *Native* Bedford *Trade* All work *Trial* Essex 21 July 1828
Offence Stealing fowls *Sentence* Life No previous convictions *Height* 5'1" Ruddy
complexion Brown hair Hazel eyes Scars in left eyebrow right cheek left upper
lip inside right arm
1829 May   To Harriet Howell
     Nov   1mo. 3cl FF — abusing mistress
     ?   Transferred to John Patrick, Campbelltown, to be with husband
1832 May   12mo. 3cl FF — violent assault on her mistress
1833 Aug   Husband convicted of theft — 12mo. in irons
1834 Jan   7 days solitary — refusing to work
     Oct   1mo. 3cl FF and returned to government — refusal of orders
1835 Sep   6wks 3cl FF — refusing to work/abusive language
1835 Sep   Husband 1mo. treadmill — idleness and neglect
1837   Convict muster — with George Brown, Illawarra
1840   TL, Illawarra district
1847 Jul   Conditional Pardon
See Chapters 10 and 12

NOTES

ABBREVIATIONS

AO NSW	Archives Office of New South Wales
ANL	Australian National Library
BNL	British Newspaper Library
CRO	Central Record Office, London
CSIL	Colonial Secretary Letters Received
CSOL	Colonial Secretary Letters Sent
FWK	Framework Knitter
HRA1	Historial Records of Australia, Series 1
ML	Mitchell Library
NCRO	Nottingham County Record Office
NL	Nottingham Library
NSW BDM	New South Wales Register of Births, Deaths and Marriages
NSW GG	*New South Wales Government Gazette*
OBSP	Old Bailey Sessions Papers
PRO	Public Record Office, London
SAG	Society of Australian Genealogists
SL NSW	State Library of New South Wales

1   INTO THE MAELSTROM

1   See Bibliography for the books on which this summary is based.

2   E. P. Thompson, *The Making of the English Working Class*, Chapter 1.

3   Information drawn from Susannah Watson's Burial Certificate, 28 October 1877 (NSW BDM) and from records of the British Lying-in Hospital Holborn. See also note 4 below.

4   The birth of Susannah's brother, Thomas, is confirmed by the following record from the British Lying-in Hospital, Holborn: Patient No: 30117, Agnes Bidy, age 40, wife of William, Blacking Maker. Entered 30 October 1807. Delivered 30 October. Child baptised 5 November, Thomas. Discharged 19 November. Order for Admission dated 18 September 1807. Recommended by S. Gambier. (Particulars of Patients Vol. 9 1797–1819.) PRO RG8/60, London. Susannah refers to 'Aunt Mary' in her letter to Mary Ann Birks 29 August 1875.

5   George Rudé, *Hanoverian London 1714–1808*, p. 116.

6   Analysis of Princess Royal Muster. AO NSW 4/4014, Reel 398. Forty-three of 100 women claimed to read and write. Another 40 said they could read only.

7   Greater London Record Office. Microfilm X23/18 Baptisms in the Parish of St Mary-

le-Bone 1816–19, No. 499, p. 630.

8   Ibid. Edward's occupation is the only one, for several pages, to be left blank. He signed his marriage certificate only with his mark.

9   Susannah Watson to Mary Ann Birks, 17 October 1876.

10   Marriages in the Parish of St Anne, Westminster 1817. Microfilm No. 24, Entry No. 308 p. 103. Westminster City Library, Archives Section of the Victoria Library, London. St Anne's was bombed during World War II and only the tower still stands between Dean and Wardour Streets.

11   Rudé, op. cit., p. 41

12   John Hayes, *London: A Pictorial History*, p. 24.

13   Rudé, op. cit., p. 189.

14   E. P. Thompson, op. cit., p. 693.

15   Ibid.

16   Recorded by Susannah Watson in the note she left for her children.

17   John Clarke, *The Price of Progress: Cobbett's England 1780–1835*, p. 71

18   A. J. Peacock, *Bread or Blood: The Agrarian Riots in East Anglia 1816*, pp. 30–31.

19   Rudé, op. cit., p. 232.

2   PITY OUR DISTRESS

1   Parish Registers, St Marys, Bulwell. NCRO.

2   M. Berg, *The Age of Manufacturers 1700–1820*, p. 211

3   Ibid., Chapter 9.

4   E. P. Thompson, *The Making of the English Working Class*, p. 584.

5   D. Liversidge, *The Luddites: Machine Breakers of the Early Nineteenth Century*, p. 42.

6   Ibid.

7   J. Stevens, *England's Last Revolution: Pentrich 1817*, Chapter 6.

8   A. D. Uppadine, 'Framework Knitters', *Nottinghamshire Family History Society*, Vol. 2, No. 12, June 1979.

9   *Nottingham Review*, 23 January 1824, p. 4. NL.

10   Liversidge, op. cit., p. 42.

11   Roy A. Church, *Economic and Social Change in a Midland Town: Victorian Nottingham 1815–1900*, p. 42.

12   Quoted by Church, ibid.

13   *Nottingham Review*, 27 October 1820, 23 January 1824, op. cit. *Nottingham and Newark Mercury*, 19 April 1828. BNL. *Nottingham Journal*, 19 April 1828. NL.

14   Emrys Bryson, *Portrait of Nottingham*, p. 93.

15   Ibid., p. 93.

16   Their address was given as 'Derry Mount, Arnold', which was a street known into the twentieth century for its rows of framework knitters' cottages, now demolished. Arnold Parish Registers, NCRO.

17   Mary Ann and William were both baptised at St Mary's Church, Bulwell. Thomas was baptised, 20 January 1828, at the church of St Mary the Virgin, Nottingham city. Parish Registers Bulwell and Nottingham, NCRO.

18   John Clarke, *The Price of Progress: Cobbett's England 1780–1815*, p. 76.

19   *Nottingham Review*, 27 October 1820, p. 4, op. cit.

20   Ibid., January 1821.

21   Ibid., 23 January 1824, p. 4.

22   Ibid, 30 April 1824, p. 4

23   OBSP March 1827, ML.

24   Susannah recorded the death of both her parents on a piece of paper, which was found with her letters by Mr L. King, Nottinghamshire. The information is confirmed by the following recorded in the Burial Register of St Margaret's, Westminster: 24 January 1824, Agnes Bidey, 59 years, Abode Strutton Ground, Westminster. Buried at Chapel Yard. 16 March 1827, William Bidy, 81 years, Abode Strutton Ground, Westminster. Buried Chapel Yard. (Chapel Yard was an extra burial ground for St Margaret's, located half-way down what is now Victoria Street. Today it is just a patch of grass, known as Broadway.) Original Parish Register of St Margaret's, Westminster, in the Muniments Room, Westminster Abbey.

25   Parish Registers of St Mary's, Nottingham, NCRO. The family's address is noted as

Dutch Alley, which was off Red Lion Street in Narrow Marsh, Nottingham.
26 Bryson, op. cit., p. 84.
27 Ibid., p. 98
28 A. J. Peacock, *Bread or Blood: The Agrarian Riots of East Anglia 1816*, pp. 43, 52.
29 Ibid.
30 *Nottingham Review*, 22 March 1828, op. cit.
31 Calendar of Prisoners in the Southwell House of Correction 1827–28. NCRO Q/CR/WZC Ref. QAG 5, Microfilm Z408.
32 *Nottingham Journal*, 29 March 1828, p. 3, op. cit.
33 Ibid., 19 April 1828.
34 *Nottingham and Newark Mercury*, 19 April 1828, op. cit.
35 Nottingham County Record Office.
36 *Nottingham and Newark Mercury*, 19 July 1828, op. cit.
37 Ibid. 26 July 1828.
38 Ibid. The 'carrier' alluded to is, of course, Edward Watson.
39 Bulwell Parish Registers, NCRO.
40 Paper found with Susannah's letters, op. cit.
41 *Nottingham and Newark Mercury*, 26 July 1828, op. cit.
42 Susannah Watson to her daughter, Hannah, 28 June 1857.
43 Ibid.
44 Ibid.
45 Home Office Criminal Papers Entry Book, 1828, PRO HO/13 Reel 3097A, ML. (26 July 1828; 30 August 1828; 5 September 1828.)
46 Ibid., Sir Robert Peel to the Mayor of Newcastle, October 1828.
47 Ibid., Sir Robert Peel to Mr Cockburn, Dean of York, 10 August 1828; William Peel to Rev. J. Graham, Rector of St Saviour, York, 2 September 1828.
48 Ibid., List forwarded to Justices of Assizes for the Home Counties, 23 August 1828.
49 Ibid., Letter to Visiting Magistrate, Presteigne, 16 September 1828.
50 Ibid., Removal Order, 20 October 1828, Recorded 23 October 1828. *Nottingham Review*, 7 November 1828, op. cit.
51 Susannah Watson to Mary Ann Birks, 17 October 1876.

3 THE FULL PENALTY OF THE LAW

1 Analysis of the Princess Royal Muster. AO NSW 4/4014.
2 Christopher Hibbert, *London: The Biography of a City*, p. 160.
3 Ibid. pp. 160–62.
4 Douglas Hill, *A Hundred Years of Georgian London*, p. 92.
5 See for instance Henry Mayhew, *London's Underworld*, pp. 31–132 for details of prostitution in London and direct quotes from many women. Although Mayhew investigated in the 1850s, little had changed in the slums since the 1820s.
6 For the development of new moral attitudes in general and concepts of female modesty in particular, see Derek Jarrett, *England in the Age of Hogarth*, Chapter 5, 'A Paradise for Women'.·
7 OBSP 1828, p. 988, ML.
8 Ibid., p. 779.
9 Ann Carrier, Elizabeth Foxall and Mary Harcourt: *Warwick and Warwickshire General Advertiser*, 16 August 1828. BNL. Ann Kirby recorded as Ann Kirley: *Bristol Mercury*, 15, 22 July 1828. BNL.
10 Princess Royal Muster, op. cit.
11 OBSP 1828, p. 862.
12 Ibid., p. 874.
13 *Hull Advertiser*, 18 July 1828. BNL.
14 *Hull Packet*, 22 July 1828. BNL.
15 Ann McGee, Margaret Coffin, Caroline Thomas: OBSP 1828, pp. 796, 802, 981. Mary Wheat: *Hull Packet*, op. cit.
16 *Dorset County Chronicle*, July 1828. BNL.
17 OBSP 1828, p. 875.
18 Mary Tilley, p. 788; Mary Connell, p. 871; Margaret Mahoney, p. 784; Sarah Quittenton, p. 804.
19 Elizabeth Stocker: *Bristol Mercury*, 20, 22 July 1828, op. cit. Ann Bowler: *Aris'*

Birmingham Gazette, 28 July 1828. BNL. Mary Ann Bates, ibid.

20 Ann Perks: *Warwick and Warwickshire General Advertiser*, op. cit.
21 *Hull Packet*, op. cit.
22 Mary Haynes: *Bristol Mercury*, 21 October 1828. BNL.
23 Ann Loydall: *Leicester and Midland Counties Journal*, 30 March 1827. BNL. Sarah Hazle: *Bristol Mercury*, 22 July 1828, op. cit.
24 *Leeds Mercury*, 20 September 1828 ANL. OBSP 1828, p. 719.
25 OBSP 1828, p. 854.
26 Dorothy Huldie, Ann Maw, Margaret Williams: Princess Royal Muster, op. cit. Sarah Hancock: ibid., plus OBSP 1828, p. 868. Elizabeth Smith, ibid., plus OBSP 1828, p. 874.
27 Mary Mahoney, OBSP 1828, p. 865; Ann Barnett, ibid., p. 960; Mary Wheat, *Hull Packet*, op. cit.
28 L. L. Robson, *The Convict Settlers of Australia*.
29 Princess Royal Muster, op. cit. Robson, op. cit., p. 145.
30 Princess Royal Muster, op. cit. Robson, op. cit., p. 9.
31 Princess Royal Muster, op. cit. Robson, op. cit., p. 76.
32 Princess Royal Muster, op. cit.
33 The fact that this was a recent statute is referred to in Ann Cheeseman's case reported in the *Hull Packet*, op. cit.
34 Ibid.
35 *Aris' Birmingham Gazette*, 18 August 1828, op. cit.
36 *Warwick and Warwickshire General Advertiser*, op. cit.
37 *Bristol Mirror*, 21 October 1828. BNL.

4 TRANSPORTED BEYOND THE SEAS

1 Charles Bateson, *The Convict Ships*, pp. 348, 384, 386.
2 Log of Surgeon Andrew D. Wilson. ML Adm.101/62, PRO Reel 3208, ML.
3 Bateson, op. cit., p. 10.
4 Ibid., pp. 50–51.
5 Ibid., p. 55.
6 Princess Royal Muster, 12 May 1829. AO NSW 4/4014, Reel 398, p. 174.
7 Home Office to Commissioners for the Navy, 7 November 1828. Criminal Papers Entry Book, 1828. PRO HO/13 Reel 3097A, ML.
8 Surgeon Wilson's Log, op. cit.
9 Deduced from Surgeon Wilson's Log, op. cit.
10 Surgeon Wilson's Log, op. cit. Agnes described herself as a widow with one child in the Princess Royal Muster, op. cit.
11 OBSP, op. cit.
12 Details of husbands recorded on Princess Royal Muster, op. cit. Sailing date and place for the *Mellish* in Bateson, op. cit., pp. 348–49.
13 Details of sailing, route, seasickness, all in Surgeon Wilson's Log, op. cit.
14 Princess Royal Muster, op. cit.
15 Mary Reiby's diary details how she and other passengers waited, in her case at Gravesend, for the ship to come down the Thames. ML.
16 AO NSW COD 22, Vessels Arrived 1829, lists the names of the passengers and their trade or profession.
17 Mitchell to Under Secretary of State for the Colonies, 22 September 1832, summarised Stapylton's explorations to that date. ML A2146 (Colonial Office 201/230) Miscellaneous letters 1832 H–Z p. 285). (Mitchell describes Stapylton as morose in his Journal. ML A332, p. 293. Robert Russell, notes written on a letter from Stapylton. ML Ar. 97/7.
18 Information gathered from letters from and about Rebecca and Stephen Owen in the Papers of Henry Nisbet, ML MSS 3093, Vols 3 and 4.
19 Surgeon Wilson's Log, op. cit., records Susan gave birth to a girl on 29 November 1828. Princess Royal Muster, op. cit., records that Susan had a child with her when she landed, but the matron of the Female Factory stated Susan's child, Elizabeth, was born on 29 November 1829, and adds she was baptised in Parramatta. There is no record of any child of Susan King or Forrester being baptised in Parramatta. I believe the child is one and the same and she was born on the ship on 29 November,

a year earlier than the Matron stated. This kind of inaccuracy or perhaps deliberate distortion was not uncommon, particularly when it might ensure the desired effect, in this case admission to the female orphan school. Female Factory to Colonial Secretary, 30 April 1832. CSIL No. 32/3467, AO NSW 4/2142.

20 All information on sailing dates and place taken from Surgeon Wilson's Log, op. cit.

21 Ibid.

22 Ship's routine, chores, rations etc., in Bateson op. cit., p. 80, and P. Cunningham, *Two Years in New South Wales*, pp. 291, 292, 293.

23 Princess Royal Muster, op. cit.

24 Cunningham, op. cit., p. 361.

25 See report of the crew's refusal to sail from Sydney, published in the *Sydney Gazette*, 11 June 1829. SL NSW.

26 Harriet Bannister, Application to Publish Banns, 16 November 1829, St John's, Parramatta. AO NSW 4/2018, Reel 717. George Hearn is the only member of the crew whose role is not recorded on the crew list. His marriage application, however, describes his trade as cabinetmaker, so I conclude he was the ship's carpenter. Princess Royal crew list, CSIL 29/4157, AO NSW 4/2031. Application to Publish Banns, St James, Sydney. AO NSW 4/2018, Reel 717.

27 Surgeon Wilson's Log, op. cit.

28 Cunningham, op. cit., Chapter XXXI.

29 OBSP 1828, op. cit.

30 Surgeon Wilson's Log, op. cit.

31 Ann Storrett, Ann Stokes, Mary Fagan, Ann Simpson, Princess Royal Muster, op. cit. Mary Tilley and Ann Barnett, ibid., plus OBSP 1828, op. cit.

32 Princess Royal Muster, ibid, for all these women.

33 Ibid., plus, OBSP, op. cit., for those from London. Many of the women did make patchwork quilts and some of them left them behind on the ship. Surgeon Wilson sent them to the Female Factory to be held for collection by their owners. Colonial Secretary to Female Factory, 25 May 1829. AO NSW 4/3718, Reel 1056.

34 Princess Royal Muster, op. cit.

35 Navy Office, London, Advice of the charter of the Princess Royal. AO NSW CSIL 1829 4/2031, CSIL No. 29/4157. William Peel to Navy Commissioners, 26 July 1828.
   Criminal Papers Entry Book, 1828, op. cit.

36 HRA1, Vol. XV p. 117.

37 Calculated from information on Princess Royal Muster, op. cit.

38 James Pitches born 2 May 1827. Colonial Secretary to Church and Land Corporation, 10 July 1830. AO NSW 4/3614, p. 130. Abigail Hartigan, born 13 September 1827, London. Protestant. Parents: William Splain, in London, and Margaret Hartigan, prisoner, Princess Royal. Female Factory to Colonial Secretary, 23 February 1831. AO NSW CSIL 1831, No. 31/1382.

39 Jane Thomas, born St Giles, London, 22 November 1819. Daughter of Thomas and Caroline Thomas. Father died May 1823. Richard Kemp to Colonial Secretary, 23 May 1829. AO NSW 4/2031, CSIL 1829, No. 29/4032. James Coffin, born 3 December 1823, in Henrietta Street, Parish of St Paul's, Covent Garden. Parents: James and Margaret Coffin, father a coachmaker. P. de Mestre to Colonial Secretary, 29 May 1829. AO NSW 4/2032, CSIL 1829, CSIL No. 29/4225.

40 Richard Mahoney, born 17 March 1820 Protestant. Father: John Mahoney in London. Mother: Margaret Mahoney a prisoner per Princess Royal. Female Factory to Colonial Secretary, 30 May 1829. AO NSW 4/2032, CSIL 1829, CSIL No. 29/4256.

41 Surgeon Wilson's Log, op. cit.

42 Ibid.

43 Ibid.

44 C. M. H. Clark, *A History of Australia*, Vol. 2, 1975 edition p. 267.

45 Bateson, op. cit., p. 277.

46 Surgeon Wilson's Log, op. cit.

5 A VERY PLEASANT TOWN

1 Colonial Secretary to Master Attendant, 20 May 1829. AO NSW 4/3778, Reel 2862.

2   Peter Cunningham, *Two Years in New South Wales*, p. 30.

3   William Hunt to Samuel Preston. *Nottingham Review*, 24 August 1827, on microfilm, NL.

4   *1828 Census*, ed. M. Sainty and K. Johnson, lists John Wright and James Haynes, identifiable by ship of arrival and other details.

5   Muster of the ship Mellish. Arrived Sydney 18 April 1829. AO NSW 4/4014, Reel 398.

6   Princess Royal Muster, AO NSW 4/4014, Reel 398, notes that William Foxall, Thomas Walton and Richard Dagnall were in Van Diemen's Land. This information given by the wives is confirmed by the following: Foxall, William Miles Muster, ML A1059/4, Reel FM 4/8481; Walton, Georgiana Muster, ML A1059/3; Dagnall, Juliana Muster, AO NSW 2/8284, Reel 2756.

7   Cunningham, op. cit.

8   *Sydney Gazette*, 9–12 May 1829, SL NSW.

9   Princess Royal Muster, op. cit.

10 Christopher Sweeney, *Transported in Place of Death*, p. 55

11 J. W. C. Cumes, *Their Chastity Was Not Too Rigid*, p. 92.

12 Princess Royal Muster, op. cit., is a typical example of the notes added by clerks in later years.

13 Princess Royal Muster, op. cit.

14 Ibid.

15 Convict Savings Bank Ledgers, May 1829. ML CO207/4 PRO, Reel 58.

16 AO NSW 4/2071, CSIL No. 30/2968 and AO NSW 4/2043, CSIL No. 29/5944 — Superintendent of Police to Colonial Secretary, 25 July 1829, confirms Georgiana Baxter still had money after she landed.

17 Principal Superintendent of Convicts to Colonial Secretary, 20 May 1829. AO NSW 4/2030, CSIL 29/3956.

18 *1828 Census*, op. cit., entry for Charles Windeyer and family.

19 Colonial Secretary to Master Attendant, op. cit.

20 Ann Simpson and Mary Palmer entered the Benevolent Asylum in 1860. They were still identified by the *Princess Royal* as ship of arrival. ML D574 Benevolent Society Admissions and Discharges.

21 Cumes, op. cit., p. 34.

22 Colonial Secretary to Principal Superintendent of Convicts, 20 May 1829. AO NSW 4/3668, Reel 1043.

23 Princess Royal Muster, op. cit., for the name and place of the women's assignments.

24 Ibid., and *1828 Census*, op. cit., for details of the employers' occupations and families.

25 Ibid.

26 Ibid.

27 Ibid.

28 Ibid.

29 Jane Lyon, per Princess Royal, died 13 August 1830, at the Hospital, Sydney. Age 33. NSW BDM E.316 V.14

30 Ticket-of-leave Butts. AO NSW 4/4138, Reel 936; Convict Death Register 1828–79. AO NSW 4/4549, COD.16 p. 174.

31 Colonial Secretary to Superintendent of Police, Sydney. 20 May 1829. AO NSW 4/3827, Reel 2807, p. 318

32 Princess Royal Muster, op. cit.

33 *1828 Census*, op. cit.

34 Ibid.

35 The details about Sydney and its people are drawn from 'A Walk through Sydney in South Asian Register, December 1828,' reproduced in F.Crowley (ed.), *A Documentary History of Australia*, Vol. 1, pp. 378–80; and Cunningham, op. cit., Letters III and IV.

36 William Hunt to Samuel Preston and to William Shaw, *Nottingham Review*, August 24 1827, on microfilm, NL.

37 Sydney Gaol Entrance Book, AO NSW 4/6431, Reel 851.

38 Correspondence between the Colonial Secretary, Superintendent of Convicts and Superintendent of Police. Petition of William Palmer. Filed together. AO NSW 4/2116, CSIL 1831, No. 31/7092 and CSOL Colonial Secretary to Female Factory, 31

July 1829, 7 April 1832, AO NSW 4/3718 and 4/3720.

39 Sydney Gaol Entrance Book, op. cit.

40 Ibid.

41 Ibid.

42 Ibid. for Sarah Hazel, Margaret Lyons, Elizabeth Wooller. *Sydney Gazette*; 21 July 1829 for Mary Bates; 18 August 1829 for Maria Allen and Ann Maw; 4, 11, 18 August 1829 for Ann Dodd.

43 Ticket-of-leave butt for Ann Dodd, AO NSW 4/4082 No. 32/241, Reel 916. NSW GG, Vol. 1, 1832, p. 11

44 Colonial Secretary to Sheriff, 23 December 1829. AO NSW 4/3896, Reel 1062, p. 274. Register of Convicts at Moreton Bay 1824–39. ML FM4/17, p. 57.

45 Colonial Secretary to Committee of the Female Factory, 11 March 1833, AO NSW 4/4320, Reel 1057.

46 Based on an extensive examination of gaol and court records for Sydney and country areas of N.S.W.

47 Applications to Publish Banns. AO NSW 4/2535.51, Reel 735.

48 *Sydney Gazette*, 11 June 1829. SL NSW.

49 Applications to Publish Banns, Harriet Bannister St John's, Parramatta, and Mary Williams, St James' Sydney. Both in AO NSW 4/2018, Reel 717.

6 ON ASSIGNMENT

1 Colonial Secretary, Returns of the Colony 1830. ML CY4/261, p. 210. P. Cunningham, *Two Years in New South Wales*, Letter III, p. 40.

2 H. Pook, *A Worker's Paradise? A History of Working People in Australia 1788–1901*, p. 12. Notice from the Committee of the Female Factory in NSW GG, 30 May 1832, p. 111.

3 *Sydney Gazette*, 30 February 1830. SL NSW.

4 Female Factory to Colonial Secretary, 26 November 1830. CSIL 1830, No. 30/8862, AO NSW 4/2087.

5 Colonial Secretary to Superintendent of Convicts, 28 May 1831, AO NSW 4/3671, Reel 2650, p. 39.

6 Ibid., 20 October 1831, AO NSW 4/3672, Reel 1044, p. 35.

7 NSW GG, 30 May 1832, p. 111.

8 *Sydney Gazette*, 2 March 1830, SL NSW.

9 Sydney Gaol Entrance Book 1829, AO NSW 4/6431, Reel 851.

10 Ibid.

11 Princess Royal Muster, AO NSW 4/4014, Reel 398. *1828 Census*, ed. M. Sainty and K. Johnson.

12 Compiled from the following sources: Sydney Gaol Entrance Book 1829–35, AO NSW 4/6431–35, Reels 851, 852; NSW GG, 2 January 1833, p. 5. Application to Publish Banns: Ann Walker, Princess Royal etc. assigned to Mrs Howell and Thomas Pearson, Brickmaker, age 26, per Asia(1), 7 years, FS. AO NSW 4/4511, 19 August 1830, AO NSW 4/2065, 12 August 1830.

13 NSW GG 1833, p. 159.

14 See the following for the policy concerning the assignment of women prisoners to penal colonies: Colonial Secretary to Female Factory, 8 March 1832, 20 March 1833. AO NSW 4/4320, Reel 1057, pp. 110, 556. Colonial Secretary to Surgeon Superintendent of the ship Pyramus, 13 March 1832. AO NSW 4/3738, Reel 2865, p. 240

15 Female Factory to Colonial Secretary, 9 August 1838. AO NSW 4/2401.1

16 Magistrate, Goulburn, to Colonial Secretary, 17 February 1831. CSIL No. 31/1531, AO NSW 4/2100. Colonial Secretary to Magistrate, Goulburn, 11 July 1833. AO NSW 4/3834, Reel 2809, p. 478.

17 Superintendent of Police to Colonial Secretary, 18 March 1831, AO NSW CSIL 1831, 4/2101 No. 31/2010.

18 Ibid., 23 October 1830. AO NSW 4/2085 No. 30/8106.

19 Superintendent of Police to Colonial Secretary, 6 October 1830, CSIL No. 30/7573, AO NSW 4/2083; CSOL 1830, AO NSW 4/3667, Reel 1043, p. 365.

20 CSIL No. 30/3808, AO NSW 4/2074.

21 Ibid., 23 October 1830. CSIL No. 30/8074, AO NSW 4/2085. Ibid., February 1831.
    CSIL 31/1453, AO NSW 4/2099
22 CSIL 1829, Nos. 29/5944, 29/6157, 29/6620 AO NSW 4/2043 and CSOL AO NSW
    4/3718, Reel 1056.
23 CSIL No. 32/3527, Superintendent of Convicts to Colonial Secretary, 2 May 1832,
    and Petition of Pearson Simpson, 17 April 1832, AO NSW 4/2143, CSOL to
    Establishments 11 May 1832, AO NSW 4/3721, Reel 1057, p. 223. CSOL to
    Superintendent of Convicts, 11 May 1832, AO NSW 4/3674, Reel 1045, p. 302.
24 Sydney Gaol Entrance Book, 25 February 1831: Louisa Caulfield, Princess Royal.
    Absent from service. 3rd Class Factory 1 month and returned to Government by her
    master, R. Walker. AO NSW 4/6432, Reel 851.
25 *Sydney Gazette*, 25 July 1831. SL NSW
26 *Sydney Herald*, 31 December 1832. SL NSW.
27 *Sydney Gazette*, 2 March 1930, op. cit.
28 Patrick Plains Bench Book, 16 November 1835, AO NSW 5/7685, Reel 679.
29 Liverpool Bench Books, 5 January 1833. AO NSW 5/2697, Reel 682.
30 *Sydney Herald*, 25 February 1833, op. cit.
31 Graham Abbott and Geoffrey Little, *The Respectable Sydney Merchant: A. B. Spark of
    Tempe*, pp. 56, 76, 92.
32 Princess Royal Muster, op. cit. Application to Publish Banns, Christ Church,
    Newcastle August 1831. AO NSW 4/2126.4, Reel 719.
33 Princess Royal Muster, op. cit.
34 Compiled from the following sources: Princess Royal Muster, op. cit. Sydney Gaol
    Entrance Book 1829–33. AO NSW 4/6431–34, Reels 851–2. Bathurst Gaol
    Entrance Book 1831–35. AO NSW 5/1093. Police Magistrate, Newcastle to Colonial
    Secretary, 23 September 1829. CSIL No. 29/7701, AO NSW 4/2048. Superintendent
    of Convicts to Colonial Secretary, 7 March 1831. CSIL No. 31/1600, AO NSW
    4/2100. Colonial Secretary to Police Superintendent, Bathurst, 9 August 1833, AO
    NSW 4/3835, Reel 2810.
35 Jane Edwards: Princess Royal Muster, op. cit., Application to Publish Banns, St
    Luke's, Liverpool, July 1831. AO NSW 4/2127.3, Reel 720. Ann Carrier: Application
    to Publish Banns, St. Philip's, Sydney, 22 June 1831. AO NSW 4/2126. Catherine
    Barrett: Princess Royal Muster, op. cit. Application to Publish Banns, St. Luke's,
    Liverpool, March 1830. AO NSW 4/2065. Ann Loydall: Princess Royal Muster,
    op. cit. Application to Publish Banns, St Philip's, Sydney, 30 March 1830. AO NSW
    4/2065.
36 Princess Royal Muster, op. cit. Applications to Publish Banns, Richmond, 16 May
    1831. AO NSW 4/2127.5, Reel 720.
37 Princess Royal Muster, op. cit. Applications to Publish Banns, Scots Church, 7
    January 1831, AO NSW 4/2125, Reel 719.
38 Princess Royal Muster, op. cit., Applications to Publish Banns, St Philip's, Sydney,
    2 August 1831. AO NSW 4/2126, Reel 719. *1828 Census*, op. cit.
39 Princess Royal Muster, op. cit. Applications to Publish Banns, Narellan, January
    1831. AO NSW 4/2127.2, Reel 720.
40 Applications to Publish Banns, St Philip's, Sydney, March 1832. AO NSW 4/2151.3,
    Reel 722.

7 THE FEMALE FACTORY — THEY MUST BE KEPT UNDER

1 NSW BDM E.83 V.14. (On several occasions, including his marriage, Charles
   described himself as 'Charles Isaac Moss Watson'.)
2 Isaac Moss (or Mofs) appears in several musters and lists from 1801 onwards. The
   1811 Muster gives the most details of his trial date, sentence and ship. AO NSW
   4/1224, Reel 1252. See also Criminal Registers, Newgate 1797–8, Series 1, No. 6.
   H026/6, Reel 2731, and OBSP April 1797. ML.
3 Lists of Convicts who have received Conditional Emancipation, in 'Miscellaneous
   Musters and Lists up to 1805', SAG B7/30/1805. Register of Conditional Pardons
   1791–1825, AONSW 4/4430 COD 19. Pay list of the Lady Nelson 1 July–31
   December 1801, King Papers, Vol. 1. ML A1976. Crew of the Lady Nelson 1801,
   1803, 1804 recorded in the logbooks of HMS *Buffalo*, partially reproduced in 'The

Logbooks of the Lady Nelson', ed. I. Lee, ML 980/M. Isaac's escape from an Aboriginal spear recounted in 'The Logbooks of the Lady Nelson', ibid.

4   Isaac Moss, sailmaker, listed in 1806 Muster. ML A4404, Lydia Moss died, 26 December 1826. NSW BDM. Isaac Moss, publican, age 72, listed in *1828 Census*, ed. M. Sainty and K. Johnson.

5   Parish Register of St Leonard's, Shoreditch, London: Isaac Moss, son of Lydia and Isaac, baptised 24 December 1794. Isaac Moss, application to purchase land. AO NSW 2/7933, Reel 1165.

6   Shipping Notices, *Sydney Gazette*, 26 June 1813, 11 March, 4 November 1815, 19 April 1817, and others. SL NSW. Ships Musters, 1816–25. AO NSW 4/4771–5, Reel 561–2. Physical description in list of absconded seamen from the brig *Governor Macquarie:* Isaac Moss, seaman, 18 years of age. 5 feet 4 inches high, sallow complexion, grey eyes and dark hair. *Sydney Gazette*, 11 September 1813. SL NSW.

7   *Sydney Gazette*, 31 May 1822, notice by Isaac Moss, Jnr., concerning illegal cutting of timber on his farm. Notice from the Sheriff: Isaac Moss, Snr. v. Isaac Moss, Jnr. *Sydney Gazette*, 15 July 1824. Moss Farm, Notice for Sale in the *Australian*, 8 April 1826, 24 May 1826. All on microfilm, SL NSW.

8   It is my conclusion that Isaac Moss, junior, is erroneously listed in the 1828 Census as: 'Isaac Moor, Came Free, Seaman, with Thomas Street', I believe he was probably at sea when the Census was taken and this explains the sparse details and the inaccurate spelling of his name. It is worth noting that his father's name at his trial at the Old Bailey was spelt by the reporter covering the Sessions as 'Morse' which is an indication of its pronunciation and further support for the spelling 'Moor' in the 1828 Census.

9   J. W. Moss, liquor license for The Mermaid, Cumberland Street, recorded in the *Australian*, 7 March 1828. SL NSW. See also memorial of Aaron Byrne and Joseph Moss, 29 June 1830. CSIL 30/5144 and AO NSW 4/2077.

10 A. Salt, *These Outcast Women*, pp. 48–49. Matron of the Female Factory to Colonial Secretary 'Many prisoners of the 3rd Class were insubordinate and riotous being drunk with spirits thrown over the wall in bladders', 1 July 1835. CSIL 1835. AO NSW 4/2277.4. Mrs Julia Leach to Mrs Elizabeth Fry, 10 April 1838. Letters concerning the Female Factory, typescript of originals in Colonial Office, London. ML MSS A1813.

11 B. H. Fletcher, *Ralph Darling: A Governor Maligned*, pp. 117–18.

12 Government figures between 11 July 1832 and 13 February 1833 ranged between 398–493, plus children, but there was still a heavy demand for women servants at that time and free female immigrants were only just beginning to arrive in the Colony. NSW GG, 11, 21 July, 4 August, 31 October 1832 and 13 February 1833. The number in residence averaged 509 women and 137 children a month in 1835. Female Factory Returns 1829–47, quoted in A. Salt, op. cit., p. 52. Governor Gipps reported the numbers of the Factory were 1,203 in July 1842, HRA 1, Vol. 22, p. 736.

13 Statement of Ellen Turner, 10 April 1830. CSIL 1830 No. 30/2968, AO NSW 4/2071.

14 A. Salt, op. cit., Chapter 6. Gipps to Glenelg, 13 March 1838, HRA 1, Vol. 19, p. 318.

15 Return of Punishments at the Female Factory, 1 January–30 June 1828. AO NSW 2/2811, Reel 2278.

16 Ibid.

17 *Sydney Gazette*, October 1827, SL NSW.

18 *Sydney Monitor*, Saturday 5 February 1831, SL NSW.

19 Factory Committee of Management to Colonial Secretary, 12 October 1832. CSIL 1833. AO NSW 4/2191.3.

20 Marsden to Colonial Secretary, 7 March 1833 CSIL 1833 No. 33/1907, AO NSW 4/2191.3.

21 Factory Management Committee to Colonial Secretary, 8 March 1833, recommending Mary Ann Jarvis per *Competitor*, for a reduction in her sentence of two months for improper conduct. The governor approved the mitigation. CSIL 1833, AO NSW 4/2191.3.

22 Marsden to Colonial Secretary, 7 March 1833, op. cit.

23 Governor Bourke, 1836, quoted in A. Salt, op. cit., p. 13.

24   *Sydney Monitor*, 5 February 1831, op. cit.
25   See Applications to Publish Banns, Parramatta, 1838. AO NSW 4/2443.1.
26   See Colonial Secretary Out Letters to the Female Factory, for instance 30 November
     1830, where the governor approves the lists submitted by Mrs Gordon, the matron.
     AO NSW 4/3719, Reel 1057. Who matched the women to the employers, at this
     period, is not clear. It was either the Convict Department or Land/Assignment
     Board in Sydney. In May 1832, the Factory committee of management requested
     employers to send all applications in future to the committee at Parramatta,
     indicating this was a new procedure. NSW GG 30 May, 1832, p. 111. ML. CSIL
     No. 32/6062 (AO NSW 4/2153) 13 August 1832, Female Factory to Colonial
     Secretary, reveals an instance when an assignment on the list was disallowed.
     Predictably, the reason was the prospective employer's immorality, rather than any
     concern with a woman prisoner's suitability. Later in the 1830s, after the committee
     was abolished, the matron again had sole power, subject only to the cursory
     inspection of the visiting magistrate.
27   Master, Male Orphan School to Colonial Secretary, 11 December 1843. AO NSW
     4/2621.3.
28   Ellen Turner's statement, op. cit. Ellen Turner incurred the enmity of the matron
     and the other staff, resulting in a fight between them outside the Factory entrance
     one evening in 1832. CSIL No. 32/1898, AO NSW 4/2137. Ellen and her husband
     Joseph, who was employed as a clerk at the Factory, resigned and left at the end of
     1832. CSIL 32/9271, AO NSW 4/2163.
29   Statement of Ellen Turner, op. cit.
30   Charlotte Anley, *The Prisoners of Australia*, p. 42. James Macarthur, evidence to the
     Select Committee on Transportation, 1837, quoted in A. Summer, *Damned Whores
     and God's Police*, p. 283. Lady Jane Franklin, quoted in Katrina Alford, *Production or
     Reproduction?* p. 167. Colonial Secretary to Visiting Justice, Female Factory, 12
     February 1838. AO NSW 4/3841, Reel 2812.
31   Colonial Secretary to Female Factory, 21 December 1830. AO NSW 4/3719, Reel
     1057, p. 156. Male Orphan Admission Book: Thomas James Watson Age 3.
     Admitted: 31 December 1830. Parents: Edward and Susannah Watson per ship
     Princess Royal. Died: 17 August 1831. AO NSW 4/352, Reel 2777.
32   J. T. Bigge, *Report on Agriculture and Trade*, p. 75. SL NSW.
33   Female Factory to Colonial Secretary, 3, 17 December 1830, 17 January 1831. AO
     NSW 4/2089, 4/2090, 4/2095. Replies, CSOL 1830–31, 20, 29 December 1830, 4,
     10 January 1831. AO NSW 4/3719.
34   Colonial Secretary to Female Factory, 7 November 1833. AO NSW 4/3723, Reel
     1058. Petition for child out of Orphanage, 2 August 1836. AO NSW 4/2363.1, Reel
     2207. Police Magistrate, Newcastle, to Colonial Secretary, 5 August 1840. CSIL
     40/7907, AO NSW 4/2506.6.
35   Factory Committee to Colonial Secretary, 3 August 1832. CSIL 32/6068, AO NSW
     4/2153. *1828 Census*, op. cit.
36   R. Kemp to Colonial Secretary, 23 May 1829. CSIL No. 29/4032, CSIL 1832, AO
     NSW 4/2031. Jane Thomas, age 9. Admitted: 28 May 1829. Left: ? Parents: John
     and Caroline Thomas. Female Orphan School. AO NSW 4/351, Reel 2777. 10 July
     1829, Caroline was sentenced to 3 months in the 3rd Class of the Factory. Sydney
     Gaol Entrance Book. AO NSW 4/6431, Reel 851.
37   P. de Mestre to Colonial Secretary, 27 May 1829. CSIL 1829, AO NSW 4/2032. Male
     Orphan School to Colonial Secretary, November 1835. CSIL No. 35/9615, AO NSW
     4/2289.2 and reply Colonial Secretary to Male Orphan School, 14 December 1835.
     AO NSW 4/3722, Reel 1058. James Coffin was apprenticed to Francis Ellard, music
     seller, Hunter Street, Sydney. Margaret returned, 29 November 1829, Sydney Gaol
     Entrance Book, op. cit.
38   *1828 Census* op. cit., 27 May 1829, Sydney Gaol Entrance Book, op. cit.,
39   Female Factory to Colonial Secretary, 30 May 1829. CSIL No. 29/4256, CSIL 1829.
     AO NSW 4/2032.
40   John Coghill to Colonial Secretary, 3 September 1830 and accompanying deposi-
     tions. CSIL No. 30/6928, CSIL 1830, AO NSW 4/2081.
41   6 September 1830, 29 November 1830. Sydney Gaol Entrance Book, op. cit.

Bathurst Gaol Entrance Book 1831–1835. AO NSW 5/1093. Princess Royal Muster, op. cit., for description of Margaret. Ticket-of-leave No. 33/536 dated 20 August 1833. AO NSW 4/4089, Reel 919.

42 Certificate of freedom No. 35/1206 dated 5 November 1835. AO NSW 4/4330, Reel 995. Police Magistrate, Bathurst, to Colonial Secretary, 24 June 1839, 4 November 1839. CSIL Nos. 39/6999, 39/12025, AO NSW 4/2646.1.

43 List of Boys for Apprenticeship, 23 July 1834, includes Richard Meeley (*sic*). Margaret's surname was described as Mahoney or Meliar on the Princess Royal Muster. The details of Richard Meeley in the Male Orphan School Admission Book tally exactly with Prosper de Mestre's letter where he gives Richard's surname as Mahoney, Male Orphan School Admission Book, ML C.200. Male Orphan School to Colonial Secretary, CSIL No. 34/5024, AO NSW 4/2246.3. Either the apprenticeship did not proceed or Richard was returned as unsatisfactory. In January 1835 he was apprenticed to James Bibb, blacksmith of Clarence Street, Sydney. List of Boys for Apprenticeship 1–31 January 1835. CSIL 35/893, AO NSW 4/2289.2

44 20 July 1831. Sydney Gaol Entrance Book. AO NSW 4/6433, Reel 851. Sydney Herald, Monday 25 July 1831. SL NSW.

45 Female Factory to Colonial Secretary, 9 July 1834. AO NSW 4/2234.5. Petition of Mary Ann Smith per Princess Royal, refers to the child she left in Parramatta with a nurse while she assigned in Maitland. CSIL No. 33/1981, CSIL 1833 Miscellaneous 'F', AO NSW 4/2195.1, Reel 2196. It appears, in the early 1830s, the situation for mothers and children was *ad hoc*, but most took their young children into assignment. By the end of the decade the government had formalised arrangements at the Parramatta Factory for separating children over 12 months from their mothers, who were then assigned. Governor Gipps advised the Bathurst Magistrate that he should do the same. Police Magistrate, Bathurst, to Colonial Secretary, 1 June 1840. CSIL No. 40/5667, AO NSW 4/2504.3.

46 NSW BDM E.1482 Vol. 15.

47 Factory Management Committee to Colonial Secretary, 3 August 1832 (CSIL No. 32/6068, AO NSW 4/2153) and reply CSOL to Factory, 18 August 1832. AO NSW 4/3675, Reel 1045, p. 124.

8 WITH HIS EXCELLENCY'S CONSENT

1 Analysis of Application to Publish Banns 1829–41, Convict Applications to Marry and NSW BDM Index and Registers pre-1856 at AO NSW.

2 Ibid.

3 Ibid. Three women were eligible to marry, but died without applying. Mary Bishop (died 1830) Jane Lyon (1830) and Jane Bailey (1833). Sarah Piper, who was crippled, did not apply. Mary Haynes and Ann Wright were reunited with husbands in the colony. Only four young, single women failed to apply: Mary Ann Clancy, Mary Ann Collins, Mary Connell and Catherine Donoghue. (See Chapter 14 for Donoghue.)

4 K. Alford, *Production or Reproduction*? p. 9.

5 B. Fletcher, *Ralph Darling: A Governor Maligned*, p. 120

6 Colonial Secretary to Superintendent of Convicts, 28 May 1831. AO NSW 4/3671, Reel 2650.

7 NSW GG, 30 May 1832, p. 111, ML.

8 Colonial Secretary to Management Committee, Female Factory, 30 February 1833. AO NSW 4/4320, Reel 1057.

9 Application to Publish Banns 1829–41, op. cit. Convict Applications to Marry, op. cit., plus Banns Applications 1830 filed in CSIL 1830, AO NSW 4/2065.

10 Sydney Police Magistrate to Colonial Secretary, March 1831, CSIL 1831, AO NSW 4/2100.

11 Sydney Police Magistrate to Colonial Secretary, 3 May 1831, CSIL No. 31/3160, AO NSW 4/2105. NSW GG, 18 July 1832, p. 191, ML. Application to Publish Banns, St Johns, Parramatta, January 1833, AO NSW 4/2174.1, Reel 724. NSW BDM Registers E.178 V.20.

12 *Sydney Gazette*, 26 September 1829, SL NSW.

13 Jane Hyde: Convict Applications to Marry, St John's, Paramatta. AO NSW 4/4509,

Reel 713. The conclusions concerning Sarah Bryant and Elizabeth Stocker are based on a study of their circumstances and the charges brought against them which caused them to be in the Factory, which I believe were caused by their involvement with the men they subsequently married.

14   Convict Applications to Marry, Bathurst, 1, 29 March 1831, AO NSW 4/4508 Reel 713. Application to Publish Banns, Bathurst, January 1831. AO NSW 4/2126.6 Reel 719. Marriage of Maria Allen and Joseph Woodcock: NSW BDM E.5170 V.3. Certificate of Freedom No. 35/1082, AO NSW 4/4330, Reel 995. Princess Royal Muster. AO NSW 4/4014, Reel 398. Death of Joseph Woodcock, 25 January 1859. Born Canterbury, England. 41 years in N.S.W. Married Bathurst to Maria James (*sic*). Issue: Nil. Informant: Maria Woodcock, wife. NSW BDM E.59 4308.

15   Princess Royal Muster, op. cit. Application to Publish Banns, Maitland 1832 and Newcastle 1832. AO NSW 4/2150.4 and 4/2150.2, Reel 721. *Sydney Monitor*, 15 August 1829. SL NSW. Sydney Gaol Entrance Book, 1829–1831. AO NSW 4/6431–3, Reel 851. Charlotte's various assignments are revealed by the Princess Royal Muster, Sydney Gaol Entrance Book, Application to Publish Banns, op. cit., and also NSW GG, 18 July 1832, p. 430, ML. Conditional Pardon No. 47/351 dated 16 April 1847. AO NSW 4/4451, Reel 783.

16   Princess Royal Muster, op. cit. Sydney Gaol Entrance Book, 1829–1831, op. cit. NSW GG 1832, pp. 180, 1660. Application to Publish Banns, St James', Sydney. AO NSW 4/2226, Reel 726. NSW BDM Registers E.505 V.18, E.537 V.19, E.367 V.32.

17   Princess Royal Muster, op. cit. Sydney Gaol Entrance Book, 3 April 1830. op. cit. Convict Applications to Marry, St John's Parramatta, 20 February 1832. AO NSW 4/4508, Reel 713. Charlotte Smith's ticket-of-leave was altered to Mudgee, 14 December 1840. Ticket-of-leave No. 38/114, AO NSW 4/4117, Reel 929. Death of Charlotte Rayner, age 67, 18 October 1857, at Broomby, near Mudgee. Informant: Samuel Rayner, husband. NSW BDM 57 3588.

18   Sydney Gaol Entrance Book, November 1830, March 1831 and February 1833. op. cit. Application to Publish Banns, Sutton Forest, 27 August 1835. AO NSW 4/2269.94, Reel 727. Application for Conditional Pardons, Queanbeyan 1846. Catherine Leonard, Princess Royal. Residence: W. Leonard. AO NSW 4/5651. NSW BDM, Births E.72 V.981 describes John Leonard as 'settler'. Death of Catherine Leonard, 3 August 1880, NSW BDM, 80 11128.

19   Princess Royal Muster, op. cit. Sydney Gaol Entrance Book, June 1831, April 1833, October, 1834. AO NSW 4/6432, Reel 851, and 4/6434–5, Reel 852. NSW GG 1833, p. 159, reveals Mary ran away from her employer in 1833. Application to Publish Banns. St James' Sydney, February 1836. AO NSW 4/2304.6, Reel 730. NSW BDM E.83 V.20. James Lockwood died 15 November 1860, age 55, stonemason, of Shadforth Street, Paddington. Married to Mary Fagan about 30 years. The certificate also lists their children by name and age. NSW BDM 60 2491. Mary died, aged 61 years, 22 March 1873. NSW BDM 73 6663.

20   Princess Royal Muster, op. cit. Application to Publish Banns, 23 November 1829, St Peter's, Campbelltown. AO NSW 4/2017, Reel 716. Superintendent of Convicts to Colonial Secretary, CSIL No. 35/3627, 18 May 1835, alterations to tickets-of-leave for Joseph Giles and Mary Ann Taylor. CSIL No. 35/3627, AO NSW 4/2276. Petition of Joseph Giles, 2 September 1839, CSIL No. 39/10262 in Petitions 1838–39 AO NSW X645–6, Reel 591. Police Magistrate, Campbelltown, to Colonial Secretary concerning a replacement for Joseph Giles in the Police Force, 21 February 1838. CSIL No. 38/1909 and 8 August 1838, concerning Giles cattle. CSIL No. 38/8438, AO NSW 4/2417.5. Mary Ann Taylor, ticket-of-leave No. 33/471 dated 20 August 1833. AO NSW 4/4089, Reel 919.

21   Georgiana Baxter: Application to Publish Banns, St James' Sydney, August 1829. (AO NSW 4/2017, Reel 718) and St James' Sydney, October 1836. CSIL No. 36/7697, AO NSW 4/2304.6, Reel 730. Harriet Bannister and Mary Williams: Marriage references cited in note 49, Chapter 5. Ann Morgan: Application to Publish Banns, Windsor, 19 June 1830. AO NSW 4/2065.

22   Princess Royal Muster, op. cit. Register of Convicts at Moreton Bay 1824–39. ML FM4/17 p. 57. Application to Publish Banns, St Mary's, Sydney, 16 March 1839. AO NSW 4/2435.51, Reel 735, and Convict Applications to Marry, 18 March 1839. AO

NSW 4/4510, Reel 713. Ticket-of-leave No. 39/697 (AO NSW 4/4128, Reel 932) and certificate of freedom No. 43/1904. AO NSW 4/4387, Reel 1015.

23 Convict Applications to Marry, August 1831. AO NSW 4/4508, Reel 713. Application to Publish Banns, St Philip's, Sydney, 2 August 1831. AO NSW 4/2126, Reel 719. Bathurst Gaol Entrance Book, 1831–35. AO NSW 5/1093. Superintendent of Convicts to Colonial Secretary, 28 October 1834 (CSIL No. 34/7925. AO NSW 4/2232) and reply CSOL re Convicts, 10 December 1834. AO NSW 4/3680, Reel 1048. Coroners inquest at Evans Plains, Bathurst, 21 January 1835. AO NSW 4/6611, Reel 190. Ticket-of-leave No. 31/683 dated 25 August 1831. AO NSW 4/4080, Reel 915. Certificate of freedom No. 35/808 dated 29 July 1835. AO NSW 4/4329, Reel 995. Convict Applications to Marry, Wellington Valley, 13 July 1835. AO NSW 4/4509, Reel 713. The governor allowed the marriage but the NSW BDM Index does not record it actually took place.

24 Ticket-of-leave No. 31/680. AO NSW 4/4081, Reel 916. Application to Publish Banns, St Philip's, Sydney, July 1832. AO NSW 4/2151.3, Reel 722. Further information on Ann and supporting documents, supplied by her descendant, Mrs Enid Bohlsen of Northmead, N.S.W.

25 Ticket of Leave No. 32/1165 dated 15 December 1832. AO NSW 4/4081, Reel 916. Hannah Solomons and James Box: Application to Publish Banns, St John's Parramatta, September 1833. AO NSW 4/2174.1, Reel 724. Hannah Solomons and Charles Smith: Application to Publish Banns, St John's Parramatta, 31 October 1837. AO NSW 4/2344.3, Reel 732. Female Factory Report, 24 December 1842, noted on Princess Royal Muster, op. cit. Certificate of freedom No. 43/694 AO NSW 4/4382, Reel 1014.

26 Application to Publish Banns, Bathurst, February 1832. AO NSW 4/2151.2 Reel 722. Police Superintendent, Bathurst, to Colonial Secretary, 9 October 1834. CSIL No. 34/7410, AO NSW 4/2249.2.

27 Application to Publish Banns, Roman Catholic Chapel, March 1830. CSIL 1830. AO NSW 4/2065. NSW BDM E.1284 V.116.

28 Application to Publish Banns, Roman Catholic Chapel, 17 November 1830. Ibid.

29 NSW GG, 27 June 1832, p. 152, ML. Application to Publish Banns, St James', Sydney, 1832. AO NSW 4/2150.1, Reel 721. Application to Publish Banns, Scots Church, Sydney, 5 October 1833. AO NSW 4/2174, Reel 724.

30 Application to Publish Banns, Pitt Town, December 1831. AO NSW 4/2174.4, Reel 720. NSW BDM V.16 E.1142.

31 Application to Publish Banns, St Philip's, Sydney. March 1832. AO NSW 4/2151.3, Reel 722. Convict Applications to Marry, 7 April 1832. AO NSW 4/4512, Reel 714. Application to Publish Banns, St James', Sydney, 1835. AO NSW 4/2270.4, Reel 728. Convict Applications to Marry, January 1835. AO NSW 4/4509, Reel 713.

32 Princess Royal Muster, op. cit. Application to Publish Banns, 3 August 1830, CSIL No. 30/45859, AO NSW 4/2079. 5 October 1830, CSIL No. 30/7555, AO NSW 4/2083. January 1831. AO NSW 4/2127.2, Reel 720. James's name is shown as Robinson in the official records, but he married and had children as Robertson. NSW BDM Register Marriage E.5254 V.3. NSW BDM Register Births, reveals James was Captain Rossi's overseer. E.586 V.16.

9 'FEMALE MARRIED'

1 CSOL to Clergy, 19 October 1836. AO NSW 4/3617.

2 E. Rogers to Colonial Secretary, 12 November 1830, AO NSW 4/2443.94, quoted by A. Atkinson, 'Convicts and Courtship' in *Families in Colonial Australia*, ed. P. Grimshaw, C. McConville, and E. McEwen, p. 19.

3 E. Fry to S. Marsden, 23 May 1832, quoted in Helen Heney, *Dear Fanny*, p. 122.

4 Rusden to Colonial Secretary, 30 June 1836. CSIL from Clergy, AO NSW 4/2303.92.

5 Princess Royal Muster, AO NSW 4/4014, Reel 398. Application to Publish Banns, Newcastle, December 1832. AO NSW 4/2150.2, Reel 721.

6 Colonial Secretary to Reverend Wilton, 1833. AO NSW 4/3616.

7 CSIL Nos. 34/9226, 34/5769, Petitions 1834, AO NSW 4/2248, Reel 2200.

8 Application to Publish Banns, Scots Church, Sydney, November 1831. AO NSW 4/2125.5, Reel 719.

9   Ann Kirby, Application to Publish Banns, Windsor July 1839. AO NSW 4/2435.93, Reel 735. Hannah Solomons: Application to Publish Banns, Parramatta 1837. AO NSW 4/2344.3, Reel 732.

10 Application to Publish Banns, Newcastle, 13 July 1830. CSIL No. 30/512, AO NSW 4/2065. Convict Applications to Marry, 28 July 1830. AO NSW 4/4511, Reel 714. Princess Royal Muster, op. cit. Application to Publish Banns, Newcastle, July 1831, AO NSW 4/2126.4, Reel 719. Extract from petition of Mary Ann Green, 11 July 1831. CSIL 31/5316, AO NSW 4/2065. Peter Cheek and Henrietta Hannaghan, Application to Publish Banns, Newcastle, December 1833. AO NSW 4/2173, Reel 723. Marriage of Peter Cheek and Henrietta Harrigan (*sic*), NSW BDM E.1399 V.18.

11 Colonial Secretary to Reverend Wilton, Schedule No. 41, 22 December 1832, and Colonial Secretary to Reverend Wilton, 5 January 1833. AO NSW 4/3616.

12 Application to Publish Banns, 1829−41, in general and specifically Maitland 1837. AO NSW 4/2343.8, Reel 732.

13 *Warwick and Warwickshire General Advertiser*, 16 August 1828, BNL.

14 Princess Royal Muster, op. cit. *Aris' Birmingham Gazette*, 17 August 1827. Ship William Miles Muster, for details of William Foxall. Tasmanian Papers ML A1059/4, Reel FM4/8481.

15 Elizabeth was in hospital 4−22 March and 30 March−5 May a total of 55 days during the voyage out Surgeon Wilson's Log. Adm.101/62 PRO, Reel 3208, ML.

16 Police Report, Parramatta, 21 December 1829. AO NSW X826, Reel 661.

17 Elizabeth Clayton stated Elizabeth was her assigned servant for three years, 10 June 1838. CSIL 38/6031, AO NSW 4/2403.3.

18 Sydney Gaol Entrance Book, 16 July 1830 and 30 November 1830 AO NSW 4/6432, Reel 851.

19 Application to Publish Banns, St Philip's, Sydney, July 1832. AO NSW 4/2151.3, Reel 722. Petition of Richard Barron, 9 July 1832. CSIL No. 32/5085. AO NSW 4/2151.3, Reel 722. Petition of Richard Barron, 9 July 1832. CSIL No. 32/5085. AO NSW 4/2194.1, Reel 2196.

20 The petitions, affidavits and official correspondence which reveal most of the story of Elizabeth Foxall are filed together CSIL 1833 Miscellaneous 'B', AO NSW 4/2194.1, Reel 2196.

21 Ibid.

22 Ibid.

23 Ibid.

24 Ibid.

25 Ibid.

26 Ibid.

27 Petition of Richard Barron, 7 February 1833. Ibid.

28 Ibid.

29 Ibid.

30 Ibid.

31 Newcastle Gaol Entrance Book, 7 October 1832: Elizabeth Foxall, assigned to John Smith. AO NSW 2/2003, Reel 755.

32 17 August 1833, Elizabeth Foxall, assigned servant of W. McFail. Newcastle Bench Book. AO NSW SZ80, Reel 2721.

33 November 1833, Sydney Gaol Entrance Book. AO NSW 4/6434, Reel 852.

34 NSW BDM E.128 V.17.

35 10 June 1835, Sydney Gaol Entrance Book, AO NSW 4/6436, Reel 852.

36 Application to Publish Banns, Roman Catholic, March 1838. AO NSW 4/2391.5, Reel 734.

37 Statement of William Greig accompanying Petition of Elizabeth Fox alias Cootes (*sic*), 10 June 1838. CSIL 1838, Miscellaneous 'C' No. 38/6031. AO NSW 4/2403.3.

38 Ibid.

39 Petition of Elizabeth Coates alias Foxall, August 1838. CSIL No. 38/9011, AO NSW 4/2391.5.

40 Ibid.

41 Colonial Secretary to Superintendent of Convicts, 22 September 1838. AO NSW 4/3685, Reel 1051.

42 Elizabeth's death is noted on the Princess Royal Muster and the Convict Death Register (AO NSW 4/4549) as 6 February 1840.

10 BEATING THE SYSTEM

1 Princess Royal Muster. AO NSW 4/4014, Reel 398.

2 Ibid.

3 Sydney Gaol Entrance Book, 29 July 1829, 22 April and 22 May 1830, 26 February and 13 July 1831. AO NSW 4/6431–32, Reel 851. *Sydney Gazette*, 25 July 1831. SL NSW. Bench of Magistrates, Goulburn, 31 August 1836, AO NSW X706, Reel 661.

4 Application to Publish Banns, Sutton Forest 1836. AO NSW 4/2304.8, Reel 730.

5 Ibid.

6 Ibid.

7 Ibid.

8 Ibid.

9 Ibid.

10 Bench of Magistrates, Goulburn 31 August 1836, op. cit. F. Allman to Colonial Secretary, 4 May 1836, filed with Application to Publish Banns, Sutton Forest, 1836, op. cit.

11 Campbelltown Cases Tried, 3 May 1837. Mary was charged with absence and sentenced to Solitary Confinement for 24 hours. ML MSS 2482/6, CY954.

12 Ticket-of-leave No. 37/614 dated 24 April 1837. AO NSW 4/4111, Reel 927. Application to Publish Banns, Goulburn, 1838. AO NSW 4/2444.2, Reel 2210.

13 Convict applications to marry, Presbyterian, Goulburn, 1838. AO NSW 4/4510, Reel 713.

14 J. J. Byles to William Hickmott, undated, but probably May 1840. Filed in CSIL from Police, Goulburn 1840. AO NSW 4/2508.8

15 Ibid.

16 Ibid.

17 Ibid.

18 Ibid.

19 Ibid.

20 Ibid.

21 Ibid.

22 NSW BDM E.534 V.24.

23 Petition of Mary Wheet (*sic*), 30 April 1832. CSIL No. 32/4052, AO NSW 4/2144.

24 Ibid.

25 Ibid.

26 Ibid. Governor Bourke noted his approval on 23 May. Mary and John Tiffin were married on 4 June. NSW BDM E.997 V.16.

27 Ellen Meares: Application to Publish Banns, Castlereagh, March 1834. AO NSW 4/2224, Reel 725. Elizabeth Smith: Application to Publish Banns, Bathurst, December 1829. CSIL 29/10,080, AO NSW 4/2057. Ann Cheeseman: Application to Publish Banns, Maitland 1832 (AO NSW 4/2150.4, Reel 721), and Parramatta 1833. AO NSW 4/2174, Reel 724.

28 Princess Royal Muster, op. cit.

29 Elizabeth O'Brian (*sic*), 9 June 1829, Sydney Gaol Entrance Book. AO NSW 4/6431, Reel 851. Application to Publish Banns, St John's, Parramatta, 1831. AO NSW 4/2126, Reel 419.

30 Assigned to J. McLoughlin, York Street, Sydney, January–March 1832. Assigned to William Lackay, Parramatta, July 1832. NSW GG, 11 July 1832. 14 November 1832, ML. Bench of Magistrates, Sydney, 26 December 1836. AO NSW X709, Reel 662. Ticket-of-leave No. 38/1942 dated 20 November 1838. AO NSW 4/4124, Reel 931.

31 Convict Applications to Marry, Windsor, 26 December 1840. AO NSW 4/4510, Reel 713.

32 Ticket-of-leave No. 42/2897 dated 1 December 1842. AO NSW 4/4169, Reel 946. Certificate of freedom No. 44/244 dated 21 February 1844. AO NSW 4/4389, Reel 1016.

33 Rachael Dagnall: NSW BDM 16 September 1835. E.412 V.123. Mary Ann Smith alias Burke: Application to Publish Banns, Maitland 30 September 1833. AO NSW

4/2174.1, Reel 724 and Maitland, March 1834, AO NSW 4/2225.4, Reel 725 and Maitland, February 1835. AO NSW 4/2270.2, Reel 728, NSW BDM 4 May 1835, E.1474 V.19. Sarah Pitches: NSW BDM Marriage E.405 V.20.

34 Ship Juliana Muster: Richard Dagnall, Tried Lancaster Assizes, 20 March 1820. Sentence: Life. Native Place: Liverpool. Trade: Ropemaker and seaman. Age: 24. Height: 5'8¼". AO NSW 2/8284, Reel 2756.

35 Ship Georgiana Muster. Arrived V.D.L. 20 April 1829. Tasmanian Papers 23 and 24, ML.

36 Ship William Miles Muster. Arrived V.D.L. 29 July 1828. William Foxall, Tried Warwick Assizes, 15 August 1827, 14 years. Offence: Stealing from the person, £7. Native: Birmingham, Trade: Wire drawer. Age: 23. Marital Status: illegible, possibly 'S'. Height: 5'3½". Tasmanian Papers, ML A1059/4, FM 4/8481.

37 Ship Mellish Muster. Arrived N.S.W., 18 April 1829. John Shannon, Tried Liverpool, 28 July 1828, 7 years, Offence: Street robbery, No previous convictions. Age: 31, Education: Read and write, Religion: Catholic, Native Place: Down Patrick, Ireland. Trade: Shoemaker. Height: 5'7". Assigned: James Busby, Sydney. AO NSW 4/4014, Reel 398. Ticket-of-leave No. 33/829 dated 1 October 1833. AO NSW 4/4090, Reel 920. Application to Publish Banns, Newcastle, 5 November 1833. AO NSW 4/2173, Reel 723. NSW BDM Marriage 1833 E.311 V.17.

38 Ann Shannon: Sydney Gaol Entrance Book 1 July 1829 and 1 February 1830. AO NSW 4/6431, Reel 851. See also 4/6434–5, Reel 852. NSW GG 1833 pp. 159, 167. ML. Certificate of freedom dated 13 November 1835, No. 35/1220. AO NSW 4/4331, Reel 996. Parramatta Gaol Entrance Book, 12 February 1836. AO NSW 4/6531, Reel 802.

39 *Sydney Gazette*, 16 June 1829. SL NSW.

40 Princess Royal Muster, op. cit. Ship Marquis of Hastings Muster, John Wright, Tried Essex, 5 December 1827, Offence: Stealing money, 7 years, No previous offences. Age: 30, Reads, Protestant, Married, One child. Trade: Groom. Native Place: Essex. Height: 5'5". AO NSW 4/4013, Reel 398. Assigned to John Patrick, Inn Keeper, Campbelltown, *1828 Census*, ed. M. Sainty and K. Johnson. John Patrick's Inn called The Marrow. CSIL No. 30/5516, AO NSW 4/2077.

41 Princess Royal Muster, op. cit. Sydney Gaol Entrance Book, 30 November 1829. AO NSW 4/6431, Reel 851. Petition of Ann Wright. CSIL No. 32/8947, AO NSW 4/2162.

42 *Bristol Mercury*, 21 October 1828, BNL. Princess Royal Muster, op. cit.

43 Ship Adamant Muster, Arrived N.S.W., 8 September 1821. James Haynes, Age 20, Native Place: Bristol, Trade: Labourer, Tried: Bristol, 13 June 1820, 7 years. Height: 5'8". AO NSW 4/4007, COD 149. No marriage recorded for James Haynes in NSW BDM pre-1856. James Haynes per Adamant, FS, Occupation: Sawyer, Employer: William Wells. *1828 Census*, op. cit. Robbery of a woman named Haines (*sic*) by Jane Umpage and Eliza Thompson reported in *Sydney Monitor*, 25 August 1830, SL NSW. Petition of Jane Wooller now Humpage, convicted of stealing from Mary Haynes, a prisoner, on 18 August 1830. CSIL 31/1154, AO NSW 4/2099. The contents of these two latter documents together indicate that Mary Haynes had come to Sydney for the first time in August 1830 and my deduction is she had been newly assigned to her husband.

44 1841 Census. Return No. 1208 James Haynes, Parish of South Coolah, Parramatta. AO NSW X948, p. 109. James Haynes, splitter, age 62, died 18 June 1862 at South Colah. Born Bristol, England. 42 years in N.S.W. Married Bristol, age 19, to Mary Robberts. Issue: Unknown. NSW BDM E.62 5233. Mary Haynes, 59, died 7 November 1862. Born Bristol, England. About 30 years in N.S.W. Married Bristol to James Haynes. 1 girl living. NSW BDM 62 01132.

45 Princess Royal Muster, op. cit. Analysis of Applications to Publish Banns, 1829–41, and NSW BDM Registers and Index pre-1856. Ann Perks' mother, Phelis Herring, petitioned the colonial secretary of V.D.L. for permission for Ann to join her. Permission was granted and Ann sailed for V.D.L. on the *Schnapper* on 13 August 1831. Colonial Secretary, V.D.L., to Colonial Secretary, Sydney, 30 April 1831. Superintendent of Convicts to Colonial Secretary, 21 July 1831, 12 August 1831. All filed at CSIL No. 31/3352. AO NSW 4/2106. Colonial Secretary to Superintendent of Convicts, 26 July 1831. AO NSW 4/3671, Reel 2650.

46 Colonial Secretary to Superintendent of Convicts quotes the Solicitor General's opinion, 21 April 1841, in the case of William Flannagan and Margaret Power. AO NSW 4/3689, Reel 1053.

47 *Nottingham Review*, 7 November 1828. NL. *Nottingham and Newark Mercury*, 1 November 1828, BNL.

48 Princess Royal Muster, op. cit. Ship Waterloo Muster, Arrived N.S.W. 9 July 1829. John Clarke, 41, Read and write, Protestant. Married, 2 children. Native Place: Stafford. Trade: Coachman. Tried Nottingham, 15 October 1828 for receiving stolen goods. Sentence: 7 years. 2 prior convictions. Height: 5'7". Brown hair. Hazel eyes. Scars both eyebrows. Assigned: Carters Barracks. AO NSW 4/4014, Reel 398.

49 The earliest evidence that Susannah used the name 'Clarke' is on the Birth Certificate of her son John in 1835. NSW BDM E.63 V.19. In the 1837 Convict Muster she is listed under Clarke alias Watson. SAG. She is recorded as 'Clarke' 'a married woman' in the Visiting Justice, Female Factory to the Colonial Secretary, 27 September 1838, which also describes her previous service as 'assigned to husband, John Clarke'. CSIL No. 38/10,235, AO NSW 4/2401.1.

50 The *Red Rover* arrived in 1832 with the first group of female immigrants for N.S.W. It was followed by other ships delivering a total of 1,908 single women by the end of 1835. F. Crowley, *Colonial Australia 1788–1840*, p. 450. NSW GG 1832 and January 1833, contains detailed lists of female prisoners assigned and transferred during the year 1832. Susannah does not appear on any of them. Visiting Magistrate, Female Factory to Colonial Secretary, 27 September 1838. AO NSW 4/2401.1

51 Waterloo, Ship's Muster. AO NSW 4/4014, Reel 398.

52 NSW GG, 13 June 1832, op. cit.

53 Waterloo Muster, op. cit.

54 *Nottingham and Newark Mercury*, 18 October 1828. BNL.

55 Entrance Books and Gaol Report for the York Hulk, 31 October 1828. Records of the Laurel, York and Hardy Hulks. HO 9/9, PRO Reel 4881. ML.

56 Waterloo Muster, op. cit.

57 NSW BDM Register E.63 V.19. AO NSW.

58 Matron of the Female Factory to Colonial Secretary, 8 June 1835. AO NSW 4/2277.4. See also, Male Orphan School Admission Book. C.200 ML.

59 30 March 1836, Bench of Magistrates, Parramatta, AO NSW X708, Reel 662.

60 Certificate of freedom No. 36/1257 dated 30 November 1836. AO NSW 4/4336, Reel 998.

61 Parramatta Gaol Entrance Book, 1837. John Clarke per Waterloo 1828 (*sic*). Entered: 21 April from Parramatta Barracks. Committed Quarter Sessions Iron Gang 2 years. Disposed of: Parramatta Stockade 11 May. AO NSW 4/6532, Reel 803. See also Sydney Gaol Entrance Book, July 1837, John Clarke per Waterloo No. 999. John appears to have, perhaps, worked his way down the road in an iron gang to Sydney and then been returned to another gang at Parramatta. AO NSW 4/6437, Reel 853.

62 NSW BDM E.644 V.21.

63 1837 Convict Muster, photocopy at the Society of Australian Genealogists, Sydney, p. 120 for Susannah, who is listed as Clarke alias Watson, and p. 122 for John.

64 Memorial of John Clarke, May 1838. CSIL Miscellaneous 'C' No. 38/4876. AO NSW 4/2403.3 It is the description of himself as an upholsterer in this memorial and also on his certificate of freedom, which is the linking proof that John Clarke, transported per *Waterloo* from Nottingham, was the father of Susannah's son, John Henry Clarke Watson. In 1871, John Henry, who called himself by all four names throughout his life, stated his father's occupation was 'upholsterer'. NSW BDM 1871 E.3356.

65 Susannah Watson to Mary Ann Birks, 28 May 1873.

66 Memorial of John Clarke, May 1838, op. cit.

67 Ibid. Thomas Blake's details revealed in Petition of Emma Blake, July 1835. CSIL 35/7799. AO NSW 4/2282, Real 2201.

68 Matron of the Female Factory to the Colonial Secretary 17 September 1838. AO NSW 4/2401.1.

69 Matron of the Female Factory to the Colonial Secretary, 11 September 1838. Ibid.

70 Matron of the Female Factory to the Colonial Secretary, 17 September 1838. Ibid.
71 P. Campbell, Visiting Justice, Female Factory to the Colonial Secretary, 27 September 1838. CSIL 38/10235. Ibid.
72 Ibid.
73 Ibid.
74 Matron of the Female Factory to the Colonial Secretary, 23 November 1838. Ibid.
75 List of children, dated 2 February 1839, from the Matron of the Female Factory to the Colonial Secretary. AO NSW 4/2451.3
76 Male Orphan School Admission Book, op. cit.
77 Quarter Sessions Register, Parramatta 1839. AO NSW 5/2997, Reel 2757. Parramatta Gaol Entrance Book, 1839, prisoner No. 127, confirms that it was John Clarke, per *Waterloo*, who was convicted. AO NSW 4/6533, Reel 803. The only evidence for the commutation of his sentence is a note beside his name in the Gaol book, 'Commuted June 2'. This may have been subject to a qualification that he leave Parramatta. I believe the following is his death, but cannot prove it: Christ Church, Newcastle. John Clarke, age 58, abode Newcastle, cottch (*sic*, couch?) manufacturer, died 26 January 1842. Accidentally shot. NSW BDM E.1127 V.26.
78 Colonial Secretary to Police Magistrate, Parramatta, 31 January 1839. AO NSW 4/3843, Reel 2812, p. 33.
79 Ticket-of-leave No. 39/1171 dated 1 July 1839. AO NSW 4/4130, Reel 933.
80 See note on ticket-of-leave No. 39/1171, ibid. Petition of Emma Blake, July 1835, op. cit., confirms she and Thomas Blake were husband and wife.
81 Petition of John Clarke, undated but received before 6 July 1839. CSIL 39/7544, AO NSW 4/2454.3, Reel 2216. Charles Watson, discharged August 1839 'to his mother'. Male Orphan School Admission Book, op. cit. The page showing young John's discharge has been torn off.

11 A DUBIOUS REFUGE

1 English case (1840) cited in J. Scutt, *Sexism in Criminal Law*, in S. Mukherjee and J. Scutt (eds) *Women & Crime*, p. 11, quoted by K. Alford in *Production or Reproduction?* p. 70n.
2 Princess Royal Muster, AO NSW 4/4014, Reel 398. 9 September 1829 Sydney Gaol Entrance Book, AO NSW 4/6431, Reel 851.
3 Application to Publish Banns, St James', Sydney, 29 October 1830, in CSIL 1830, AO NSW 4/2065.
4 4 September 1833 Sydney Quarter Sessions Papers, July (*sic*) 1833, Case No. 97, AO NSW 4/8458.
5 25 January 1834 Sydney Quarter Sessions Papers, April 1834, Case No. 40, AO NSW 4/8460.
6 Ibid.
7 24 February 1834, Sydney Quarter Sessions Papers, April 1834, Case No. 41, AO NSW 4/8460.
8 Ibid.
9 Petition of Mary Ann Neary, 11 September 1835. CSIL No. 35/8034. AO NSW 4/2296.
10 Ibid. Ticket-of-leave No. 35/972 dated 28 November 1835. AO NSW 4/4100, Reel 923.
11 Robert Neary died 28 January 1838, aged six weeks. NSW BDM E.2103 V.22.
12 Walter Neary, per Hercules, now Free, charged with housebreaking and robbery. 19 June 1838. Supreme Court depositions, 1838, Case No. 56. AO NSW 9/6315. 14 August 1838, Walter Neary: Sentence 14 years transportation to Norfolk Island. Supreme Court Returns of persons tried and convicted. AO NSW X43, Reel 2756.
13 NSW BDM E.697 V.25.
14 Application to Publish Banns, St Philip's, Sydney, 18 August 1829. AO NSW 4/2017, Reel 716. NSW BDM E.4646 V.3. Isaac White's burial certificate reveals he was a brassfounder. NSW BDM E.337 V.20. Absconded from husband: Sydney Gaol Entrance Book. AO NSW 4/6431–32, Reel 851 and 4/6434, Reel 852. Sought protection from husband: Police Register of Arrests 1833. ML MSS 2481.
15 Applications to Publish Banns, Newcastle 1831. AO NSW 4/2126.4, Reel 719.

16 9 October 1835, Newcastle Bench Book, p. 156. AO NSW 4/5608, Reel 2721.

17 October 1834, Newcastle Bench Book, p. 407. AO NSW SZ80, Reel 2721.

18 27 January 1835, ibid. p. 514.

19 Application to Publish Banns, Newcastle, June 1830. AO NSW 4/2065.

20 Princess Royal Muster, op. cit. Sir Robert Peel to the Dean of York, 10 August 1828, and William Peel to Rev. R. Graham, York, 2 September 1828, in Criminal Papers Entry Book. HO/13 PRO, Reel 3097A, ML. *Hull Packet*, 22 July 1828. BNL.

21 Application to Publish Banns, Newcastle, June 1830, op. cit.

22 G. Wyndham to Colonial Secretary, 16 December 1833. CSIL No. 33/8211. AO NSW 4/2197.4, Reel 2197.

23 2 April 1834, Ann Simpson, now Prentice from Newcastle to 1st Class Factory. Sydney Gaol Entrance Book. AO NSW 4/6435, Reel 852.

24 Princess Royal Muster, op. cit.

25 Application to Publish Banns, Newcastle, 29 January 1830. CSIL 1830, AO NSW 4/2065. Ann's assignment to her husband is deduced by me from the documents concerning her and with awareness of the official policy. There is, however, no specific reference to it.

26 Patrick Plains Bench Book, 1835. AO NSW 5/7685, Reel 679, p. 180.

27 Colonial Secretary to Female Factory, 21 December 1832. AO NSW 4/4320, Reel 1057, p. 473. Colonial Secretary to Magistrate, Penrith, 21 December 1832. AO NSW 4/3833, Reel 2809, p. 481.

28 *Sydney Monitor*, 6 May 1839, SL NSW.

29 2 December 1830. Sydney Gaol Entrance Book. AO NSW 4/6432, Reel 851.

30 Maitland Quarter Sessions Papers, 1833. AO NSW 4/8406, Reel 2406.

31 Ann Kingsmill (*sic*) No. 217. Newcastle Gaol Entrance Bok, January 1833. AO NSW 2/2004, Reel 755.

32 16 January 1835, Memorandum of the Colonial Secretary, filed with CSIL 35/122, AO NSW 4/2291.1.

33 Memorandum of Colonial Secretary, 16 January 1835 and Police Magistrate, Maitland, to Colonial Secretary, 6 January 1835. CSIL 35/122. Ibid. Colonial Secretary to Police Magistrate, Maitland, 30 January 1835. AO NSW 4/3837, Reel 2810, p. 98.

34 Newcastle Gaol Entrance Book. In: Ann Kingsmill now Hoskins, from Sydney and Factory. To be returned to her husband. Out: 25 March to Maitland, to be with her husband. Conduct: Orderly. AO NSW 2/2005, Reel 756.

35 Certificate of freedom No. 35/786 dated 23 July 1835. AO NSW 4/4329, Reel 995.

36 Police Magistrate, Maitland, to Colonial Secretary, 31 December 1839. CSIL No. 40/815. AO NSW 4/2506.6.

37 Princess Royal Muster, op. cit. Application to Publish Banns, Liverpool, 13 August 1831. AO NSW 4/2127.3, Reel 720.

38 13 December 1832, Liverpool Bench Book. AO NSW 5/2697, Reel 682. 10 December 1834, ticket-of-leave torn up for repeated drunkenness. Ticket-of-leave No. 33/298. AO NSW 4/4088, Reel 919.

39 Petition of John Smith, December 1832 and attached case depositions. CSIL No. 32/9427, AO NSW 4/2163.

40 Died at Bathurst, 20 July 1834. Noted on indent for John Smith, ship *Glory* Muster, AO NSW 4/4006, COD 144.

41 Surgeon Wilson's Log, Ad.101/62, PRO Reel 3208, ML. 24 August 1830, Sydney Gaol Entrance Book. AO NSW 4/6431, Reel 851.

42 16 October 1833, ticket-of-leave cancelled for Drunkenness and insolence. Ticket-of-leave No. 33/498. AO NSW 4/4089, Reel 919. Coroner's Report on Susan Gilbert, 28 October 1840. AO NSW 4/6612, Reel 190.

43 22 May 1829, Drunk and Improper Conduct. 12 March 1831, Drunk and Disorderly. 9 May 1831, Drunk and Disorderly. Sydney Gaol Entrance Book, AO NSW 4/6431 and 4/6433, Reel 851. Application to Publish Banns, Bathurst, March 1832. AO NSW 4/2151.2, Reel 722. 30 September 1831, No. 572 Thomas Brothers and No. 573 Martha Clare, plus many subsequent convictions for Martha in Bathurst Gaol Entrance Book 1831–35. AO NSW 5/2093.

44 Princess Royal Muster, op. cit. Application to Publish Banns, St James' Sydney,

February 1830. AO NSW 4/2065. See notation on ticket-of-leave No. 37/1927. AO NSW 4/4116, Reel 928.

45 Application to Publish Banns, Parramatta, November 1829. AO NSW 4/2018, Reel 717.

46 20 November 1830. Sydney Gaol Entrance Book. AO NSW 4/6432, Reel 851.

47 The Sydney Gaol Entrance Book records that he had gone to England, not New Zealand, 4 July 1831. AO NSW 4/6432, Reel 851.

48 Sydney Police to Colonial Secretary, 21 June and 4 July 1831, filed at CSIL No. 31/5043, AO NSW 4/2110. Colonial Secretary to Sydney Police, 29 June 1831. AO NSW 4/3830, Reel 2808, p. 169 To Female Factory, 7 July 1831. AO NSW 4/3719 Reel 1057. *Sydney Herald*, 20 June 1831. SL. Sydney Gaol Entrance Book, 14 July 1831. AO NSW 4/6432, Reel 851.

49 *Sydney Herald*, 24 November 1831, SL. NSW GG, 11 July 1832. ML. Ibid, 2 January 1833, 27 February, 1833. Convict Death Register. AO NSW 4/4549, COD 16 p. 222 and NSW BDM Burials E.230 V.17

50 Princess Royal Muster, op. cit. Application to Publish Banns, St. James' Sydney, 1829. AO NSW 4/2018, Reel 718. Quarter Sessions Papers, Sydney, April 1830. AO NSW 4/8451.

51 15 March 1830, 4 October 1831, Sydney Gaol Entrance Book. AO NSW 4/6432, Reel 851.

52 Application to Publish Banns, Scots Church, Sydney, November 1831. AO NSW 4/2125.5, Reel 719.

53 Petition of Joseph Irving, 10 April 1838. CSIL No. 38/3813 and other documents filed at CSIL No. 38/4522. AO NSW 4/2421.2

54 Princess Royal Muster. AO NSW 4/4014, Reel 398. OBSP 1828, p. 804. ML.

55 Princess Royal Muster, ibid. Application to Publish Banns, Bathurst, 9 December 1830. CSIL 1830, AO NSW 4/2065, and St Philip's, Sydney, February 1831. AO NSW 4/2126, Reel 719.

56 Application to Publish Banns, St Philip's, Sydney, ibid.

57 Petition of Daniel Riddiford, 16 August 1830. CSIL No. 30/6148, AO NSW 4/2080.

58 NSW BDM E.5164 V.3.

59 Sydney Quarter Sessions Papers, October 1835, Case No. 68. AO NSW 4/8467.

60 Ibid.

61 Sydney Quarter Sessions Papers, October 1835, Case No. 48 Sarah Whittington (*sic*) stealing a cap the property of Raphael Clint. AO NSW 4/8466. Sydney Gaol Entrance Book, 1835, No. 2203 Sarah Whittington, *Princess Royal*, and other details which are the same as Sarah Quittenton in the Princess Royal Muster. AO NSW 4/6435, Reel 852. Sarah's name is also spelt Quidenton, Quittendon and Quindenton. I have adopted the one used marginally more often. Daniel's name also varies between Reddiford and Riddiford to Redaford and Ruddiford. More details of Sarah's theft were reported in the *Sydney Gazette*, 24 October 1835. SL NSW.

62 Sydney Quarter Sessions Papers, October 1835, Case No. 67. AO NSW 4/8466.

63 Ibid.

64 The charge of stealing a barrow of leather was stood over until the quarter sessions in January 1836, when somebody noted on the front of the papers 'Q? if the same man transported on the Sophia, vide 27.'

65 Sydney Quarter Sessions Papers, October 1835, Case No. 48, op. cit.

66 Ibid, Case No. 67.

67 NSW BDM E.1479 V.44.

68 Sarah Quittenton, died 17 October 1838 of Natural Causes, Campbelltown. Certified by Coroner F. Allman, 25 October 1838. Coroners Inquest, AO NSW 4/6612, Reel 190.

69 Princess Royal Muster, op. cit. Details of Sarah's father and his profession were supplied by Sarah for her second marriage. NSW BDM 61 1827. The items she stole were mentioned in the *Bath and Cheltenham Gazette*, 22 July 1828. BNL.

70 Application to Publish Banns, Parramatta, 17 November 1830. AO NSW 4/2065.

71 Application to Publish Banns, Parramatta, 14 October, 17 November 1830. Ibid.

72 Ibid.

73 Quarter Sessions Papers, Sydney, July 1831, Case No. 11. AO NSW 4/8453.

74 Quarter Sessions Papers, Sydney, October 1831, Case No. 20. AO NSW 4/8453.

75 Charles Foley, born 29 September 1831, Sydney. John Foley, born 8 June 1833, Sydney. Police Magistrate, Bathurst to Colonial Secretary, 16 June 1836. CSIL No. 36/5072. AO NSW 4/2329.1.

76 Quarter Sessions Papers, Bathurst, February 1836, Case No. 3. AO NSW 4/8380, Reel 2397.

77 Memorial of John Foley, 16 September 1835. CSIL No. 35/8033. AO NSW 4/2296.

78 Colonial Secretary to Superintendent of Convicts, 10 February 1830. AO NSW 4/3669, Reel 1044.

79 Notes on Memorial of John Foley, 16 September 1835, op. cit.

80 Quarter Sessions Papers, Bathurst, February 1836. op. cit.

81 Ibid.

82 Colonial Secretary to Sheriff, 9 October 1836. AO NSW 4/3900, Reel 1064.

83 Colonial Secretary to Superintendent of Convicts, 8/9 May 1837. AO NSW 4/3683, Reel 1050.

84 Colonial Secretary to Sheriff, 24 November 1837. AO NSW 4/3700, Reel 1064.

85 John mentions the memorial, which got lost, in his petition, 10 September 1838. **CSIL No. 38/10,155, AO NSW 4/2402.2**

86 Sheriff to Colonial Secretary, 13 August 1838. CSIL 38/8480. Ibid.

87 Mr Robertson, Colonial Surgeon, to Colonial Secretary, 26 September 1838. CSIL 38/10,155. Ibid.

88 Memorial of John Foley, 10 September 1838. CSIL No. 38/10,155. Ibid.

89 Ibid.

90 Ibid.

91 Ibid.

92 Police Magistrate, Bathurst to Colonial Secretary, 16 June 1836. CSIL No. 36/5072, op. cit. Charles and John Foley are mentioned specifically by name and the magistrate adds 'the mother has a third child nursing'. In CSIL 39/10,647, AO NSW 4/2464.1, Margaret is mentioned by name and her birth is given as 20 November 1836. The two references don't compute. It is my belief the latter date should be 1835 and Margaret's age had been put back a year because Sarah was trying to keep her out of the orphan school. Margaret's birth is not recorded in the NSW BDM.

93 Police Magistrate, Bathurst, to Colonial Secretary, 16 June 1836. Ibid.

94 Colonial Secretary to Police Magistrate, Bathurst, 30 November 1836. AO NSW 4/3839, Reel 2811. Male Orphan School Admission Book, C.200 ML.

95 Ticket of Leave No. 37/1678 dated 2 December 1837. AO NSW 4/4114, Reel 928.

96 Police Magistrate, Bathurst to Colonial Secretary, 1 January 1838. CSIL No. 38/56, AO NSW 4/2394.

97 Ibid.

98 Male Orphan School Admission Book, op. cit.

99 Police Magistrate, Bathurst to Colonial Secretary, 24 September 1839. CSIL No. 39/10,647, AO NSW 4/2464.1

100 Police Magistrate, Bathurst to Colonial Secretary, 14 October 1839. CSIL 39/11,470. Ibid.

101 Police Magistrate, Bathurst to Colonial Secretary, 4 November 1839. CSIL 39/12,025. Ibid.

102 Ibid.

103 Male Orphan School Admission Book, op. cit.

104 Notes on Ticket of Leave No. 43/2026 dated 11 August 1843. AO NSW 4/1833, Reel 949.

105 Colonial Secretary to Female Factory, 20 February 1847. AO NSW 4/3727, Reel 1060.

106 Female Factory Discharge Register, 23 February 1847. List of belongings received by Sarah Bryant, Princess Royal. AO NSW 6/5347.

107 Ticket-of-leave No. 49/298 dated 17 July 1849. AO NSW 4/4217, Reel 962.

108 Conditional pardon No. 53/207, dated 10 December 1853, noted on ticket-of-leave No. 49/298. Ibid.

109 Application to Publish Banns, Wollongong, 26 August 1833. CSIL 33/5607, AO NSW 4/2186. Convict Applications to Marry, Bathurst, 20 August 1833. AO NSW 4/4509, Reel 713. Louisa's assignment to Captain Waldron, June 1832, also detailed in NSW GG, 7 November 1832, p. 393, and that she absconded from him almost immediately, NSW GG 27 June 1832, p. 169. ML.

110 Quarter Sessions Papers, Campbelltown, August 1834, Case No. 25. AO NSW 4/3890, Reel 2401, p. 255.

111 Ibid.

112 Quarter Sessions Calendar, Campbelltown, 1834. AO NSW 5/2996, Reel 2727.

113 Campbelltown Cases Tried, 22 October 1836. ML MSS 2482/6, CY954.

114 Louisa Caulfield, *Princess Royal*, age 40. Died 4 October 1839, Parramatta Hospital. Noted on Princess Royal Muster, op. cit., and in Convict Death Register, AO NSW 4/4549, COD 16.

12 DIFFERENT JOURNEYS

1 Princess Royal Muster. AO NSW 4/4014, Reel 398. Ship Marquis of Hastings (1828) Muster. AO NSW 4/4013, Reel 398. Petition of Ann Wright, 29 October 1832. CSIL No. 32/8947, AO NSW 4/2162.

2 *1828 Census*, ed. M. Sainty and K. Johnson, gives details of John Patrick and his family. CSIL No. 30/5516 reveals Patrick's inn at Campbelltown was called The Marrow. AO NSW 4/2077.

3 Marquis of Hastings Muster, op. cit., gives John's trade. Reference of Thomas Reddall personally vouches for John's 'industrious habits'. Filed with John's petition dated 20 December 1833. CSIL No. 34/1683, AO NSW 4/2247.

4 Princess Royal Muster, op. cit. Marquis of Hastings Muster, op. cit.

5 Petition of Ann Wright, 29 October 1832, op. cit.

6 Ibid.

7 Petition of John Wright, 20 December 1833, op. cit.

8 Ibid.

9 Ibid.

10 Thomas Reddall to J. C. Harrington, 14 March 1834, and covering note from F. H. Hely, superintendent of convicts, to Harrington, the colonial secretary. These letters are unregistered and filed with other unregistered notes near CSIL No. 34/634 in AO NSW 4/2229. Petition of John Wright, 19 March 1834. CSIL No. 34/2431, AO NSW 4/2247, Reel 2199.

11 14 January 1834, Campbelltown Register of Convicts Tried 1832–37. ML Mss 2482/6, CY 954.

12 Ticket-of-leave No. 33/949, dated 1 December 1833. AO NSW 4/4091, Reel 920.

13 25 October 1834, Campbelltown Register of Convicts Tried, op. cit.

14 1828 Census, op. cit., lists William Eggleton as a servant at John Patrick's inn. He was then aged 13.

15 8 September 1835 (Ann Wright) and 30 September 1835 (John Wright). Campbelltown Register of Convicts Tried, op. cit.

16 John Patrick, per Pitt, free by servitude, buried 11 May 1835. NSW BDM E.2295 V.19.

17 1837 Muster at Society of Australian Genealogists, Sydney.

18 John Wright, Certificate of freedom No. 40/679, dated 13 April 1840. AO NSW 4/4357, Reel 1005.

19 Ann Wright: ticket-of-leave No. 40/257, dated 20 January 1840. AO NSW 4/4136, Reel 935. Conditional pardon No. 47/895, dated 30 July 1847, noted on Princess Royal Muster, op. cit.

20 OBSP 1828, p. 839. ML

21 The Princess Royal Muster shows Catherine as 26 and, on her marriage applications in December 1829 and May 1834 she stated she was 26 and 31 respectively, both of which are relatively consistent. Her death certificate makes her one year older again than her age in the latter application.

22 OBSP, op. cit.

23 Princess Royal Muster. AO NSW 4/4014, Reel 398.

24 Ibid.

25 Ibid.

26 Sydney Gaol Entrance Book, 8 June 1829, Catherine Stevens (*sic*) Princess Royal is returned to the first class. AO NSW 4/6431, Reel 851.
27 Application to Publish Banns, Narellan, 24 December 1829. AO NSW 4/2065.
28 Ibid. Also, Convict Applications to Marry, 1 January 1830. AO NSW 4/4508, Reel 713.
29 NSW BDM: Caroline E.10247 V.1 and Elizabeth E.616 V.17.
30 Application to Publish Banns, Narellan, 5 May 1834, Rev. Hassall states Peter Riglin died 'about December 1833 and was interred at Hebe Chapel Burial Ground'. AO NSW 4/2225, Reel 725. NSW BDM confirms E.600 V.17.
31 Information about John's Irish background and date of transportation obtained from his descendant, Mr G. Squires of Longacre, Mittagong Road, Bowral, N.S.W. Mr Squires' research also revealed John disputed the length of his sentence, claiming it was for seven years, not life. John Dorman's employment at Emu Plains and Wellington Valley is detailed in the following: Petition of John Dorman 1829. CSIL No. 29/6732, AO NSW 4/2043. Superintendent of Convicts to Colonial Secretary, 1 April 1830. CSIL No. 30/3425, AO NSW 4/2073. Superintendent of Emu Plains to Colonial Secretary, 8 June 1831 (CSIL No. 31/4346, AO NSW 4/2108) and ibid, 13 September 1831. CSIL No. 31/7259, AO NSW 4/2116.
32 Application to Publish Banns, Narellan, 5 May 1834. op. cit.
33 Application to Publish Banns, Narellan, 5 May 1834. Ibid.
34 NSW BDM E.1352 V.18
35 Revealed by 1837 Convict Muster (HO10/32–35 PRO, SAG) and Burial and Baptism entries as cited below in note 36.
36 William and Daniel Dorman born *circa* February 1837. Daniel died aged three months, 14 May 1837. William died aged 20 months, 11 September 1838. NSW BDM E.2740 V.21 and E.3154 V.22. Jane Dorman, born 29 October 1838. Returns of Births, Deaths and Marriages, Narellan, 24 December 1838. AO NSW 4/2389.4, Reel 734.
37 Register of Prisoners Tried, Quarter Sessions, Sydney, 1841: Catherine Dorman alias Steele, Bond, Princess Royal. Committed Sydney 2 August 1841. Charge: Larceny. Witnesses: Bridget Buckley, James Spears, William Walker and Mary Holmes. Defence witnesses: Requires none. Trial 18 August 1841. Guilty: 4 calendar months imprisonment, hard labour Sydney gaol. Solitary Confinement every four weeks. No case papers have survived to provide further details of Catherine's offence. AO NSW Vol. 2916, Reel 2431.
38 This is a conclusion based on the following: Johanna began her assigned service in Sydney and prisoners who were returned or punished passed through the Sydney gaol. The gaol records, 1829–31, are available and she does not appear in them at all until July 1831. The entry, dated 30 July 1831, does not, however, specifically name Durant as her employer. Sydey Gaol Entrance Book AO NSW 4/4631–4632, Reel 851.
39 Ibid. 24 August 1831.
40 Ibid. 5 October 1831.
41 Colonial Secretary to Superintendent of Convicts, 20 October 1831. AO NSW 4/3672, Reel 1044, p. 34.
42 25 October 1831, Sydney Gaol Entrance Book.
43 Johanna's sentence is listed 5 December 1831 in Sydney Gaol Entrance Book. Her offence is described in the *Sydney Herald*, 12 December 1831. SL NSW. The fact that she was returned to government is deduced from her subsequent assignment and from a letter in the colonial secretary's files, which reveals Elizabeth Edwards was arranging to transfer Johanna to the service of Elizabeth Raine. Colonial Secretary to Superintendent of Convicts, 10 December 1831. AO NSW 4/3672, Reel 1044, p. 227.
44 Johanna's assignment to Mr Brooks, January–March 1832 is listed in NSW GG, 11 July 1832, p. 177. ML. All female assignments and transfers for 1832 were published in the *Gazette*. Johanna does not appear again for that year.
45 Runaways Aprehended, NSW GG, 22 May 1833. ML.
46 30 November 1836, Bench of Magistrates, Sydney. AO NSW X709, Reel 662.
47 Colonial Secretary to Police Magistrate, Port Macquarie, 15 January 1839. AO NSW 4/3842, Reel 2812.

48 Ibid, April 1840. AO NSW 4/3845, Reel 2813, p. 103.

49 Convict Death Register 4/4549, COD 16, p. 174.

50 Application to Publish Banns, Port Macquarie, 21 March 1839. AO NSW 4/2442.7, Reel 2215.

51 Ibid.

52 Application to Publish Banns, Port Macquarie, 7 July 1840. AO NSW 4/2480.9, Reel 736. NSW BDM V.44 E.138.

53 Certificate of freedom No. 44/400 dated 14 March 1844. AO NSW 4/4390, Reel 1016.

54 Sydney Gaol Entrance Book Prisoner No. 436, 26 March 1843. AO NSW 4/6440, Reel 854.

55 Sydney Gaol Entrance Book, 1842–44 and 1844–49. AO NSW 4/6440 and 4/6441, Reel 854.

56 Benevolent Society Index 1852: Johanna Brown, Admitted 28 July, Discharged 31 July. ML D562–4. Benevolent Society Admissions and Discharges 1857–61: Johanna Hunt, admitted 26 October 1857 (ML D574) and Benevolent Society Index 1859, op. cit. Johanna Hunt, admitted 12 June, discharged 25 June. These records have been examined in a general sense, but not minutely. Johanna probably appears on other occasions.

57 Benevolent Society Inmates Journals 1860. (ML A7231) and Admissions and Discharges 1857–61, op. cit.

58 Information on Catherine's descendants and home at Pomeroy supplied by Mr G. Squires, Longacre, Mittagong Road, Bowral N.S.W. Her death confirmed by NSW BDM E.62 3629. John died, aged 73, in 1865. NSW BDM E.65 3713.

59 The Coroner's verdict is recorded on Johanna's Death Certificate. NSW BDM E.69 7469.

13   SOME EVIDENCE OF AFFECTION

1 Susannah Watson to Hannah Watson, 28 June 1857.

2 Maria Allen, Charlotte Tither and Georgiana Baxter, see Chapter 8 and notes 14, 15 and 21. Mary Williams alias Chambers, see Chapter 11 and note 14. Susannah Turbitt, application to marry Daniel Bullock, 22 September 1829, St James' Sydney. AO NSW 4/4511, Reel 714.

3 J. F. O'Connell, *Residence of Eleven Years in New Holland...*, quoted in F. Crowley, *Colonial Australia 1788–1840*, p. 309.

4 Harriet Bannister, see Chapter 12. Sarah Bryant, Chapter 14. Sarah Hazle, see note 50 below. Elizabeth Stocker: Application to Publish Banns, Parramatta, 1832. AO NSW 4/2150.3, Reel 721. Betty Brian, see Chapter 10. Ann Cheeseman, see Chapter 14. Jane Hyde, see Chapter 8. Margaret Williams, see note 15 below.

5 John Potter, see Chapter 8, note 15. Gregory Howe, see Chapter 8, note 26. James Neale, see Chapter 8, note 25. Joseph Giles, see Chapter 8.

6 Isaac White, see Chapter 11, note 14. John Foley, see Chapter 11. Thomas Tollis, see Chapter 8, note 23. Peter Riglin, see Chapter 12.

7 Peter Tyler, Application to Publish Banns, St Philip's, Sydney 1833. AO NSW 4/2174.1, Reel 724. CSIL No. 29/1784 confirms it is the same Peter Tyler, who was a political football between Governor Darling and Tyler's employer, Edward Smith Hall. AO NSW 4/2069.

8 James Lake, see note 50 below. Richard Turton, Quarter Sessions Papers, Sydney, 1831, Case No. 20, AO NSW 4/8453, and Application to Publish Banns, CSIL 30/6858, AO NSW 4/2081. Walter Neary, see Chapter 12. Henry Latham Application to Publish Banns, Scots Church, Sydney, 1832. AO NSW 4/2150.5, Reel 721. William Mason, see Chapter 6, note 37. Joseph Woodcock, see Chapter 8, note 14.

9 Barron/Foxall see Chapter 9. Reddiford/Quittenton; see Chapter 11. Hoskins/ Kinsman see Chapter 11 and note 26, plus Police Magistrate, Maitland, to Colonial Secretary, 6 January 1835. CSIL 35/122. AO NSW 4/2291.1. Mason/McPherson see Chapter 6, note 37, and Burial Certificate of Jane Mason, NSW BDM E.5287 V.122.

10 Thomas Pearks to Superintendent of Convicts, 7 April 1830, enclosed with Superintendent of Convicts to Colonial Secretary, April 1830, CSIL No. 30/2859, AO NSW 4/2071.

11 The crew's rebellion reported in the *Sydney Gazette*, 11 June 1829. Application to Publish Banns for Harriet Wright, St John's, Parramatta, November 1829. AO NSW 4/2018, Reel 718.

12 See Chapters 7 and 4 respectively.

13 Police Magistrate, Newcastle, to Colonial Secretary, 23 March 1840, CSIL No. 40/3062, passes on the complaint of Reverend Wilton that Ann Birmingham, per *Margaret*, used pages from the New Testmanent for curl papers. AO NSW 4/2506.6.

14 See Chapter 6, note 8.

15 Application to Publish Banns, Maitland, December 1830. AO NSW 4/2126.5, Reel 719. Convict Applications to Marry, 4 January 1831. AO NSW 4/4512, Reel 714.

16 Colonial Secretary to George Brooks, Police Magistrate, Newcastle, 1 March 1831. AO NSW 4/3829, Reel 2808, p. 447.

17 George Brooks to Colonial Secretary, 14 March 1831. CSIL No. 31/1976, filed with 31/1473. AO NSW 4/2099.

18 Application to Publish Banns, Parramatta, September 1832. AO NSW 4/2150.3, Reel 721.

19 Mary had left a girl, 14 years in 1835 and a boy, 10, in England. Joseph was trying to get them on the ship *Florentina* as assisted immigrants, but the regulations specifically excluded convicts' families from this help. Petition of Joseph Irving, 14 November 1835, CSIL 35/9107. AO NSW 4/2283, Reel 2202.

20 Deposition of Thomas Clements, 14 February 1838. CSIL 38/4522, AO NSW 4/2421.2.

21 Ibid and Petition of Joseph Irving, 10 April 1838. CSIL 38/3813. Ibid.

22 Ibid.

23 Bathurst Gaol Entrance Book, 1831–35, 29 November 1833, Elizabeth Glover, assault, and 1 May 1834, Peter Glover, a debtor. AO NSW 5/1093.

24 Application to Publish Banns, Bathurst, January 1830. AO NSW 4/2065. 10 June 1834, Bathurst Gaol Entrance Book, op. cit.

25 John Godfrey, 19 June 1834, and Mary Godfrey late Hilsley, 15 August and 16 December 1834, Sydney Gaol Entrance Book. AO NSW 4/6435, Reel 852. Supreme Court Session Returns, November 1834: John Godfrey, 27 August 1834, Receiving stolen sheep, Guilty, Norfolk Island 14 years. AO NSW X731, Reel 2389.

26 Quarter Sessions Papers, Maitland 1835. AO NSW 4/8415, Reel 2408.

27 Ibid.

28 Return of Sentences Passed. Ibid.

29 NSW BDM E.1407 V.24.

30 Ann Loydall: NSW BDM V.14 E.73. Sarah Pitches: NSW BDM V.20 E.405.

31 Catherine Steele and Johanna Brown: Old Bailey Session Papers, 1828. ML. Ann Cheeseman and Ann Simpson: *Hull Advertiser*, 18 July 1828, and *Hull Packet*, 22 July 1828. BNL. Mary Hart: Surgeon Wilson's Log, Adm. 101/62, PRO Reel 3208. ML.

32 Captain Allman see Chapter 10. Rev. Sowerby, see Chapter 10. Rev. Rusden see Chapter 9. George Wyndham see Chapter 11.

33 Petition of Mary Smith, 11 March 1833. CSIL No. 33/1981, AO NSW, CSIL 1833 Miscellaneous 'F', 4/2195.1, Reel 2196.

34 Ann Burke assignment to Walter Rotten: Application to Publish Banns, Maitland, 30 September 1833. AO NSW 4/2174.1, Reel 724.

35 Sydney Gaol Entrance Book, 9 July, 5 September 1829. AO NSW 4/6431, Reel 851.

36 Application to Publish Banns, Newcastle, 6 December 1829. AO NSW 4/2817, Reel 716.

37 Colonial Secretary to Superintendent of Convicts, 15 November 1834. AO NSW 4/3680, Reel 1048, p. 257.

38 Certificate of freedom No. 35/998, dated 7 September 1835. AO NSW 4/4330, Reel 995.

39 8 January 1844. Mary Cranford (*sic*), *Princess Royal*. Newcastle Gaol Discharge Book, AO NSW 2/2018. 8 July 1856, Mary Cranfield, *Princess Royal*, Newcastle/Maitland Gaol Entrance Book, AO NSW 2/2009. Reel 757.

40 Separation of children at 12 months: Magistrate, Bathurst, to Colonial Secretary, 1 June 1840, and Governor Gipps note on the flap. CSIL No. 40/5667, AO NSW 4/2504.3. Children to Moreton Bay: Colonial Secretary to Sheriff, 30 May 1836. AO NSW 4/3899, Reel 1063, p. 427.

41 The following are documents which demonstrate the government's attitude to releasing children from the orphan schools and the reluctance to abandon apprenticeship: Colonial Secretary to Orphan Schools, March 1836. AO NSW 4/3722, Reel 1058, pp. 261, 266. Colonial Secretary to Male Orphan School, 25 April 1837. AO NSW 4/3724, Reel 1059, p. 16. Colonial Secretary to Magistrates, 11 June 1842. AO NSW 4/3847, Reel 2814, p. 426.

42 Female Factory to Colonial Secretary, 30 April 1832. AO NSW 4/2142. Reply to the Factory, 2 May 1832. AO NSW 4/3720, Reel 1057, p. 207. Application to Publish Banns, St James' Sydney, May 1832. AO NSW 4/2150.1, Reel 721.

43 Ibid. There is no record that Susan married Edward Sinnott, who was the other party in this application. Susan was assigned in May 1832 to G. Pearce, Sydney, and in July 1832 to W. H. Pettit, Sydney. NSW GG 24 October, 14 November 1832. ML.

44 Ticket-of-leave No. 33/498 dated 20 August 1833. AO NSW 4/4089, Reel 919. Application to Publish Banns, St Philip's, Sydney, 24 February 1835. AO NSW 4/2270.3, Reel 728. Marriage of Susan King and George Gilbert, 31 March 1835. NSW BDM E.1143 V.19. Burial of Eliza King, six years, at Parramatta Orphan Institution, 5 May 1835. NSW BDM E.1591 V.19. Susan Gilbert died 2 September 1840. Coroner's Inquest, 28 October 1840. AO NSW 4/6612, Reel 190, and NSW BDM E.80, V.24.

45 See Chapter 7.

46 G. Abbott and G. Little, *The Respectable Sydney Merchant: A. B. Spark of Tempe*, pp. 20, 85, 87, 99, 103, 116, 123.

47 Sydney Gaol Entrance book, 10 July 1829, 7 February, 22 August, 29 December 1831. AO NSW 4/6431–2, Reel 851. 5 January 1833, Liverpool Bench Book, AO NSW 5/2697, Reel 682.

48 Caroline Thomas, Certificate of Freedom No. 36/836, dated 30 August 1836. AO NSW 4/4329, Reel 995. Application to Publish Banns, Liverpool, December 1834. AO NSW 4/2225, Reel 725.

49 Caroline Myers of Liverpool, buried 2 July 1837. Age 43. Ship Princess Royal. Wife of Mr Myer, Butcher. NSW BDM 1837 E.2676 V.21. Jacob remarried to Ann Clegg on 20 November 1837. NSW BDM E. 1684 V.21.

50 Jane Thomas married John Kent, 28 October 1839. NSW BDM E.328 V.23.

51 Female Factory to Colonial Secretary, 23 February 1831. CSIL No. 31/1382, AO NSW 4/2099.

52 Application to Publish Banns, Newcastle, September 1831. AO NSW 4/2126.4, Reel 719. Margaret Hartigan married John Smith, 3 November 1831. NSW BDM E.1210 V.15. Chapter 11 describes their marriage.

53 Colonial Secretary to Superintendent of Convicts, 4/11 April 1839, answer re Petition No. 39/3571. AO NSW 4/3686, Reel 1051.

54 Female Orphan School to Colonial Secretary, September 1838. CSIL No. 38/10309, AO NSW 4/2413.2 and reply Colonial Secretary to Orphan School, 4 October 1838, AO NSW 4/3724, Reel 1059, p. 280. Margaret Hartigan Ticket of Leave No. 39/114 dated 1 February 1839. AO NSW 4/4126, Reel 932.

55 Application to Publish Banns, Parramatta, 1832. AO NSW 4/2150.3, Reel 721.

56 Memorial of Sarah Hazell, May 1832. CSIL 32/4050, AO NSW 4/2144.

57 Ibid.

58 Princess Royal Muster, op. cit.

59 Ibid.

60 Memorial of Ann Bowler, October 1831. CSIL No. 31/7986, AO NSW 4/2118.

61 Ticket-of-leave No. 33/480 1833. AO NSW 4/4089, Reel 919.

62 Memorial of Ann Bowler, 30 December 1836. CSIL 37/1249, AO NSW 4/2375.2

63 Ibid. Absolute pardon dated 3 January 1840, noted on Princess Royal Muster, op. cit.

64 Princess Royal Muster. AO NSW 4/4014, Reel 398.

65 Ibid. Female Factory to Colonial Secretary, 5 July 1830. CSIL No. 30/5170, James Pitches, born 2 May 1827. Parents: James and Sarah Pitches, the latter a convict per Princess Royal. AO NSW 4/2077.

66 Princess Royal Muster. op. cit.

67 Female Factory to Colonial Secretary, 5 July 1830. op. cit.

68 Sydney Gaol Entrance Book, 13 September 1830, 8 August 1831. AO NSW 4/6432,

Reel 851. NSW GG, 7 November 1832, p. 395, 21 November 1832, p. 416. ML.
69 *Sydney Gazette*, 22 November 1832. SL NSW.
70 8 January 1835, Newcastle Bench Book. AO NSW SZ80, Reel 2721, p. 490 and Newcastle Gaol Entrance Book, No. 127 1835. AO NSW 2/2005, Reel 756. Sarah's surname in the Bench Book is recorded as Bridges, but the Gaol records her as 'Bridges name Pitches'.
71 Sarah is described as 'Free by Servitude' in the Newcastle Bench Book in October 1835, but her Certificate is dated 20 February 1837 No. 37/156 and was not sent to Newcastle until 1840. On the evidence of her life in the colony, the discrepancy would appear simply to be either a bureaucratic delay or, more likely, that Sarah herself did not go through the procedures necessary to ensure she received the actual certificate near the due date.
72 8 October 1835, Newcastle Bench Book. AO NSW 4/5608, Reel 2721, p. 136.
73 Ibid.
74 William Turvey married Harriet Kinder, E.1332 V.18. Harriet Turvey, burial E.2216 V.18. William Turvey married Sarah Pitchers, E.405 V.20. NSW BDM.
75 Memorial of William Turvey, 5 June 1839. CSIL 39/6368, AO NSW 4/2463.2
76 Sworn statement of William Turvey, 31 May 1839, Ibid.
77 Ibid.
78 Male Orphan School to Colonial Secretary, 14 June 1839. CSIL No. 39/6735. Ibid. Male Orphan School Admission Book. ML C200.
79 William Turvey, burial, E.932 V.29. James Pitcher, burial, E.958 V.29. NSW BDM.
80 Sarah Turvey married William Price, 22 November 1852. E.856a V.38. NSW BDM.
81 Sarah Price, died at Morpeth Street, Maitland, 12 February 1868, aged 68, wife of William Price, labourer. Born County Derry, Ireland. In N.S.W. 41 years. Married East Maitland aged 48 years to William Price. NSW BDM 68 4726.

14 CAUGHT IN THE SYSTEM
 1 Princess Royal Muster. AO NSW 4/4014, Reel 398.
 2 23 September 1829, 12 November 1830, Sydney Gaol Entrance Book. AO NSW 4/6431, Reel 851.
 3 B. Lloyd to Colonial Secretary, 13 November 1830. CSIL No. 30/8505, AO NSW 4/2087 and Colonial Secretary to Sheriff, 15 November 1830. AO NSW 4/3896, Reel 1062.
 4 22 November 1830. Sydney Gaol Entrance Book, AO NSW 4/6431, Reel 851.
 5 Petition of Ann Huldie, undated, but some time late July/early August 1831, CSIL No. 31/7795, AO NSW 4/2118.
 6 Ibid.
 7 Colonial Secretary to Sheriff, 23 August 1831. AO NSW 4/3897, Reel 1062. Moreton Bay Monthly Returns, 1829–37, p. 85. ML FM4/18.
 8 Certificate of Freedom 40/2077, dated 19 December 1840. AO NSW 4/4356, Reel 1005.
 9 Sydney Quarter Sessions Register, 1841, Case No. 30. Ann White alias Dorothy Holiday (*sic*) FS, Princess Royal, Committed Sydney 25 January 1841. Charge, Larceny. Tried 19 February 1841. Guilty. 6 months, hard labour, Female Factory. AO NSW Vol. 2916, Reel 2431.
10 Note on Certificate of freedom No. 40/2077, op. cit.
11 11 April 1846, Sydney Gaol Entrance Book. AO NSW 4/6441., Reel 854. NSW BDM, Marriages E.4020 V.74. Death of Richard Challenor E.283 V.105. Death of Anne Challenor, 5907790.
12 Princess Royal Muster, op. cit. Surgeon Wilson's Log. PRO Adm. 101/62, Reel 3208. ML.
13 8 June, 5 October 1829, 3 and 8 May 1830. Sydney Gaol Entrance Book, AO NSW 4/6431, Reel 851.
14 27 and 29 November 1830. Sydney Gaol Entrance Book, AO NSW 4/6431–2, Reel 851.
15 NSW GG 1832. ML.
16 Police Magistrate, Port Macquarie, to Colonial Secretary, 9 October and 25 October 1833. CSIL No. 33/8884 and 7176, AO NSW 4/2208.

17 15 October 1833, Sydney Gaol Entrance Book. AO NSW 4/6434, Reel 852. Colonial Secretary to Sheriff, 18 October 1833. AO NSW 4/3898, Reel 1063, p. 463.

18 Ibid. 29 October 1833.

19 Colonial Secretary to Female Factory, 12 November 1833. AO NSW 4/3723, Reel 1058.

20 Extract from records at Port Macquarie of assaults committed by prisoners on officers of Justice during the last 12 months. Enclosed with letter from Police Magistrate to Colonial Secretary, 25 October 1833, op. cit.

21 Princess Royal Muster, op. cit., and Convict Death Register, AO NSW 4/4549, COD 16.

22 Princess Royal Muster, op. cit.

23 Compiled from the following sources: Princess Royal Muster, op. cit. Sydney Gaol Entrance Book, 1829–36. AO NSW 4/6431–36, Reels 851, 852. NSW GG, 1832, op. cit. Colonial Secretary to Police Magistrate, Newcastle, October 1832. AO NSW 4/3833, Reel 2809, p. 267 and Colonial Secretary to Sheriff, October 1832, AO NSW 4/3898, Reel 1063, p. 70. Convict Applications to Marry, Newcastle, November 1832, February 1835, July 1839. AO NSW 4/4309–10, Reel 713. Application to Publish Banns, Newcastle, October 1832, and Newcastle, February 1835. AO NSW 4/2150.2, Reel 721 and 4/2269.9, Reel 727. Newcastle Bench Book, March 1835, AO NSW SZ80, Reel 2721, p. 550, and September 1837. AO NSW 4/5608, Reel 2722, p. 321. Complaints Against Convicts, Newcastle, February and April 1833. AO NSW, COD 120. Patrick Plains Bench Book, March 1833. AO NSW 7/3714, Reel 681. Newcastle Gaol Entrance Book, 1831–39. AO NSW 2/2003–6. Newcastle Gaol Discharge Book, 1840–46. AO NSW 2/2018, Reel 760. Newcastle Gaol, Females Received and Discharged, 1838–46. AO NSW 5/1240, Reel 761.

24 Newcastle Bench Book, September 1837, op. cit.

25 Ibid.

26 Certificate of Freedom No. 38/1118 dated 27 December 1838. AO NSW 4/4345, Reel 1002.

27 NSW BDM V.26 E.504

28 Princess Royal Muster, op. cit. *Hull Advertiser*, 18 July 1828 and *Hull Packet*. 22 July 1828. BNL.

29 11 June 1829, Sydney Gaol Entrance Book. AO NSW 4/6431, Reel 851.

30 Application to Publish Banns, Maitland, January 1832, reveals Ann was drunk in February 1830. AO NSW 4/2150.4, Reel 721 25 September 1830, Sydney Gaol Entrance Book. AO NSW 4/6432, Reel 851.

31 23 July 1831, Sydney Gaol Entrance Book. AO NSW 4/6432, Reel 851. 8 August 1831, Newcastle Gaol Entrance Book — 'assigned to Mr Ogilvie'. AO NSW 2/2003, Reel 755. 12 June 1832. Newcastle Gaol Entrance Book — '10 days solitary'. AO NSW 2/2004, Reel 755.

32 Application to Publish Banns, March and July 1833, Parramatta. AO NSW 4/2174, Reel 724.

33 Sydney Gaol Entrance Book. AO NSW 4/6434–5, Reel 852.

34 Sydney Gaol Entrance Book. AO NSW 4/6435, Reel 852. Bench of Magistrates, Sydney. AO NSW X709, Reel 662.

35 Application to Publish Banns, Maitland, 1832, op. cit.

36 Application to Publish Banns, Parramatta, March and July 1833, op. cit.

37 Compiled from the following: Newcastle Gaol Entrance Book. AO NSW 2/2006, Reel 756. Newcastle Gaol Discharge Book. AO NSW 2/2018, Reel 760. Newcastle Gaol, Females Received and Discharged. AO NSW Vol. 1240, Reel 761.

38 Newcastle Gaol, Females Received and Discharged, 8–14 August 1841, op. cit.

39 Sydney Gaol Entrance Book. AO NSW 4/6432, and 4/6433. But see also 4/6296 where the physical descriptions do not fit.

40 23 July 1831. Ibid.

41 Ticket-of-leave No. 42/2895 dated 1 December 1842. AO NSW 4/4169, Reel 946. Certificate of Freedom No. 44/188 dated 9 February 1844. AO NSW 4/4389, Reel 1016.

42 See Chapter 11.

43 Newcastle Bench Book, July 1838. AO NSW 4/5608, Reel 2722.

44 Newcastle Gaol Entrance Book, 25 January, 1838, 'assigned to Mr Wainwright'. AO NSW 2/2006, Reel 755.
45 Ibid, 3 July 1838.
46 Ibid, 18 October and 18 December 1838.
47 Ibid. 16 January 1839.
48 Police Magistrate, Newcastle, to Colonial Secretary, 14 September 1839. CSIL No. 39/10207, AO NSW 4/2506.6
49 Ibid, 8 November 1839 and Colonial Secretary to Police Magistrate, Maitland, 26 November 1839. AO NSW 4/3844, Reel 2813, p. 319.
50 Police Magistrate, Maitland, 31 December 1839. CSIL No. 40/815, AO NSW 4/2506.6
51 Ibid.
52 Ibid.
53 Colonial Secretary to Police Magistrate, Maitland, 13 February 1840. AO NSW 4/3844, Reel 2813, p. 473.
54 Ticket of Leave No. 41/1520 dated 25 July, 1841. AO NSW 4/4153, Reel 941. A note on the ticket-of-leave concerning the expiry of Ann's sentence and reference to correspondence with the magistrate in Queanbeyan is the evidence for her presence in that district. Certificate of freedom No. 44/1818 dated 11 December 1844. AO NSW 4/4395, Reel 1018.

15 SURVIVORS AND VICTIMS

1 B. H. Fletcher, *Ralph Darling, A Governor Maligned*, p. 120
2 The eight women and the dates of their tickets were: Georgiana Baxter, Isabella Errington, Mary Ann Smith, Hannah Solomons — all 1832; Ann Bowler, Susan King, Jane Edwards, Mary Ann Taylor — 1833. The reason for Georgiana Baxter's ticket is specified in NSW GG, 27 June 1832, p. 152. ML.
3 Princess Royal Muster, AO NSW 4/4014, Reel 398.
4 Ibid. Details of William Hodges listed in *1828 Census*, edited Sainty and Johnson. The reason for Isabella's ticket is given in NSW GG, 27 June 1832, op. cit.
5 Princess Royal Muster, op. cit.
6 Marriage of Isabella Gibson in Northumberland listed in the International Genealogists Index, ML. There are two facts which mitigate against this conclusion. First, Isabella received a 14 year sentence but the marriage certificate shows no consent from the governor. NSW BDM E.436 V.73. Second, the death certificate of Isabella Bath shows her age as only 39. NSW BDM E.68 V.109. However, ages on death certificates were consistently unreliable and with exceptionally good behaviour on Isabella's part and the assistance of her ex-convict employer, it is quite feasible this is the same woman. Isabella Errington is not listed in the 1837 Muster.
7 The only evidence concerning a *Princess Royal* woman relates to Mary Ann Clancy, who was returned by her employer 2 April 1830 and sent to the second class of the Factory 'for being pregnant'. Sydney Gaol Entrance Book, AO NSW 4/6432, Reel 851.
8 Conditional pardon No. 40/168, dated 10 October 1839. Noted on Princess Royal Muster, op. cit.
9 Charlotte Tither and Hannah Solomons, see Chapter 8.
10 NSW BDM E.316 V.14.
11 NSW BDM E.24 V.14.
12 Princess Royal Muster, op. cit.
13 Ibid.
14 Female Factory to Colonial Secretary, April 1831. CSIL 31/3003. AO NSW 4/2105.
15 Susannah Turbitt: Application to Publish Banns, St James', Sydney, August 1829. AO NSW 4/2018, Reel 718. Marriage: NSW BDM E.806 V.13. Burial: Susannah Bullock: NSW BDM E.1405 V.16. Mary Hart: Application to Publish Banns, Castlereagh, September, 1830. AO NSW 4/2065. Marriage: NSW BDM E.137 V.14. Burial: 3 May 1833, Mary Winter, per *Princess Royal*, at St Giles, Bathurst Plains. Wife of Jacob Winter, Bricklayer. NSW BDM E.634 V.17. Mary Hilsley: Chapter 13 for details of her marriage. Ticket-of-leave No. 36/275 dated 8 March 1836. AO NSW 4/4101, Reel 965. Died 28 March 1837. Convict Death Register, AO NSW 4/4549, COD 16. Jane Bailey, per *Princess Royal*, died Sydney hospital, buried 18

March 1833. NSW BDM E.169 V.17.

16 Harriet Wright, see Chapter 11. Caroline Thomas and Susan King or Forrester see Chapter 13

17 Sarah Quittenton and Louisa Caulfield, see Chapter 11. Catherine Donoghue, see Chapter 14. Elizabeth Foxall, see Chapter 9.

18 Jane Edwards: ticket-of-leave No. 33/298 and No. 42/2901. AO NSW 4/4088, Reel 919, and 4/6169, Reel 946. Betty Brian: ticket-of-leave No. 38/1942 and No. 42/2897. AO NSW 4/4124, Reel 931 and 4/4169, Reel 946. Ann Kirby: Application to Publish Banns, Roman Catholic, Windsor, July 1839. AO NSW 4/2435.93, Reel 735. Tickets-of-leave Nos 39/581, 39/1152. AO NSW 4/4128, Reel 932 and 4/4130, Reel 930.

19 Jane Edwards: Certificate of freedom No. 43/1569. AO NSW 4/4385, Reel 1015. Betty Brian: Certificate of freedom No. 44/244. AO NSW 4/4389, Reel 1016.

20 Note on ticket-of-leave No. 43/2026. AO NSW 4/1833, Reel 949. Conditional pardon No. 53/207 dated 10 December 1853, noted on Princess Royal Muster, op. cit.

21 Martha Turner: Application to Publish Banns, St James', Sydney, February 1830. AO NSW 4/2065. Tickets-of-leave No. 37/1927 and No. 40/1159. AO NSW 4/4116, Reel 928 and 4/4138, Reel 936.

22 Petition of Martha Turner, 10 March 1840. AO NSW 4/2513, Reel 2245.

23 Ibid.

24 Conditional Pardon No. 47/199, dated 30 January 1847. Noted on Princess Royal Muster, op. cit.

25 The note on Susannah's ticket-of-leave reads: Cancelled per P.M. [Police Magistrate] Parramatta, letter dated 2 June 1840, Watson having been sent to the Factory for six months for obtaining bread under false pretences. Ticket-of-leave No. 39/1171. AO NSW 4/4130, Reel 933. The NSW GG repeated this information 1 July 1840, p. 621. ML.

26 Colonial Secretary to Mr Long Innes, JP, 21 September 1841. AO NSW 4/3847, Reel 2814, p. 129.

27 F. Crowley, *Colonial Australia 1788–1840*, p. 589.

28 L. L. Robson, *The Convict Settlers of Australia*, p. 4.

29 A. G. L. Shaw, *Convicts and the Colonies*, pp. 351, 358.

30 Robson, op. cit.

31 HRA 1, Vol. 22, p. 740.

32 Ibid. pp. 458, 739.

33 Ibid. p. 740.

34 Ibid. p. 736.

35 Ibid. p. 737.

36 NSW BDM V.26 E.663. Burials, St John's, Parramatta. Agnes Ellen Watson, died 4 January 1842 at General Hospital, Parramatta. Buried 4 January. Age 4 years.

37 NSW BDM E.1744 V.76. The proof it is the correct Susannah Watson, who married William Woollard is a note on Susannah's Certificate of Freedom. A clerk began to record, as he was supposed to do, 'wife of William . . .' Someone, who stood by as he wrote and conscious of her legal bigamy, stopped him from finishing the sentence and persuaded him to scribble it out. The words, however, remained, just legible.

38 The solicitor general's opinion is quoted by the colonial secretary in a letter to the superintendent of convicts, 21 April 1841, in the case of William Flannagan and Margaret Power. AO NSW 4/3689, Reel 1053.

39 I have been unable to prove the date and location of John Clarke's death. See Chapter 10 and particularly note 77 for the likely explanation of his end.

40 Ship Grenada (2) Muster, arrived Sydney, 16 September 1821. William Woollard, tried Essex Assizes, 4 March 1820. Sentence, Life. Native Place, Essex. Labourer. Age, 24. Height, 5'2¾" Complexion, dark and florid. Hair, Brown. Eyes, Brown. AO NSW 4/4007, COD 149 p. 387.

41 Ticket-of-leave No. 32/1172, William Woollard, gardener. Valid for Liverpool. AO NSW 4/4086, Reel 918. Ticket mutilated and reissued No. 35/951, altered to Prospect district. AO NSW 4/4100, Reel 923. Conditional Pardon No. 42/252 dated 1 July 1841, noted on Ticket-of-leave No. 35/951, op. cit.

42 Certificate of freedom No. 44/1069 dated 16 July 1844. AO NSW 4/4392, Reel 1017.

43 Obituary of Charles Watson. The *Bulletin*, 3 April 1886.

44 NSW BDM E.725 V.34B.

45 Sydney Gaol Entrance Book, 9, 15 October 1834, 12 December 1835, 6 September 1836, 6 August 1839, 8 October 1841. AO NSW 4/6435−6, 4/6439−40, Reels 852−4. After Ann's marriage, there is no death recorded for a Patrick McMahon until 1853, NSW BDM E.201 V.119.

46 Sheriff to Colonial Secretary, 4 October 1838. CSIL No. 38/10491, AO NSW 4/2649.2

47 Martha was convicted of drunkenness 12 times in Bathurst between September 1831 and April 1835. See Bathurst Gaol Entrance Book. AO NSW 5/1093.

48 Bench of Magistrates. Bathurst, 8 February 1836. AO NSW 2/8325, Reel 1259. William Boyler had been Martha's employer at the time she married. He gave his permission but somewhat grudgingly. On this occasion when she abused him, it was two days after the Bathurst Bench forwarded her application for a certificate of freedom. (Noted on Princess Royal Muster, op. cit.) It seems probable that Mr Boyler's opinion or reference had been sought in connection with that application and he had in some way jeopardised Martha's potential freedom.

49 Thomas Brothers' death: NSW BDM E.1106 V.26. Martha Brothers' death: NSW BDM E.1009 V.37.

50 Catherine Steele, see Chapter 12. Sarah Turton: Sydney Gaol Entrance Book, 12 July 1842. AO NSW 4/6440, Reel 854. *Sydney Herald*, 18 July 1842. SL NSW. Supreme Court Depositions 1842. AO NSW 9/6325.

51 Margaret Coffin: ticket-of-leave No. 42/777. Valid for the District of Hunter. AO NSW 4/4161, Reel 943. James Coffin apprenticed, November 1835. CSIL No. 35/9615, AO NSW 4/2289.2. Margaret Coffin died Hospital, Parish of St Luke, Liverpool, 1 October 1841. Age 44. Bond per ship Princess Royal. NSW BDM E.1191 V.25.

52 Mary Wheat marriage, see Chapter 10. Certificate of Freedom No. 35/1120 dated 8 October 1835. AO NSW 4/4330, Reel 995. Mary married John Tiffin at Liverpool, south-west of Sydney in 1832. A John Tiffin died 28 April 1838 at Bungonia, which is approximately 80 miles further south-west. He was roughly the right age. NSW BDM E.3248 V.22. Sydney Gaol Entrance Book, 16 November 1840, 5 August 1846. AO NSW 4/6439, Reel 853 and 4/6441, Reel 854. Parramatta Bench Book, 11 March 1847. AO NSW 4/5612, Reel 2733. *Hull Packet*, 15 July 1828. BNL.

53 Maitland Gaol Entrance Book, 8 July 1856. AO NSW 2/2009, Reel 757.

54 See Chapter 11 for Ann Kinsman's story. Marriage to Phillip Field at Clarence Town, Parish of Uffington, 20 May 1846. NSW BDM E.495 V.31.

55 Dungog Bench Book, 22 March 1853. AO NSW 4/5537, Reel 668.

56 Maitland Gaol Entrance Book, 31 March 1853, No. 93. AO NSW 2/2009, Reel 757. Maitland Gaol Description Book, Prisoner No. 93. AO NSW 2/2017, Reel 759.

57 Maitland Gaol Discharge Book. Prisoner No. 93. AO NSW 2/2019, Reel 760. Tarban Creek Lunatic Asylum, 25 April 1853. AO NSW 4/7200, Reel 746.

58 Ann Field alias Hosking, age 61 years, died 7 May 1861, at lunatic asylum, Parramatta. Cause: Insanity, Bronchitis, Debility. Buried: St Patrick's Cemetery, Parramatta. NSW BDM 61 04221.

59 Princess Royal Muster, op. cit. For Mary Gregory's offences, see Sydney Gaol Entrance Book. AO NSW 4/6431−2 and 4/6434−5, Reels 851−52. Parramatta Gaol Entrance Book, 4 October 1834. AO NSW 4/5430, Reel 1260. Benevolent Asylum House Committee Minutes, 18 October 1854. A.7191 ML.

60 Princess Royal Muster, op. cit. Benevolent Asylum House Committee Minutes, 14 December 1854, op. cit.

61 Ann Maw died 12 November 1858. NSW BDM 58 1371. Mary Gregory: Benevolent Asylum Inmates Journals, 9 April 1858. A.7230 ML. Mary Gregory died 19 January 1861. NSW BDM 61 00062.

62 Benevolent Society Inmates Journals, 17 January 1860. A.7231 ML. William Hickman (*sic*) died 1 March 1853. NSW BDM E.2077 V.39. Mary Hickmatt (*sic*) died 31 October 1863. NSW BDM 63 01336.

63 Ann Simpson, ticket-of-leave No. 41/1520 dated 25 July 1841, valid for Goulburn

District. AO NSW 4/4153, Reel 941. Ann Simpson, widow, married John Stone, at St Saviour, Goulburn, 21 November 1842. NSW BDM E.614 V.26. John Prentice, Butcher, died Maitland, 1 August 1848. NSW BDM E.1078 V.33.

64 Benevolent Society Inmates Journals, 25 September 1860. A.7231 ML. Benevolent Society Admissions and Discharges, 1860–62. D.574 and 575 ML.

65 Jane Simpson, 58 years, died at Hyde Park asylum, 28 October 1867. NSW BDM 67 01905.

66 John Foley, tailor, 57, died 4 July 1860. Father: Patrick Foley. Born: Limerick, Ireland. NSW BDM 60 03924.

67 Sarah Ann Foley, widow, 46, married Francis Tunnicliff, Bachelor, 49, 12 July 1861. Both of Little Diamond, near Binda. Sarah's parents: Charles Bryant, musician and Mary Ann Clark. Witnesses: William Elliott and M. A. Skelly. NSW BDM 61 1827.

68 Sarah Ann Tunnicliffe, 63, died 8 February 1879 at Diamond Swamp, Binda. Born Bath, England. In N.S.W. 48 years. Father: Charles Bryant, painter (*sic*), Issue: 1 girl living, 2 boys deceased. Informant: Francis Skelly, grandson, of Diamond Swamp. NSW BDM 79 5459.

69 Joseph Giles, 53, died 20 September 1847. Farmer, Denham Court. NSW BDM V.32 E.672. Mary Ann Giles, widow of Denham Court, married William Banford, bachelor, 18 May 1848. NSW BDM V.33 E.162.

70 Sarah's certificate of freedom is marked 'Scone'. Certificate of freedom No. 43/1210 dated 27 July 1843. AO NSW 4/4384, Reel 1014. Sarah Lake died 4 July 1853 at Scone. Wife of James Lake. NSW BDM E.1455 V.39. James Lake, butcher, died Scone, 7 February 1860. NSW BDM 60 05884.

71 Princess Royal Muster, op. cit. Ann Phillips died 7 August 1856 at 636 Parramatta Street, Sydney. Informant: George Phillips, husband, a dealer. NSW BDM 56 00569.

72 Elizabeth Potter, widow, died 9 November 1857, at Sussex Street, Sydney. Informant: John Potter, shoemaker. Parents: John Jones and Elizabeth. NSW BDM 57 1045. Elizabeth's son, John, was born at Sussex Street, 24 February 1834. NSW BDM E.505 V.18.

73 James Lockwood, died 15 November 1860 at Shadforth Street, Paddington. Married 'about 30 years to Mary Fagan'. Informant: Matthew Lockwood, son. NSW BDM 60 2491. Mary Lockwood, died 22 March 1873, at Hospital Gladesville. Informant: Matthew Lockwood, son. Parents: . . . Fagan, a carpenter. NSW BDM 73 6663.

74 Mary Tilley: NSW BDM E.1284 V.116. Jane McPherson: NSW BDM E.5287 V.122.

75 NSW BDM E.183 V.80

76 Susannah Watson to Hannah Watson or Birkin, 28 June 1857.

16 AN AFFECTIONATE MOTHER

1 All original letters from Susannah Watson to her daughter, in the possession of Mr Leslie King, Nottinghamshire. Photographic copies in the possession of the author. No envelope survived with this letter to Hannah. This letter is the only one written in Susannah's own hand — the capitals, punctuation and spelling are her own.

2 25 August 1860, at Joiners Hill, Bulwell, Hannah Watson, 42 years, seamstress. Cause of Death: dropsy. Certificate No. DX 360935, GRO London.

3 I found no evidence of marriage between Hannah Watson and Emmanuel Birkin. After an extensive examination of the Bulwell Registers the following all seem to be their children: Maria (1834), Elizabeth (1835), Hannah (1839), daughters of Emmanuel and Hannah Birkin, Bulwell. Thomas (1838), Edmund (1841), Sarah Ann (1842), children of Emmanuel and Hannah Watson (*sic*). Bulwell Parish Registers of Births at NCRO and NL.

4 Joiners Hill in Bulwell, where Hannah died, is the address where Susannah sent her future letters to Mary Ann when she was married to Abraham Birks. It is very possible Birks is a contraction or variation of Birkin and they were related.

5 Mary Ann Watson, born 19 January 1823. Bulwell Parish Registers, op. cit. 7 October 1845, Reuben Povey, FWK, of South Street, Radford, son of George Povey, FWK, married Mary Ann Watson of North Street, Radford, daughter of Edward Watson, FWK. Certificate No. MX 045938, GRO, London.

6 Edwin Povey, born 6 November 1847, Byron Street, Snenton, Nottinghamshire. Mother, Mary Ann Povey, formerly Watson. Father, Reuben Povey, FWK, of Byron

Street, Snenton. Certificate No. BCA 146254, GRO, London. Reuben Povey, age 24, FWK, of South Street, Radford. Died of typhus fever, 18 January 1849. Informant: X the mark of Mary Ann Povey, present at the death, South Street, Radford. Certificate No. DX 361001, GRO, London.

7 2 March 1850, William Kirk, Widower, FWK, of Bulwell, father Charles Kirk, warper, married Mary Povey, widow, of Bulwell, father Edward Watson, FWK. Bulwell Parish Register, op. cit.

8 Edwin Povey's birth, op. cit. Sarah, daughter of William and Mary Kirk, Bulwell, baptised 9 October 1853. Father: FWK. Bulwell Parish Register, op. cit. The presence of all the family at Main Street, Bulwell, is deduced from all available facts including Edward Watson's death certificate, dated 26 November 1859, Certificate No. DX 799694, GRO, London. See details, note 10 below.

9 16 April 1838, Edward Watson, Widower, FWK, of Basford, father Edward Watson, labourer, married Marry Hopkinson, Widow, of Basford, father Thomas Potter, miller, Signed: Edward Watson X his mark and Mary Hopkinson X her mark. Bulwell was in the registration district of Basford. The two parishes adjoin. Certificate No. MX 045828, GRO, London.

10 26 November 1859, Main Street, Bulwell, Edward Watson age 75 years, Cotton Glove Maker. Cause of death: Old age. Informant: X The mark of William Kirk, in attendance, Main Street, Bulwell. Op. cit.

11 Braidwood and District Goldfields by Richard Kennedy, reproduced in *Braidwood Gold Fields*, compiled by R. H. Maddrell, p. 18.

12 Ibid, plus Susannah Watson to Hannah Watson, 28 June 1857.

13 Founding date deduced from copies of the *Braidwood Daily News* in ML.

14 The date of James Allen's move to Braidwood is recorded by the Canberra District Historical Association — An Excursion to Braidwood. ML.

15 OBSP 1836 pp. 1072–73, ML. By curious coincidence, John Bodin Yates (sic), son of Joseph and Mary, was baptised 19 July 1812, at St Anne's Church, Soho, where Susannah was married 5 years later. St Anne's Parish Register, Westminster Library, Victoria, London.

16 Muster of Ship Mangles. AO NSW 2/8268, Reel 2424 and Printed Indent Reel 908. Other details which shed light on John Yeates' career are included in Braidwood Bench Books 1838–52. AO NSW 4/5516, Reel 663. His ticket-of-leave No. 41/1817 (AO NSW 4/4154, Reel 941) and his certificate of freedom No. 44/1741. (AO NSW 4/4389, Reel 1016).

17 John Yeates, 26, Mangles 1837, Bond, with Robert Huntley. Hitherto industrious and well behaved, and Mary O'Driscol, 25, Duchess of Northumberland 1836, (Came) Free with Robert Huntley. Steady and honest. Application to Publish Banns, Goulburn 1838. AO NSW 4/2390.40, Reel 734. Marriage: NSW BDM E.564 V.75.

18 John Yeates became the Parish Clerk, which is recorded on his tombstone in the Braidwood Cemetery. In this role he was active in the church from the mid-1850s onwards.

19 Charles as a reporter details some of his activities through the *Braidwood Daily News*, copies of which — 1859, 1862 and 1864 — are in ML.

20 Obituary of Charles Watson in the *Bulletin*, 3 April 1886. SL NSW.

21 Charles Isaac Watson married Eliza Yeates, 31 August 1861, St Andrew's Church, Braidwood. NSW BDM 61 1488. Charles John Boden Watson born 28 April 1864, and Walter Watson born 11 October 1865, at Braidwood. Information recorded in a family Bible. Photostat in the author's possession.

22 Susannah Watson to Mary Ann Birks, Joiners Hill, Bulwell, 21 August 1867.

23 I could not find the record of William Kirk's death, but the following proves it: Born 7 September 1865, at Brick Row, Bulwell, William, son of William Kirk, deceased, and Mary Ann Kirk, formerly Watson, previously Povey. Father: Silk Glove Maker. Original certificate in the possession of Mr L. King of 'Ridgeway', Ashlockton, Nottinghamshire. Sighted by the author.

24 Abraham Birks, 54, Widower, of New Basford, married Mary Ann Kirk, 43, Widow, of New Basford, on 23 October 1865. Bride's father: Edward Watson. MX045742, GRO.

25 Recalled by Eliza's grandson, the late Mr Crompton Hall of Nowra, who told the author.

26   *Shoalhaven News,* founded 4 February 1867. William A. Bayley, *Shoalhaven: History of the Shire of Shoalhaven,* p. 86.
27   Susannah Watson to Mary Ann Birks, 12 February 1872.
28   Ibid, 1 September 1869.
29   William A. Bayley, op. cit., p. 92.
30   Ibid.
31   Photographs of John and Mary Yeates in the possession of the author's family. After Susannah's death, John Watson sent her certificate of freedom to Mary Ann and, in an accompanying letter, explained why it was so dirty. John Watson to Mary Ann Birks, 1 June 1880.
32   Susannah Watson to Mary Ann Birks, 18 March 1871.
33   John Henry Clarke Watson married Susannah Bean, a widow, daughter of Thomas Muldoon, in Queanbeyan, N.S.W., 1 February 1871. NSW BDM 71 03356.
34   John's occupations included: campkeeper (gold commissioner's camp, Stoney Creek), baker, carrier, builder, railway worker, shearers' cook, shoemaker, farmer. All evidenced by certificates of births, deaths and marriages and, after 1895, by the electoral rolls.
35   Susannah Watson to Sarah Kirk, 6 February 1872, and to Mary Ann Birks, same date.
36   Susannah Watson to Mary Ann Birks, 12 February 1872.
37   Ibid, 28 May 1873.
38   Ibid, 7 April 1874
39   Ibid, 29 January 1875.
40   John Watson to Mary Ann Birks, 29 August 1875 and Susannah Watson to Mary Ann Birks, same date.
41   Susannah Watson to Mary Ann Birks, 29 August 1875.
42   Ibid.
43   Ibid.
44   Ibid., 12 March 1876.
45   Ibid.
46   Ibid., 17 October 1876.
47   John Watson to Mary Ann Birks, 17 February 1878.
48   H. Saxby, Eden Villa, Gunning, to Mary Ann Birks, 28 October 1877.

17   A SECOND CHANCE

1   This writing exercise is on the back of the note recording details of Susannah's family, found with her letters by Mr L. King, Ashlockton, Nottinghamshire. Photographic copy in the possession of the author.
2   Obituary of Charles Watson, *Bulletin,* 3 April 1886. SL NSW.
3   On the masthead of *Shoalhaven News,* copies in ML.
4   Charles Isaac Watson, journalist, 57 years, (*sic*), died 24 February 1886. Born: Hawkesbury, N.S.W., (*sic*). Father: — Mother: Susannah. Buried: Nowra. NSW BDM 86 13720.
5   John Henry Watson, farmer, 88 years, died 18 October 1923. Born: Parramatta, N.S.W. Father: John Watson (*sic*), labourer. Mother: Unknown. Buried: Muringo, N.S.W. NSW BDM 1923 20067.
6   Mary Ann Birks, 70, died 30 December 1893, at Bulwell, Nottingham. Informant: William Kirk, son, 57 Joiners Hill, Bulwell. Certificate No. DX 361850, GRO London.
7   The evidence for the reunion is the discovery by Mr L. King of Nottinghamshire of photographs of Australian soldiers in World War 1 with members of his family. The photographs were destroyed before their significance was realised.
8   Henry Mayhew, *London's Underworld,* p. 50.
9   Ibid., pp. 34, 46.
10   Ibid. p. 45.
11   For an interesting explanation of the development of the concept of female modesty in the late eighteenth century, see D. Jarrett, *England in the Age of Hogarth,* Chapter 5.
12   C. Anley, *The Prisoners of Australia,* p. 17.
13   *Sydney Monitor,* 18 September 1829. SL NSW.

14 Stephen Jay Gould, *The Mismeasure of Man*, Chapter 4, particularly pp. 124–41.

15 P. Cunningham, *Two Years in New South Wales*, p. 15.

16 Walter Tollis, born 1842, second son of Ann Barnett and Thomas Tollis. Information supplied by Mrs Enid Bohlsen of Northmead, N.S.W. descendant of Ann and Thomas Tollis. See also Obituary of Walter Tollis, *Maitland Weekly Mercury*, 21 August 1926.

17 Patrick O'Farrell (ed.), *Letters from Irish Australia 1825–1929*, pp. 11, 17.

18 Ex-convict Mary Macdonald, formerly Mrs Oliver, to her daughter Barbara. Quoted by Helen Heney, *Dear Fanny*, p. 33. Source: Bonwick Transcripts, Box 19, p. 277: Bigge Report Appendix.

19 The author's father, Bruce P. Macfarlan, was the judge concerned. He was the son of Amy Emma Macfarlan, née Watson, daughter of Charles and Eliza Watson.

20 Susannah Watson to Hannah Watson or Birkin, 28 June 1857.

BIBLIOGRAPHY

ARCHIVAL SOURCES

Archives Office of New South Wales

Alphabetical Register of Pardons 1828–62, 6/884.

Applications for Free Passages for Families of Convicts 1831–34, 4/2188, 4/2136; and Returns of Convicts' Applications for Families 1837–43, 4/4492.

Applications to Publish Banns 1828–41, in Colonial Secretary Letters Received. See Information Leaflet No. 4, AO NSW.

Bathurst Gaol Entrance Books 1831–35, 5/1093; 1837–54, 4/8490–1; Description Book 1837–44, 5/1096; Bench Books 1832–36, 2/8324–5; Court Book 1829–41, 9/2640; Summons Case Register 1829–39, 9/2640; Ticket-of-Leave Holders 1843 and 1846; Ticket-of-Leave Muster Roll 1838–44, 2/8320–1.

Benches of Magistrates: Monthly Returns of Summary Trials of Convicts 1832–36, X706–9.

Berrima Bench Books 1833–36, 4/5667.

Braidwood Bench Books 1838–56, 4/5516–7.

Certificate of Freedom Butts 1829–1846, 4/4298–4/4406.

Consents of the Governor and Declarations for Presbyterian Marriages 1826–60, 5/7691.

Convict Death Register 1828–79, 4/4549.

Convicts' Savings Bank Ledgers 1824–48, 2/8390.

Dungog Bench Books 1834–35, 4/7569; 1843–53, 4/5536–7.

Female Factory: Reports of the Board of Management June and December 1829, 4/2094; Returns of Punishments 1827–28, 2/8211; Returns 1829, 1831, 1833–35, 1837–48, 4/7327; Monthly Reports of the Visiting Justice, 1845–48, 4/7199; Record of Females Discharged 1846–48, 6/5347.

Orphan School Admission Books, 4/7208, 4/352–3; Applications for Children out of the Schools 1830–32, 4/334.

Hyde Park Barracks Court of General Sessions 1830–1848, 2/670, 4/5721.

List of Convicts Transported to Moreton Bay 1824–31, 4/3794.

Liverpool Bench Books 1832–33, 5/2697; Punishment Book 1833–34 4/2772.5; Report of Prisoners Before Bench July 1831, 4/2138 filed at CSIL 32/2347.

Lunatic Asylums, Tarban Creek and Parramatta: See Convict Guide, AO NSW, pp. 78 and 79.

Mudgee Bench Books 1846–56, 4/5591.

Muswellbrook (Merton) Bench Books 1832–36 and 1838–43, 4/5599–602.

New South Wales Convict Ships' Indents and Musters 1800–33, 4/3999, 4/4005–4/4017.

New South Wales Index and Registers of Births Deaths and Marriages 1788–1900.

Newcastle: Gaol List of Women to be Assigned 1831, 4/3897; and Weekly Reports of Female Prisoners Received or Discharged 1838–46, 5/1240; Bench Books 1833–38, SZ80, 4/5607–8; Return of Trials Before the Bench 1826–34, 4/8543; Return of Convicts Tried Before the Bench 1835 and 1836, X708; Newcastle and Maitland Gaol Entrance Books 1829–53, 2/2003–9; Description Books 1832–53, 2/2010–17; Discharge Books 1840–53, 2/2018–9.

Parramatta Bench Books 1846–52, 4/5612–13; Copies of Letters Sent 1843–52, 4/5620–21.

Parramatta Gaol Entrance Books 1830–48, 4/6529–35; Description Books 1831–42, 4/6553–6.

Picton (Stonequarry) Bench Books 1829–43, 4/7572–3, 4/5626–7.

Quarter Sessions Calendar of Criminal Cases Tried: Liverpool and Campbelltown 1825–38, 5/2996; Sydney 1835–43, 4/6448, X852; Registers of Quarter Sessions Parramatta 5/2997; Windsor 1839–43, 5/3008; Depositions and Other Papers 1829–36: see Clerk of the Peace Guide AO NSW.

Queanbeyan Bench Books 1841–c.1845, 4/5652–3.

Register of Conditional Pardons 1791–1825, 4/4430.

Registers of Convicts' Applications to Marry 1825–51, 4/4508–14, 4/117.4.

Registers of Convicts Recommended for Conditonal Pardons 1826–56, 4/4478–4/4480.

Register of Coroners' Inquests and Magisterial Inquiries 1834–59, 4/6611.1–4/6612.

Register of Sentences Remitted or Commuted 1838–41, 4/4544.

Scone (Invermein) Bench Books 1833–37, 7/90 and 4/7553.

Singleton (Patricks Plains) Bench Book 1835–44, 5/7685–6, 4/5662; also Register of Convicts Tried 1833–39, 7/3714.

Supreme Court: Session Returns of Persons Tried and Convicted X728–31, X43; Returns of Criminal Convictions 1829–38, X732A and B; Annual Returns of Prisoners Tried 1829–41, X727, X48, X67; Selected Papers and Depositions.

Sydney Gaol Entrance Books 1829–49, 4/6431–41; Description Books 1831–54, 4/6419–21; 1869, 4/6312; Discharge Books 1835–51 4/6361; Weekly List of Prisoners 1836 4/6977 C–D; Police Reports of Prisoners Tried 1827–33, X821–6; Police Deposition Book 1834, 4/5668.

Ticket-of-Leave Butts 1829–50, 4/4073–4/4224.

Windsor Bench Book 1836–40, 4/5697; Windsor Gaol Weekly Transcripts of Entrance Book 1838, X42.2.

Yass Bench Books 1835–c.1841, 4/5709, 4/5703.

Colonial Secretary, Letters Received

All Departments: 1829, 4/2031–58, 4/2062; 1830, 4/2063–9.1; 1831, 4/2095–99, 4/2059.2; 4/2100–24; 1832, 4/2130–66.2.

Benevolent Asylum 1836–39, 4/2303.2, 4/2342.4, 4/2388.3, 4/2434.3.

Convicts 1833–49, 4/2179.2–4/2187, 4/2229–32, 4/2275–78, 4/2307.3, 4/2308, 4/2296, 4/2309–12, 4/2335.2, 4/2351–53, 4/2375.2, 4/2394–95, 4/2425, 4/2439.2, 4/2440, 4/2442.1, 4/2486.2, 4/2487, 4/2526.2, 4/2567.2, 4/2590.3, 4/2602, 4/2720.2, 4/2721.1, 4/2761, 4/2762.1, 4/2714.1, 4/2513, 4/2706.2

Female Factory 1833–48, 4/2191.3, 4/2234.5, 4/2277.4, 4/2317.2, 4/2359.1, 4/2401.1, 4/2451.3, 4/2492.1, 4/2530.2, 4/2574.1, 4/2610.1, 4/2649.2, 4/2688.4, 4/2727.2, 4/2766.2, 4/2804.2

Male and Female Orphan Schools 1833–45, 4/2201.1, 4/2246.3–.4, 4/2289.1–.2, 4/2328.1–.2, 4/2369.1–.2, 4/2413.2–.3, 4/2463.2, 4/2504.1–.2, 4/2541.3, 4/2621.3, 4/2659.2, 4/2701.5.

Medical 1835–40, 4/2281, 4/2359.3, 4/2402.2, 4/2453.2, 4/2493.2.

Miscellaneous Persons 1833–47, 4/2193.3–4/21198.1, 4/2238.2–4/2242.4, 4/2282.1–4/2285.2, 4/2320.2–4/2323.6, 4/2361.1–4/2365.2, 4/2403.3, 4/2406.1–4/2408.2, 4/2454.1–4/2460.1, 4/2494.1–4/2497.5, 4/2532, 4/2579, 4/2558, 4/4561–4/4563, 4/2653–4/2655, 4/2731–4/2732, 4/2734.2, 4/2737.4/.5, 4/2769, 4/2770.1–2).

Moreton Bay 1840, 4/2499.2

Petitions 1834–46, 4/2247–48, 4/2328.3, 4/2369.3, 4/2414, 4/2415.1, X645–46, 4/2664.1, 4/2736.2.

Police 1833–46; Bathurst, 4/2201.2, 4/2249.2, 4/2289.3, 4/2329.1, 4/2369.4, 4/2461.2, 4/2464.1, 4/2504.3; Patricks Plains, 4/2202.3, 4/2292.1, 4/2369.4, 4/2371.7; Liverpool, 4/2203.1, 4/2251.1, 4/2290.7, 4/2330.3, 4/2371.1; Maitland, 4/2203.3, 4/2291.1, 4/2246.2, 4/2330.4, 4/2371.2, 4/2418.5, 4/2543.6; Parramatta, 4/2204.2, 4/2252.1, 4/2291.4, 4/2371.5, 4/2419.3, 4/2466.5, 4/2506.7, 4/2543.9; Sydney, 4/2205, 4/2421.2, 4/2508.5, 4/8028; Windsor, 4/2206.1, 4/2373.2, 4/2509.3, 4/2587.5; Port Macquarie, 4/2208; Campbelltown, 4/2249.6, 4/2202.1, 4/2329.5, 4/2417.5, 4/2465.1; Newcastle, 4/2204.1, 4/2251.4, 4/2291.3, 4/2330.6, 4/2371.4, 4/2419.2, 4/2455.4, 4/2506.6, 4/2586.1; Wollongong, 4/2470.3, 4/2509.6; Goulburn, 4/2505.8, 4/2543.2; Mudgee, 4/2543.7; Merton, 4/2543.8; Queanbeyan, 4/2586.7, 4/2624.7, 4/2663.5.

Presbyterian Clergy 1842–43, 4/2561.3, 4/2599.1

Colonial Secretary, Letters Sent

To Clergy 1828–43, 4/3615–21.
To Establishments 1829–1848, 4/3718–4/3727.
To Individuals 1846–47, 4/3551–52.
To Magistrates, Police, etc. 1829–1847, 4/3827–4/3852.
To Master Attendant, Harbour Master, etc. 1829 4/3778.
To Sheriff 1829–38, 4/3737–40, 4/3896–3900.
To Superintendent of Convicts 1829–1845, 4/3668–91.

The Mitchell Library

Bathurst Hospital: Register, Ledgers, Letters Sent, Monthly Return of Patients, Mss. 2478.

Benches of Magistrates, Monthly Returns of Summary Trials, Uncat. Mss. 508 No. 6c

Benevolent Society: Acting Committee 1833–36, A7167–70; House Committee 1837–38, A7182–85; Admissions and Discharges 1857–67, D574–5; Indexes, D562–64; Inmates Journals, A7230–31.

Campbelltown Register of Convicts Tried before the Bench 1832–37, Mss. 2482/6, CY954.

1806 Muster, A4404.

Female Factory Papers including correspondence between Mrs Julia Leach and Mrs Elizabeth Fry — typescript of originals in the Colonial Office, London, Mss. A1813.

Goulburn Bench Books, Letters and Depositions received, Mss. 2482.

King Papers Vol. 1. A1976 (Pay list of the *Lady Nelson* July–December 1801).

Male Orphan School Admission Book, C200; Male Orphan School Letter Book, C201.

Sir Thomas Mitchell Journal, A332.

New South Wales Government Gazette 1832–44.

Henry Nisbet Papers, Vols. 3–4, Mss. 3093.

Old Bailey Sessions Papers 1797, 1813–28.

Register of convicts at Moreton Bay 1828–39, Microfilm FM4/17 (Original in Oxley Memorial Library, Brisbane).

Mary Reiby's Diary.

G. W. C. Stapylton letter to Robert Russell, Ar. 97/7.

Superintendent of Convicts, Copies of Letters to Goulburn Magistrates 1831–50, A664.

Sydney Police Register of Arrests 1833, Mss. 2481.

Tasmanian Papers, A1059/4.

Windsor (North Richmond) Letters sent by Magistrates 1828–32, A1397–8.

Public Records Office Documents on Microfilm Through the Australian Joint Copying Project:

Admiralty

Adm. 101/62 Journal of Andrew Douglas Wilson, Surgeon Superintendent of the Princess Royal 3 September 1828–24 May 1829.

Colonial Office

CO201/230 (A2146) Miscellaneous Letters H–Z 1832

Home Office

HO 9/9 Registers of the Laurel, York and Hardy Hulks 1805–30.
HO10/5 General Muster 1811.
HO10/19 General Muster 1825.
HO10/29 Alphabetical list prisoners who arrived 1828–1832.
HO13/51–52 Criminal Papers Entry Books 1828.
HO16/6 Old Bailey Sessions — Return of Prisoners Convicted 1835–37.
HO26/6, 42, 19–34 HO27/13–38 Criminal Registers Middlesex and other countries.

THE SOCIETY OF AUSTRALIAN GENEALOGISTS

1837 Convict Muster (photocopy of HO10/32–35 PRO ML) and the Index prepared by members of the Society.
The International Genealogical Index of baptisms and marriages.

NEWSPAPERS

England

Aris' Birmingham Gazette
Bath and Cheltenham Gazette
Bristol Mercury
Bristol Mirror
Chester Chronicle
Dorset County Chronicle and Somersetshire Gazette
Hampshire Chronicle and Sussex Chronicle
Hull Advertiser
Hull Packet
Leeds Mercury
Leicester and Midland Counties Journal and General Advertiser
Liverpool Mercury
Manchester Courier and Lancashire General Advertiser
Manchester Mercury and Harrop General Advertiser
Morning Chronicle
Nottingham and Newark Mercury
Nottingham Journal
Nottingham Review
Portsmouth Telegraph and Sussex and General Advertiser for Hants, Sussex, Dorset and Wilts
The Times
Warwick and Warwickshire General Advertiser and Leamington Gazette

New South Wales

Araluen Star
Australian
Braidwood News
Hue and Cry
Maitland Mercury
Monitor
Parramatta Chronicle
Shoalhaven News
Sydney Gazette
Sydney Herald

BIBLIOGRAPHY

BOOKS

Abbott, Graham and Little, Geoffrey, *The Respectable Sydney Merchant: A. B. Spark of Tempe*, Sydney University Press, 1976.

Alford, Katrina, *Production or Reproduction? An Economic History of Women in Australia 1788–1850*, Oxford University Press, Melbourne 1984.

Anley, C., *The Prisoners of Australia: A Narrative*, Hatchard and Son, London 1841. (ML)

Barnard, Marjorie, *A History of Australia*, Angus and Robertson, Sydney 1962.

Bateson, Charles, *The Convict Ships 1787–1868*, A. H. & A. W. Reed, Artarmon 1974.

Bayley, William A., *Shoalhaven: History of the Shire of Shoalhaven*, Shoalhaven Shire Council, 1983.

Berg, Maxine, *The Age of Manufacturers 1700–1820*, Fontana, London 1985.

Bryson, Emrys, *Portrait of Nottingham*, 2nd ed. Hale, London 1978.

Christian, Roy, *Nottinghamshire*, Batsford, London 1974.

Church, Roy A., *Economic and Social Change in a Midland Town: Victorian Nottingham 1815–1900*, Frank Cass & Co Ltd, London 1966.

Clark, C. M. H., *A History of Australia*, vols 1–3, Melbourne University Press, 1979.

Clarke, John, *The Price of Progress: Cobbett's England 1780–1835*, Granada, London 1977.

Clarke, Patricia, *The Life and Times of a Colonial Woman: Mary Braidwood Mowle*, Allen & Unwin, Sydney 1986.

Cole, C. D. H. and Postgate, Raymond, *The Common People 1746–1946*, Methuen, London 1971.

Cooper, Leonard, *The Age of Wellington: The Life and Time of the Duke of Wellington 1769–1852*, Macmillan, London 1964.

Crowley, Frank, *A Documentary History of Australia*, Vols 1 and 2, Nelson, Melbourne 1980.

Cumes, J. W. C., *Their Chastity Was Not Too Rigid: Leisure Times in Early Australia*, Longman Cheshire, Melbourne 1979.

Cunningham, Peter, *Two Years in New South Wales* (1827), ed. David S. Macmillan, Angus and Robertson, Sydney 1966.

Currey, Charles Herbert, *Sir Francis Forbes: The First Chief Justice of the Supreme Court of New South Wales*, Angus and Robertson, Sydney 1968.

Daniels, Kay (ed.), *So Much Hard Work: Women and Prostitution in Australian History*. Fontana/Collins, Sydney 1984.

Daniels, Kay and Murnane, Mary, *Uphill All the Way: A Documentary History of Women in Australia*, University of Queensland Press, St Lucia 1980.

Dixson, Miriam, *The Real Matilda: Woman and Identity in Australia 1788 to the Present*, Penguin, Ringwood 1984.

Dow, Gwyneth, *Samuel Terry: The Botany Bay Rothschild*, Sydney University Press, 1974.

Dutton, Geoffrey, *The Squatters*, Currey O'Neil, Melbourne 1985.

Edwards, J. R., *British History 1815–1939*, Bell & Hyman, London 1970.

Evans, L. and Nicholls, P., *Convicts and Colonial Society 1788–1868*, 2nd ed, Macmillan, Melbourne 1984.

Fletcher, Brian, H. *Ralph Darling: A Governor Maligned*, Oxford University Press, Melbourne 1984.

Fowles, Joseph, *Sydney in 1848*, facsimile of the original text and with an index and annotations to the plates, Ure Smith, Sydney 1962.

Gould, Stephen Jay, *The Mismeasure of Man*, Pelican, Harmondsworth 1987.

Grant, James, *The Narrative of a Voyage of Discovery Performed in His Majesty's Vessel The Lady Nelson 1800 1801 and 1802 to New South Wales*, Libraries Board of South Australia, Adelaide 1973.

Grimshaw, P., McConville, C. and McEwen, E. (eds), *Families in Colonial Australia*, George Allen and Unwin, Sydney 1985.

Grocott, Allan M., *Convicts Clergymen and Churches: Attitudes of Convicts and Ex-Convicts Towards the Churches and Clergy in New South Wales from 1788 to 1851*, Sydney University Press, 1980.

Hainsworth, D. R., *The Sydney Traders: Simeon Lord and his Contemporaries 1788–1821*, Cassell, Melbourne 1971.

Harris, Alexander, *Settlers and Convicts: Recollections of Sixteen Years' Labour in the Australian Backwoods* (1847) Melbourne University Press, 1977.

Hayes, John, *London: A Pictorial History*, Batsford, London 1969.

Heney, Helen, *Australia's Founding Mothers* Nelson, Melbourne 1978.

Heney, Helen, *Dear Fanny*, Australian National University Press, Sydney 1985.

Hibbert, Christopher, *London: The Biography of a City*, Longman Cheshire, London 1969.

Hill, Douglas, *A Hundred Years of Georgian London*, Macdonald, London 1970.

Hirst, J. B., *Convict Society and Its Enemies: A History of Early New South Wales*, Allen & Unwin, Sydney 1983.

Hodgkinson, R., *Eber Bunker*, Roebuck Society Publication No. 15, Canberra 1975.

Horn, Pamela, *The Rural World 1750–1850; Social Change in the English Countryside*, Hutchinson, London 1980.

Hughes, Robert, *The Fatal Shore*, Collins Harvil, London 1987.

Inglis, K., *The Australian Colonists: An Exploration of Social History 1788–1870*, Melbourne University Press, 1974.

Irvine, Nance, *Mary Reibey — Molly Incognita*, Library of Australian History, Sydney 1982

Jarrett, Derek, *England in the Age of Hogarth*, Hart-Davis MacGibbon, London 1974.

Kerr, James Semple, *Design for Convicts*, Library of Australian History, Sydney 1984.

King, Hazel, *Elizabeth Macarthur and Her World*, Sydney University Press, 1980.

Lane, Peter, *The Industrial Revolution 1750–1830*, Batsford, London 1972.

Liversidge, Douglas, *The Luddites: Machine Breakers of the Early Nineteenth Century*, Franklin Watts, London 1972.

Lysons, Rev. D., *The Environs of London*, Vol. 2 Part 1, printed by T. Cadell and W. Davies, Strand 1811. (SL NSW)

Mackinolty, J. and Radi, H. (eds), *In Pursuit of Justice: Australian Women and the Law 1788–1979*, Hale and Iremonger, Sydney 1979.

Mayhew, Henry, *London's Underworld* (London 1862) ed. Peter Quennell, Bracken Books, London 1983.

Meredith, Louisa (Mrs Charles), *Notes and Sketches of New South Wales During a Residence in that Colony from 1839 to 1844* (1844), Ure Smith, Sydney 1973.

Mortlock, John F., *Experiences of a Convict Transported for Twenty-One Years* (London 1864–65) eds G. A. Wilkes and A. G. Mitchell, Sydney University Press, 1965.

Mudie, James, *The Felonry of New South Wales: Being a Faithful Picture of the Real Romance of Life in Botany Bay* (London 1837), Melbourne 1964.

New South Wales Calendar and General Post Office Directory, 1832.

O'Farrell, Patrick, *Letters from Irish Australia 1825–1929*, New South Wales University Press, Sydney 1984.

Peacock, A. J., *Bread or Blood: The Agrarian Riots of East Anglia 1816*, London 1965.

Perrott, Monica, *A Tolerable Good Success: Economic Opportunities for Women in New South Wales 1788–1830*, Hale & Iremonger, Sydney 1983.

Pook, Henry, *A Worker's Paradise? A History of Working People in Australia 1788–1901*, Oxford University Press, Melbourne 1981.

Revitt, J., *Gundaroo: A Relic of Nineteenth Century Australia* (ML)

Ritchie, J., *Punishment and Profit: The Reports of Commissioner John Bigge on the Colonies of New South Wales* and *Van Diemen's Land 1822–1823*, Heinemann, Melbourne 1970.

Ritchie, J., *The Evidence of the Bigge Reports: New South Wales under Governor Macquarie*, 2 vols, Heinemann, Melbourne 1971.

Robinson, Portia, *The Hatch and Brood of Time: A Study of the First Generation of Native-Born White Australians 1788–1828*, Vol. 1, Oxford University Press, Melbourne 1985.

Robson, L. L., *The Convict Settlers of Australia*, Melbourne University Press, 1976.

Rudé, George, *Hanoverian London 1714–1808*, Secker & Warburg, London 1971.

Rudé, George, *Protest and Punishment: The Story of the Social and Political Protesters Transported to Australia 1788–1868*, Oxford University Press, Oxford 1978.

Sainty, Malcolm R. and Johnson, Keith A., *Census of New South Wales November 1828*, Library of Australian History, Sydney 1980.

Salt, Annette, *These Outcast Women: The Parramatta Female Factory 1821–1848*, Hale & Iremonger, Sydney 1984.

Shaw, A. G. L., *Convicts and the Colonies*, Melbourne University Press, 1977.

Stevens, John, *England's Last Revolution: Pentrich 1817*, Moorland Buxton, Derbyshire 1977.

Sturma, Michael, *Vice in a Vicious Society: Crime and Convicts in Mid-Nineteenth Century New South Wales*, University of Queensland Press, Brisbane 1983.

Summers, Anne, *Damned Whores and God's Police: The Colonisation of Women in Australia*, Penguin, Ringwood 1975.

Sweeney, Christopher, *Transported in Place of Death: Convicts in Australia*, Macmillan, London 1981.

Teale, Ruth (ed.), *Colonial Eve: Sources on Women in Australia 1788–1914*, Oxford University Press, Melbourne 1978.

Thompson, E. P., *The Making of the English Working Class*, Penguin, Harmondsworth 1980.

Uppadine, A. Douglas, 'Framework Knitters', Nottingham Family History Society, Vol. 2, No. 12, June 1979.

Walker, R. B., *The Newspaper Press in New South Wales 1803–1920*, Sydney University Press, 1976.

Yarwood, A. T., *Samuel Marsden: The Great Survivor*, Melbourne University Press, 1977.

INDEX